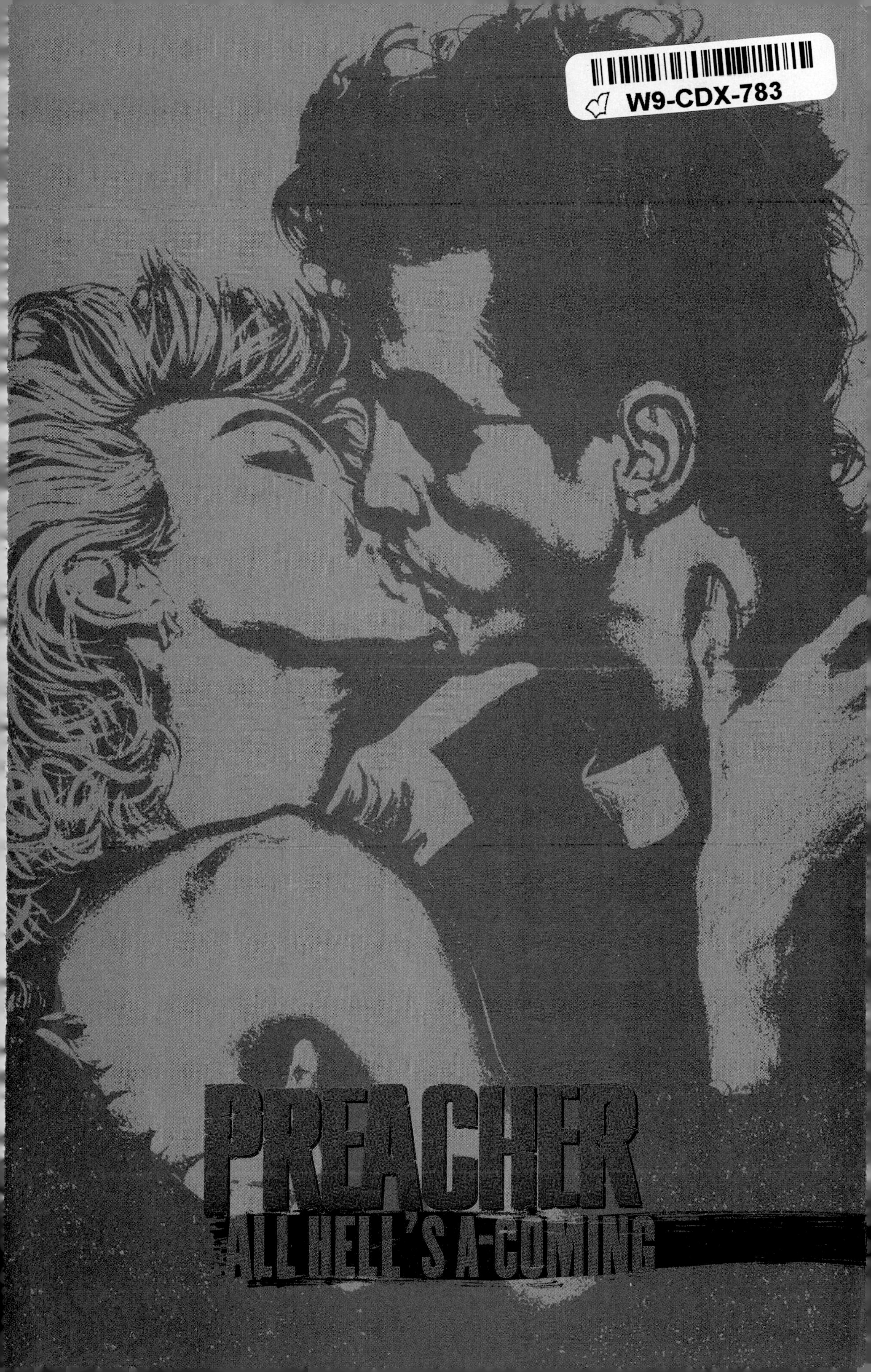
PREACHER
ALL HELL'S A-COMING

GARTH ENNiS
WRiTER

STEVE DiLLON
PENCiLS

STEVE DiLLON
JOHN McCREA
iNKS

PAMELA RAMBO
PATRiCiA MULViHiLL
COLORiSTS

CLEM ROBiNS
LETTERER

GLENN FABRY
ORiGiNAL COVERS

PREACHER created by GARTH ENNiS and STEVE DiLLON

PREA

ALL HELL'S A-COMING

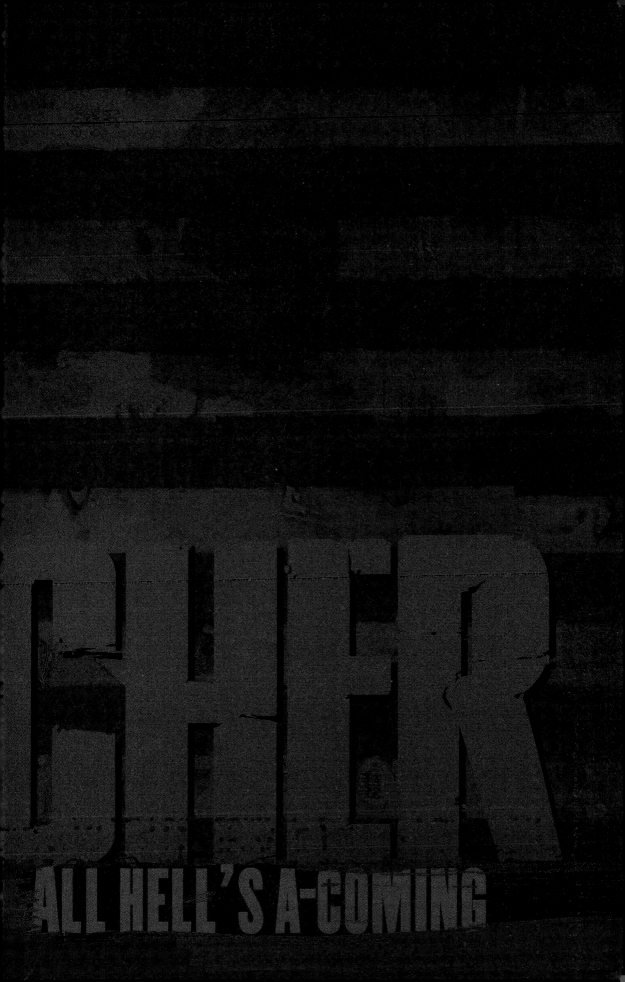

PREACHER: ALL HELL'S A-COMING

Published by DC Comics.
Cover, introduction and compilation copyright © 2000 DC Comics. All Rights Reserved.
Originally published in single magazine form as PREACHER 51-58, PREACHER: TALL IN THE SADDLE. Copyright
© 1999, 2000 Garth Ennis & Steve Dillon. All Rights Reserved. All characters, their distinctive
likenesses and related indicia featured in this publication are trademarks of Garth Ennis & Steve Dillon.
The stories, characters, and incidents featured in this publication are entirely fictional.
DC Comics, 1700 Broadway, New York, NY 10019 A division of Warner Bros. –
A Time Warner Entertainment Company
Printed in Canada. Second Printing.
ISBN:1-56389-617-6
Cover illustration by Glenn Fabry.
Publication design by Louis Prandi.

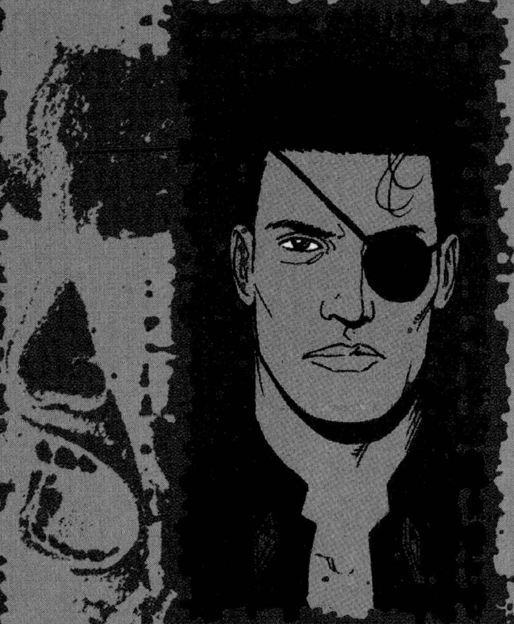

REVEREND JESSE CUSTER

Possessed by the entity Genesis—a child born of a union between Heaven and Hell that should never have existed—Jesse Custer's on a quest to find God and the reason He's abandoned his post. Because of Genesis, Jesse's voice is the literal Word of God, commanding those who hear him to do whatever he says. Jesse drinks too much, smokes too much and has a peculiar habit of taking advice from the spirit of John Wayne.

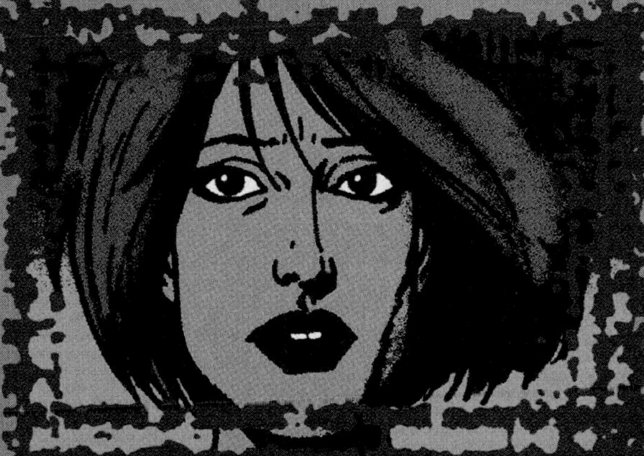

TULIP O'HARE

Five years ago, Tulip and Jesse were pretty much joined at the hip — that is, until Jesse was hauled back to his childhood home of Angelville by good ol' boys Jody and T.C., disappearing on Tulip. Since that time, Tulip made a bungling attempt to be a paid assassin to pay the bills and forget about Jesse Custer. Guns came easy, forgetting Jesse didn't. Now, after bearing witness to the apparent death of her one true love, Tulip again tries to pick up the pieces of her shattered life.

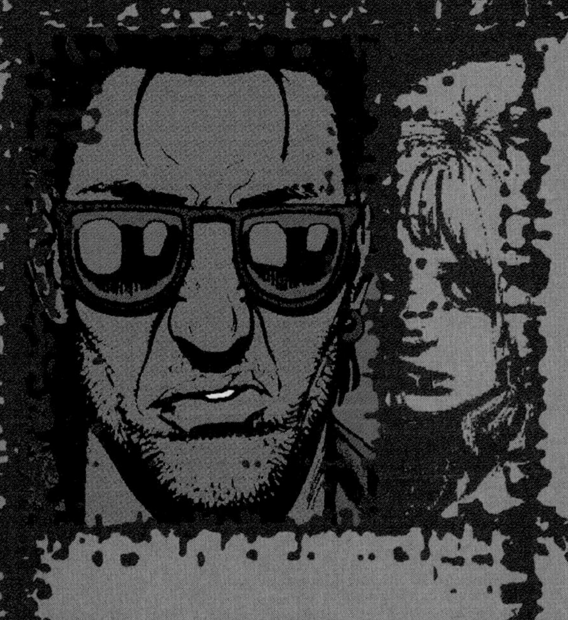

CASSIDY

A hard-drinkin' Irish vampire nearly a hundred years old, Proinsias Cassidy rode with Jesse and Tulip from the time Tulip tried to steal his truck after a botched hit in Texas until Jesse's apparent death in a nuclear firestorm. With Jesse out of the picture, Cassidy now makes his play for his best friend's girl. Call him Cassidy, Cass, or even a total wanker. Just don't ever call him Proinsias.

STARR

Recruited by the centuries-old Grail, Starr rose through the ranks to become the order's most respected agent, answering only to Allfather D'Aronique. Starr killed D'Aronique, realizing that the Grail's efforts were wasted on a tainted messiah. In Jesse Custer, Starr sees the future of the Grail...a future the newly risen Allfather Starr would gladly kill to see a reality.

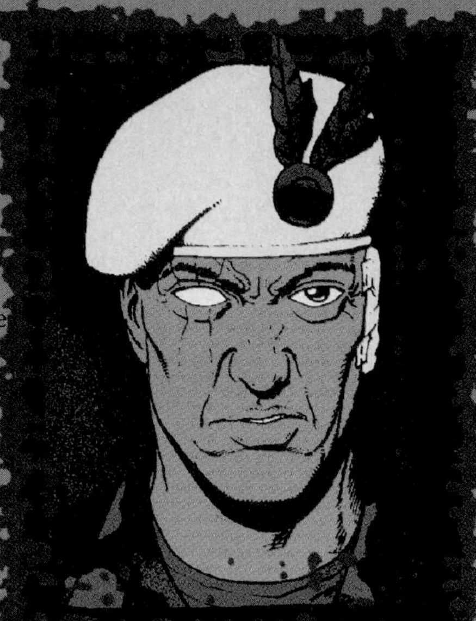

ARSEFACE

Sheriff Hugo Root's only son decided life wasn't worth livin' when Nirvana frontman Kurt Cobain up and killed himself. His father's 12-gauge missed all the vital stuff, and six operations rebuilt the rest. Arseface blamed Jesse Custer for Sheriff Root's suicide, but Jesse and Cass convinced him otherwise. They even got him laid, and helped him land a recording contract. Now he's a pop icon...with a face like an arse. Go figure.

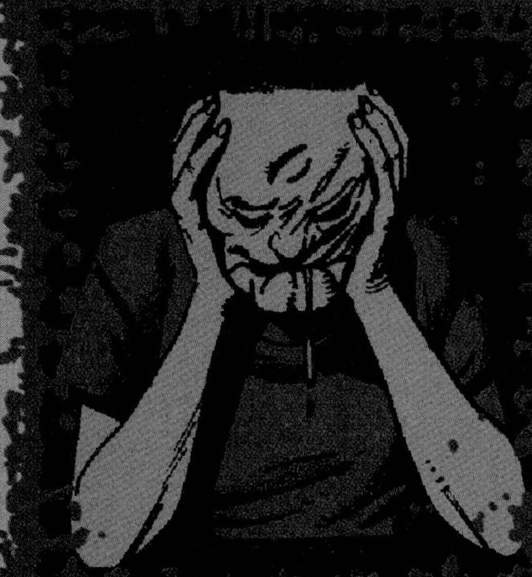

SKEETER

Man's best friend.

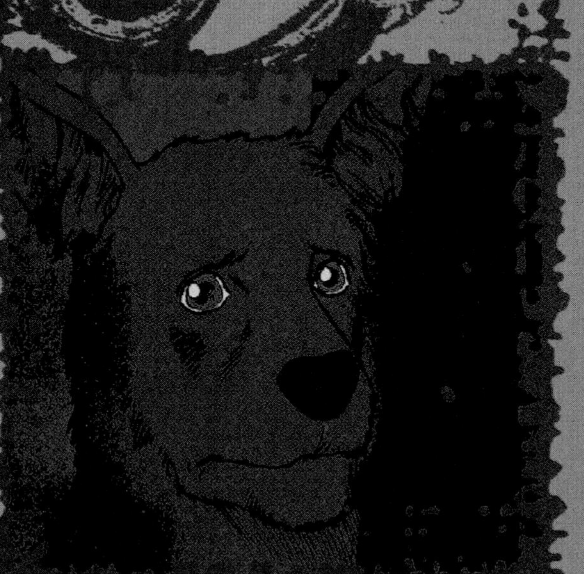

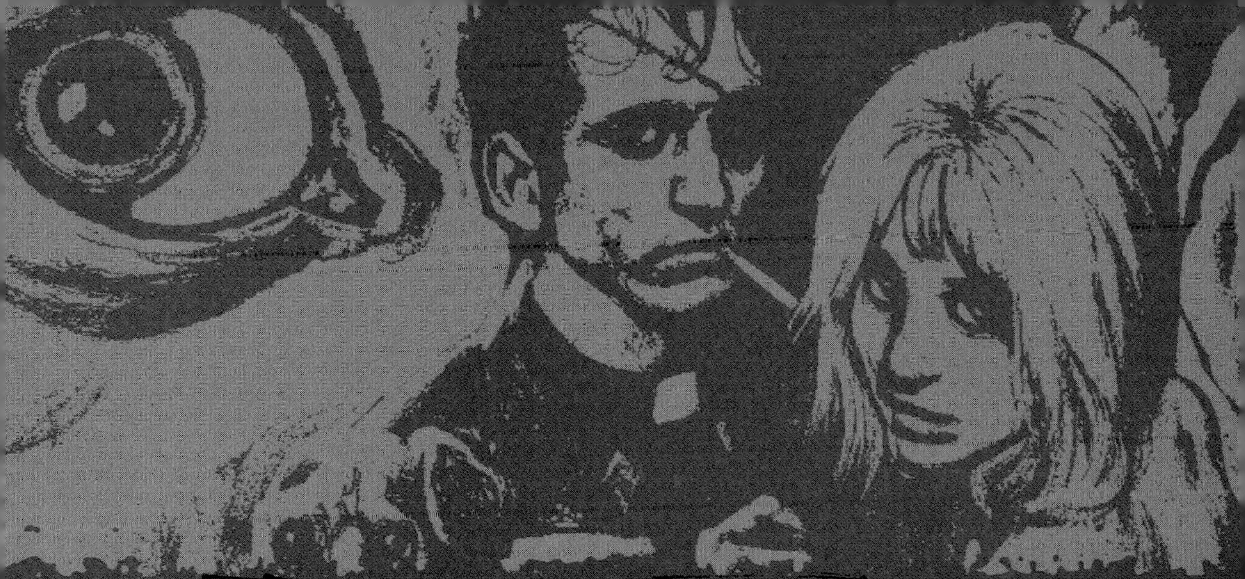

THE STORY SO FAR

The Reverend Jesse Custer may not have been the best minister there ever was, but he was a good man. A drinker with a mouth like a sailor, but a good man all the same.

Then came Genesis.

The spirit conceived from the union of angel and demon, Genesis was a power unlike any other in creation. And when it freed itself from its heavenly fetters, the spirit crash-landed in a small Texas parish, killing everyone except its preacher, Jesse, who somehow bonded with Genesis and assumed its powerful Word of God.

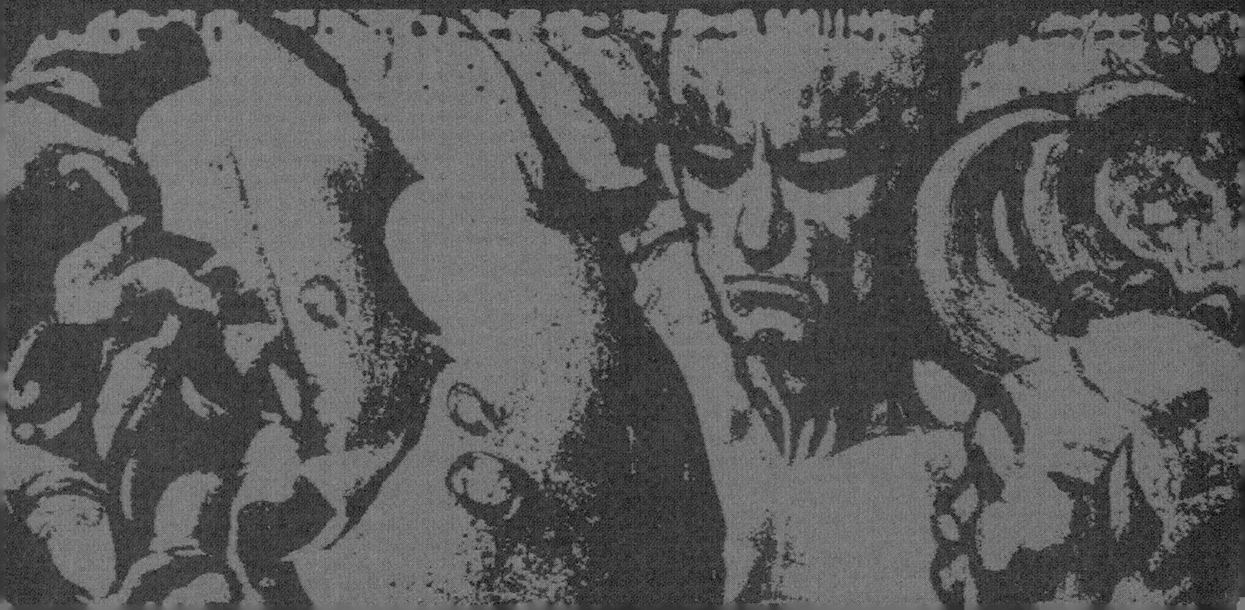

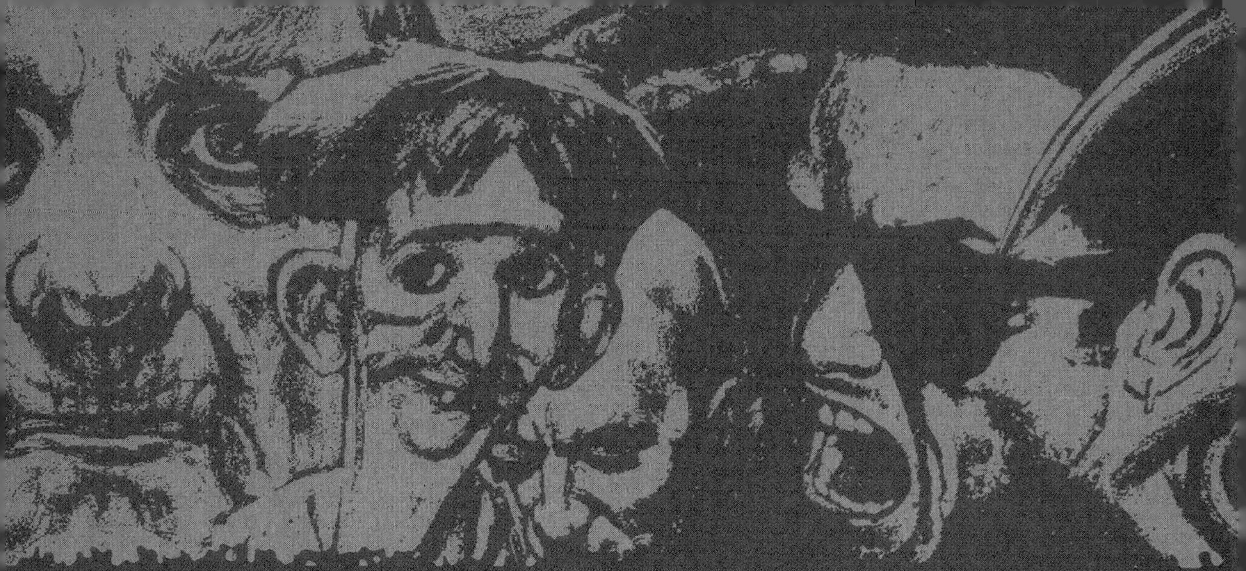

With the help of his long-lost lover, an assassin named Tulip O'Hare, and a hard-drinking Irish vampire named Cassidy, Jesse set out to find God and hold him accountable for his sins. But somewhere along the way, the mission meandered — due in no small part to the machinations of Herr Starr, an agent of a secret society known as the Grail. The Grail sought to manipulate the imminent Armageddon by maintaining control of the new messiah. Starr had his own designs, as he hoped to replace the Grail's messiah with one of his own — Jesse.

But Jesse would not submit to Starr, and their conflict continued to escalate until the day they met in Monument Valley, where Starr attempted to wipe out his foes in a nuclear firestorm. With Jesse presumed dead, Tulip found solace in booze, drugs and the all-too-willing arms of Cassidy. And when Jesse finally found his comrades, he was shocked to discover that they were now lovers, though he had no idea of the many torments this brought for Tulip. And as he left to find himself both as a drifter and a sheriff, Tulip lay wasted in her own personal hell.

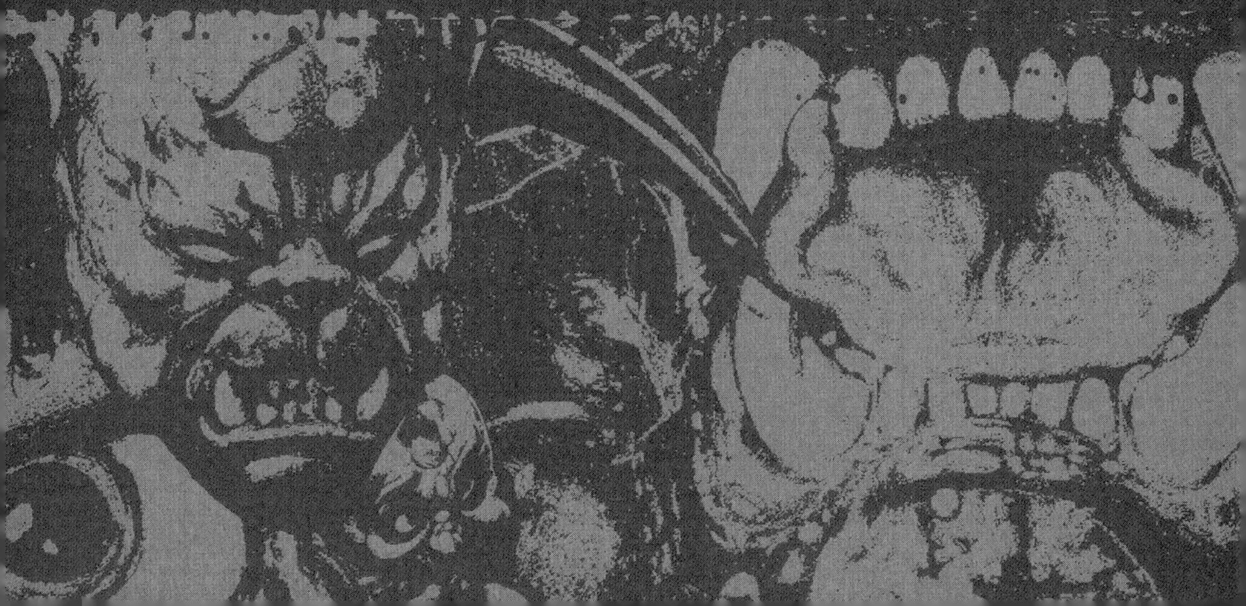

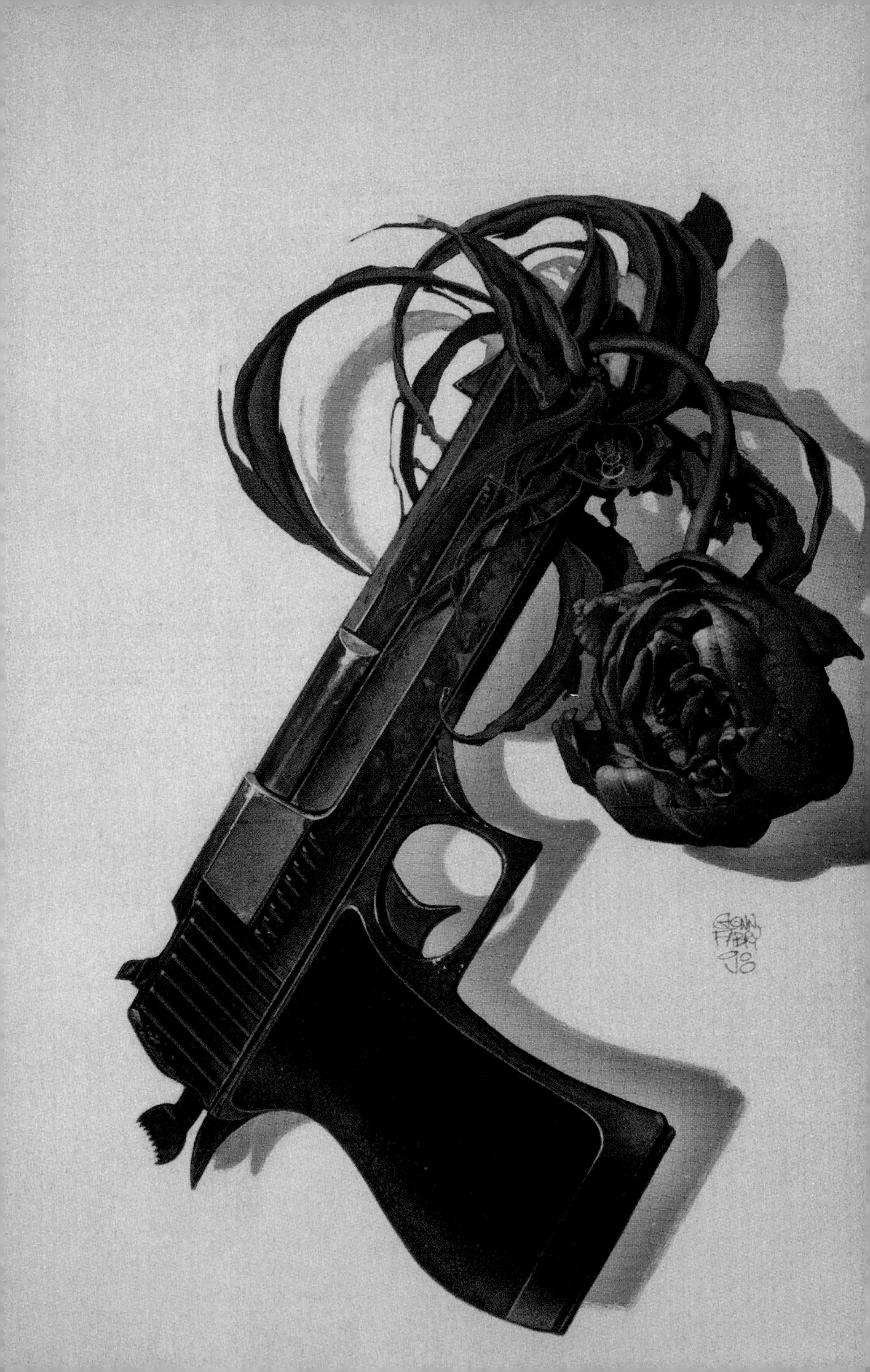
GLENN FABRY
98

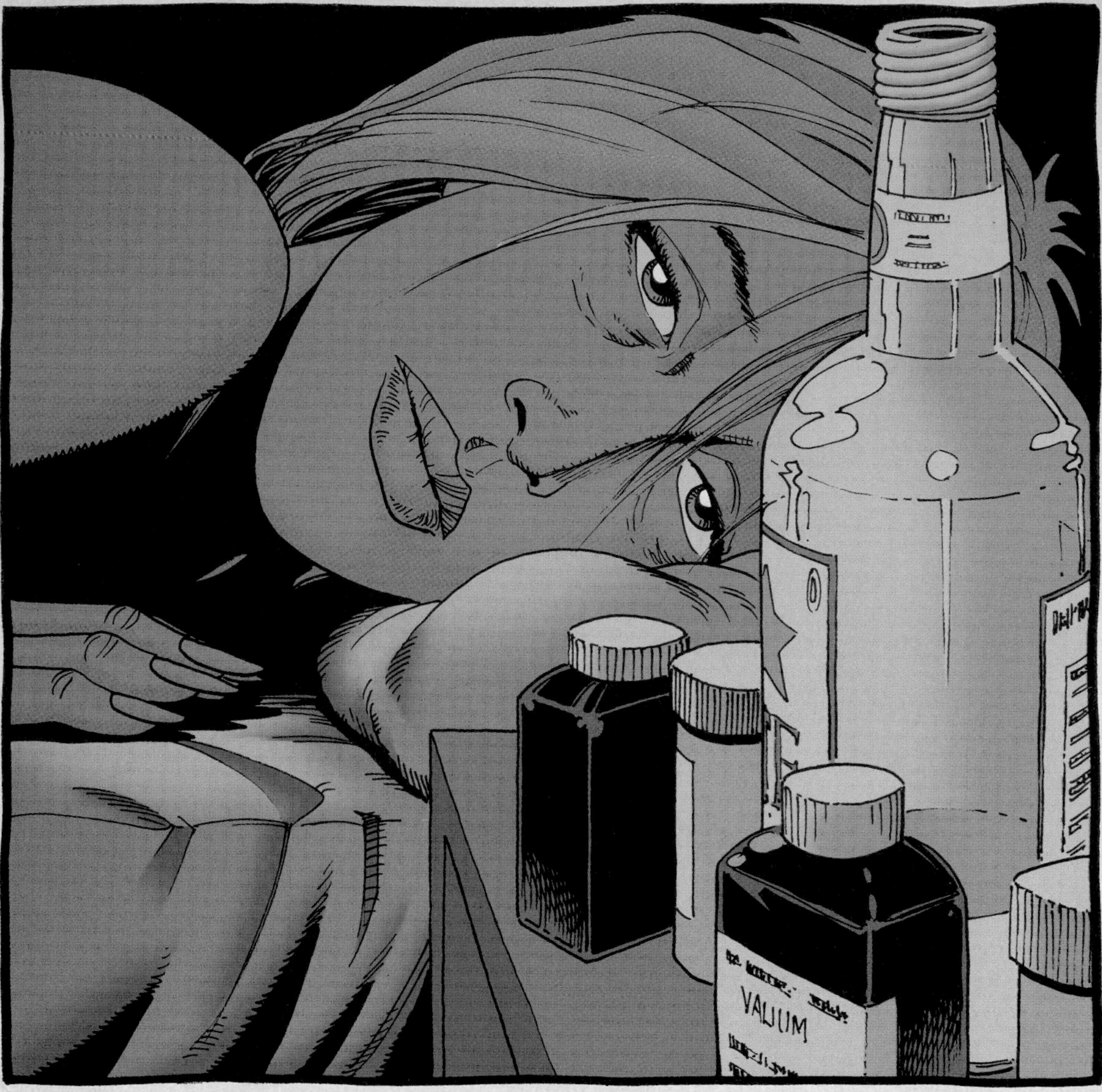
VALIUM

FREEDOM'S JUST ANOTHER WORD FOR NOTHING LEFT TO LOSE

GARTH ENNIS - Writer STEVE DILLON - Artist

PAMELA RAMBO - Colorist CLEM ROBINS - Letterer AXEL ALONSO - Editor

PREACHER created by GARTH ENNIS and STEVE DILLON

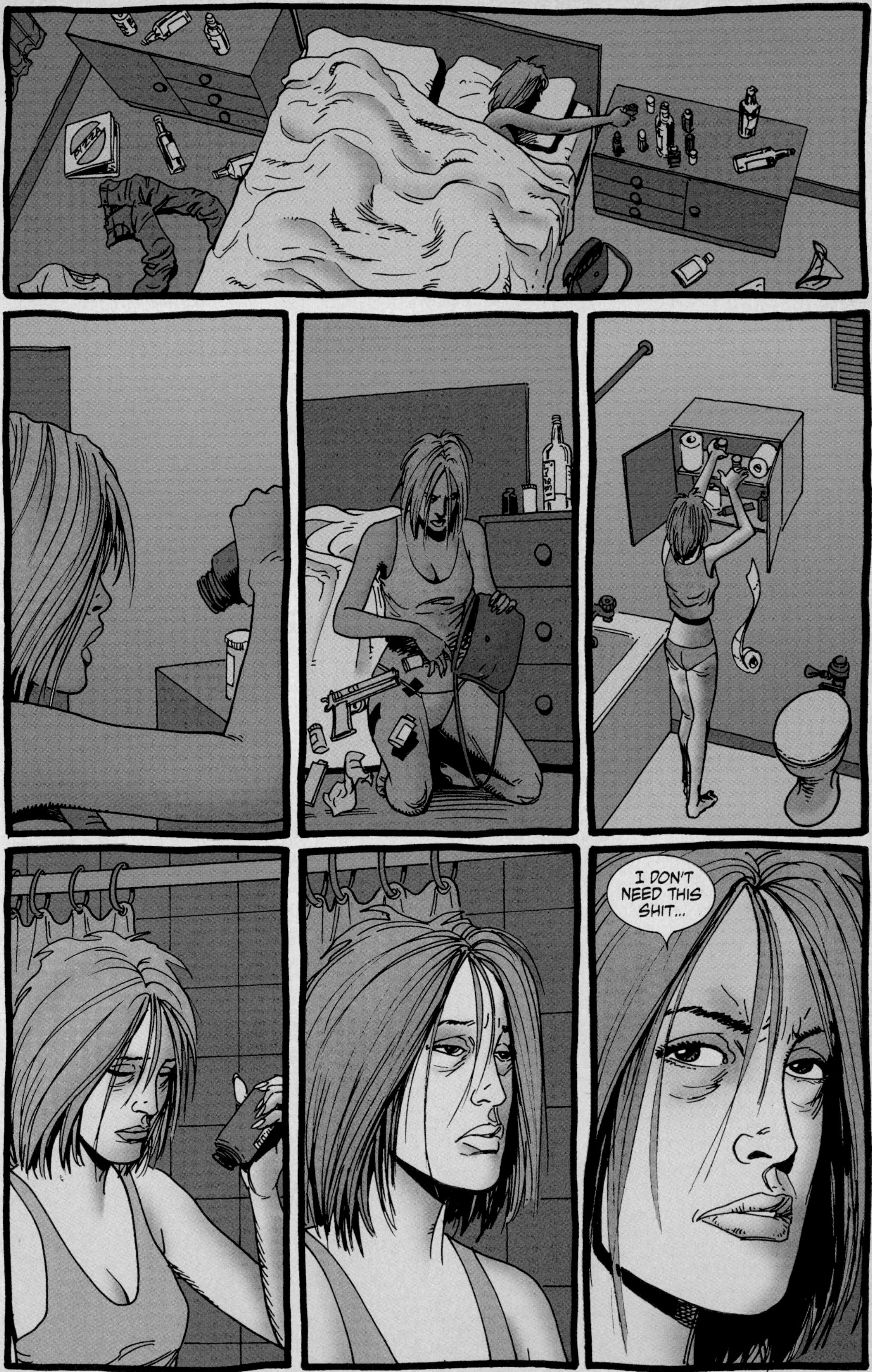
I DON'T NEED THIS SHIT...

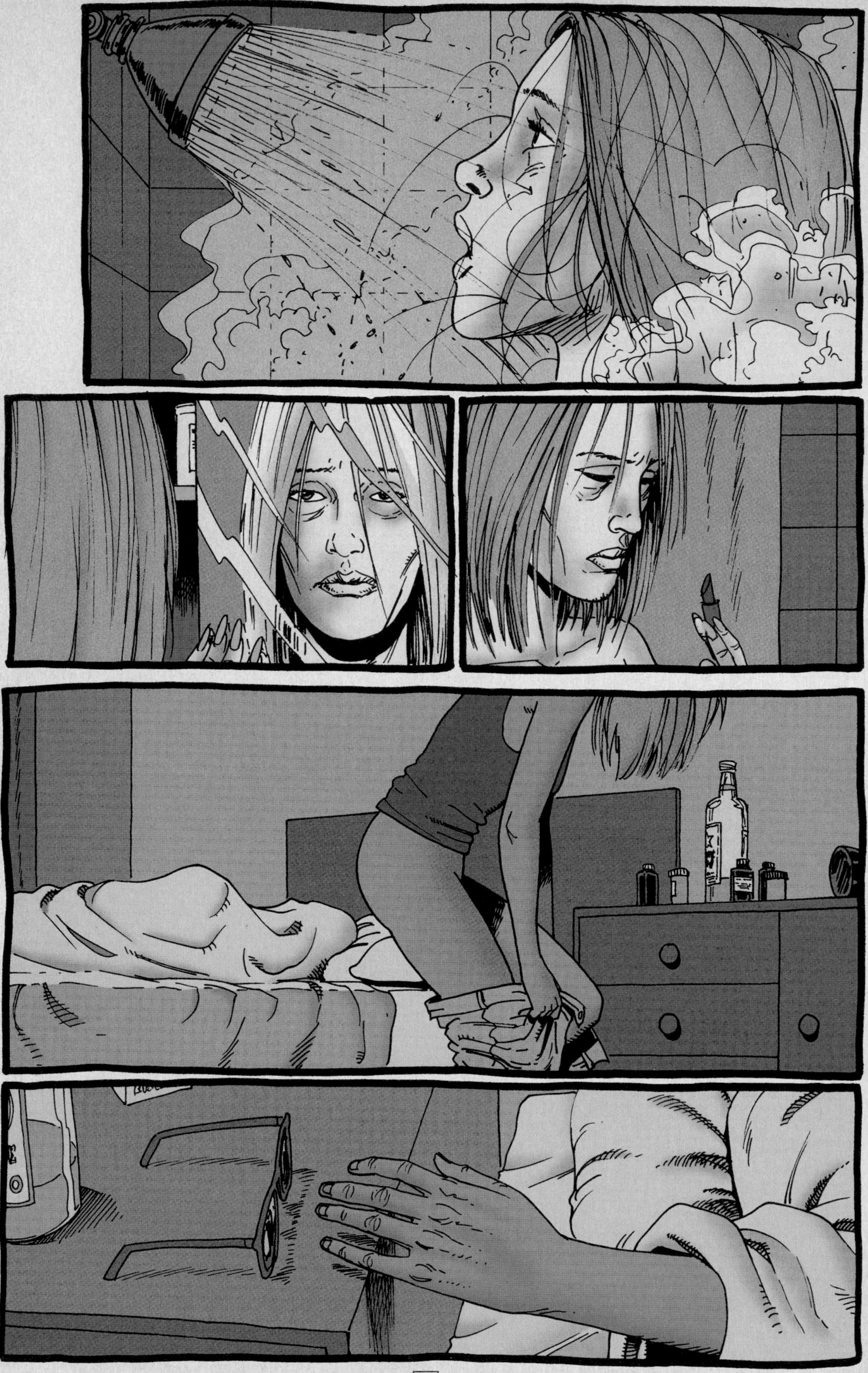

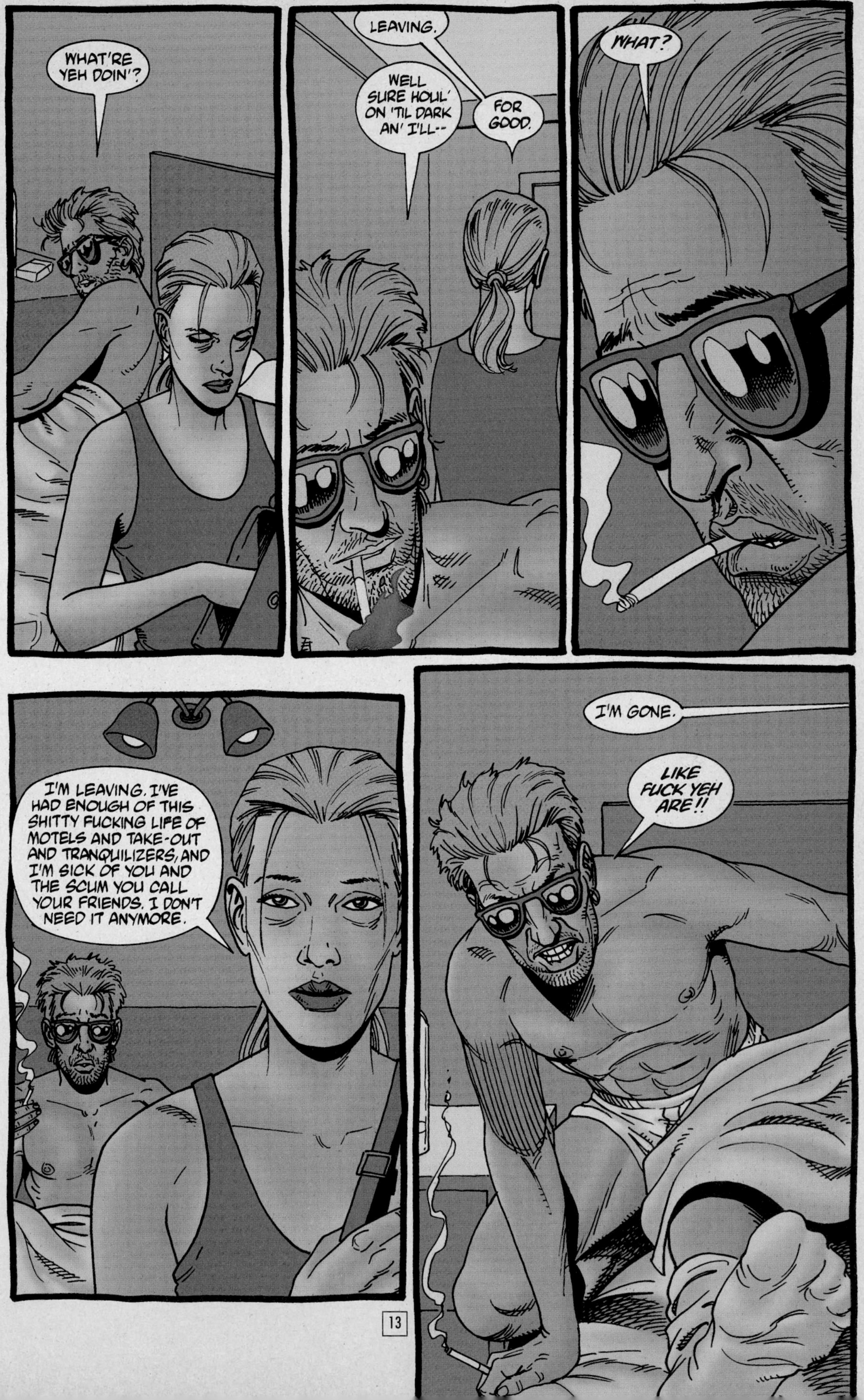
WHAT'RE YEH DOIN'?
LEAVING.
WELL SURE HOUL' ON 'TIL DARK AN' I'LL--
FOR GOOD.
WHAT?
I'M LEAVING. I'VE HAD ENOUGH OF THIS SHITTY FUCKING LIFE OF MOTELS AND TAKE-OUT AND TRANQUILIZERS, AND I'M SICK OF YOU AND THE SCUM YOU CALL YOUR FRIENDS. I DON'T NEED IT ANYMORE.
I'M GONE.
LIKE FUCK YEH ARE!!

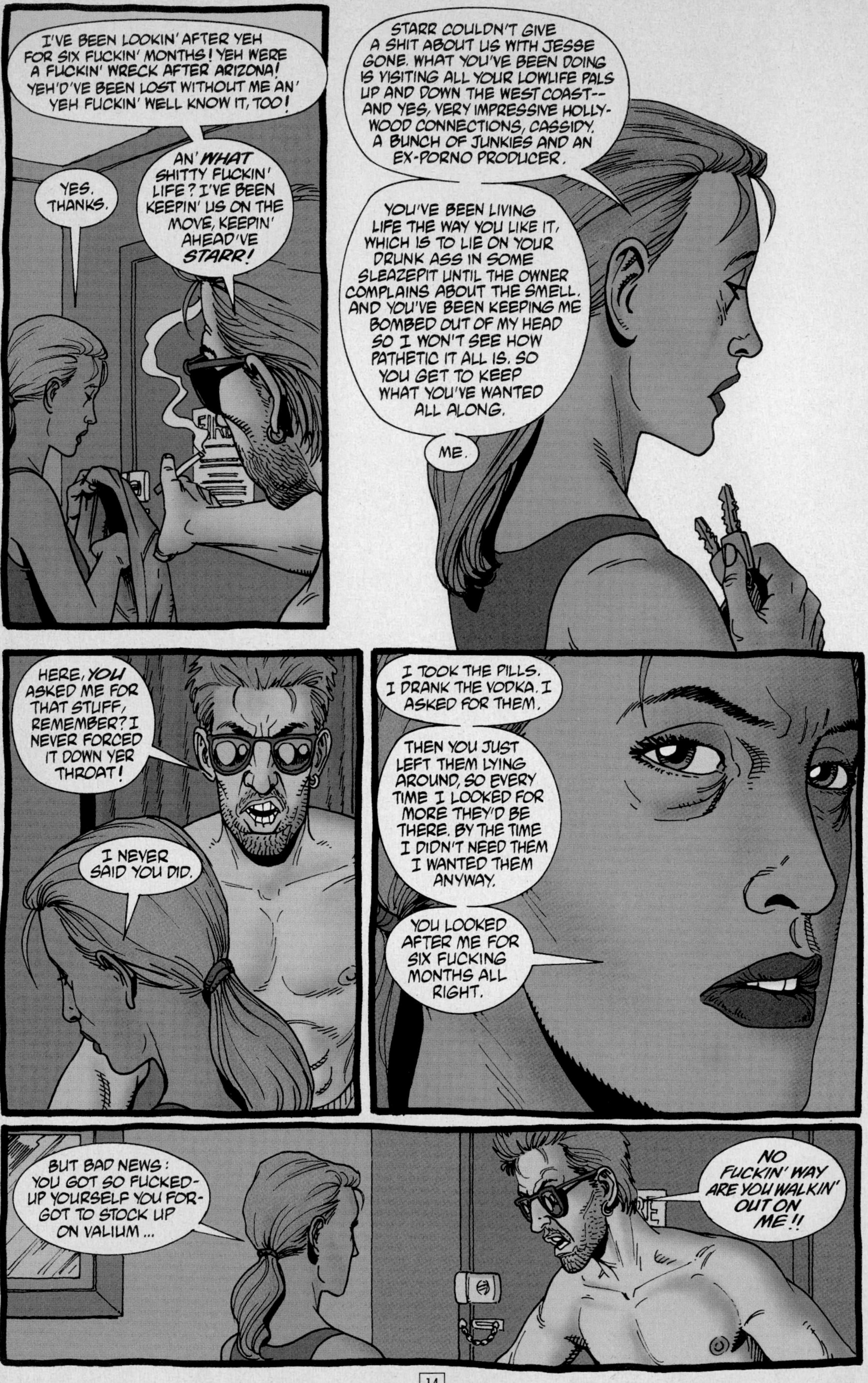

I'VE BEEN LOOKIN' AFTER YEH FOR SIX FUCKIN' MONTHS! YEH WERE A FUCKIN' WRECK AFTER ARIZONA! YEH'D'VE BEEN LOST WITHOUT ME AN' YEH FUCKIN' WELL KNOW IT, TOO!
YES. THANKS.
AN' WHAT SHITTY FUCKIN' LIFE? I'VE BEEN KEEPIN' US ON THE MOVE, KEEPIN' AHEAD'VE STARR!
STARR COULDN'T GIVE A SHIT ABOUT US WITH JESSE GONE. WHAT YOU'VE BEEN DOING IS VISITING ALL YOUR LOWLIFE PALS UP AND DOWN THE WEST COAST-- AND YES, VERY IMPRESSIVE HOLLY-WOOD CONNECTIONS, CASSIDY. A BUNCH OF JUNKIES AND AN EX-PORNO PRODUCER.
YOU'VE BEEN LIVING LIFE THE WAY YOU LIKE IT, WHICH IS TO LIE ON YOUR DRUNK ASS IN SOME SLEAZEPIT UNTIL THE OWNER COMPLAINS ABOUT THE SMELL. AND YOU'VE BEEN KEEPING ME BOMBED OUT OF MY HEAD SO I WON'T SEE HOW PATHETIC IT ALL IS. SO YOU GET TO KEEP WHAT YOU'VE WANTED ALL ALONG.
ME.
HERE, YOU ASKED ME FOR THAT STUFF, REMEMBER? I NEVER FORCED IT DOWN YER THROAT!
I NEVER SAID YOU DID.
I TOOK THE PILLS. I DRANK THE VODKA. I ASKED FOR THEM.
THEN YOU JUST LEFT THEM LYING AROUND, SO EVERY TIME I LOOKED FOR MORE THEY'D BE THERE. BY THE TIME I DIDN'T NEED THEM I WANTED THEM ANYWAY.
YOU LOOKED AFTER ME FOR SIX FUCKING MONTHS ALL RIGHT.
BUT BAD NEWS: YOU GOT SO FUCKED-UP YOURSELF YOU FOR-GOT TO STOCK UP ON VALIUM...
NO FUCKIN' WAY ARE YOU WALKIN' OUT ON ME!!

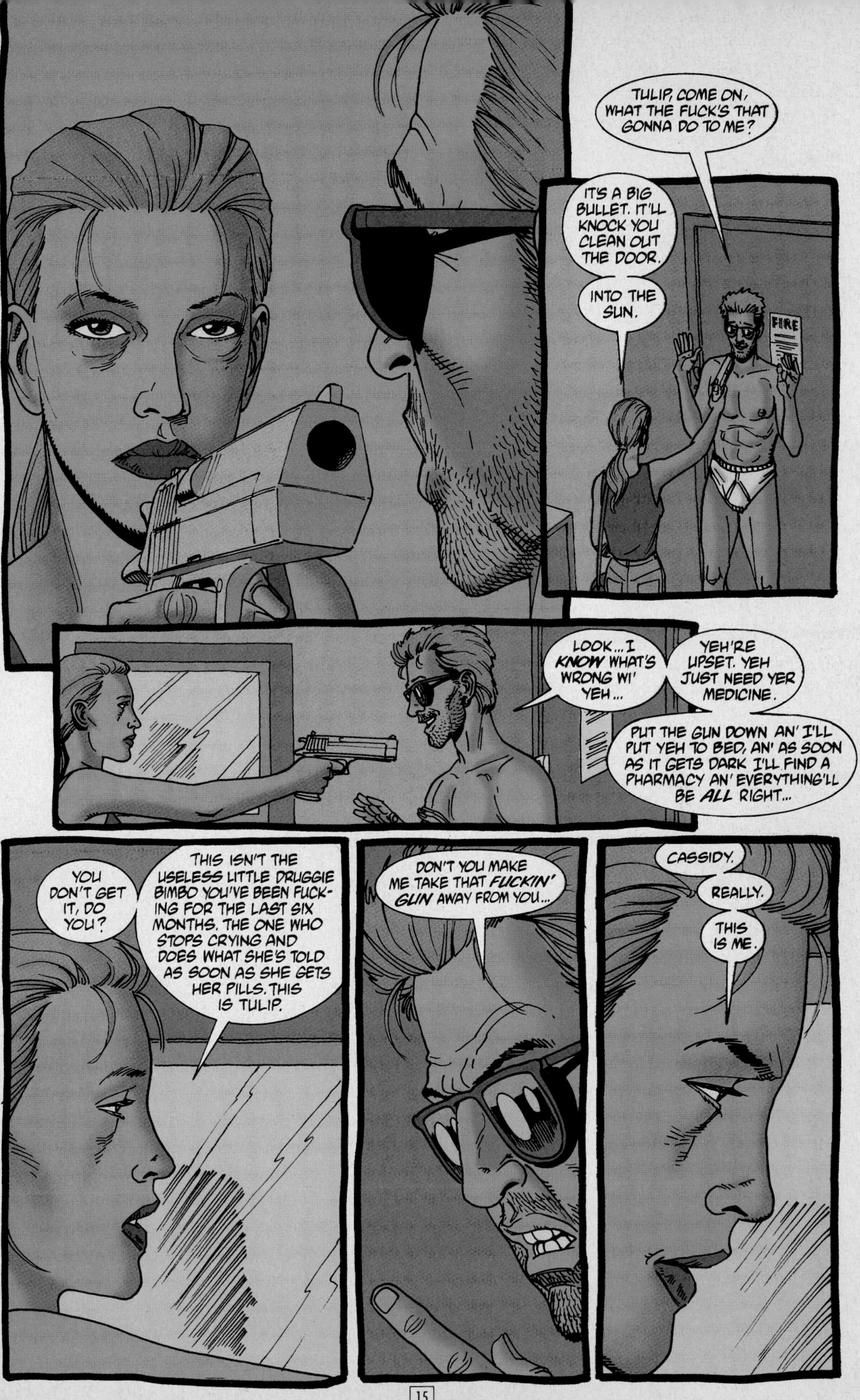
TULIP, COME ON, WHAT THE FUCK'S THAT GONNA DO TO ME?
IT'S A BIG BULLET. IT'LL KNOCK YOU CLEAN OUT THE DOOR.
INTO THE SUN.
FIRE
LOOK... I KNOW WHAT'S WRONG WI' YEH...
YEH'RE UPSET. YEH JUST NEED YER MEDICINE.
PUT THE GUN DOWN AN' I'LL PUT YEH TO BED, AN' AS SOON AS IT GETS DARK I'LL FIND A PHARMACY AN' EVERYTHING'LL BE ALL RIGHT...
YOU DON'T GET IT, DO YOU?
THIS ISN'T THE USELESS LITTLE DRUGGIE BIMBO YOU'VE BEEN FUCKING FOR THE LAST SIX MONTHS. THE ONE WHO STOPS CRYING AND DOES WHAT SHE'S TOLD AS SOON AS SHE GETS HER PILLS. THIS IS TULIP.
DON'T YOU MAKE ME TAKE THAT FUCKIN' GUN AWAY FROM YOU...
CASSIDY.
REALLY.
THIS IS ME.

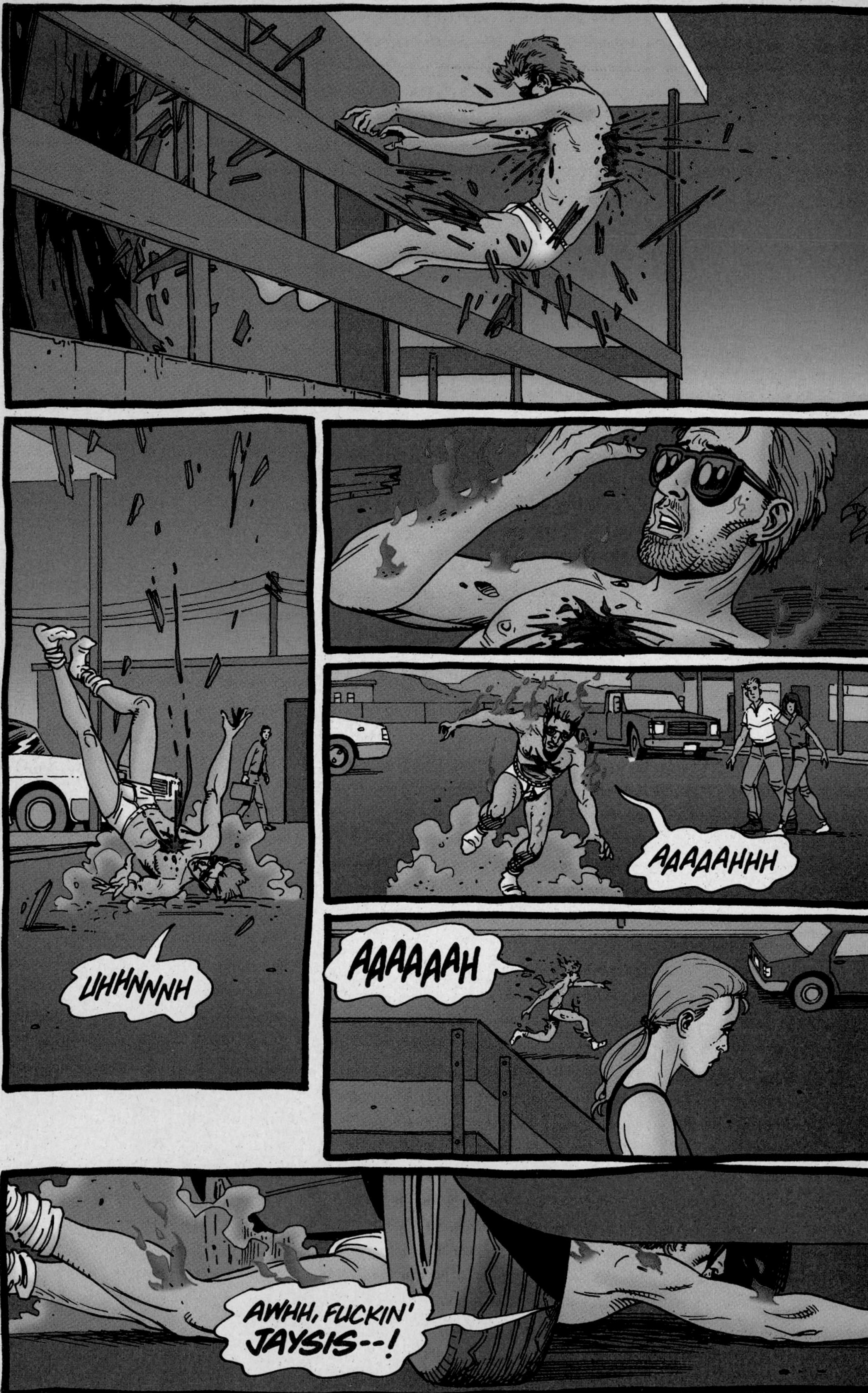
UHHNNNH
AAAAAHHH
AAAAAAH
AWHH, FUCKIN' JAYSIS--!

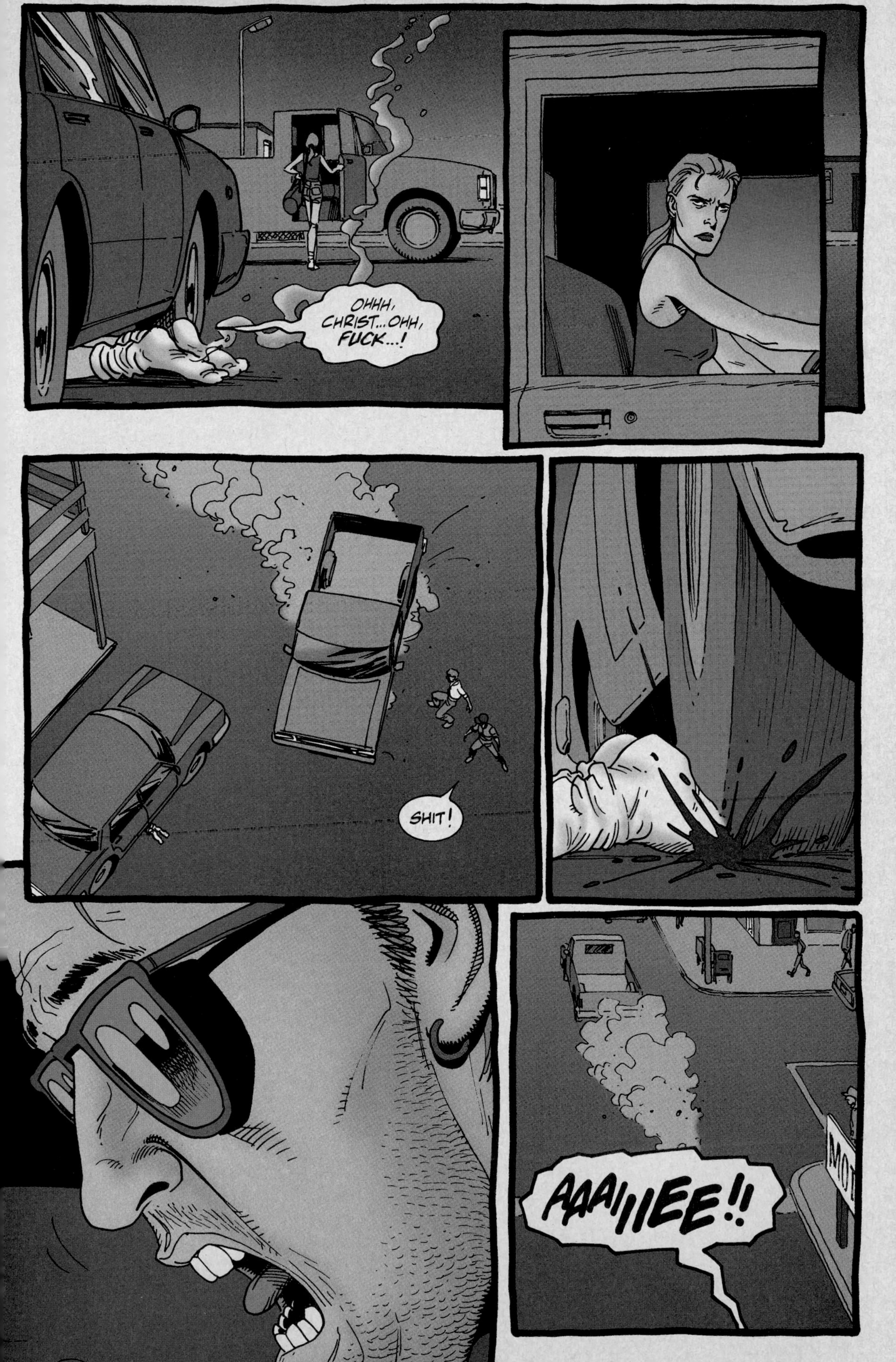
OHHH, CHRIST...OHH, FUCK...!
SHIT!
AAAIIIEE!!

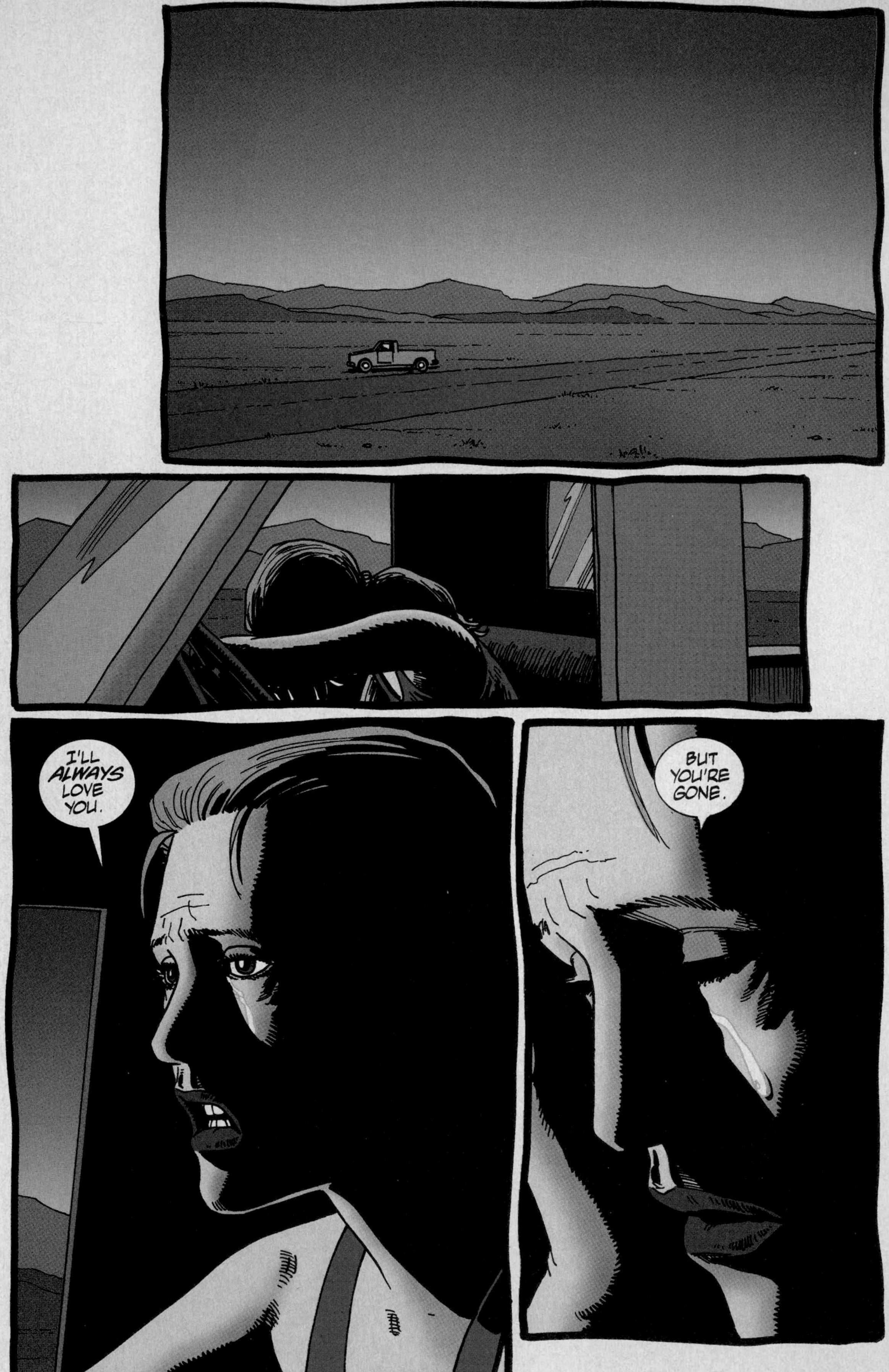
I'LL ALWAYS LOVE YOU.
BUT YOU'RE GONE.

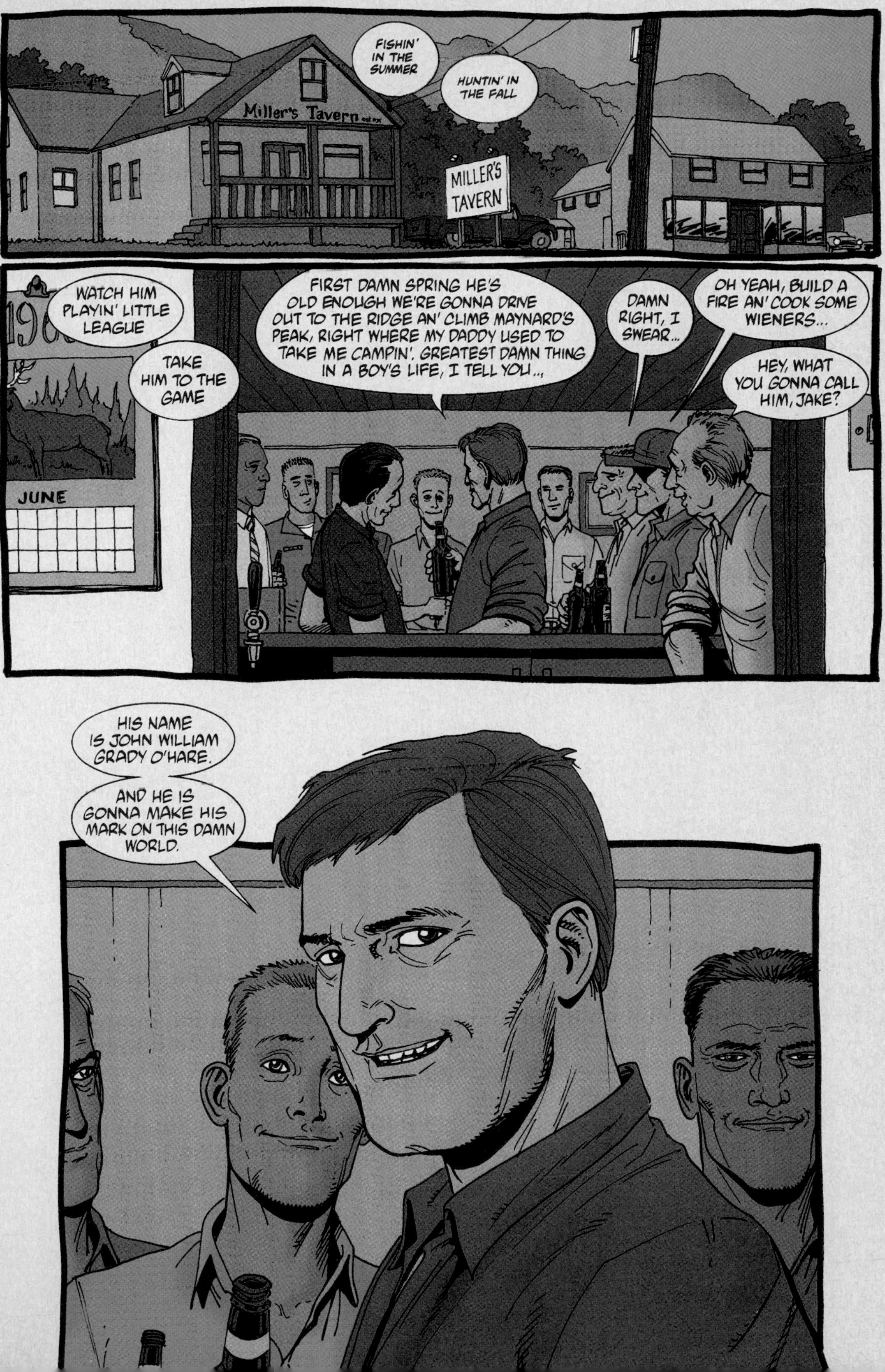
FISHIN' IN THE SUMMER
HUNTIN' IN THE FALL
Miller's Tavern
MILLER'S TAVERN
WATCH HIM PLAYIN' LITTLE LEAGUE
TAKE HIM TO THE GAME
FIRST DAMN SPRING HE'S OLD ENOUGH WE'RE GONNA DRIVE OUT TO THE RIDGE AN' CLIMB MAYNARD'S PEAK, RIGHT WHERE MY DADDY USED TO TAKE ME CAMPIN'. GREATEST DAMN THING IN A BOY'S LIFE, I TELL YOU...
DAMN RIGHT, I SWEAR...
OH YEAH, BUILD A FIRE AN' COOK SOME WIENERS...
HEY, WHAT YOU GONNA CALL HIM, JAKE?
JUNE
HIS NAME IS JOHN WILLIAM GRADY O'HARE.
AND HE IS GONNA MAKE HIS MARK ON THIS DAMN WORLD.

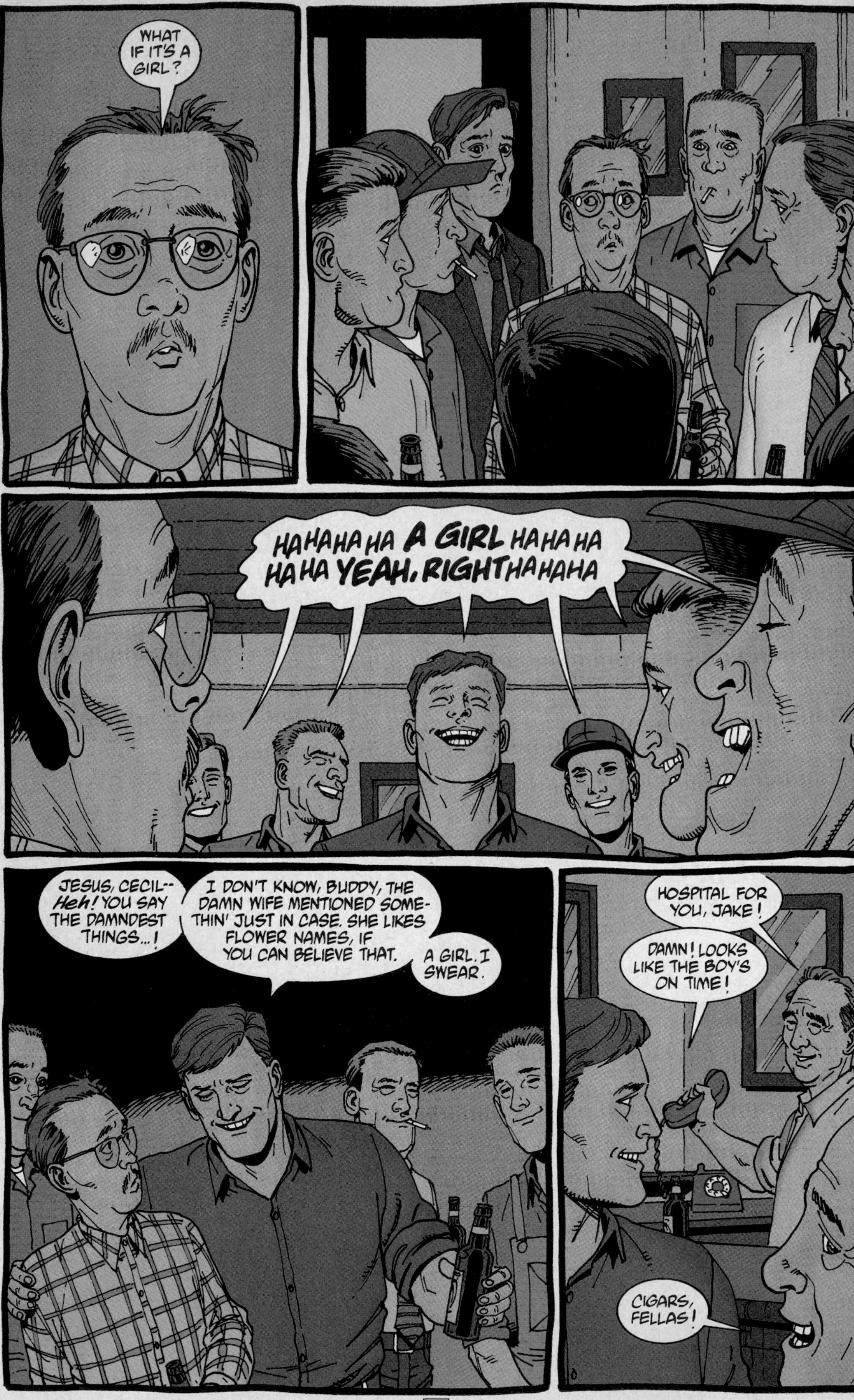
WHAT IF IT'S A GIRL?
HAHAHAHA A GIRL HAHAHA HAHA YEAH, RIGHT HAHAHA
JESUS, CECIL-- Heh! YOU SAY THE DAMNDEST THINGS...!
I DON'T KNOW, BUDDY, THE DAMN WIFE MENTIONED SOMETHIN' JUST IN CASE. SHE LIKES FLOWER NAMES, IF YOU CAN BELIEVE THAT.
A GIRL. I SWEAR.
HOSPITAL FOR YOU, JAKE!
DAMN! LOOKS LIKE THE BOY'S ON TIME!
CIGARS, FELLAS!

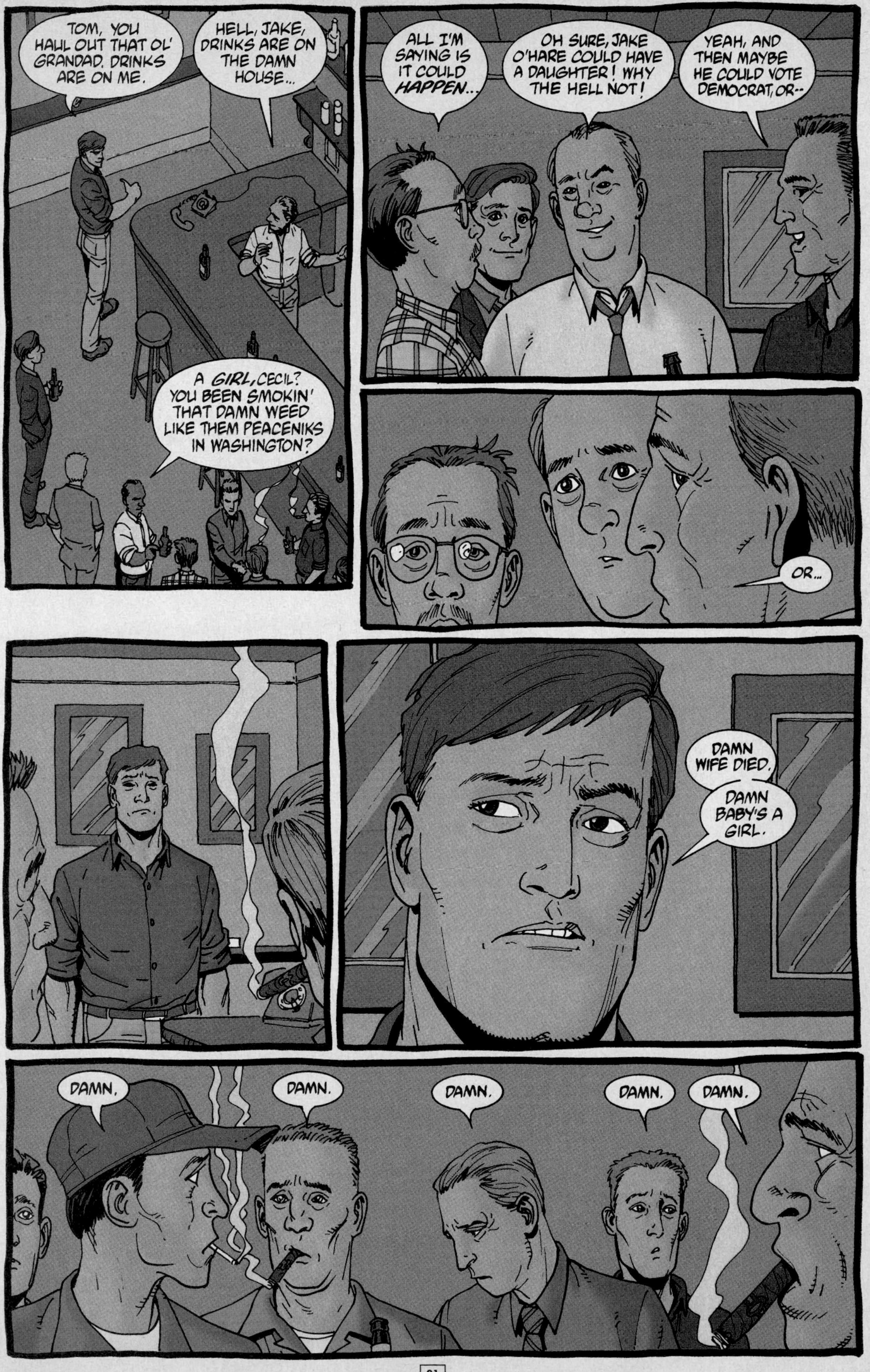
TOM, YOU HAUL OUT THAT OL' GRANDAD. DRINKS ARE ON ME.
HELL, JAKE, DRINKS ARE ON THE DAMN HOUSE...
A GIRL, CECIL? YOU BEEN SMOKIN' THAT DAMN WEED LIKE THEM PEACENIKS IN WASHINGTON?
ALL I'M SAYING IS IT COULD HAPPEN...
OH SURE, JAKE O'HARE COULD HAVE A DAUGHTER! WHY THE HELL NOT!
YEAH, AND THEN MAYBE HE COULD VOTE DEMOCRAT, OR--
OR...
DAMN WIFE DIED.
DAMN BABY'S A GIRL.
DAMN.
DAMN.
DAMN.
DAMN.
DAMN.

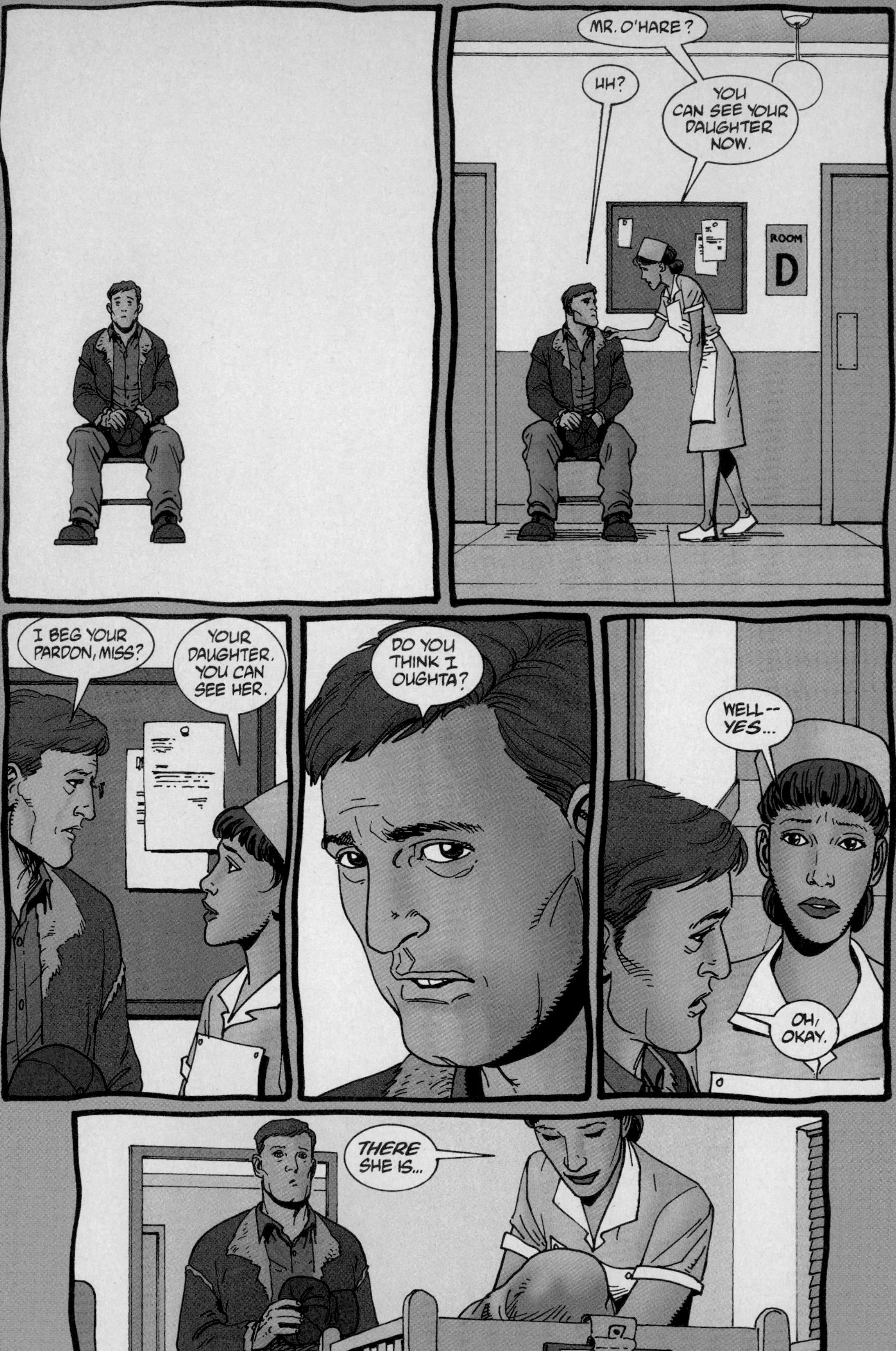
MR. O'HARE?
UH?
YOU CAN SEE YOUR DAUGHTER NOW.
ROOM D
I BEG YOUR PARDON, MISS?
YOUR DAUGHTER. YOU CAN SEE HER.
DO YOU THINK I OUGHTA?
WELL-- YES...
OH, OKAY.
THERE SHE IS...
O'HARE, TULIP

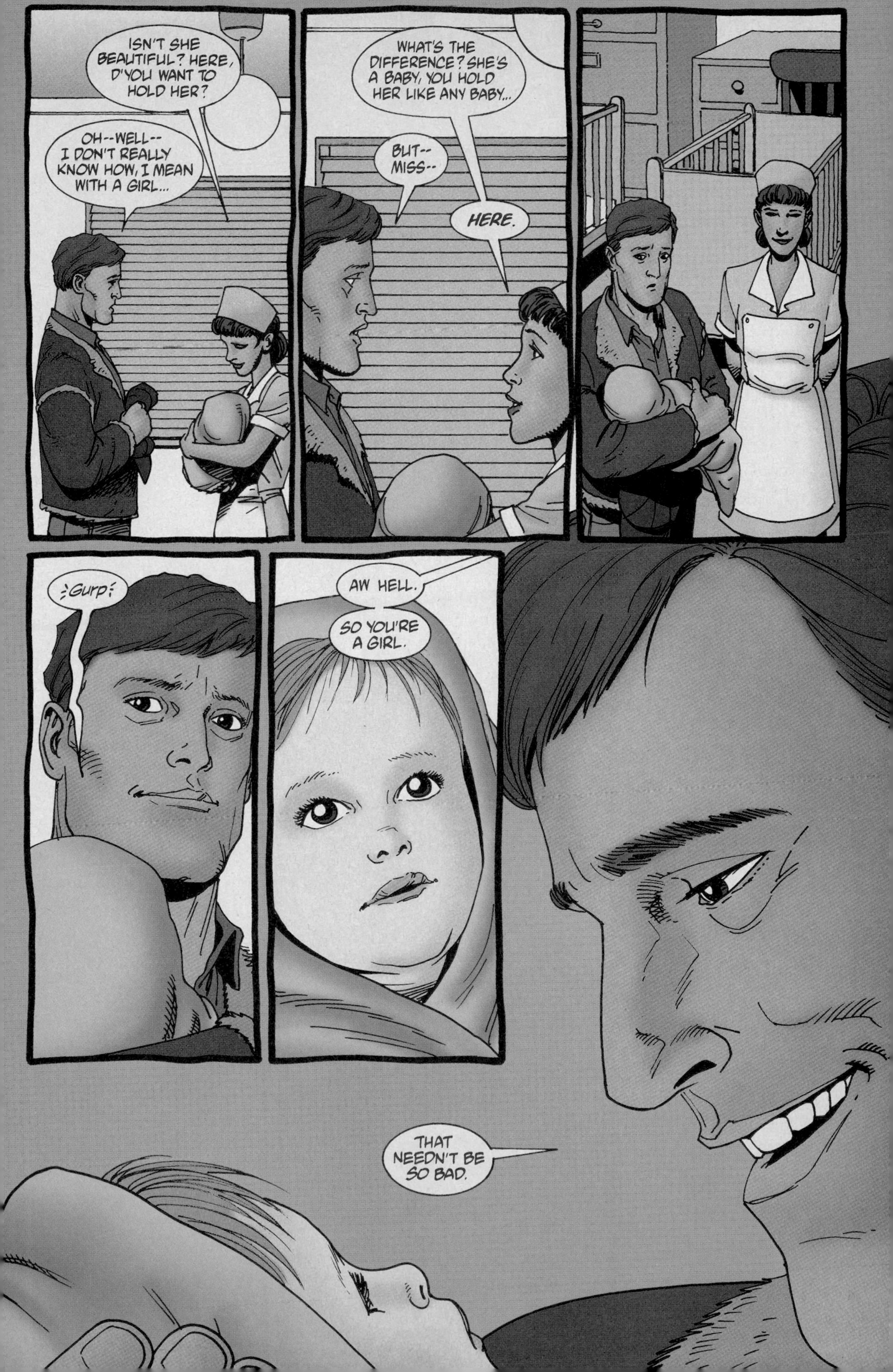
ISN'T SHE BEAUTIFUL? HERE, D'YOU WANT TO HOLD HER?
OH--WELL-- I DON'T REALLY KNOW HOW, I MEAN WITH A GIRL...
WHAT'S THE DIFFERENCE? SHE'S A BABY, YOU HOLD HER LIKE ANY BABY...
BUT-- MISS--
HERE.
Gurp
AW HELL.
SO YOU'RE A GIRL.
THAT NEEDN'T BE SO BAD.

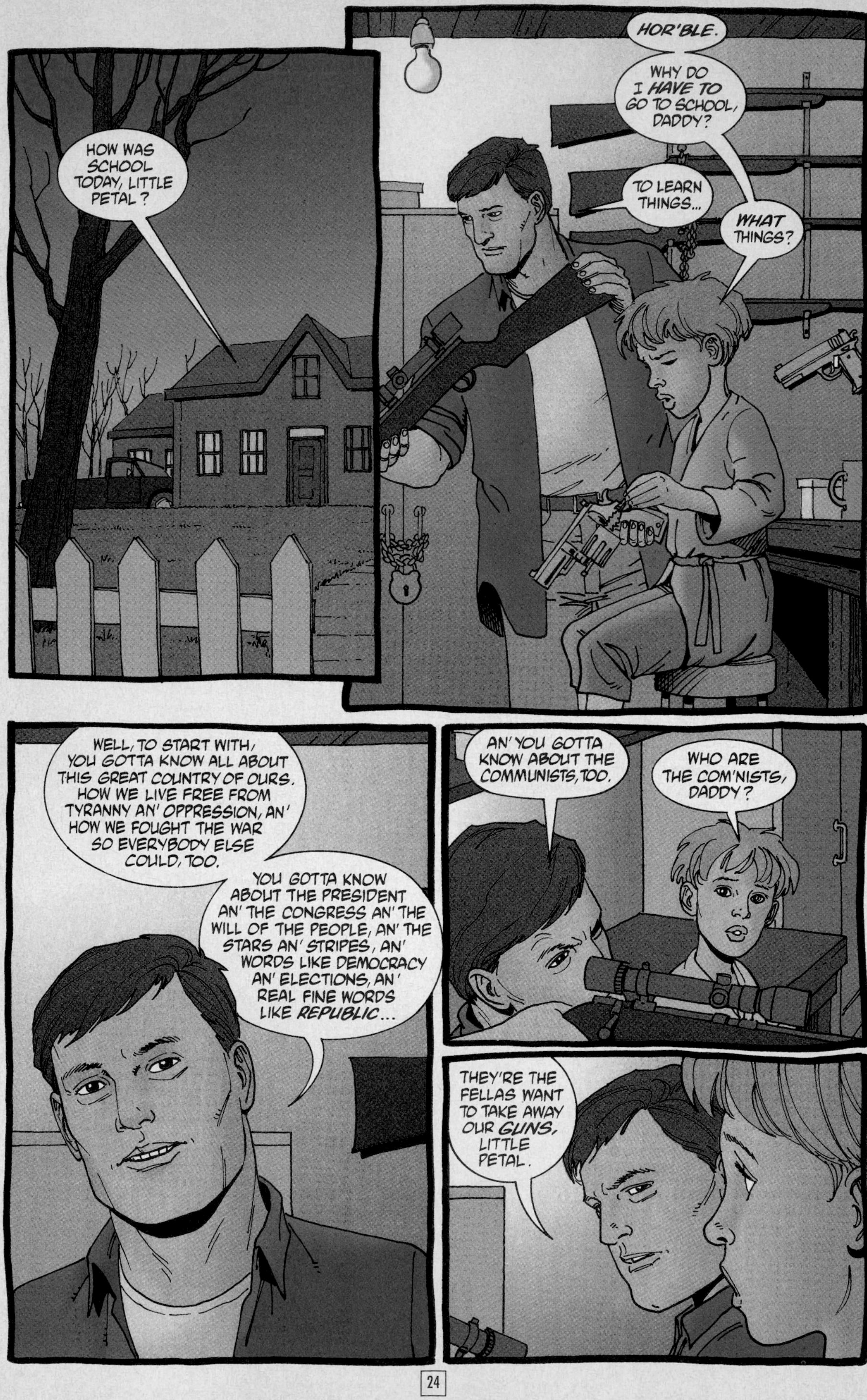
HOW WAS SCHOOL TODAY, LITTLE PETAL?
HOR'BLE.
WHY DO I HAVE TO GO TO SCHOOL, DADDY?
TO LEARN THINGS...
WHAT THINGS?
WELL, TO START WITH, YOU GOTTA KNOW ALL ABOUT THIS GREAT COUNTRY OF OURS. HOW WE LIVE FREE FROM TYRANNY AN' OPPRESSION, AN' HOW WE FOUGHT THE WAR SO EVERYBODY ELSE COULD, TOO.
YOU GOTTA KNOW ABOUT THE PRESIDENT AN' THE CONGRESS AN' THE WILL OF THE PEOPLE, AN' THE STARS AN' STRIPES, AN' WORDS LIKE DEMOCRACY AN' ELECTIONS, AN' REAL FINE WORDS LIKE REPUBLIC...
AN' YOU GOTTA KNOW ABOUT THE COMMUNISTS, TOO.
WHO ARE THE COM'NISTS, DADDY?
THEY'RE THE FELLAS WANT TO TAKE AWAY OUR GUNS, LITTLE PETAL.

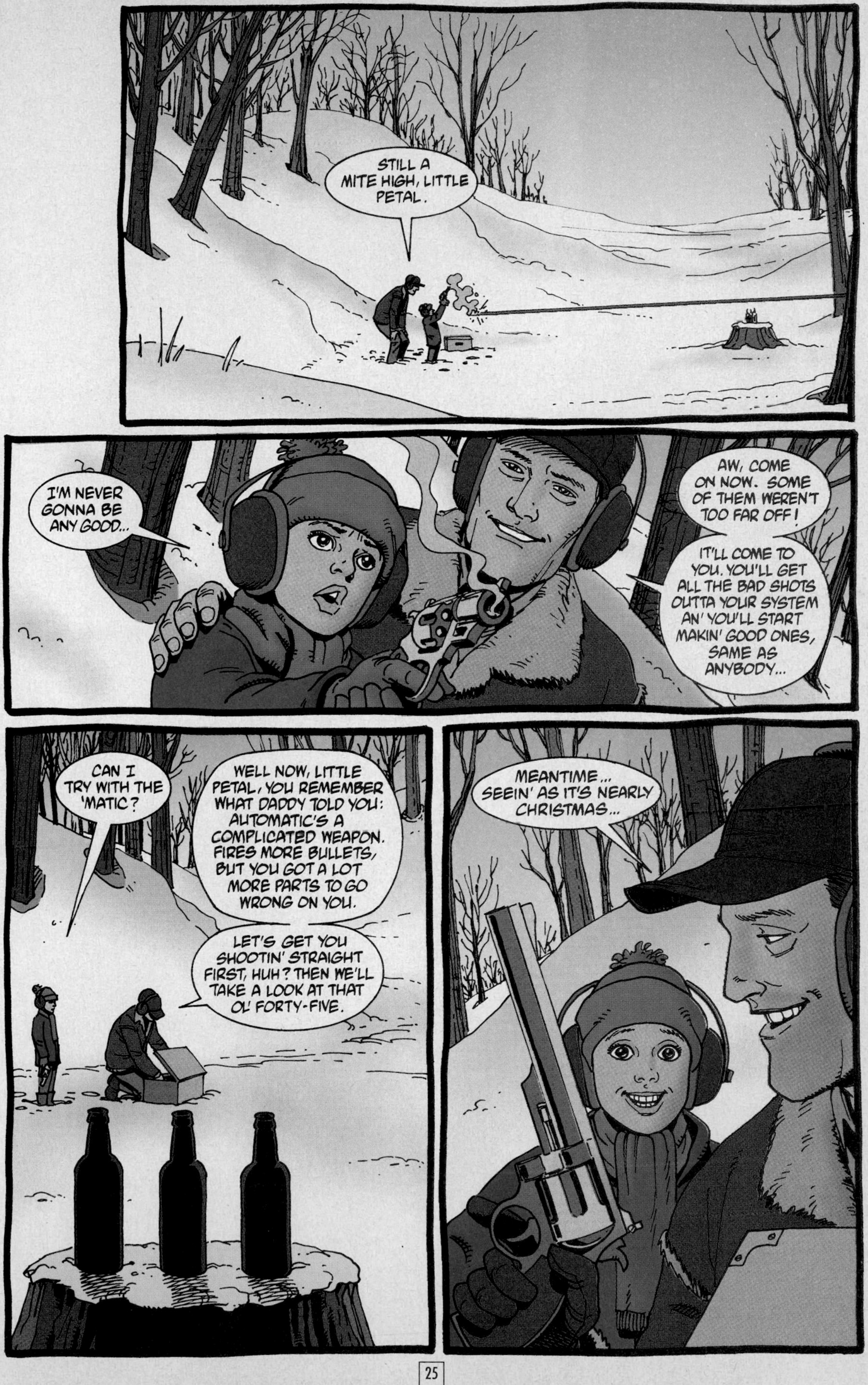
STILL A MITE HIGH, LITTLE PETAL.
I'M NEVER GONNA BE ANY GOOD...
AW, COME ON NOW. SOME OF THEM WEREN'T TOO FAR OFF!
IT'LL COME TO YOU. YOU'LL GET ALL THE BAD SHOTS OUTTA YOUR SYSTEM AN' YOU'LL START MAKIN' GOOD ONES, SAME AS ANYBODY...
CAN I TRY WITH THE 'MATIC?
WELL NOW, LITTLE PETAL, YOU REMEMBER WHAT DADDY TOLD YOU: AUTOMATIC'S A COMPLICATED WEAPON. FIRES MORE BULLETS, BUT YOU GOT A LOT MORE PARTS TO GO WRONG ON YOU.
LET'S GET YOU SHOOTIN' STRAIGHT FIRST, HUH? THEN WE'LL TAKE A LOOK AT THAT OL' FORTY-FIVE.
MEANTIME... SEEIN' AS IT'S NEARLY CHRISTMAS...

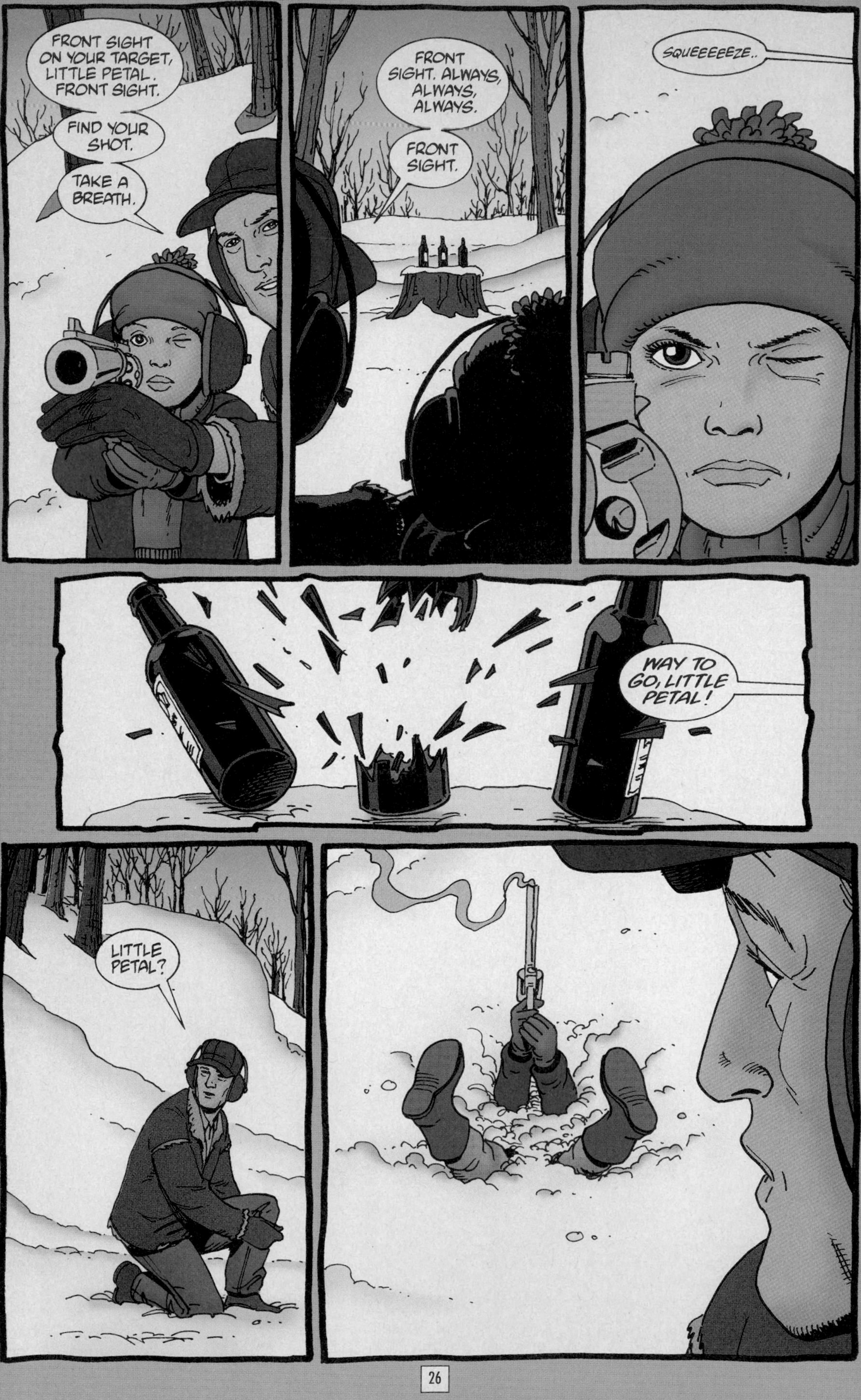
FRONT SIGHT ON YOUR TARGET, LITTLE PETAL. FRONT SIGHT.
FIND YOUR SHOT.
TAKE A BREATH.
FRONT SIGHT. ALWAYS, ALWAYS, ALWAYS.
FRONT SIGHT.
SQUEEEEEEZE..
WAY TO GO, LITTLE PETAL!
LITTLE PETAL?

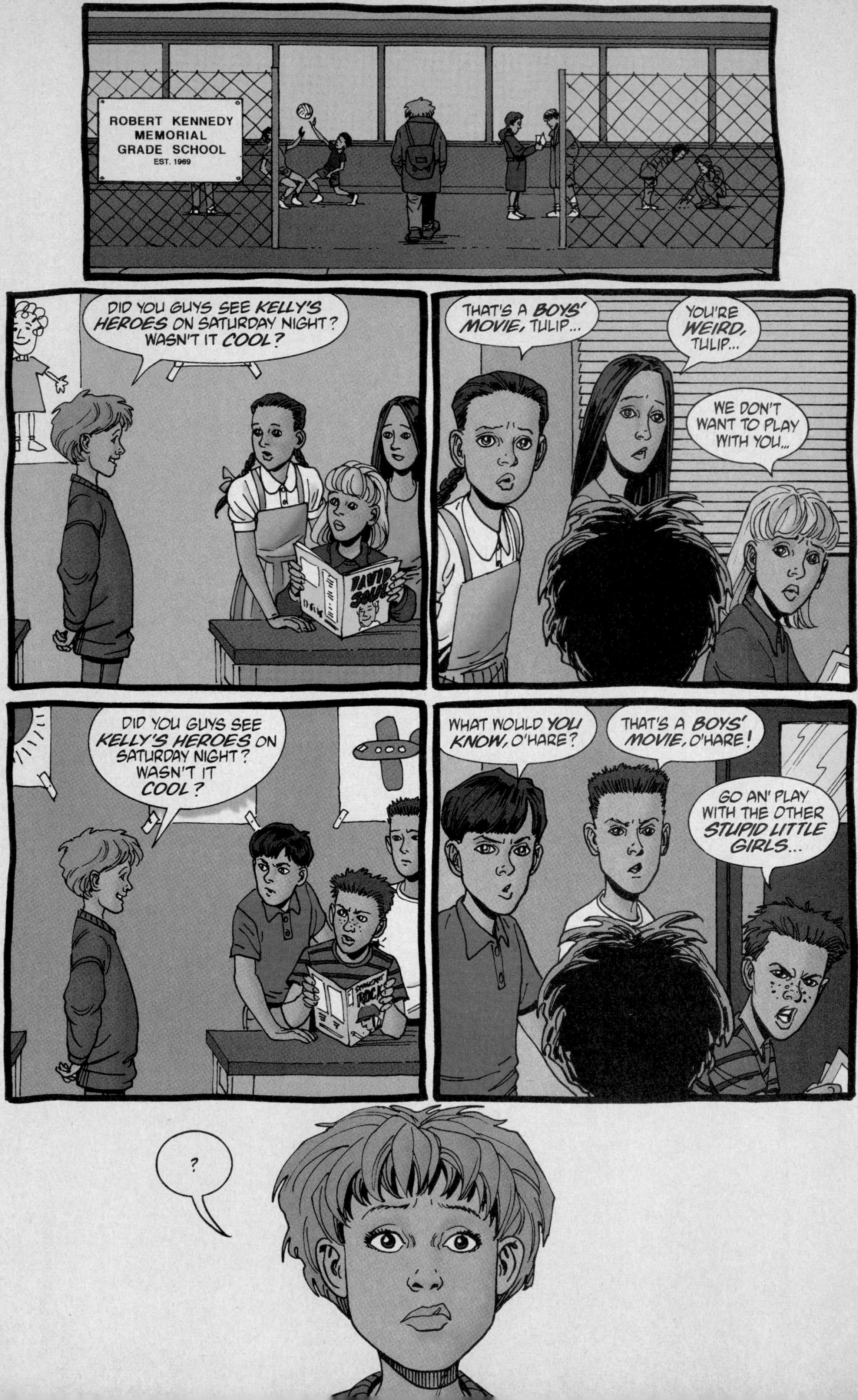
ROBERT KENNEDY MEMORIAL GRADE SCHOOL EST. 1969
DID YOU GUYS SEE KELLY'S HEROES ON SATURDAY NIGHT? WASN'T IT COOL?
THAT'S A BOYS' MOVIE, TULIP...
YOU'RE WEIRD, TULIP...
WE DON'T WANT TO PLAY WITH YOU...
DID YOU GUYS SEE KELLY'S HEROES ON SATURDAY NIGHT? WASN'T IT COOL?
WHAT WOULD YOU KNOW, O'HARE?
THAT'S A BOYS' MOVIE, O'HARE!
GO AN' PLAY WITH THE OTHER STUPID LITTLE GIRLS...
?

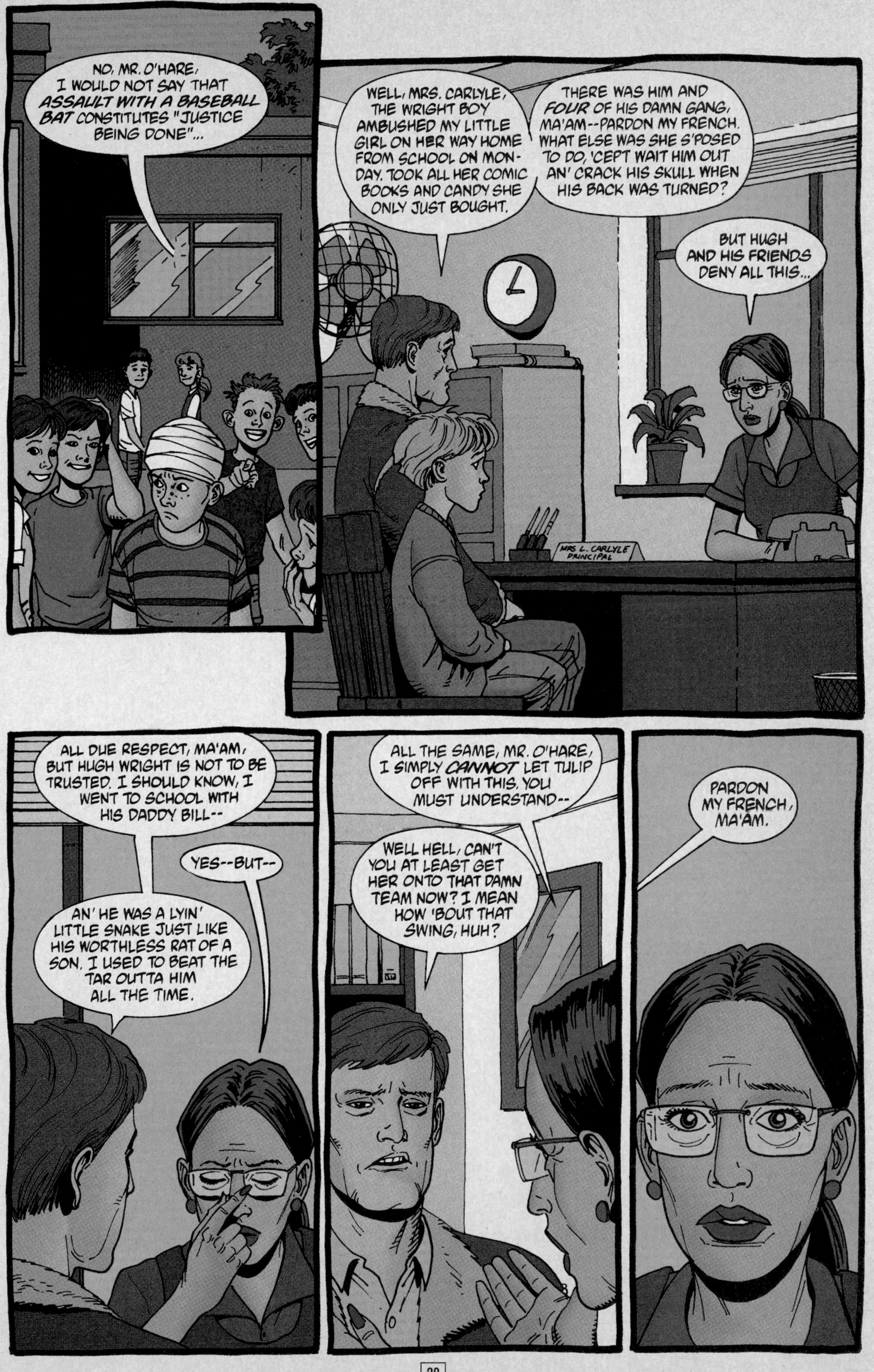
NO, MR. O'HARE, I WOULD NOT SAY THAT ASSAULT WITH A BASEBALL BAT CONSTITUTES "JUSTICE BEING DONE"...
WELL, MRS. CARLYLE, THE WRIGHT BOY AMBUSHED MY LITTLE GIRL ON HER WAY HOME FROM SCHOOL ON MONDAY. TOOK ALL HER COMIC BOOKS AND CANDY SHE ONLY JUST BOUGHT.
THERE WAS HIM AND FOUR OF HIS DAMN GANG, MA'AM--PARDON MY FRENCH. WHAT ELSE WAS SHE S'POSED TO DO, 'CEPT WAIT HIM OUT AN' CRACK HIS SKULL WHEN HIS BACK WAS TURNED?
BUT HUGH AND HIS FRIENDS DENY ALL THIS...
MRS L. CARLYLE PRINCIPAL
ALL DUE RESPECT, MA'AM, BUT HUGH WRIGHT IS NOT TO BE TRUSTED. I SHOULD KNOW, I WENT TO SCHOOL WITH HIS DADDY BILL--
YES--BUT--
AN' HE WAS A LYIN' LITTLE SNAKE JUST LIKE HIS WORTHLESS RAT OF A SON. I USED TO BEAT THE TAR OUTTA HIM ALL THE TIME.
ALL THE SAME, MR. O'HARE, I SIMPLY CANNOT LET TULIP OFF WITH THIS. YOU MUST UNDERSTAND--
WELL HELL, CAN'T YOU AT LEAST GET HER ONTO THAT DAMN TEAM NOW? I MEAN HOW 'BOUT THAT SWING, HUH?
PARDON MY FRENCH, MA'AM.

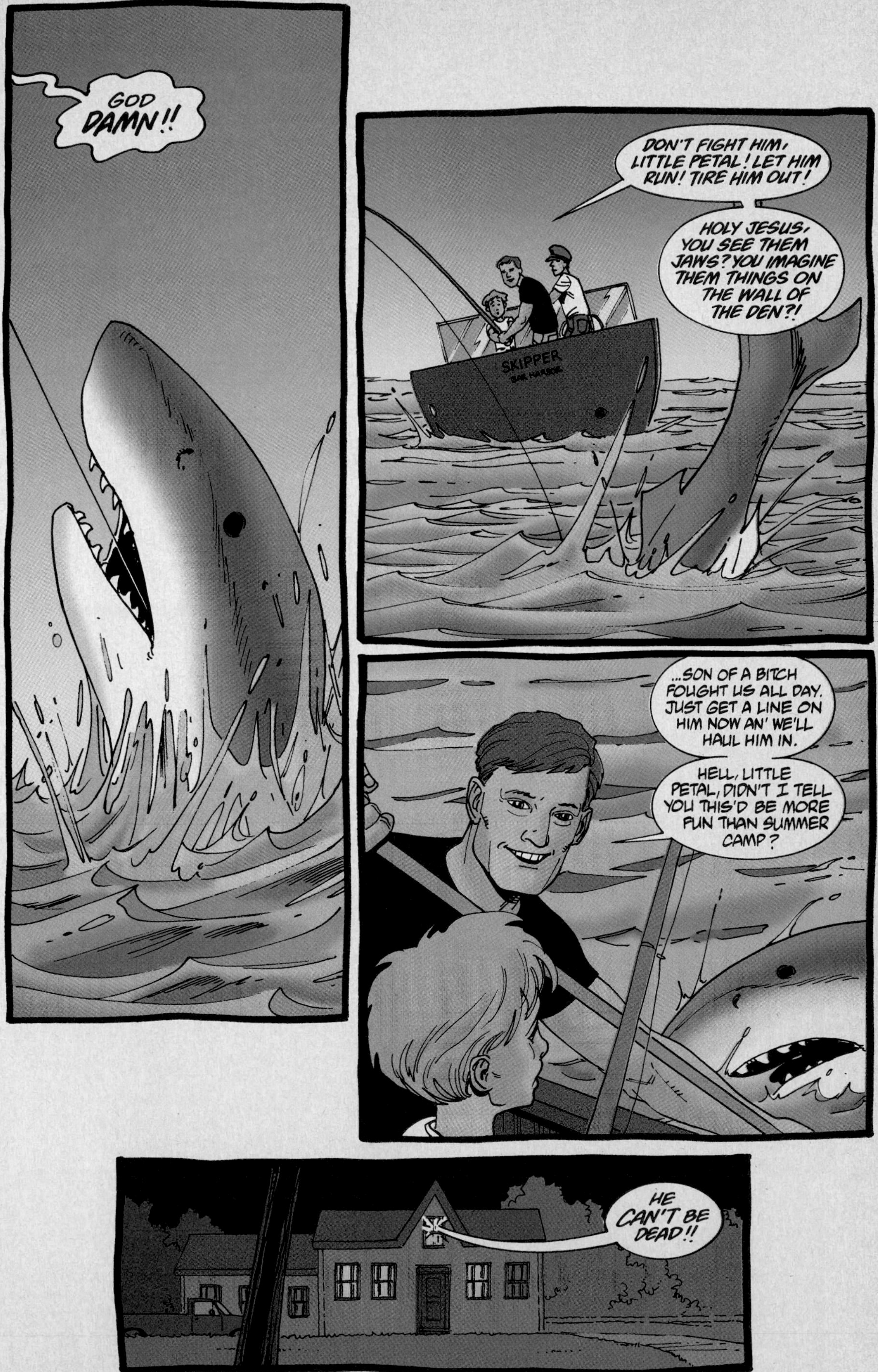
GOD DAMN!!
DON'T FIGHT HIM, LITTLE PETAL! LET HIM RUN! TIRE HIM OUT!
HOLY JESUS, YOU SEE THEM JAWS? YOU IMAGINE THEM THINGS ON THE WALL OF THE DEN?!
SKIPPER
...SON OF A BITCH FOUGHT US ALL DAY. JUST GET A LINE ON HIM NOW AN' WE'LL HAUL HIM IN.
HELL, LITTLE PETAL, DIDN'T I TELL YOU THIS'D BE MORE FUN THAN SUMMER CAMP?
HE CAN'T BE DEAD!!

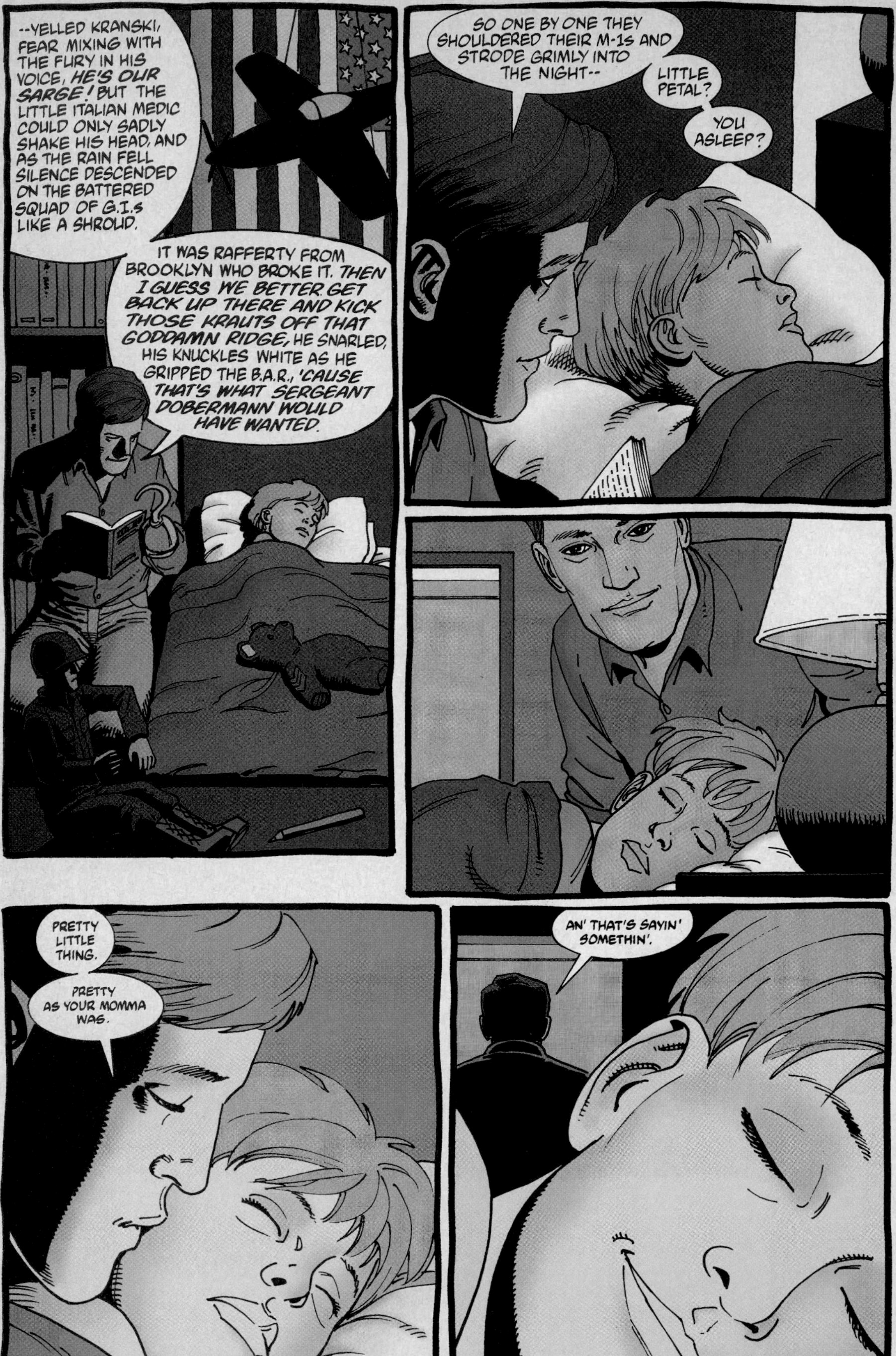
--YELLED KRANSKI, FEAR MIXING WITH THE FURY IN HIS VOICE, HE'S OUR SARGE! BUT THE LITTLE ITALIAN MEDIC COULD ONLY SADLY SHAKE HIS HEAD, AND AS THE RAIN FELL SILENCE DESCENDED ON THE BATTERED SQUAD OF G.I.s LIKE A SHROUD.
IT WAS RAFFERTY FROM BROOKLYN WHO BROKE IT. THEN I GUESS WE BETTER GET BACK UP THERE AND KICK THOSE KRAUTS OFF THAT GODDAMN RIDGE, HE SNARLED, HIS KNUCKLES WHITE AS HE GRIPPED THE B.A.R., 'CAUSE THAT'S WHAT SERGEANT DOBERMANN WOULD HAVE WANTED.
SO ONE BY ONE THEY SHOULDERED THEIR M-1s AND STRODE GRIMLY INTO THE NIGHT--
LITTLE PETAL?
YOU ASLEEP?
PRETTY LITTLE THING.
PRETTY AS YOUR MOMMA WAS.
AN' THAT'S SAYIN' SOMETHIN'.

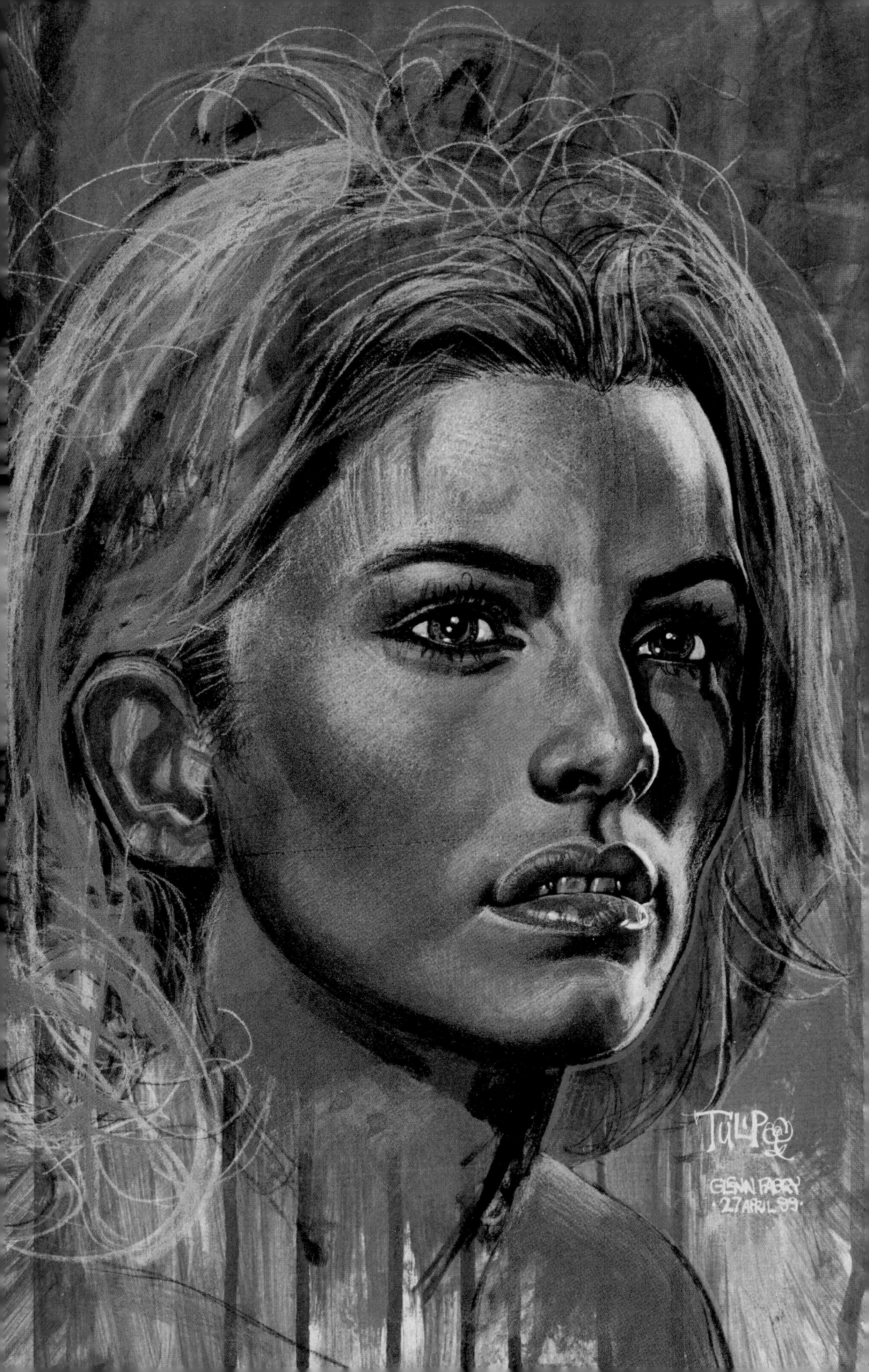
TULIP
GLENN FABRY
·27 APRIL 99·

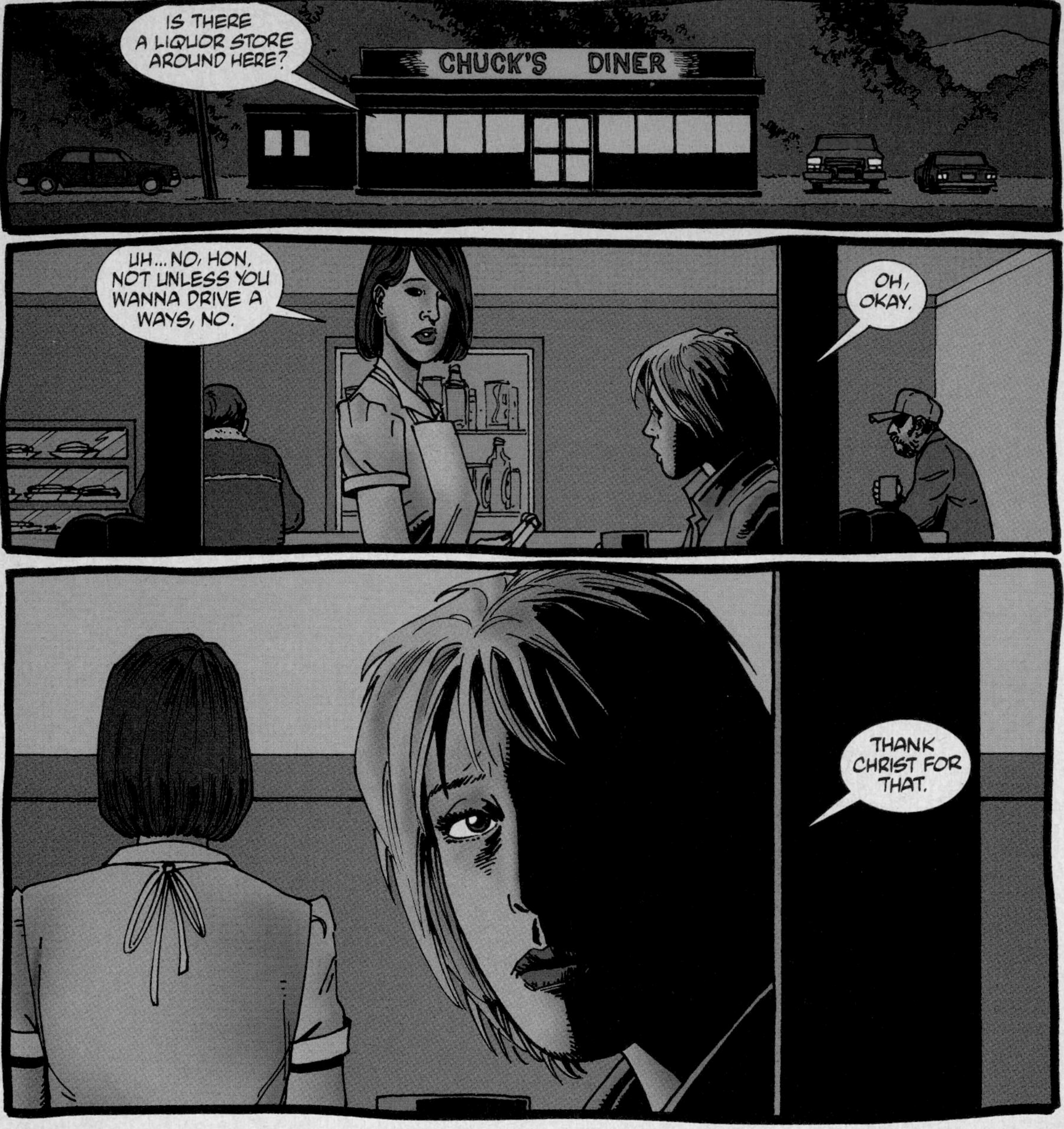
IS THERE A LIQUOR STORE AROUND HERE?
CHUCK'S DINER
UH... NO, HON, NOT UNLESS YOU WANNA DRIVE A WAYS, NO.
OH, OKAY.
THANK CHRIST FOR THAT.

EVEN HITGIRLS GET THE BLUES

GARTH ENNIS - Writer STEVE DILLON - Artist

PAMELA RAMBO - Colorist CLEM ROBINS - Letterer AXEL ALONSO - Editor

PREACHER created by GARTH ENNIS and STEVE DILLON

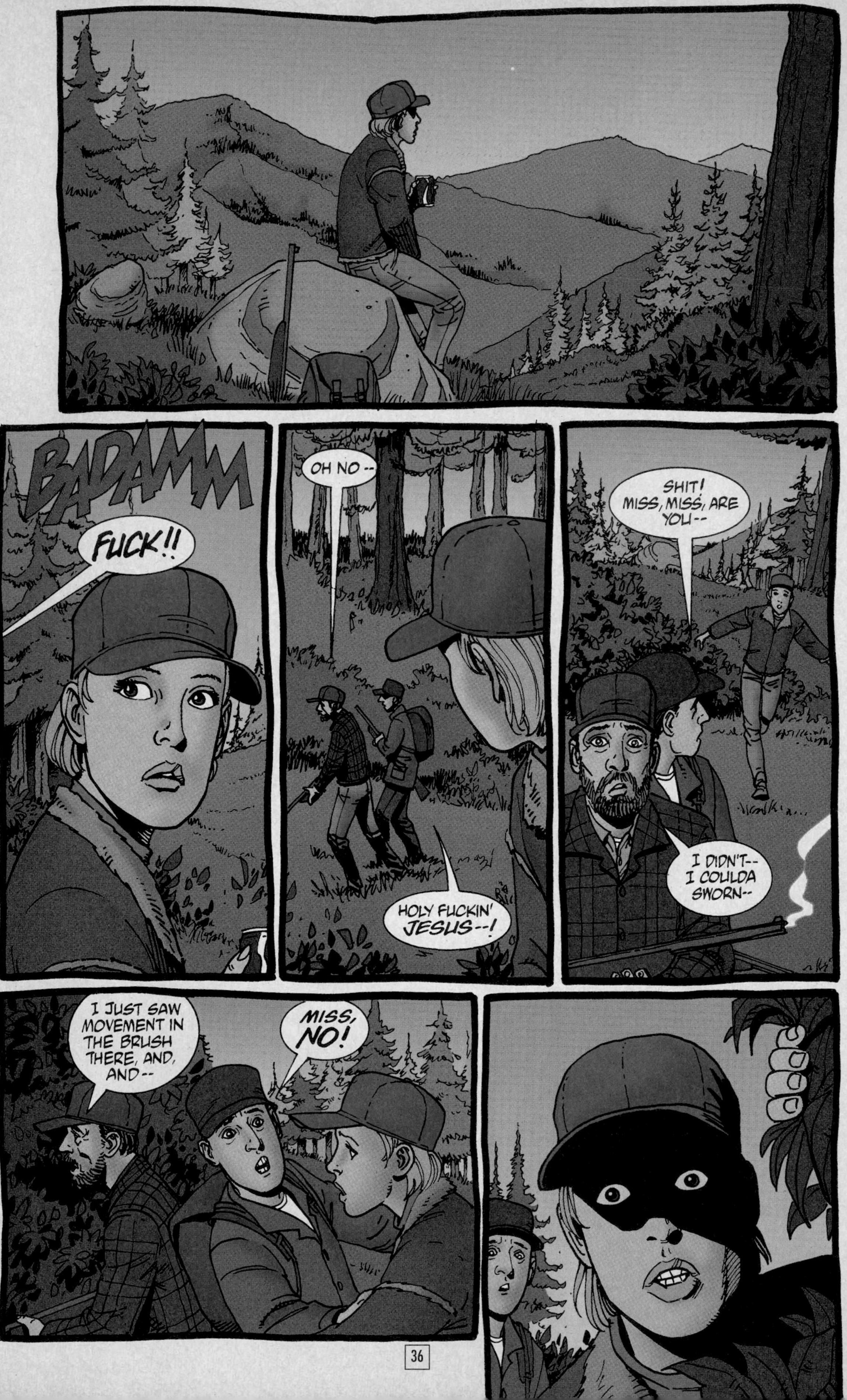
BADAMM
FUCK!!
OH NO --
HOLY FUCKIN' JESUS --!
SHIT! MISS, MISS, ARE YOU --
I DIDN'T -- I COULDA SWORN --
I JUST SAW MOVEMENT IN THE BRUSH THERE, AND, AND --
MISS, NO!

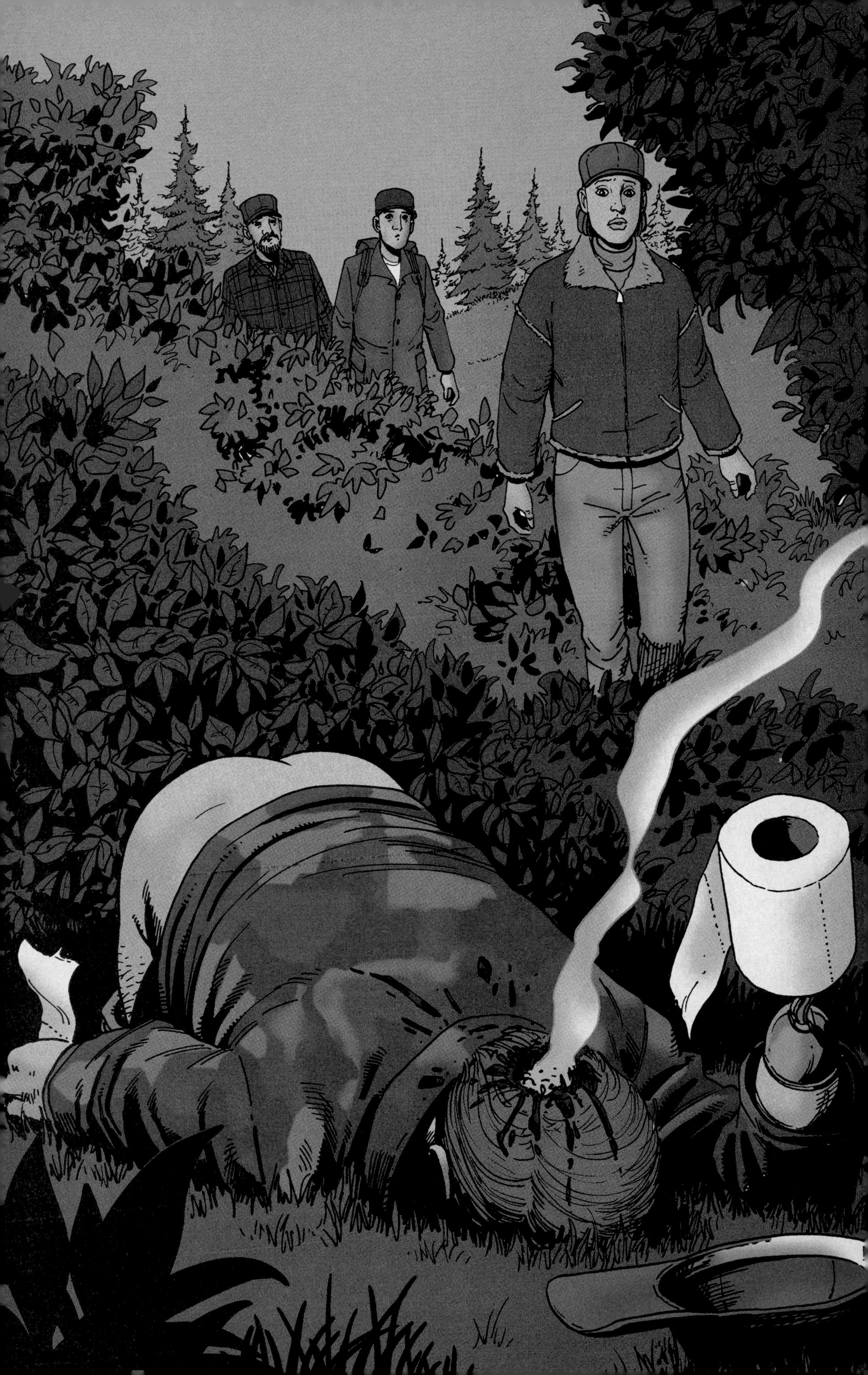

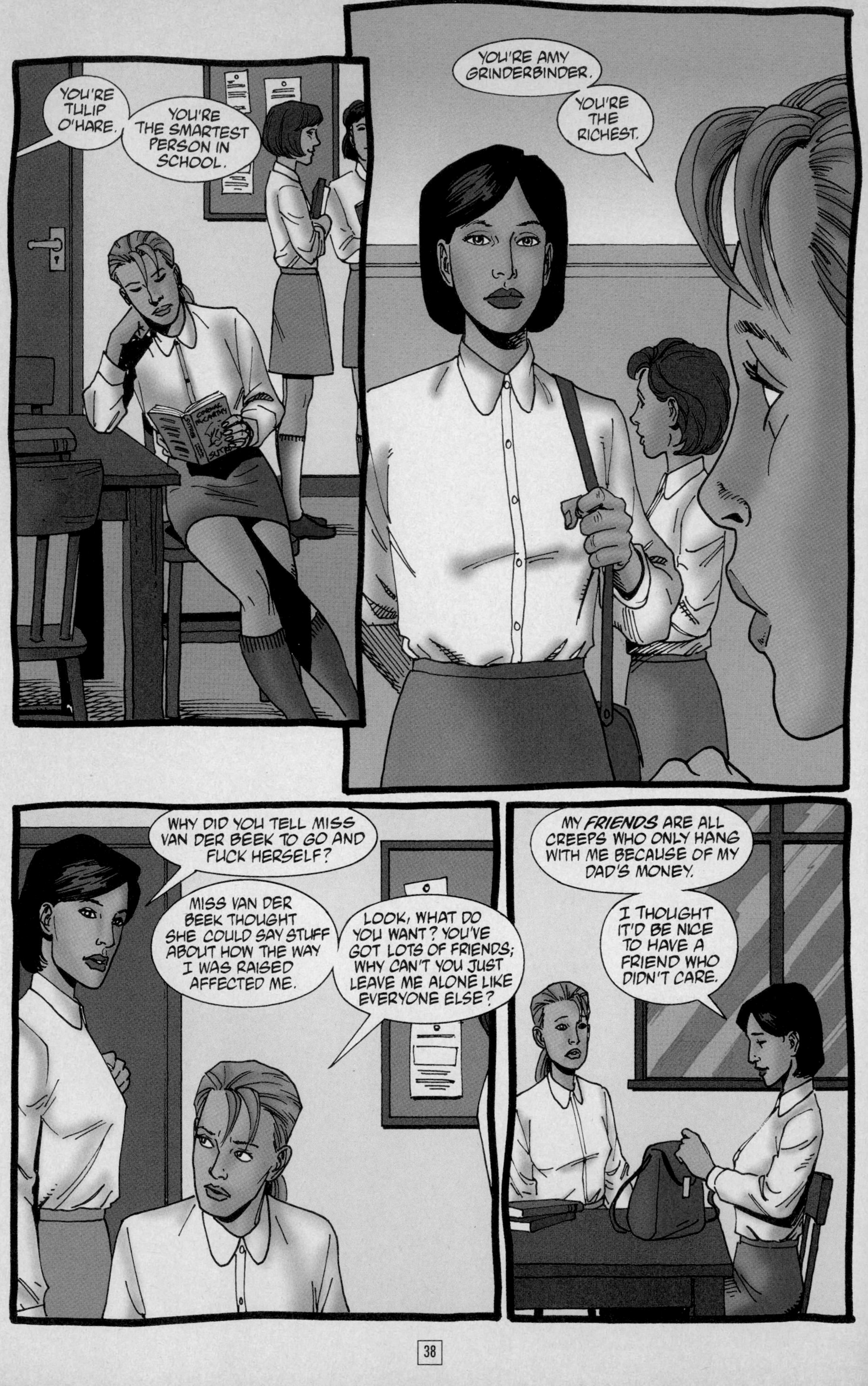

YOU'RE TULIP O'HARE.
YOU'RE THE SMARTEST PERSON IN SCHOOL.
CORMAC McCARTHY SUTTREE
YOU'RE AMY GRINDERBINDER.
YOU'RE THE RICHEST.
WHY DID YOU TELL MISS VAN DER BEEK TO GO AND FUCK HERSELF?
MISS VAN DER BEEK THOUGHT SHE COULD SAY STUFF ABOUT HOW THE WAY I WAS RAISED AFFECTED ME.
LOOK, WHAT DO YOU WANT? YOU'VE GOT LOTS OF FRIENDS; WHY CAN'T YOU JUST LEAVE ME ALONE LIKE EVERYONE ELSE?
MY *FRIENDS* ARE ALL CREEPS WHO ONLY HANG WITH ME BECAUSE OF MY DAD'S MONEY.
I THOUGHT IT'D BE NICE TO HAVE A FRIEND WHO DIDN'T CARE.

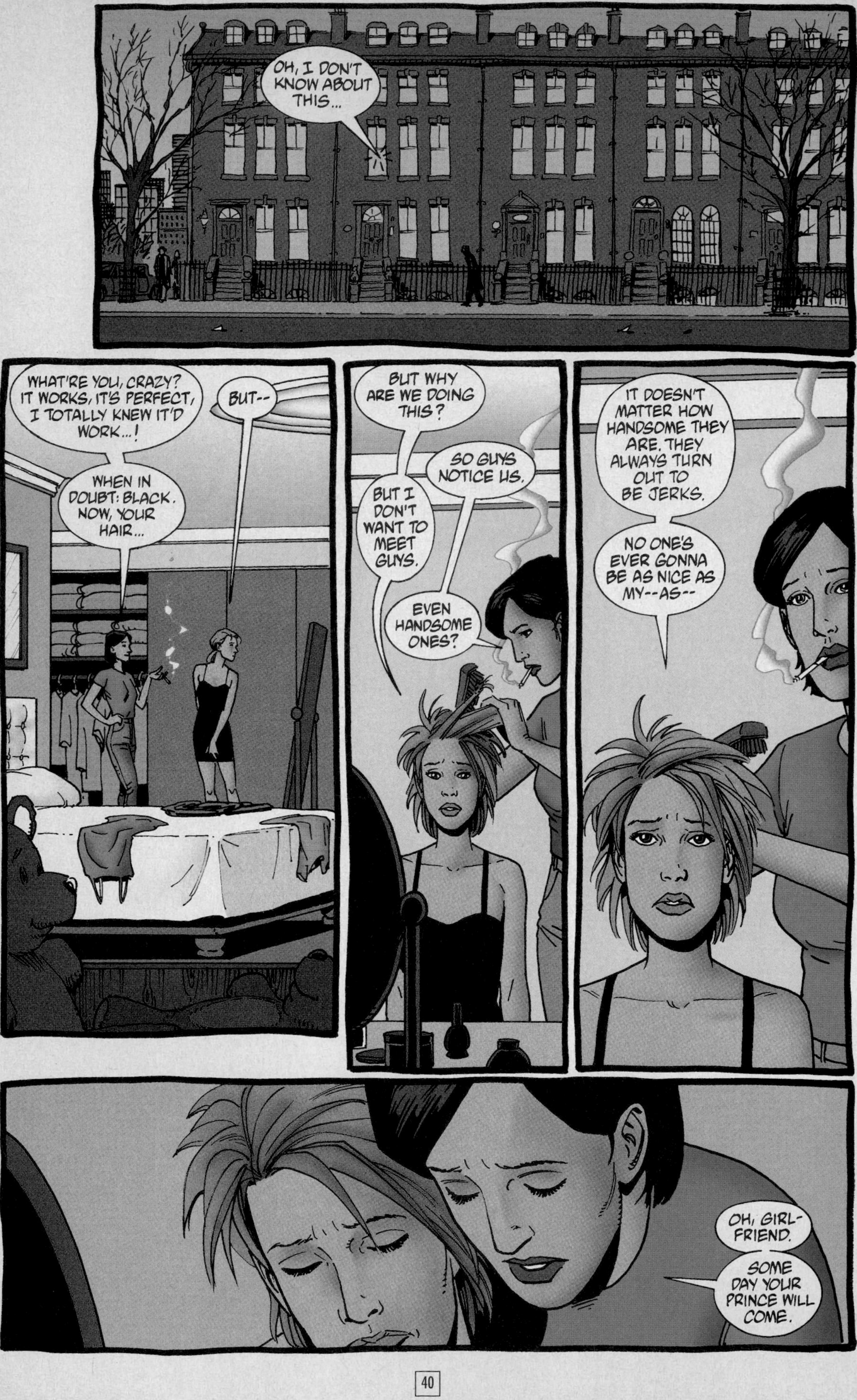

OH, I DON'T KNOW ABOUT THIS...
WHAT'RE YOU, CRAZY? IT WORKS, IT'S PERFECT, I TOTALLY KNEW IT'D WORK...!
BUT--
WHEN IN DOUBT: BLACK. NOW, YOUR HAIR...
BUT WHY ARE WE DOING THIS?
SO GUYS NOTICE US.
BUT I DON'T WANT TO MEET GUYS.
EVEN HANDSOME ONES?
IT DOESN'T MATTER HOW HANDSOME THEY ARE. THEY ALWAYS TURN OUT TO BE JERKS.
NO ONE'S EVER GONNA BE AS NICE AS MY--AS--
OH, GIRL-FRIEND.
SOME DAY YOUR PRINCE WILL COME.

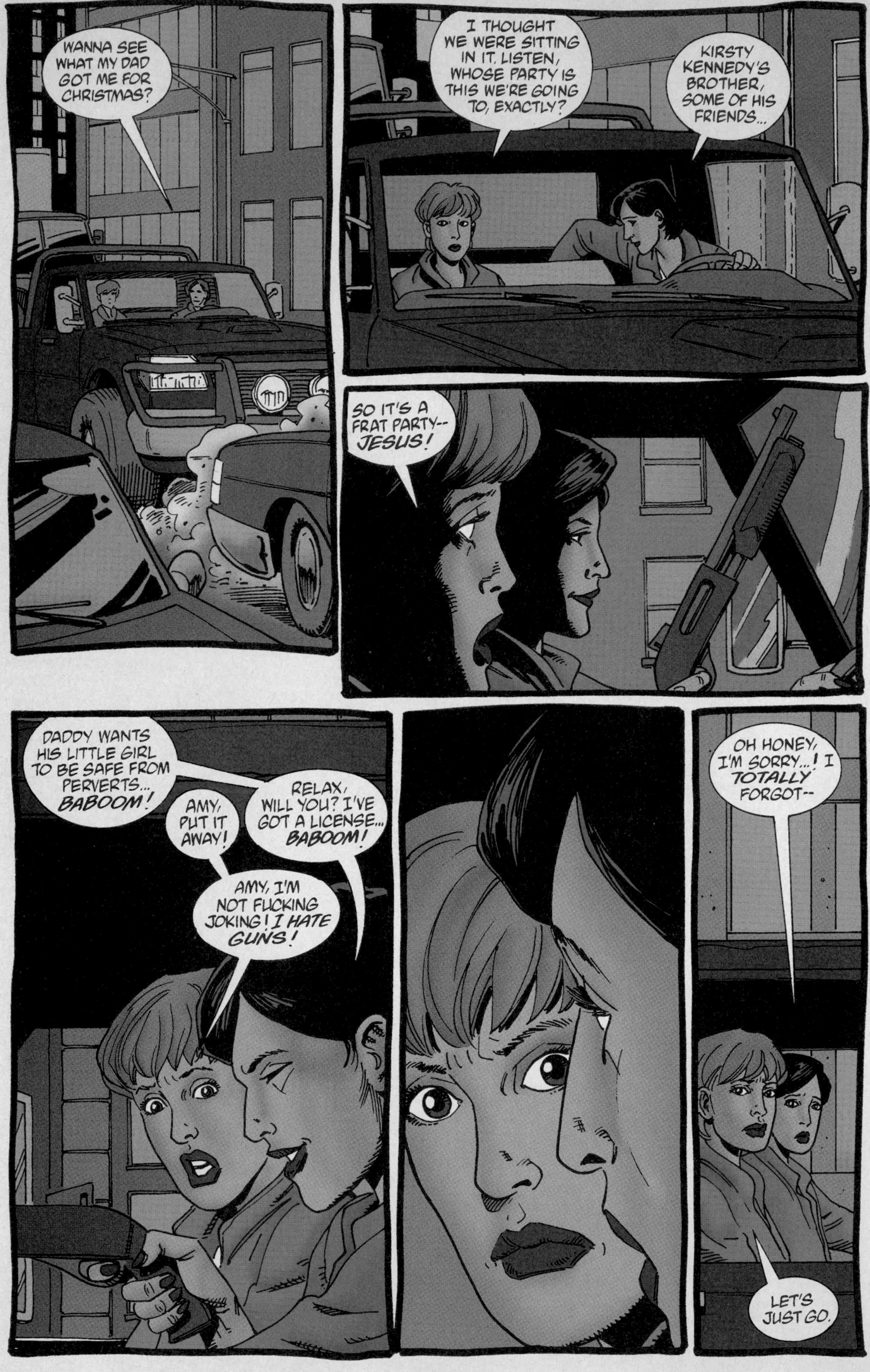
WANNA SEE WHAT MY DAD GOT ME FOR CHRISTMAS?
I THOUGHT WE WERE SITTING IN IT. LISTEN, WHOSE PARTY IS THIS WE'RE GOING TO, EXACTLY?
KIRSTY KENNEDY'S BROTHER, SOME OF HIS FRIENDS...
SO IT'S A FRAT PARTY-- JESUS!
DADDY WANTS HIS LITTLE GIRL TO BE SAFE FROM PERVERTS... BABOOM!
AMY, PUT IT AWAY!
RELAX, WILL YOU? I'VE GOT A LICENSE... BABOOM!
AMY, I'M NOT FUCKING JOKING! I HATE GUNS!
OH HONEY, I'M SORRY...! I TOTALLY FORGOT--
LET'S JUST GO.

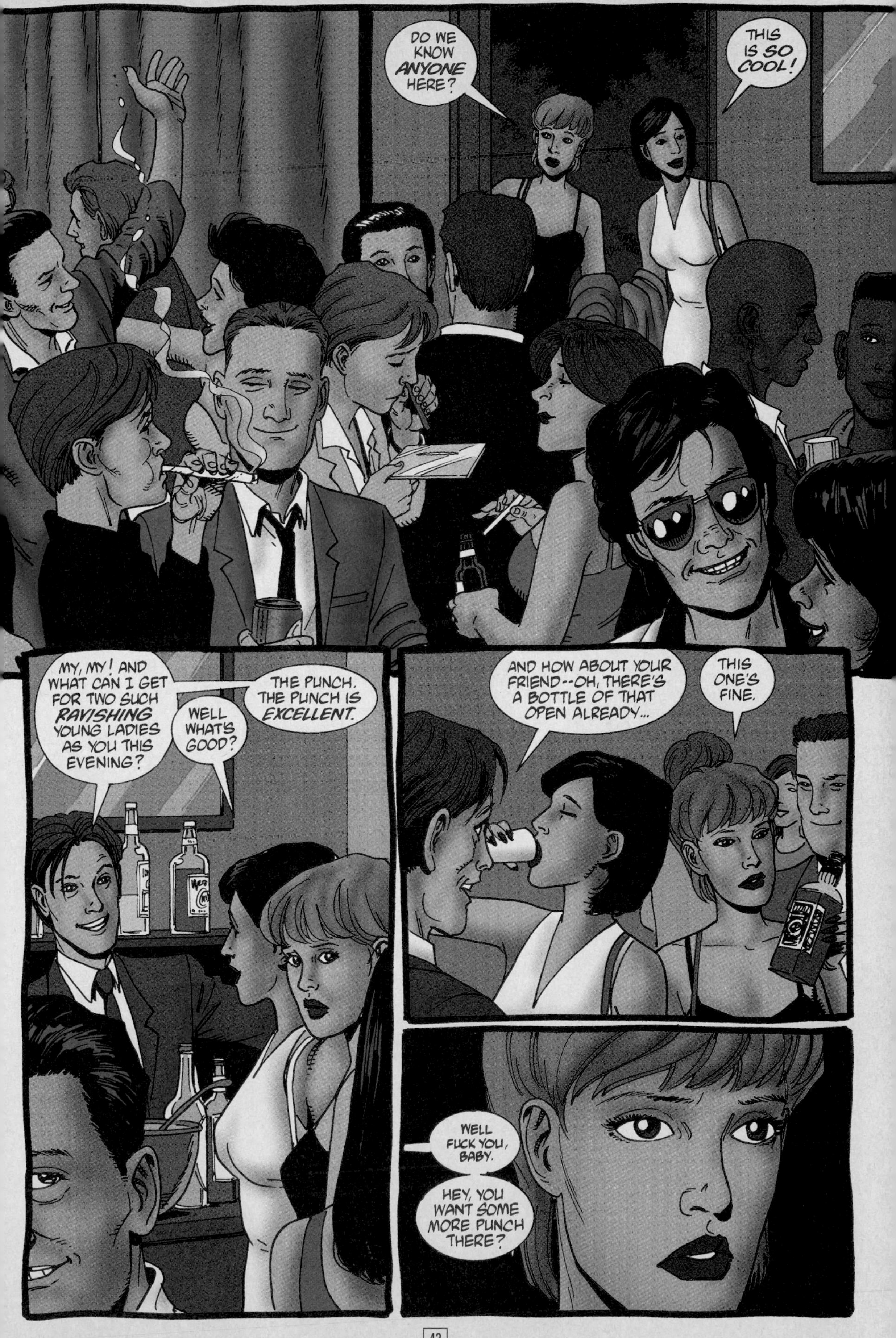
DO WE KNOW ANYONE HERE?
THIS IS SO COOL!
MY, MY! AND WHAT CAN I GET FOR TWO SUCH RAVISHING YOUNG LADIES AS YOU THIS EVENING?
WELL WHAT'S GOOD?
THE PUNCH. THE PUNCH IS EXCELLENT.
AND HOW ABOUT YOUR FRIEND--OH, THERE'S A BOTTLE OF THAT OPEN ALREADY...
THIS ONE'S FINE.
WELL FUCK YOU, BABY.
HEY, YOU WANT SOME MORE PUNCH THERE?

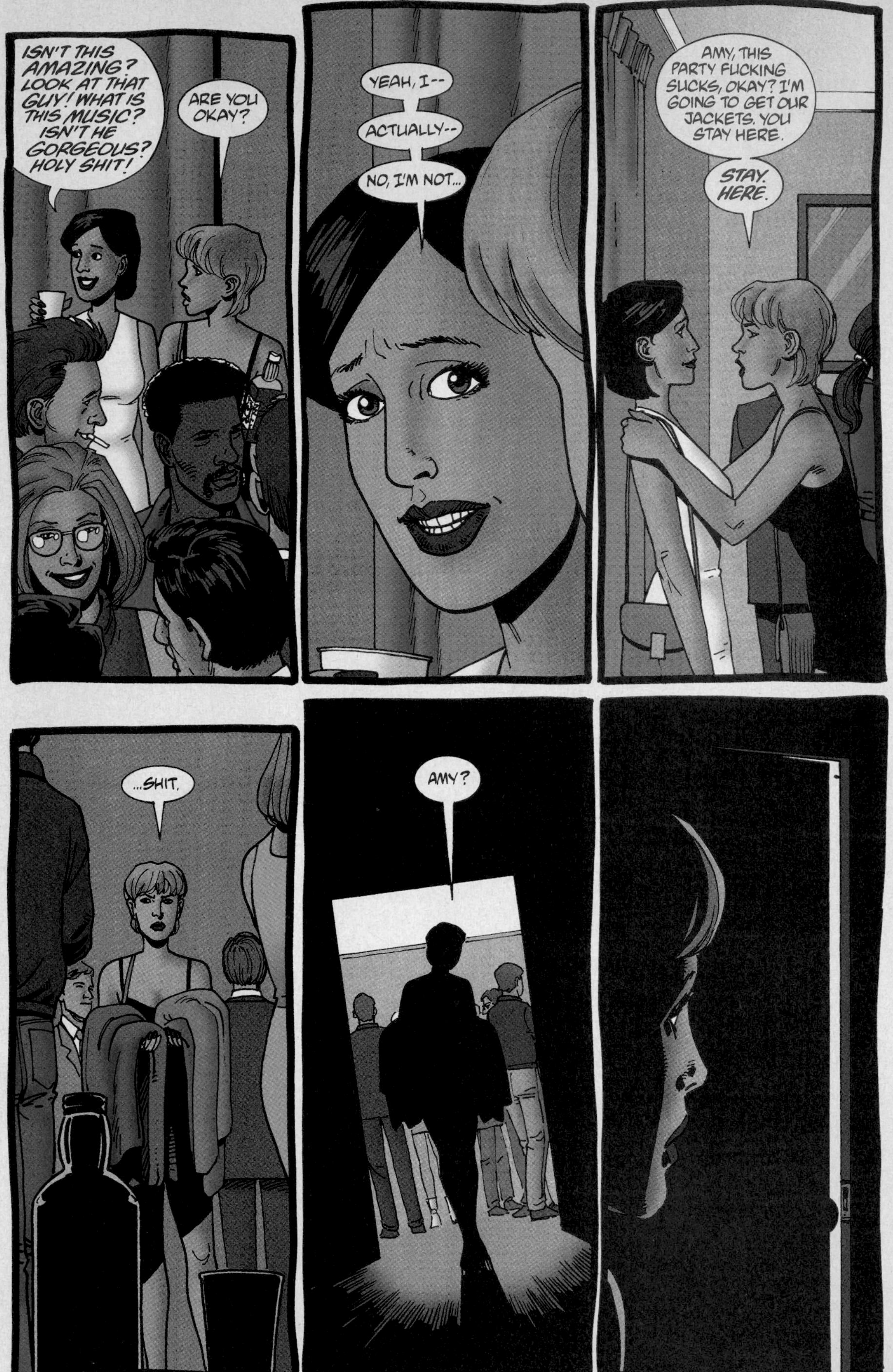

ISN'T THIS AMAZING? LOOK AT THAT GUY! WHAT IS THIS MUSIC? ISN'T HE GORGEOUS? HOLY SHIT!
ARE YOU OKAY?
YEAH, I--
ACTUALLY--
NO, I'M NOT...
AMY, THIS PARTY FUCKING SUCKS, OKAY? I'M GOING TO GET OUR JACKETS. YOU STAY HERE.
STAY. HERE.
...SHIT.
AMY?

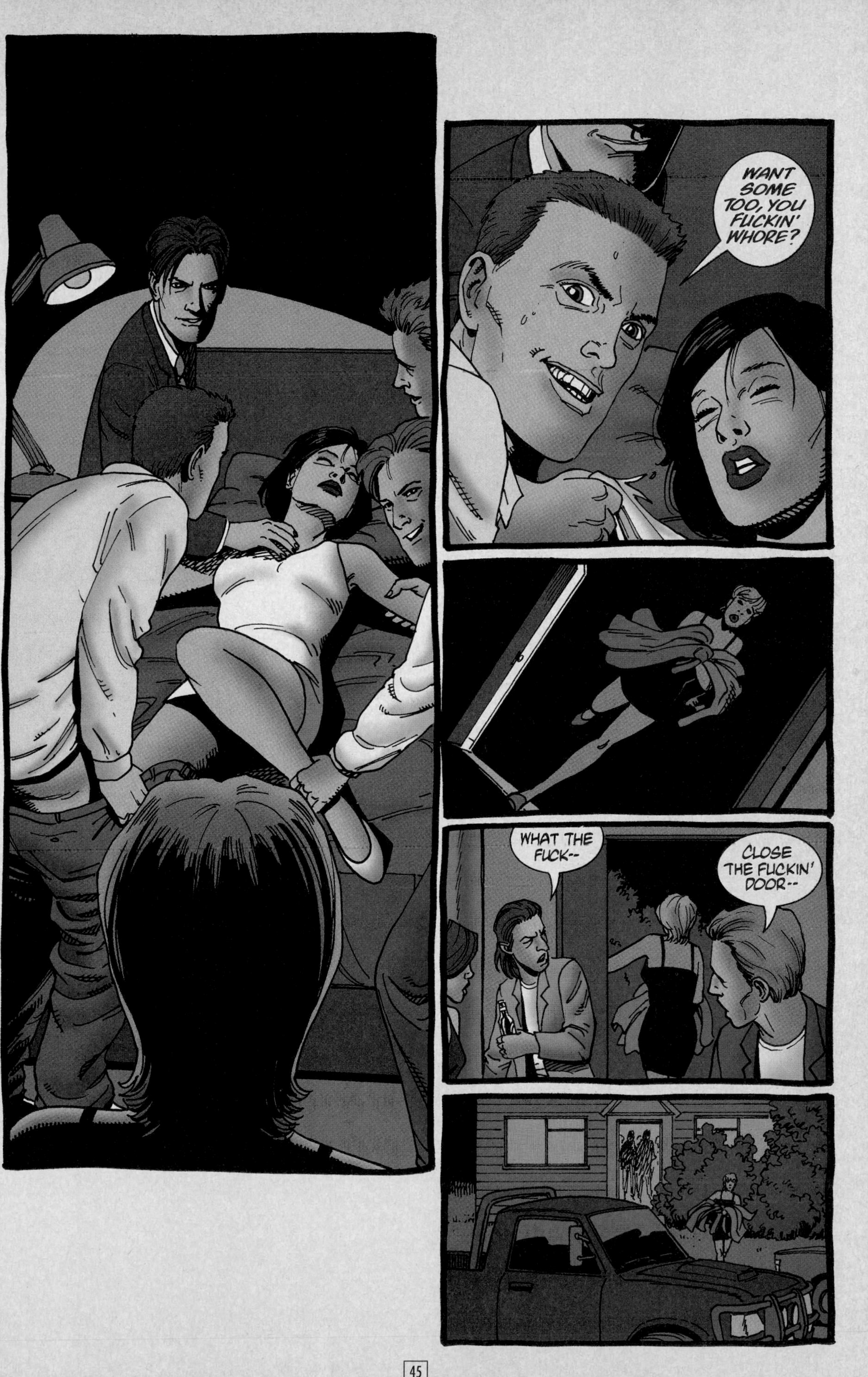
WANT SOME TOO, YOU FUCKIN' WHORE?
WHAT THE FUCK--
CLOSE THE FUCKIN' DOOR--

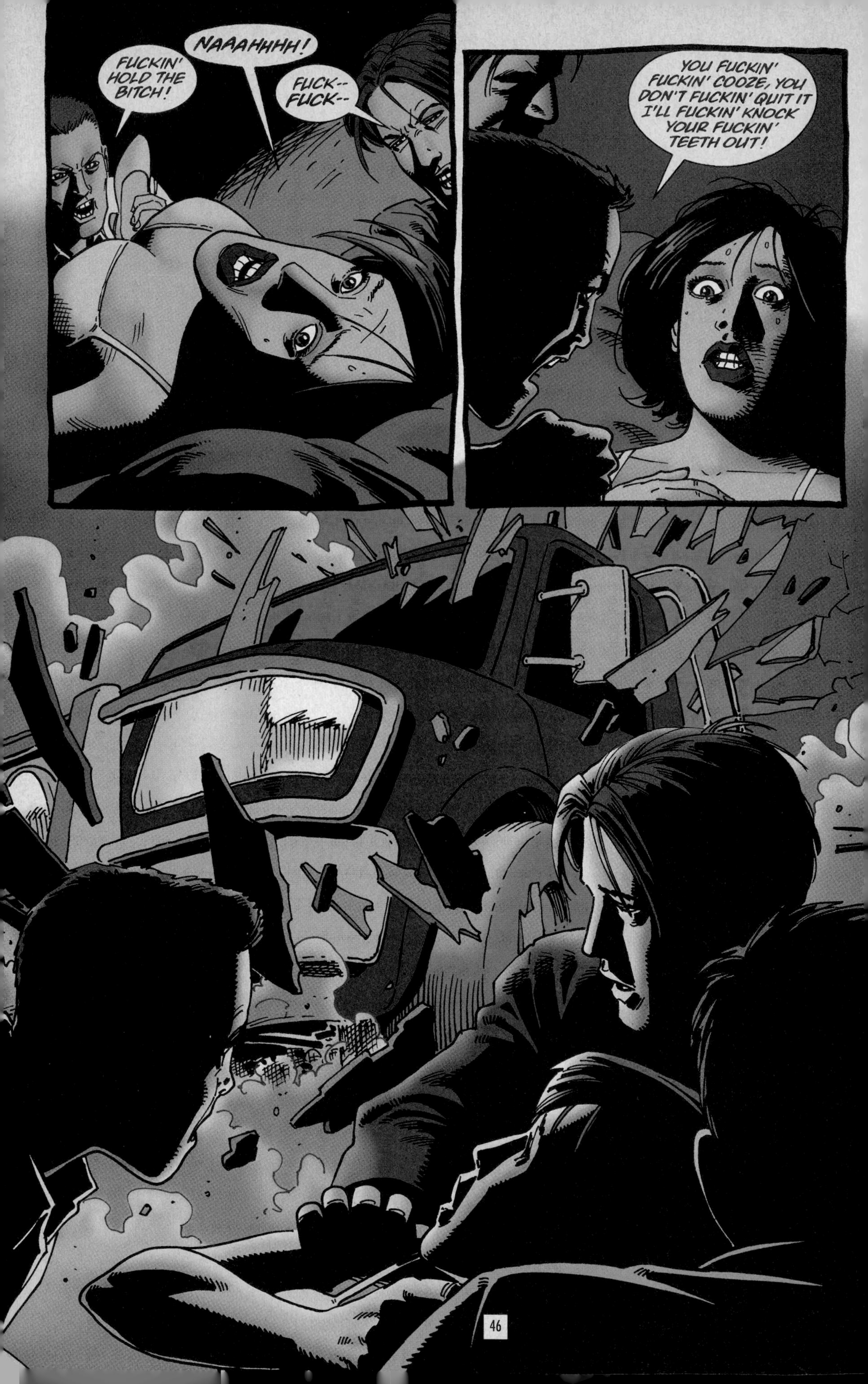
FUCKIN' HOLD THE BITCH!
NAAAHHHH!
FUCK-- FUCK--
YOU FUCKIN' FUCKIN' COOZE, YOU DON'T FUCKIN' QUIT IT I'LL FUCKIN' KNOCK YOUR FUCKIN' TEETH OUT!

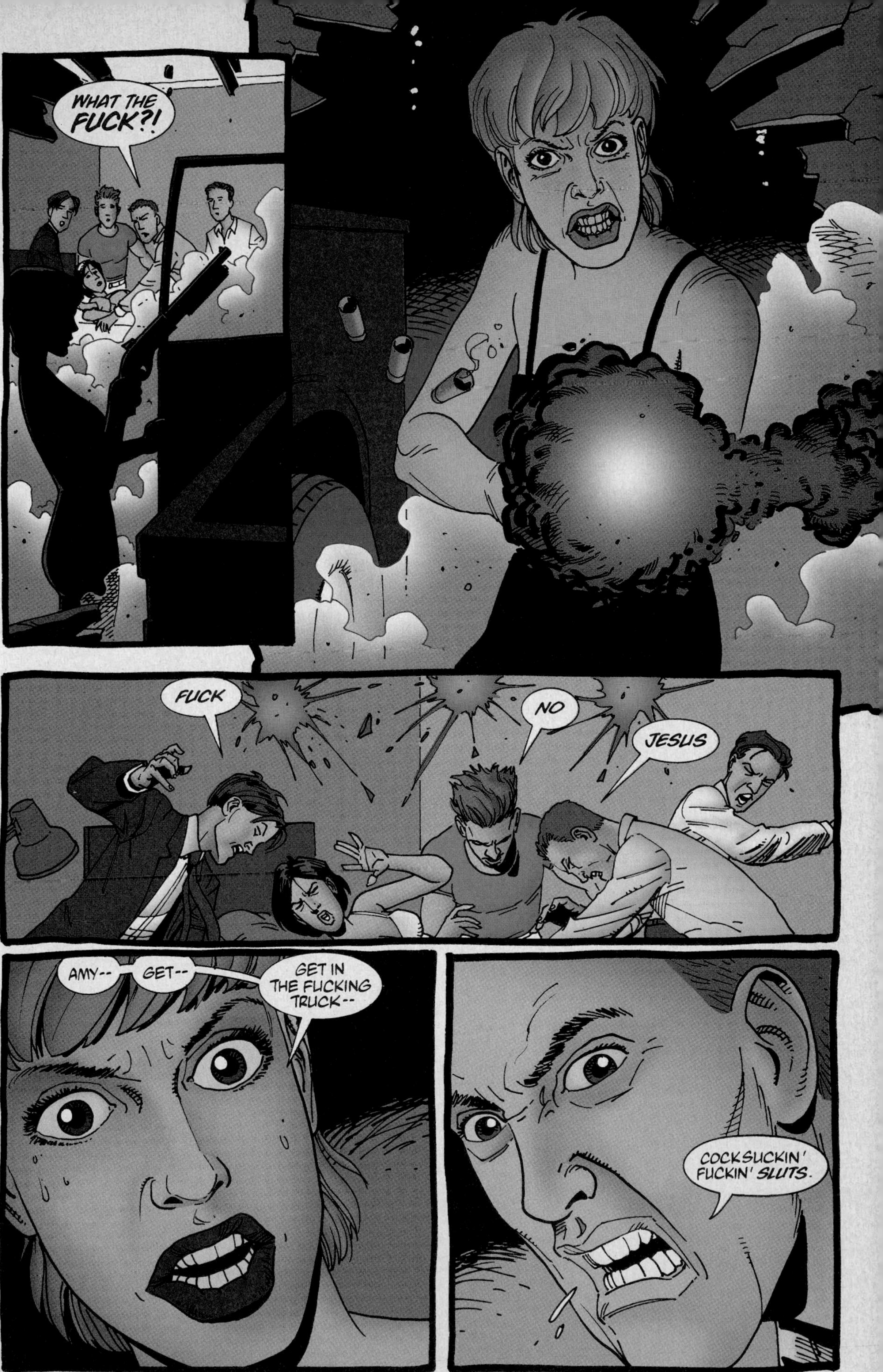
WHAT THE FUCK?!
FUCK
NO
JESUS
AMY--
GET--
GET IN THE FUCKING TRUCK--
COCKSUCKIN' FUCKIN' SLUTS.

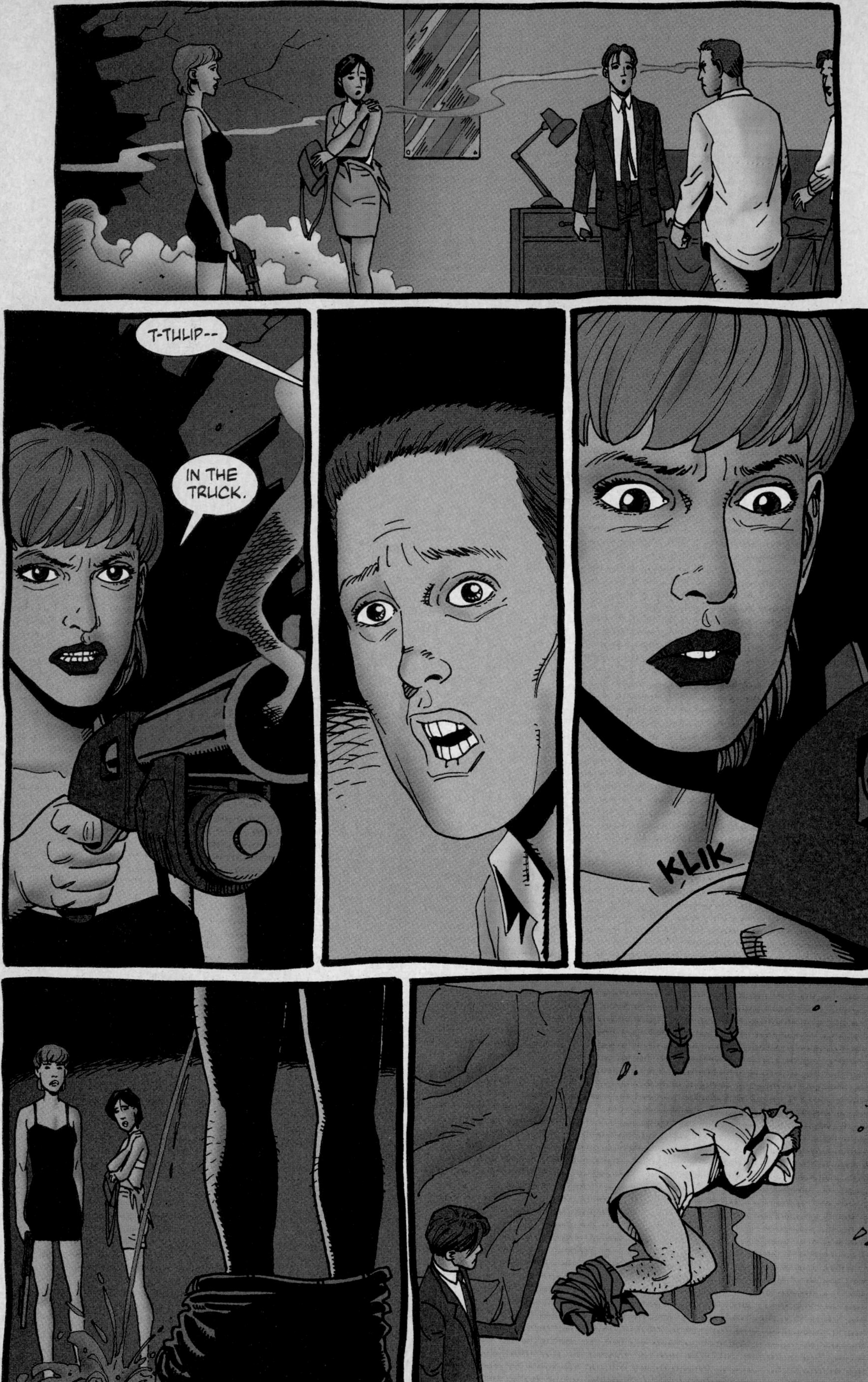
T-TULIP--
IN THE TRUCK.
KLIK

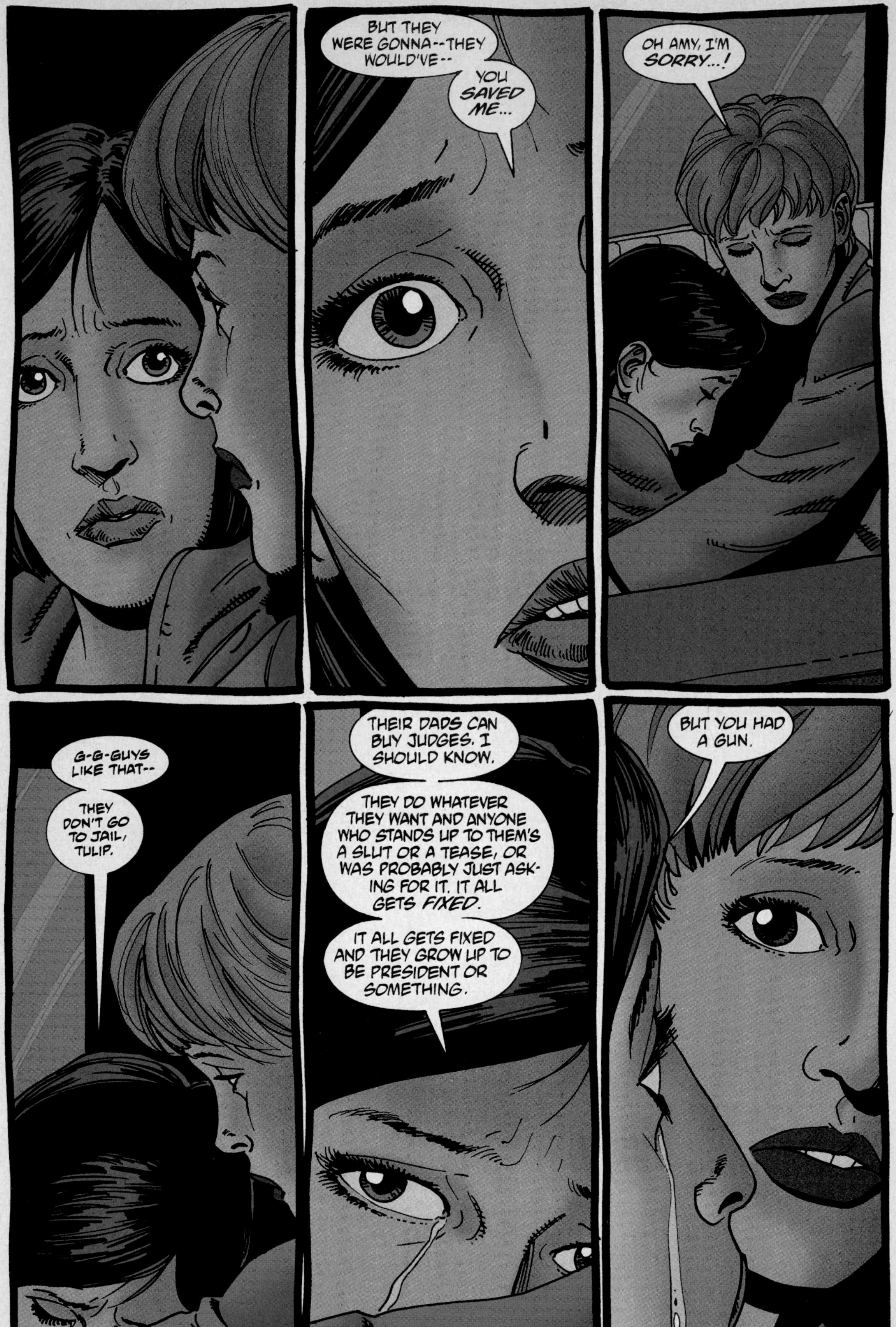
BUT THEY WERE GONNA--THEY WOULD'VE--
YOU *SAVED* ME...
OH AMY, I'M *SORRY*...!
G-G-GUYS LIKE THAT--
THEY DON'T GO TO JAIL, TULIP.
THEIR DADS CAN BUY JUDGES. I SHOULD KNOW.
THEY DO WHATEVER THEY WANT AND ANYONE WHO STANDS UP TO THEM'S A SLUT OR A TEASE, OR WAS PROBABLY JUST ASKING FOR IT. IT ALL GETS *FIXED*.
IT ALL GETS FIXED AND THEY GROW UP TO BE PRESIDENT OR SOMETHING.
BUT YOU HAD A GUN.

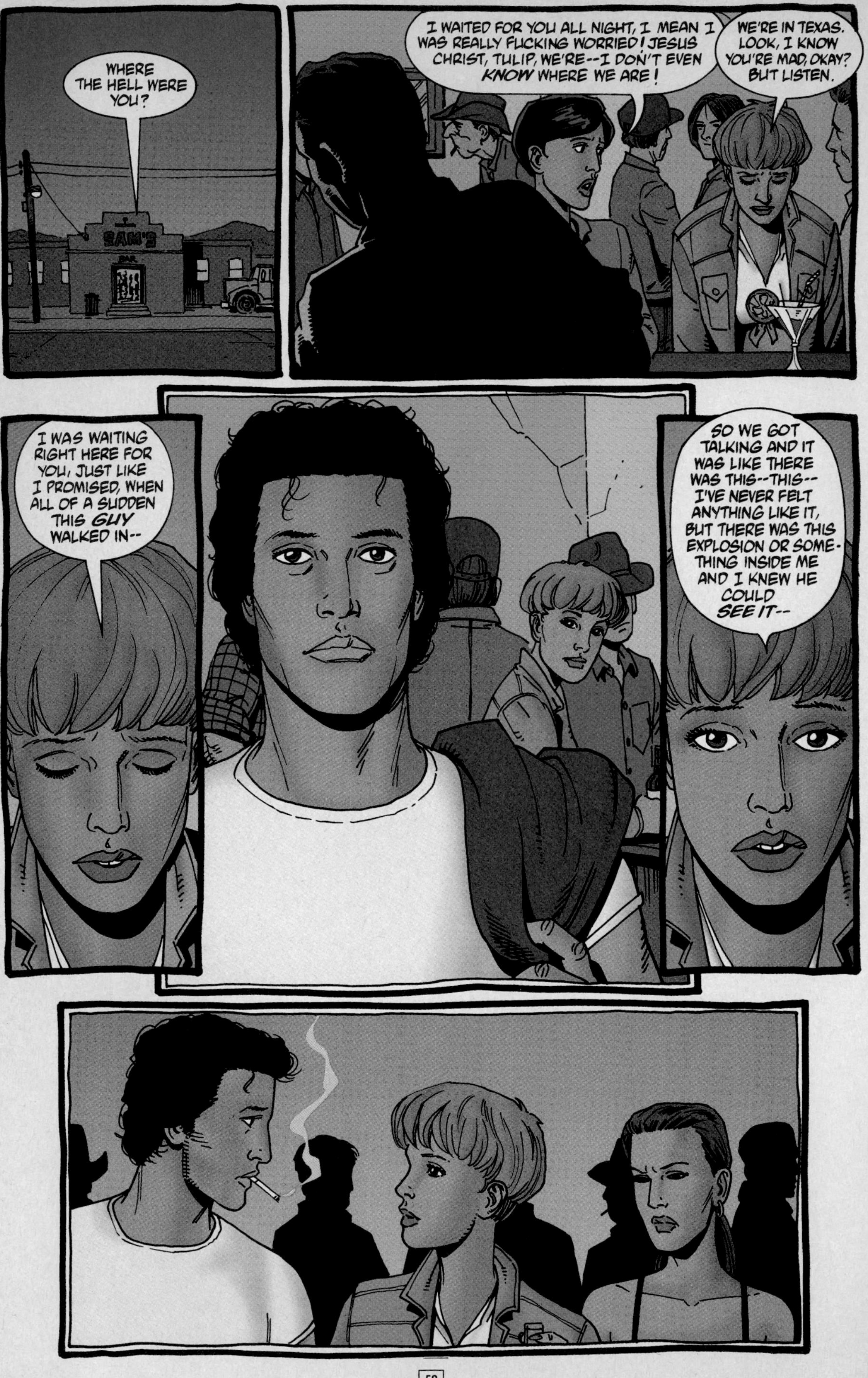
WHERE THE HELL WERE YOU?
SAM'S
I WAITED FOR YOU ALL NIGHT, I MEAN I WAS REALLY FUCKING WORRIED! JESUS CHRIST, TULIP, WE'RE--I DON'T EVEN KNOW WHERE WE ARE!
WE'RE IN TEXAS. LOOK, I KNOW YOU'RE MAD, OKAY? BUT LISTEN.
I WAS WAITING RIGHT HERE FOR YOU, JUST LIKE I PROMISED, WHEN ALL OF A SUDDEN THIS GUY WALKED IN--
SO WE GOT TALKING AND IT WAS LIKE THERE WAS THIS--THIS-- I'VE NEVER FELT ANYTHING LIKE IT, BUT THERE WAS THIS EXPLOSION OR SOME-THING INSIDE ME AND I KNEW HE COULD SEE IT--

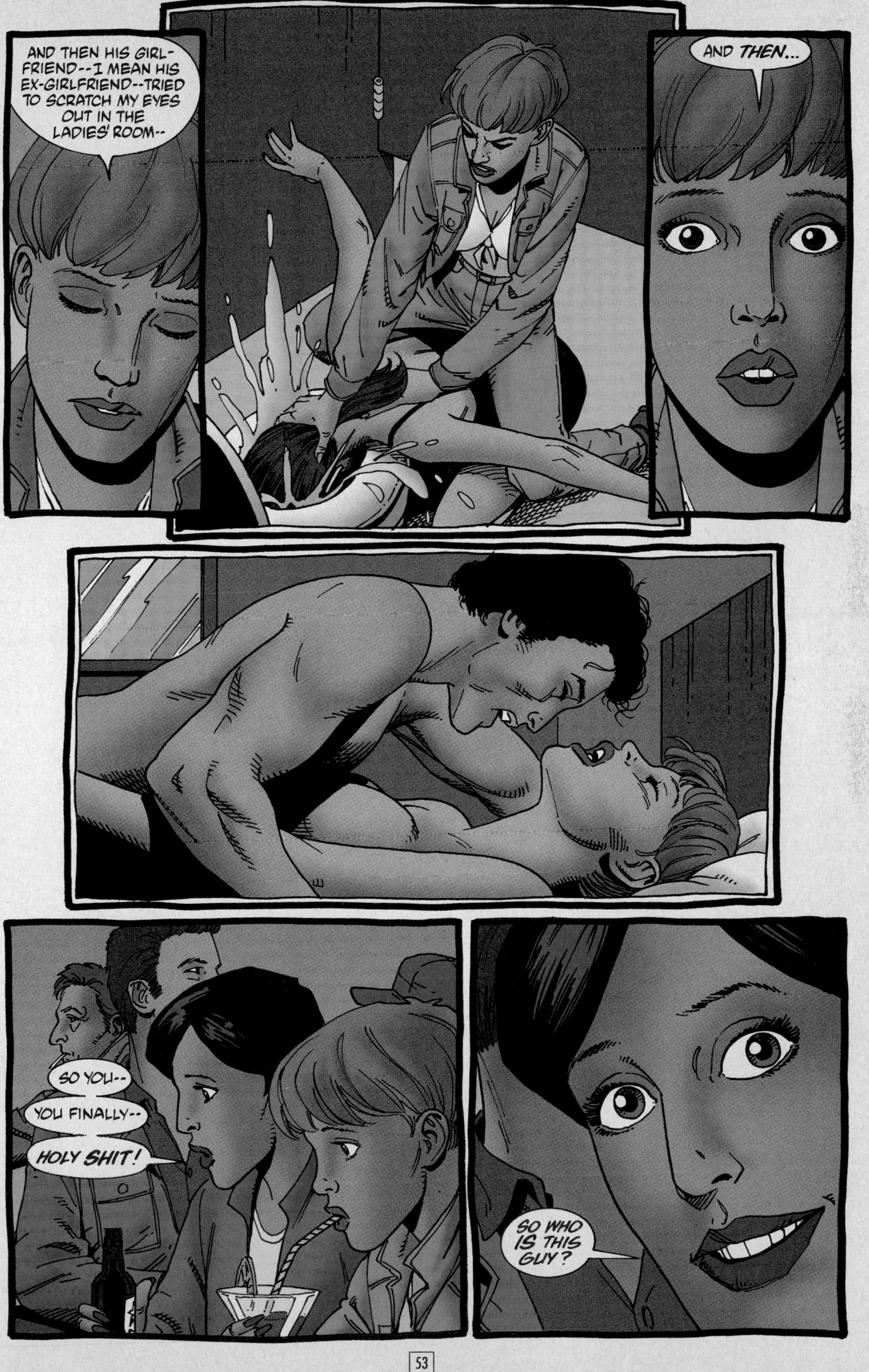
AND THEN HIS GIRL-FRIEND--I MEAN HIS EX-GIRLFRIEND--TRIED TO SCRATCH MY EYES OUT IN THE LADIES' ROOM--
AND *THEN...*
SO YOU--
YOU FINALLY--
HOLY SHIT!
SO WHO *IS* THIS GUY?

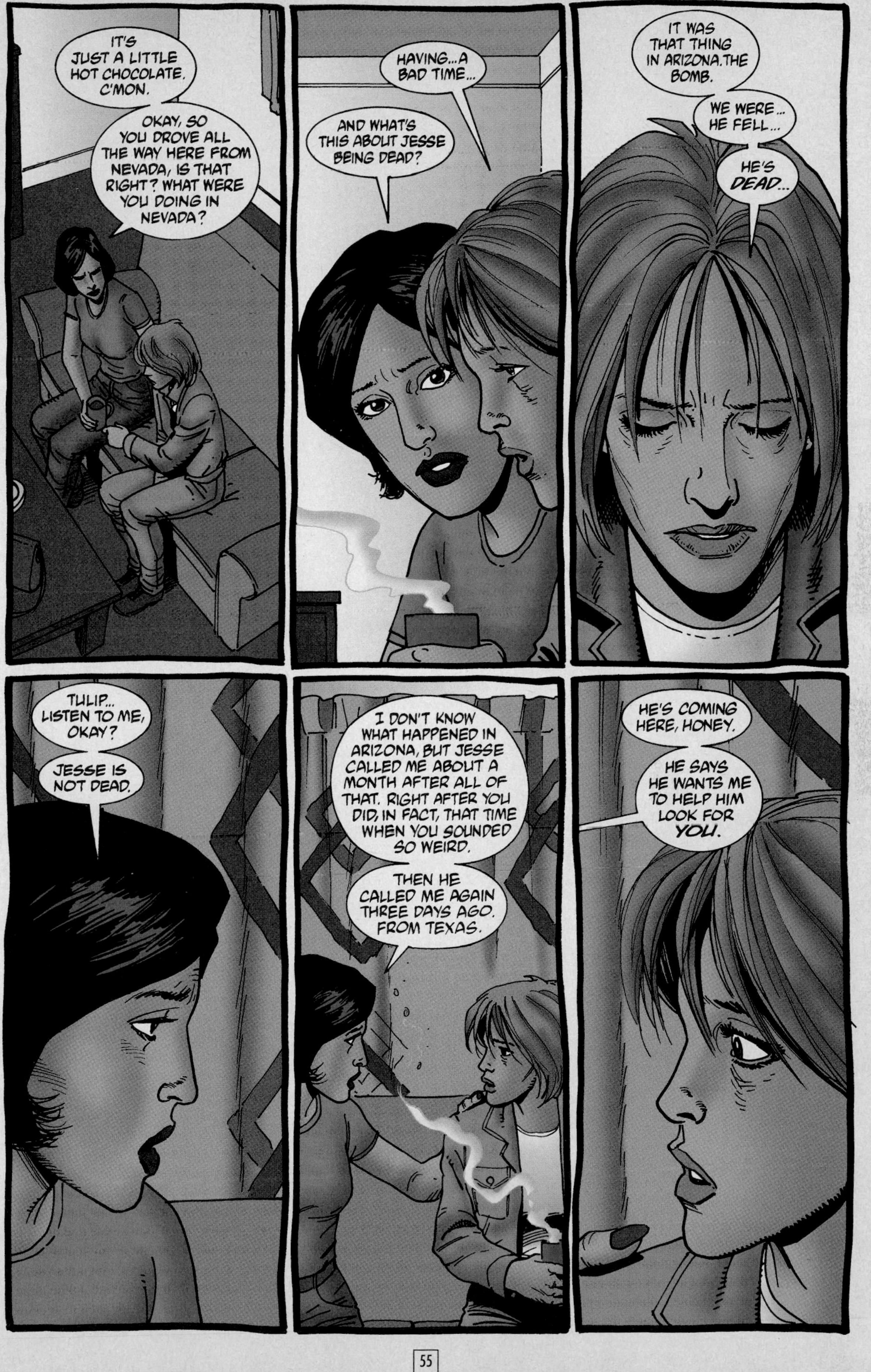
IT'S JUST A LITTLE HOT CHOCOLATE. C'MON.
OKAY, SO YOU DROVE ALL THE WAY HERE FROM NEVADA, IS THAT RIGHT? WHAT WERE YOU DOING IN NEVADA?
HAVING...A BAD TIME...
AND WHAT'S THIS ABOUT JESSE BEING DEAD?
IT WAS THAT THING IN ARIZONA.THE BOMB.
WE WERE... HE FELL...
HE'S DEAD...
TULIP... LISTEN TO ME, OKAY?
JESSE IS NOT DEAD.
I DON'T KNOW WHAT HAPPENED IN ARIZONA, BUT JESSE CALLED ME ABOUT A MONTH AFTER ALL OF THAT. RIGHT AFTER YOU DID, IN FACT, THAT TIME WHEN YOU SOUNDED SO WEIRD.
THEN HE CALLED ME AGAIN THREE DAYS AGO. FROM TEXAS.
HE'S COMING HERE, HONEY.
HE SAYS HE WANTS ME TO HELP HIM LOOK FOR YOU.

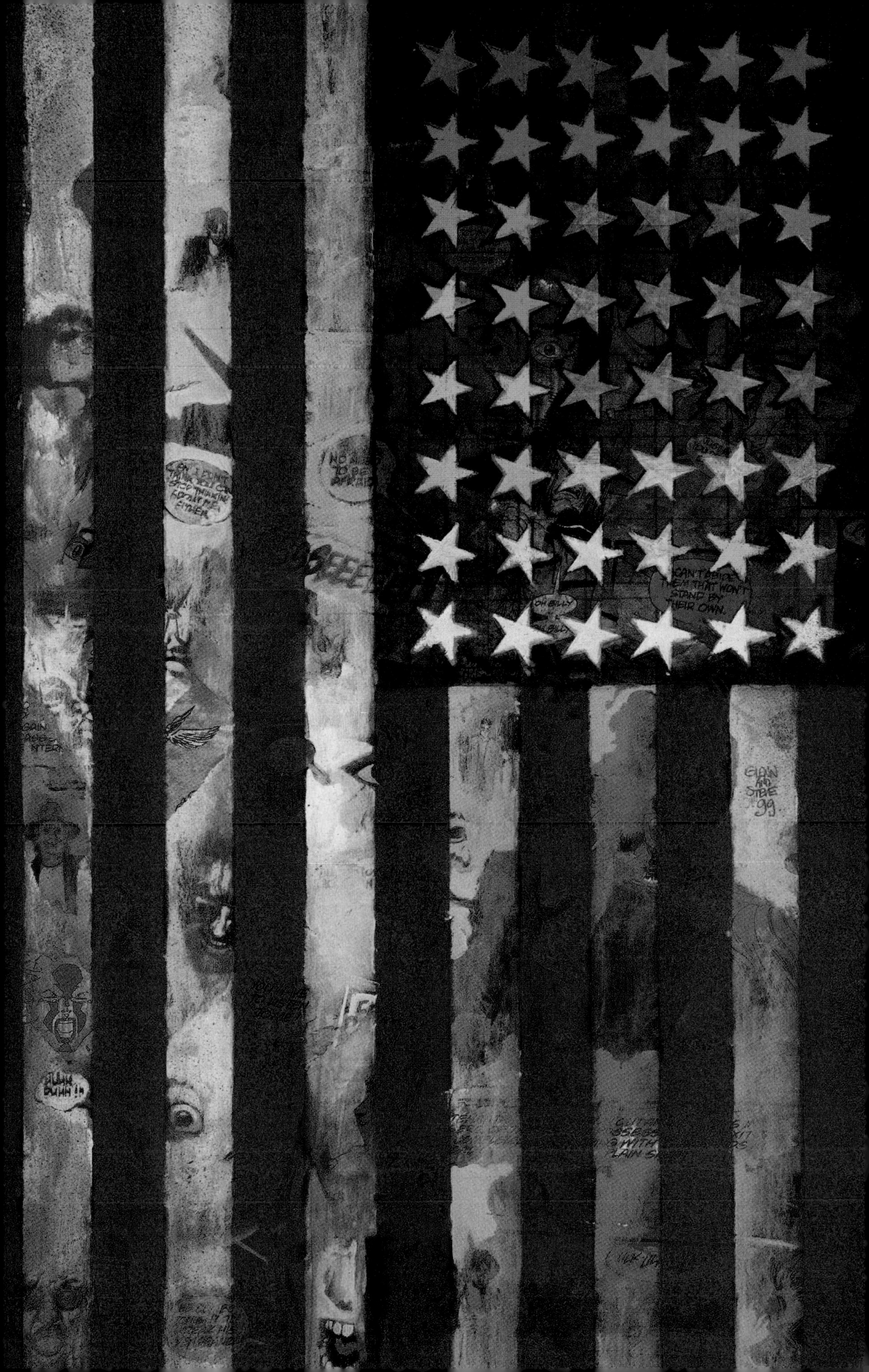

OH BILLY
I CAN'T ABIDE THEM THAT WON'T STAND BY THEIR OWN.

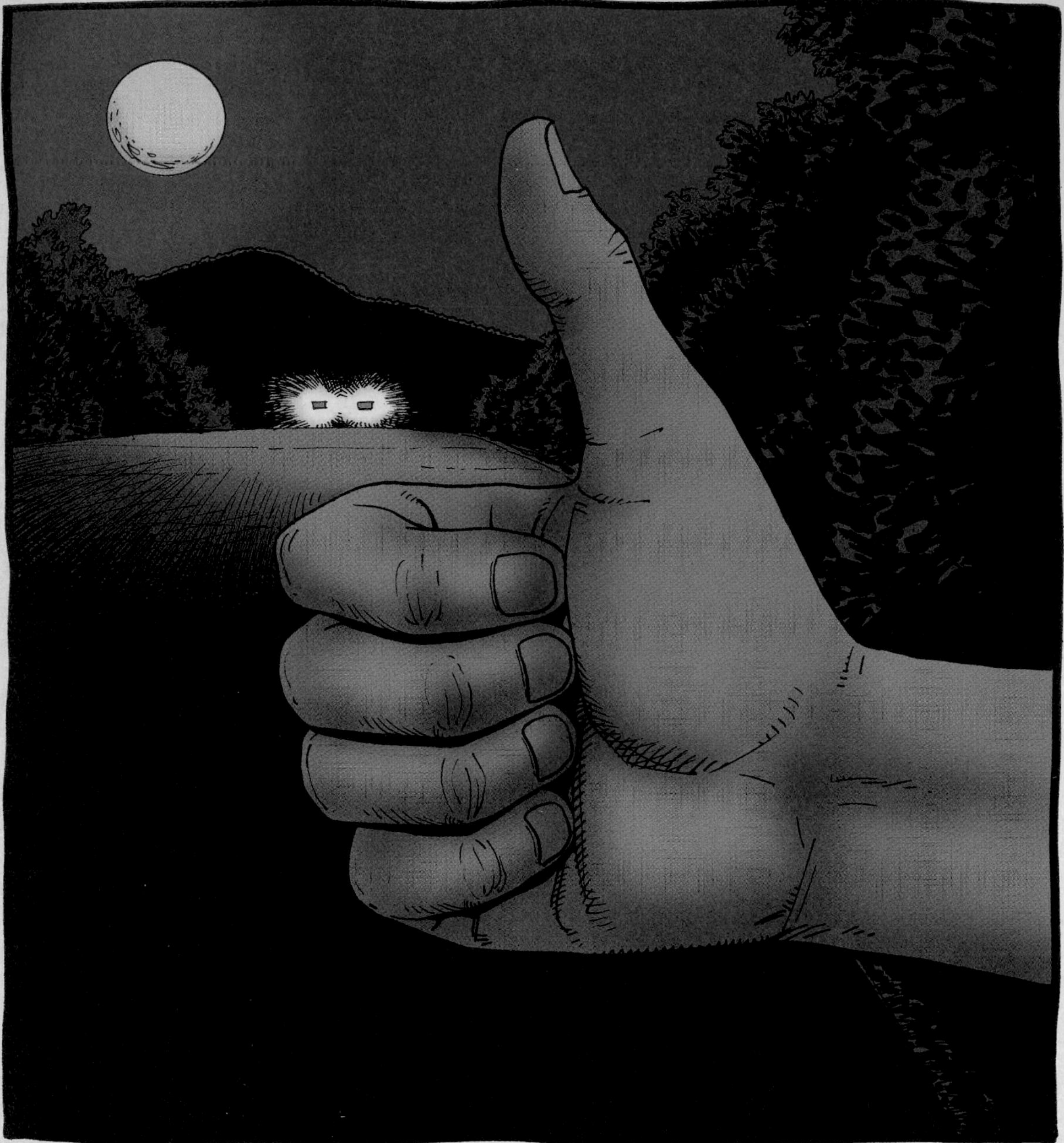

TOO DUMB FOR NEW YORK CITY AND TOO UGLY FOR L.A.

GARTH ENNIS - Writer   STEVE DILLON - Artist

PAMELA RAMBO - Colorist   CLEM ROBINS - Letterer   AXEL ALONSO - Editor

PREACHER created by GARTH ENNIS and STEVE DILLON

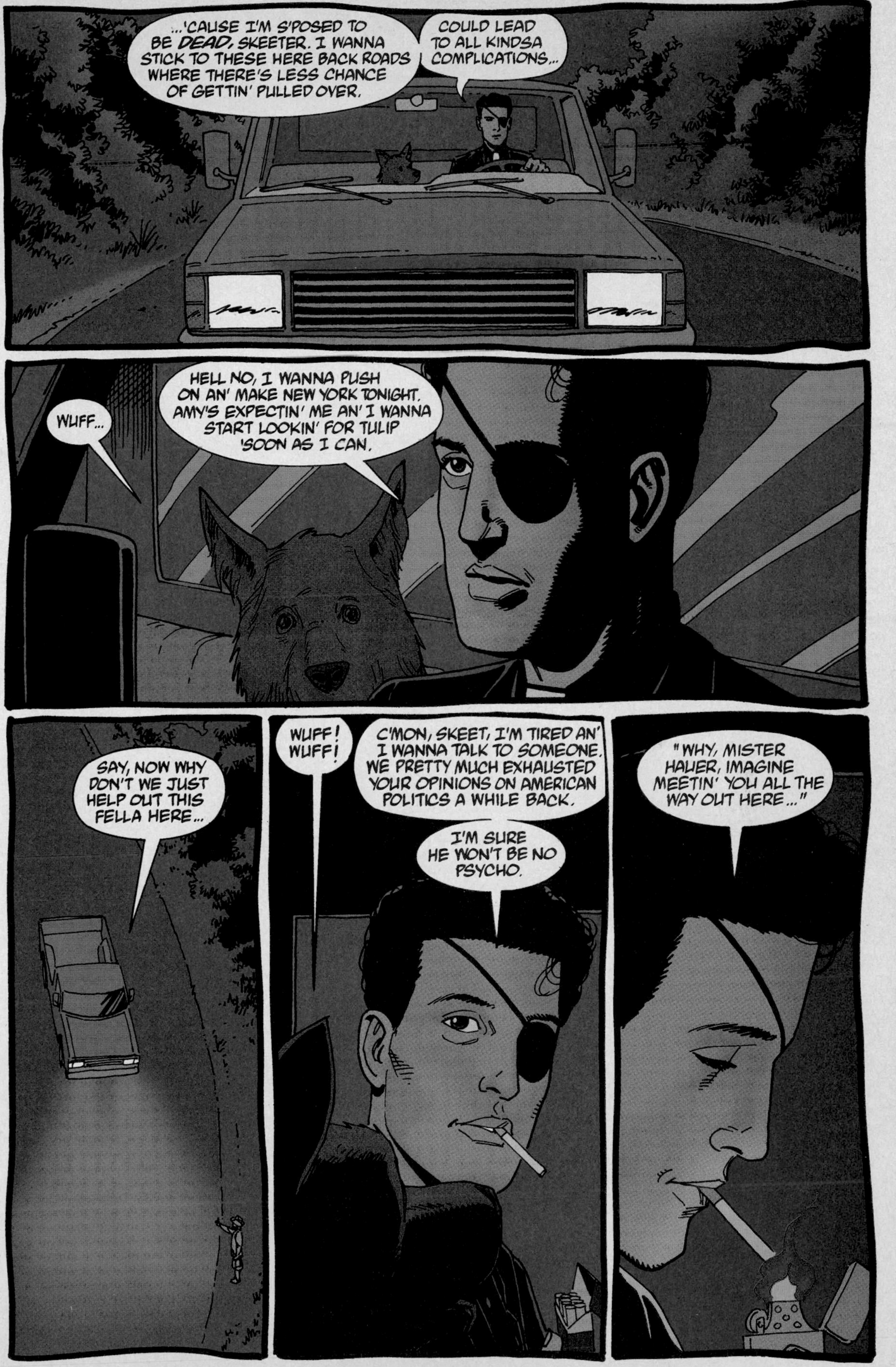
...'CAUSE I'M S'POSED TO BE DEAD, SKEETER. I WANNA STICK TO THESE HERE BACK ROADS WHERE THERE'S LESS CHANCE OF GETTIN' PULLED OVER.
COULD LEAD TO ALL KINDSA COMPLICATIONS...
WUFF...
HELL NO, I WANNA PUSH ON AN' MAKE NEW YORK TONIGHT. AMY'S EXPECTIN' ME AN' I WANNA START LOOKIN' FOR TULIP 'SOON AS I CAN.
SAY, NOW WHY DON'T WE JUST HELP OUT THIS FELLA HERE...
WUFF! WUFF!
C'MON, SKEET, I'M TIRED AN' I WANNA TALK TO SOMEONE. WE PRETTY MUCH EXHAUSTED YOUR OPINIONS ON AMERICAN POLITICS A WHILE BACK.
I'M SURE HE WON'T BE NO PSYCHO.
"WHY, MISTER HAUER, IMAGINE MEETIN' YOU ALL THE WAY OUT HERE..."

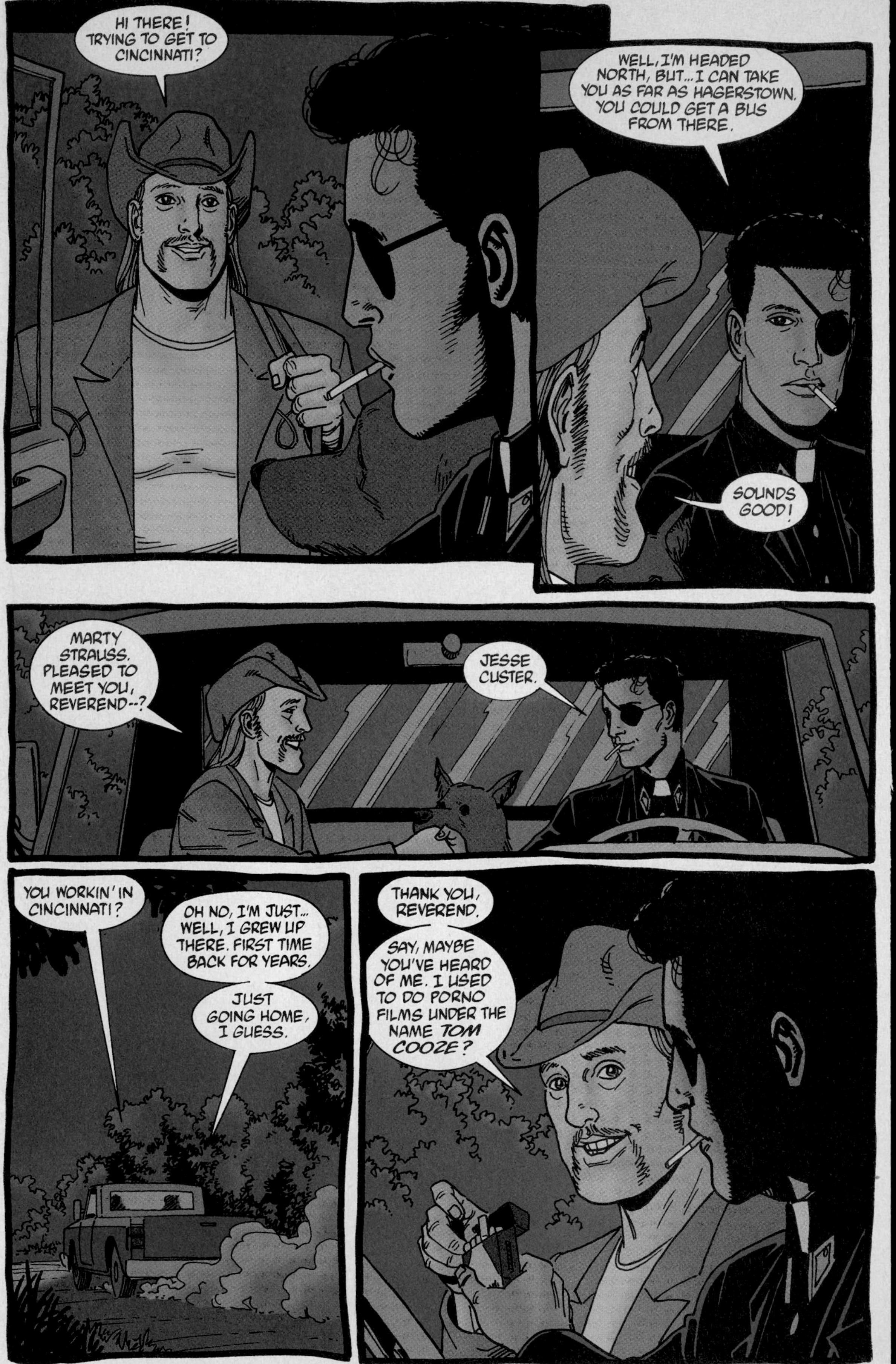
HI THERE! TRYING TO GET TO CINCINNATI?
WELL, I'M HEADED NORTH, BUT... I CAN TAKE YOU AS FAR AS HAGERSTOWN. YOU COULD GET A BUS FROM THERE.
SOUNDS GOOD!
MARTY STRAUSS. PLEASED TO MEET YOU, REVEREND--?
JESSE CUSTER.
YOU WORKIN' IN CINCINNATI?
OH NO, I'M JUST... WELL, I GREW UP THERE. FIRST TIME BACK FOR YEARS.
JUST GOING HOME, I GUESS.
THANK YOU, REVEREND.
SAY, MAYBE YOU'VE HEARD OF ME. I USED TO DO PORNO FILMS UNDER THE NAME *TOM COOZE*?

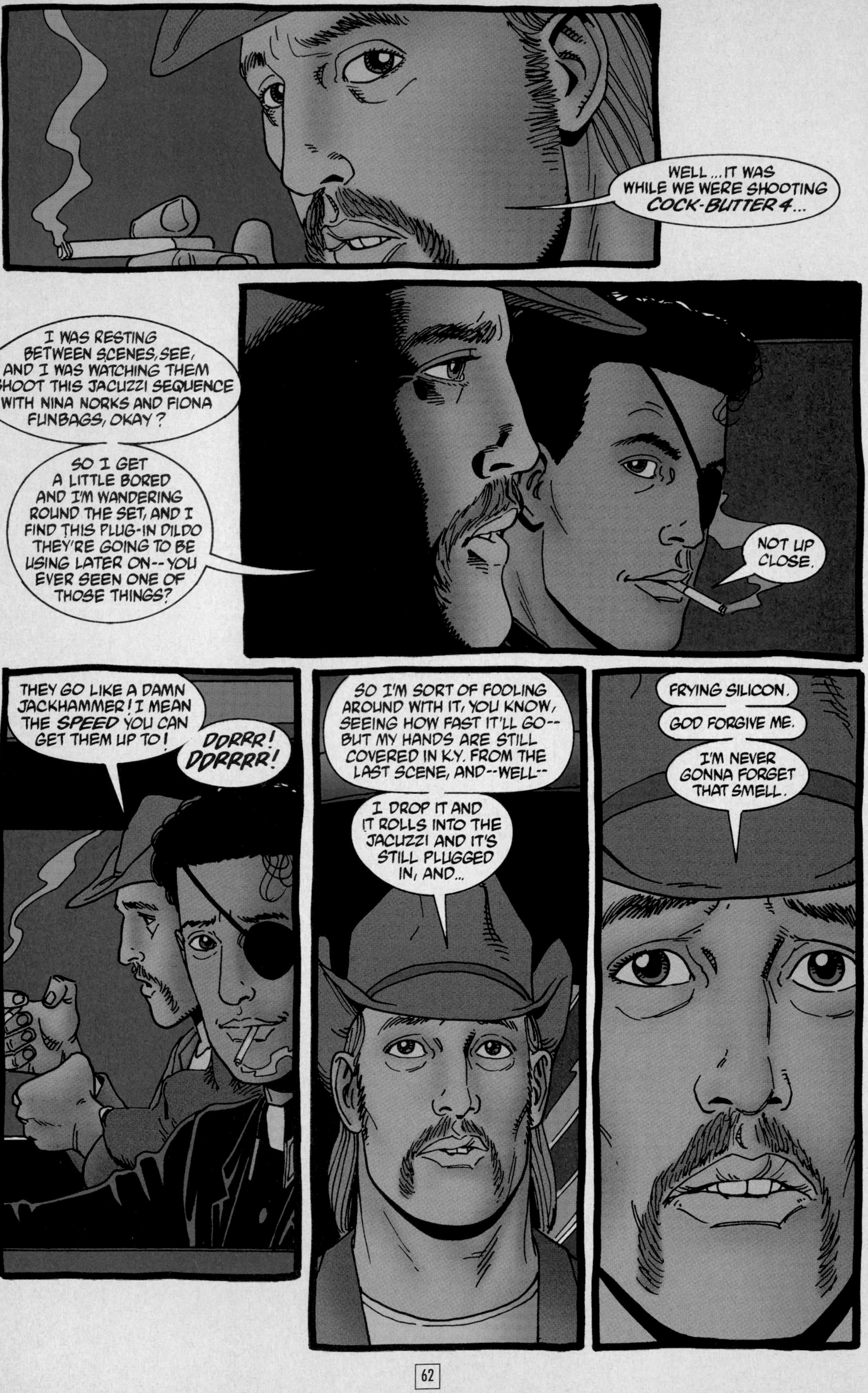
WELL ... IT WAS WHILE WE WERE SHOOTING COCK-BUTTER 4...
I WAS RESTING BETWEEN SCENES, SEE, AND I WAS WATCHING THEM SHOOT THIS JACUZZI SEQUENCE WITH NINA NORKS AND FIONA FUNBAGS, OKAY?
SO I GET A LITTLE BORED AND I'M WANDERING ROUND THE SET, AND I FIND THIS PLUG-IN DILDO THEY'RE GOING TO BE USING LATER ON--YOU EVER SEEN ONE OF THOSE THINGS?
NOT UP CLOSE.
THEY GO LIKE A DAMN JACKHAMMER! I MEAN THE SPEED YOU CAN GET THEM UP TO!
DDRRR! DDRRRR!
SO I'M SORT OF FOOLING AROUND WITH IT, YOU KNOW, SEEING HOW FAST IT'LL GO-- BUT MY HANDS ARE STILL COVERED IN K.Y. FROM THE LAST SCENE, AND--WELL--
I DROP IT AND IT ROLLS INTO THE JACUZZI AND IT'S STILL PLUGGED IN, AND...
FRYING SILICON.
GOD FORGIVE ME.
I'M NEVER GONNA FORGET THAT SMELL.

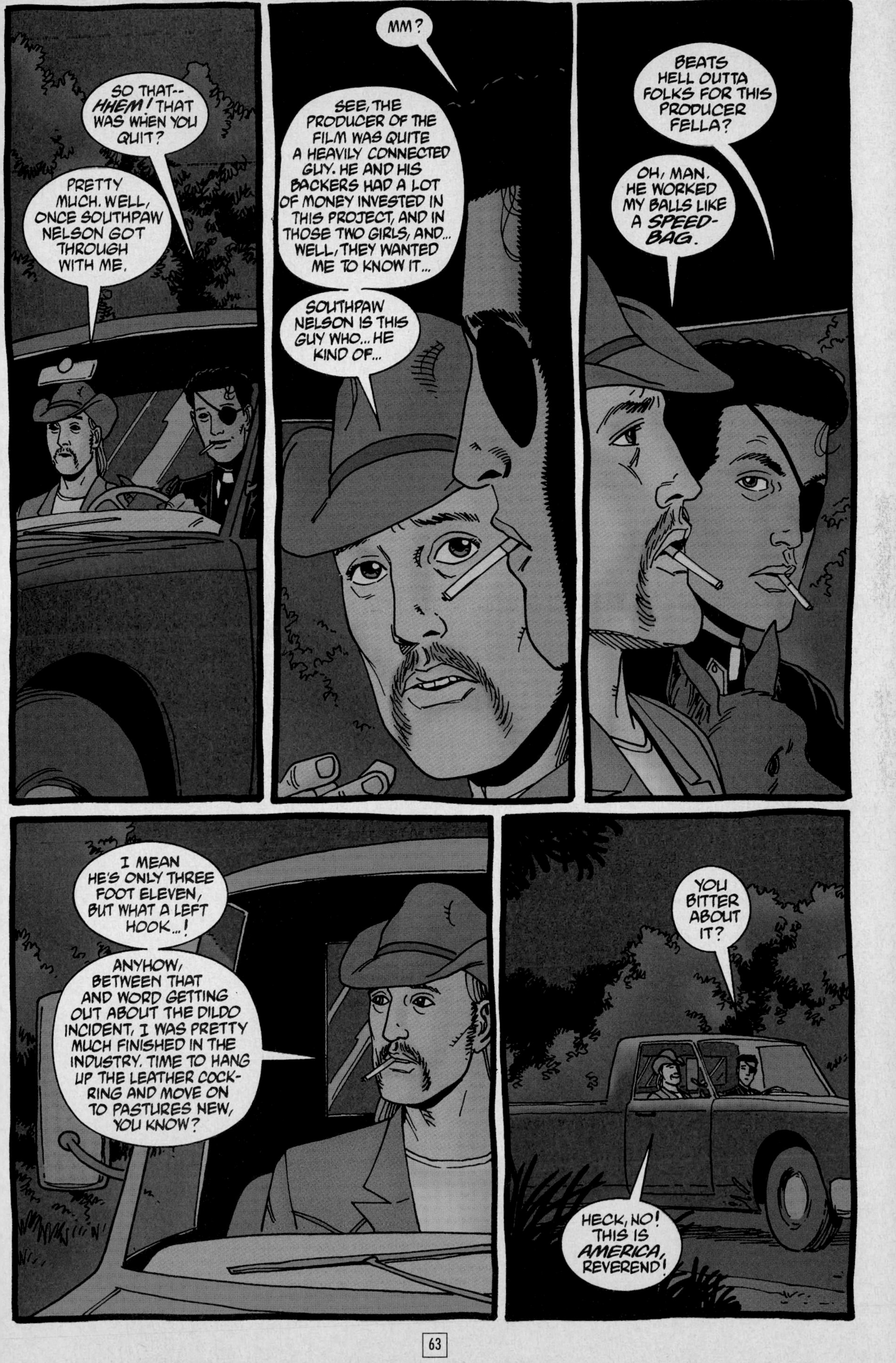
SO THAT-- HHEM! THAT WAS WHEN YOU QUIT?
PRETTY MUCH. WELL, ONCE SOUTHPAW NELSON GOT THROUGH WITH ME.
MM?
SEE, THE PRODUCER OF THE FILM WAS QUITE A HEAVILY CONNECTED GUY. HE AND HIS BACKERS HAD A LOT OF MONEY INVESTED IN THIS PROJECT, AND IN THOSE TWO GIRLS, AND... WELL, THEY WANTED ME TO KNOW IT...
SOUTHPAW NELSON IS THIS GUY WHO... HE KIND OF...
BEATS HELL OUTTA FOLKS FOR THIS PRODUCER FELLA?
OH, MAN. HE WORKED MY BALLS LIKE A SPEED-BAG.
I MEAN HE'S ONLY THREE FOOT ELEVEN, BUT WHAT A LEFT HOOK...!
ANYHOW, BETWEEN THAT AND WORD GETTING OUT ABOUT THE DILDO INCIDENT, I WAS PRETTY MUCH FINISHED IN THE INDUSTRY. TIME TO HANG UP THE LEATHER COCK-RING AND MOVE ON TO PASTURES NEW, YOU KNOW?
YOU BITTER ABOUT IT?
HECK, NO! THIS IS AMERICA, REVEREND!

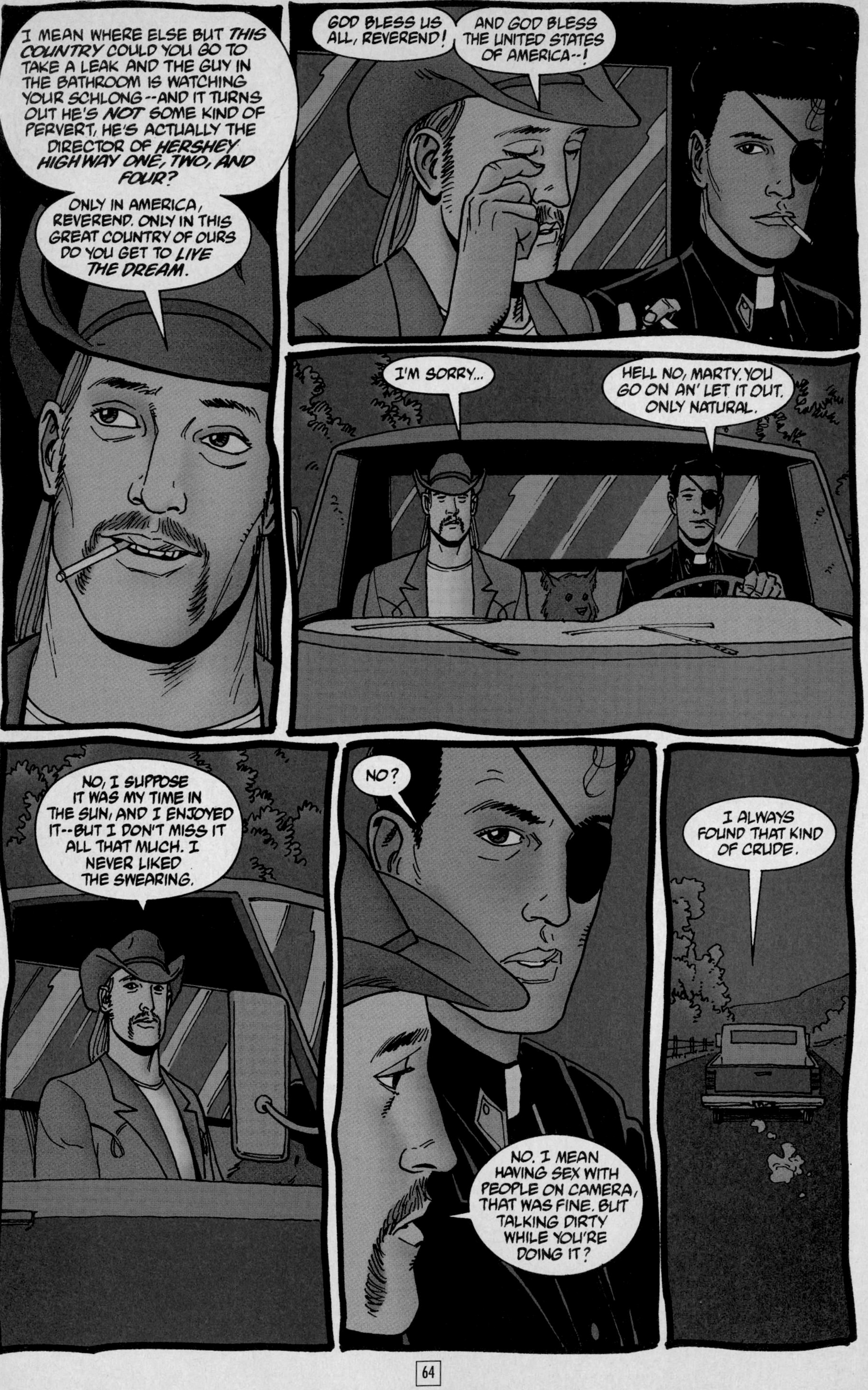
I MEAN WHERE ELSE BUT *THIS COUNTRY* COULD YOU GO TO TAKE A LEAK AND THE GUY IN THE BATHROOM IS WATCHING YOUR SCHLONG--AND IT TURNS OUT HE'S *NOT* SOME KIND OF PERVERT, HE'S ACTUALLY THE DIRECTOR OF *HERSHEY HIGHWAY ONE, TWO, AND FOUR?*
ONLY IN AMERICA, REVEREND. ONLY IN THIS GREAT COUNTRY OF OURS DO YOU GET TO *LIVE THE DREAM*.
GOD BLESS US ALL, REVEREND!
AND GOD BLESS THE UNITED STATES OF AMERICA--!
I'M SORRY...
HELL NO, MARTY. YOU GO ON AN' LET IT OUT. ONLY NATURAL.
NO, I SUPPOSE IT WAS MY TIME IN THE SUN, AND I ENJOYED IT--BUT I DON'T MISS IT ALL THAT MUCH. I NEVER LIKED THE SWEARING.
NO?
NO. I MEAN HAVING SEX WITH PEOPLE ON CAMERA, THAT WAS FINE. BUT TALKING DIRTY WHILE YOU'RE DOING IT?
I ALWAYS FOUND THAT KIND OF CRUDE.

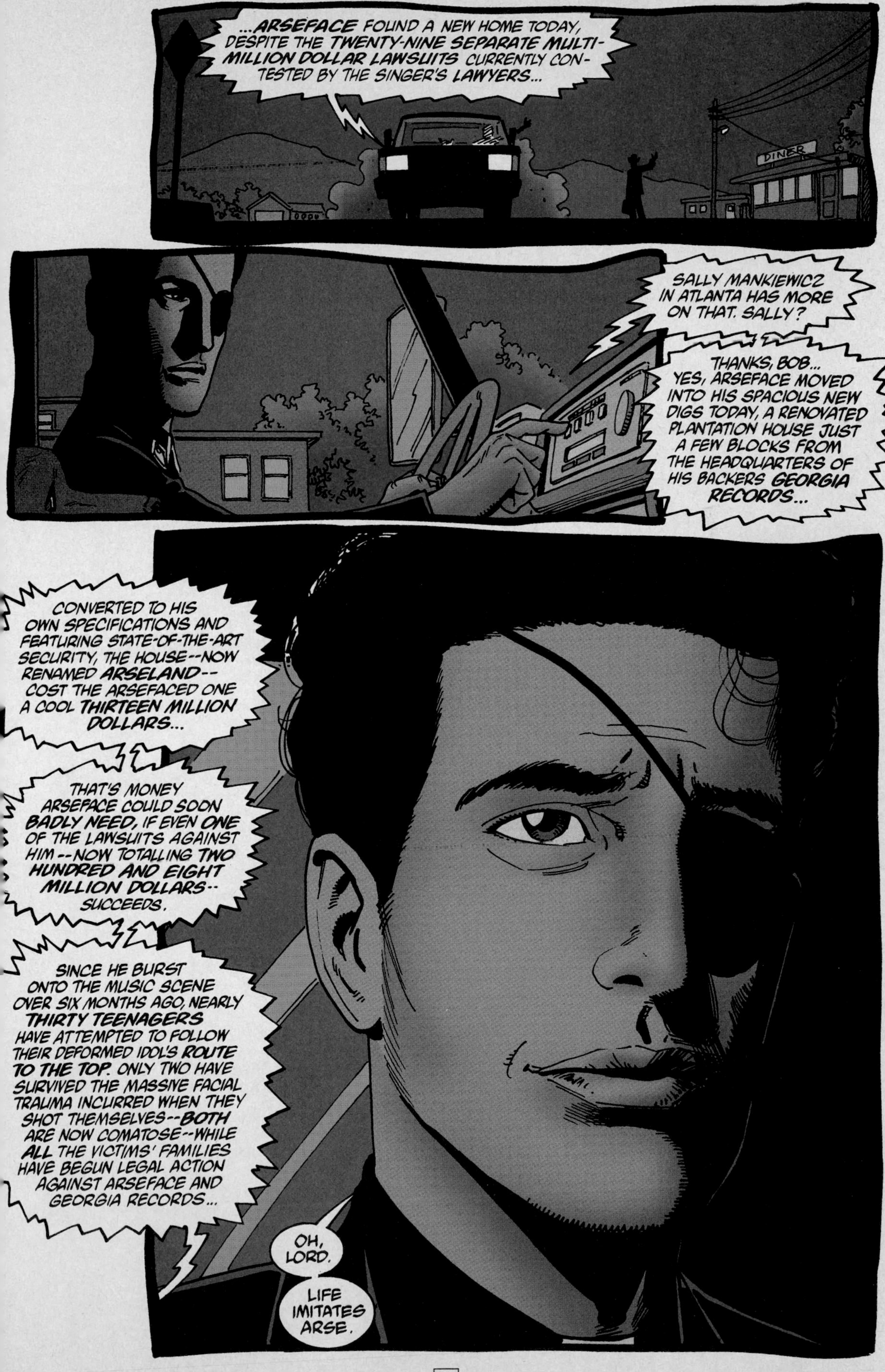

...ARSEFACE FOUND A NEW HOME TODAY, DESPITE THE TWENTY-NINE SEPARATE MULTI-MILLION DOLLAR LAWSUITS CURRENTLY CON-TESTED BY THE SINGER'S LAWYERS...
DINER
SALLY MANKIEWICZ IN ATLANTA HAS MORE ON THAT. SALLY?
THANKS, BOB... YES, ARSEFACE MOVED INTO HIS SPACIOUS NEW DIGS TODAY, A RENOVATED PLANTATION HOUSE JUST A FEW BLOCKS FROM THE HEADQUARTERS OF HIS BACKERS GEORGIA RECORDS...
CONVERTED TO HIS OWN SPECIFICATIONS AND FEATURING STATE-OF-THE-ART SECURITY, THE HOUSE--NOW RENAMED ARSELAND--COST THE ARSEFACED ONE A COOL THIRTEEN MILLION DOLLARS...
THAT'S MONEY ARSEFACE COULD SOON BADLY NEED, IF EVEN ONE OF THE LAWSUITS AGAINST HIM--NOW TOTALLING TWO HUNDRED AND EIGHT MILLION DOLLARS--SUCCEEDS.
SINCE HE BURST ONTO THE MUSIC SCENE OVER SIX MONTHS AGO, NEARLY THIRTY TEENAGERS HAVE ATTEMPTED TO FOLLOW THEIR DEFORMED IDOL'S ROUTE TO THE TOP. ONLY TWO HAVE SURVIVED THE MASSIVE FACIAL TRAUMA INCURRED WHEN THEY SHOT THEMSELVES--BOTH ARE NOW COMATOSE--WHILE ALL THE VICTIMS' FAMILIES HAVE BEGUN LEGAL ACTION AGAINST ARSEFACE AND GEORGIA RECORDS...
OH, LORD.
LIFE IMITATES ARSE.

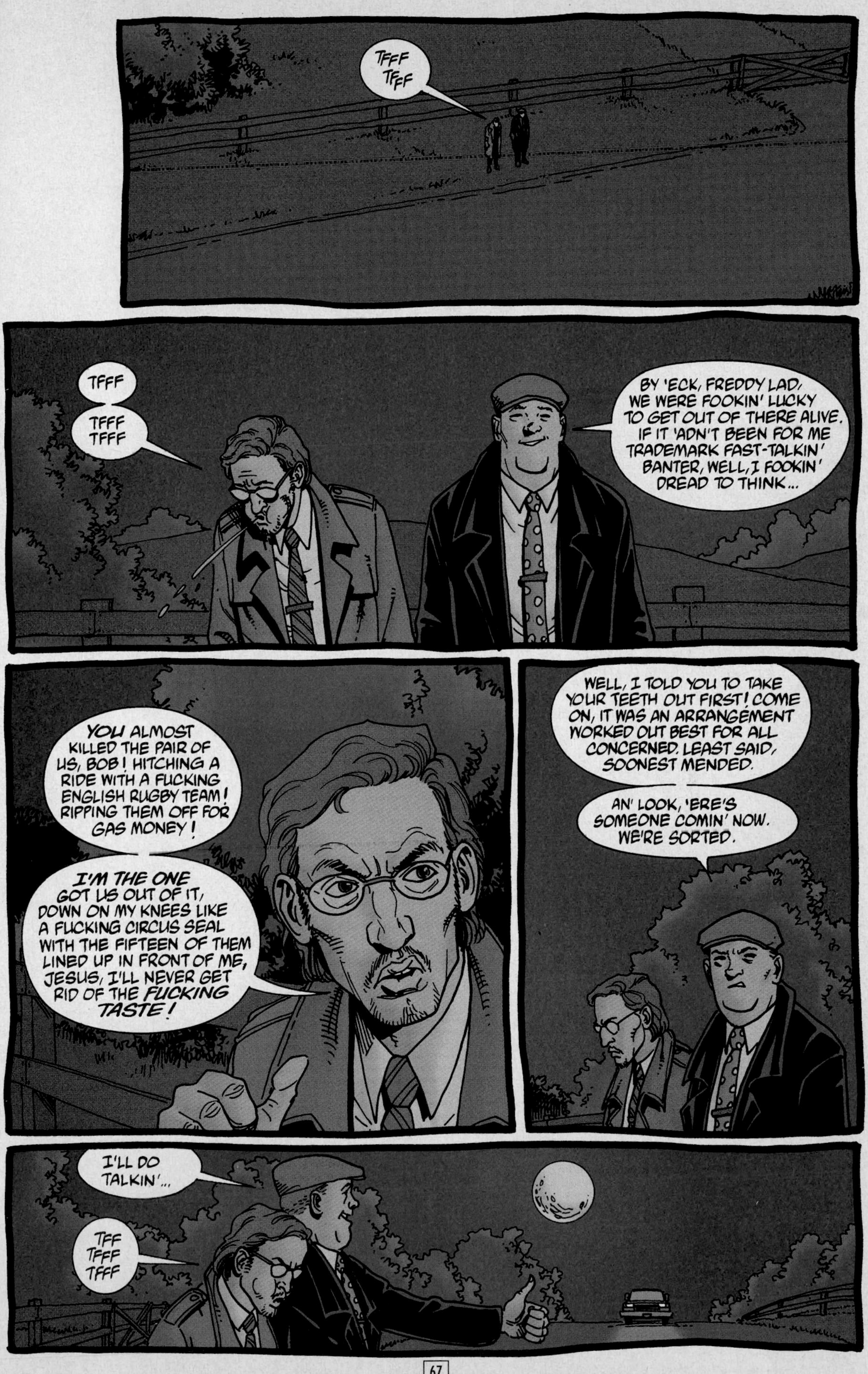
TFFF TFFF
TFFF
TFFF TFFF
BY 'ECK, FREDDY LAD, WE WERE FOOKIN' LUCKY TO GET OUT OF THERE ALIVE. IF IT 'ADN'T BEEN FOR ME TRADEMARK FAST-TALKIN' BANTER, WELL, I FOOKIN' DREAD TO THINK...
YOU ALMOST KILLED THE PAIR OF US, BOB! HITCHING A RIDE WITH A FUCKING ENGLISH RUGBY TEAM! RIPPING THEM OFF FOR GAS MONEY!
I'M THE ONE GOT US OUT OF IT, DOWN ON MY KNEES LIKE A FUCKING CIRCUS SEAL WITH THE FIFTEEN OF THEM LINED UP IN FRONT OF ME, JESUS, I'LL NEVER GET RID OF THE FUCKING TASTE!
WELL, I TOLD YOU TO TAKE YOUR TEETH OUT FIRST! COME ON, IT WAS AN ARRANGEMENT WORKED OUT BEST FOR ALL CONCERNED. LEAST SAID, SOONEST MENDED.
AN' LOOK, 'ERE'S SOMEONE COMIN' NOW. WE'RE SORTED.
I'LL DO TALKIN'...
TFF TFFF TFFF

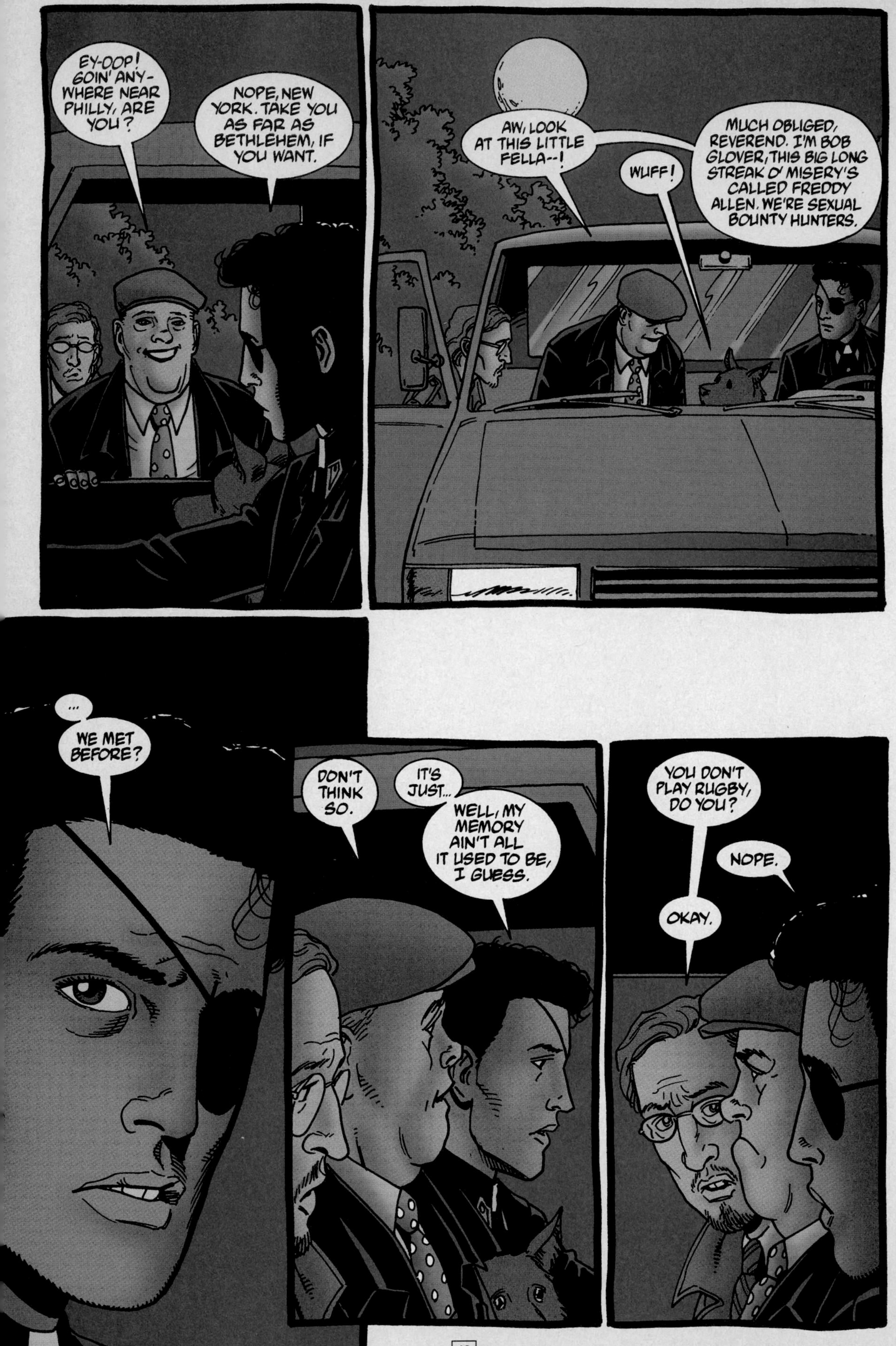
EY-OOP! GOIN' ANY-WHERE NEAR PHILLY, ARE YOU?
NOPE, NEW YORK. TAKE YOU AS FAR AS BETHLEHEM, IF YOU WANT.
AW, LOOK AT THIS LITTLE FELLA--!
WUFF!
MUCH OBLIGED, REVEREND. I'M BOB GLOVER, THIS BIG LONG STREAK O' MISERY'S CALLED FREDDY ALLEN. WE'RE SEXUAL BOUNTY HUNTERS.
...
WE MET BEFORE?
DON'T THINK SO.
IT'S JUST...
WELL, MY MEMORY AIN'T ALL IT USED TO BE, I GUESS.
YOU DON'T PLAY RUGBY, DO YOU?
NOPE.
OKAY.

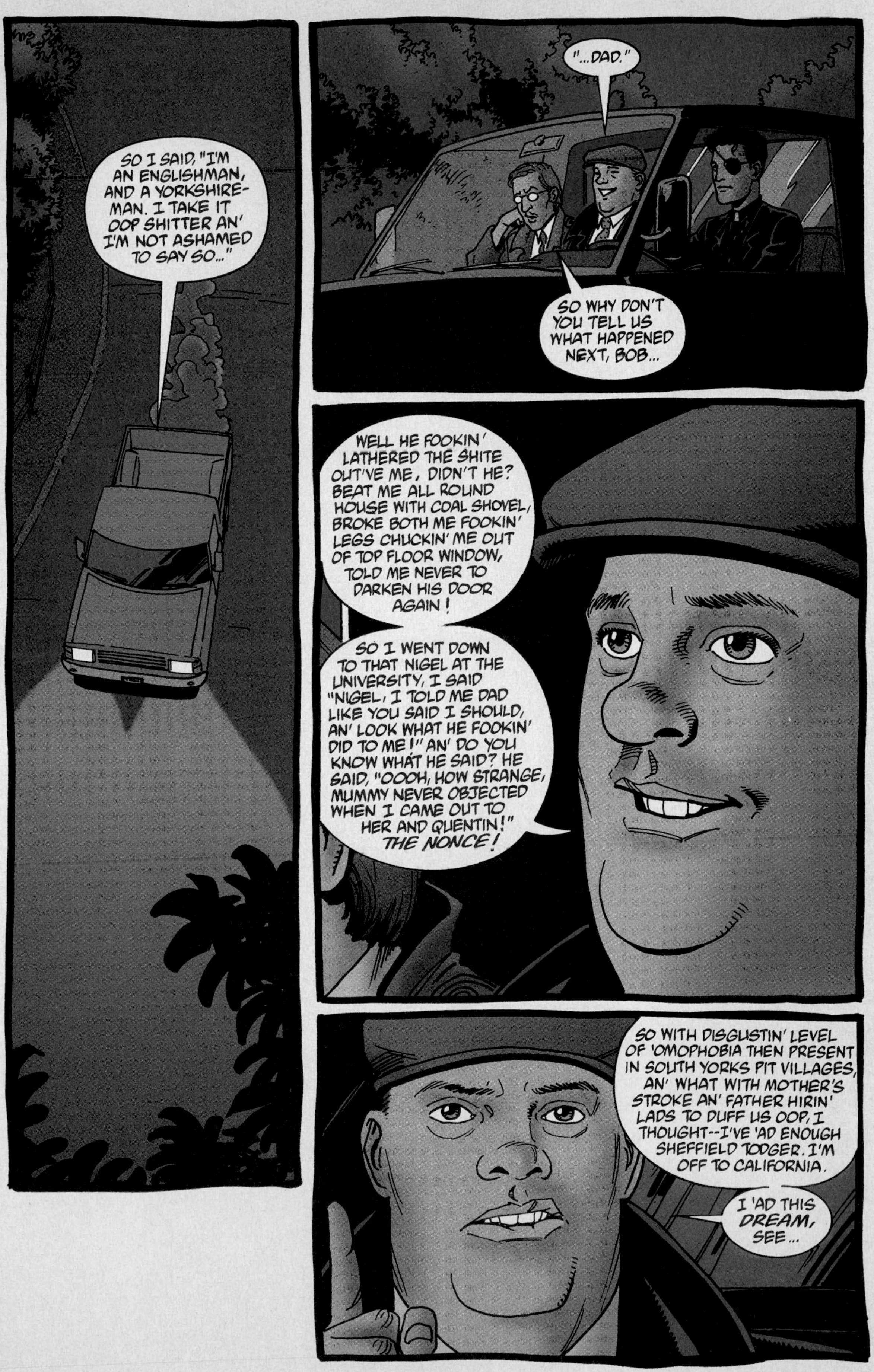
SO I SAID, "I'M AN ENGLISHMAN, AND A YORKSHIRE-MAN. I TAKE IT OOP SHITTER AN' I'M NOT ASHAMED TO SAY SO..."
"...DAD."
SO WHY DON'T YOU TELL US WHAT HAPPENED NEXT, BOB...
WELL HE FOOKIN' LATHERED THE SHITE OUT'VE ME, DIDN'T HE? BEAT ME ALL ROUND HOUSE WITH COAL SHOVEL, BROKE BOTH ME FOOKIN' LEGS CHUCKIN' ME OUT OF TOP FLOOR WINDOW, TOLD ME NEVER TO DARKEN HIS DOOR AGAIN!
SO I WENT DOWN TO THAT NIGEL AT THE UNIVERSITY, I SAID "NIGEL, I TOLD ME DAD LIKE YOU SAID I SHOULD, AN' LOOK WHAT HE FOOKIN' DID TO ME!" AN' DO YOU KNOW WHAT HE SAID? HE SAID, "OOOH, HOW STRANGE, MUMMY NEVER OBJECTED WHEN I CAME OUT TO HER AND QUENTIN!" THE NONCE!
SO WITH DISGUSTIN' LEVEL OF 'OMOPHOBIA THEN PRESENT IN SOUTH YORKS PIT VILLAGES, AN' WHAT WITH MOTHER'S STROKE AN' FATHER HIRIN' LADS TO DUFF US OOP, I THOUGHT--I'VE 'AD ENOUGH SHEFFIELD TODGER. I'M OFF TO CALIFORNIA.
I 'AD THIS DREAM, SEE...

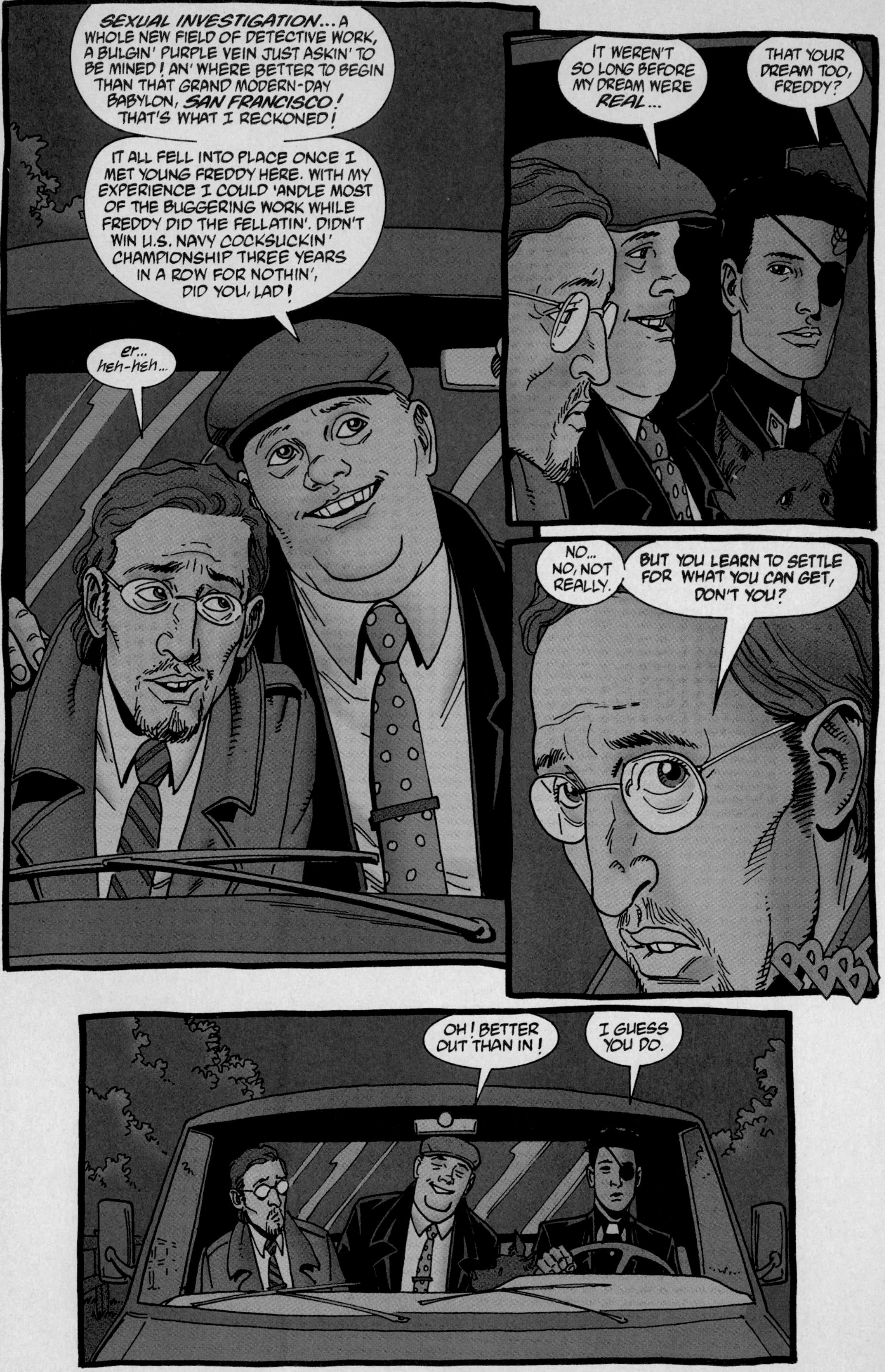
SEXUAL INVESTIGATION... A WHOLE NEW FIELD OF DETECTIVE WORK, A BULGIN' PURPLE VEIN JUST ASKIN' TO BE MINED! AN' WHERE BETTER TO BEGIN THAN THAT GRAND MODERN-DAY BABYLON, SAN FRANCISCO! THAT'S WHAT I RECKONED!
IT ALL FELL INTO PLACE ONCE I MET YOUNG FREDDY HERE. WITH MY EXPERIENCE I COULD 'ANDLE MOST OF THE BUGGERING WORK WHILE FREDDY DID THE FELLATIN'. DIDN'T WIN U.S. NAVY COCKSUCKIN' CHAMPIONSHIP THREE YEARS IN A ROW FOR NOTHIN', DID YOU, LAD!
er... heh-heh...
IT WEREN'T SO LONG BEFORE MY DREAM WERE REAL...
THAT YOUR DREAM TOO, FREDDY?
NO... NO, NOT REALLY.
BUT YOU LEARN TO SETTLE FOR WHAT YOU CAN GET, DON'T YOU?
PBBBT
OH! BETTER OUT THAN IN!
I GUESS YOU DO.

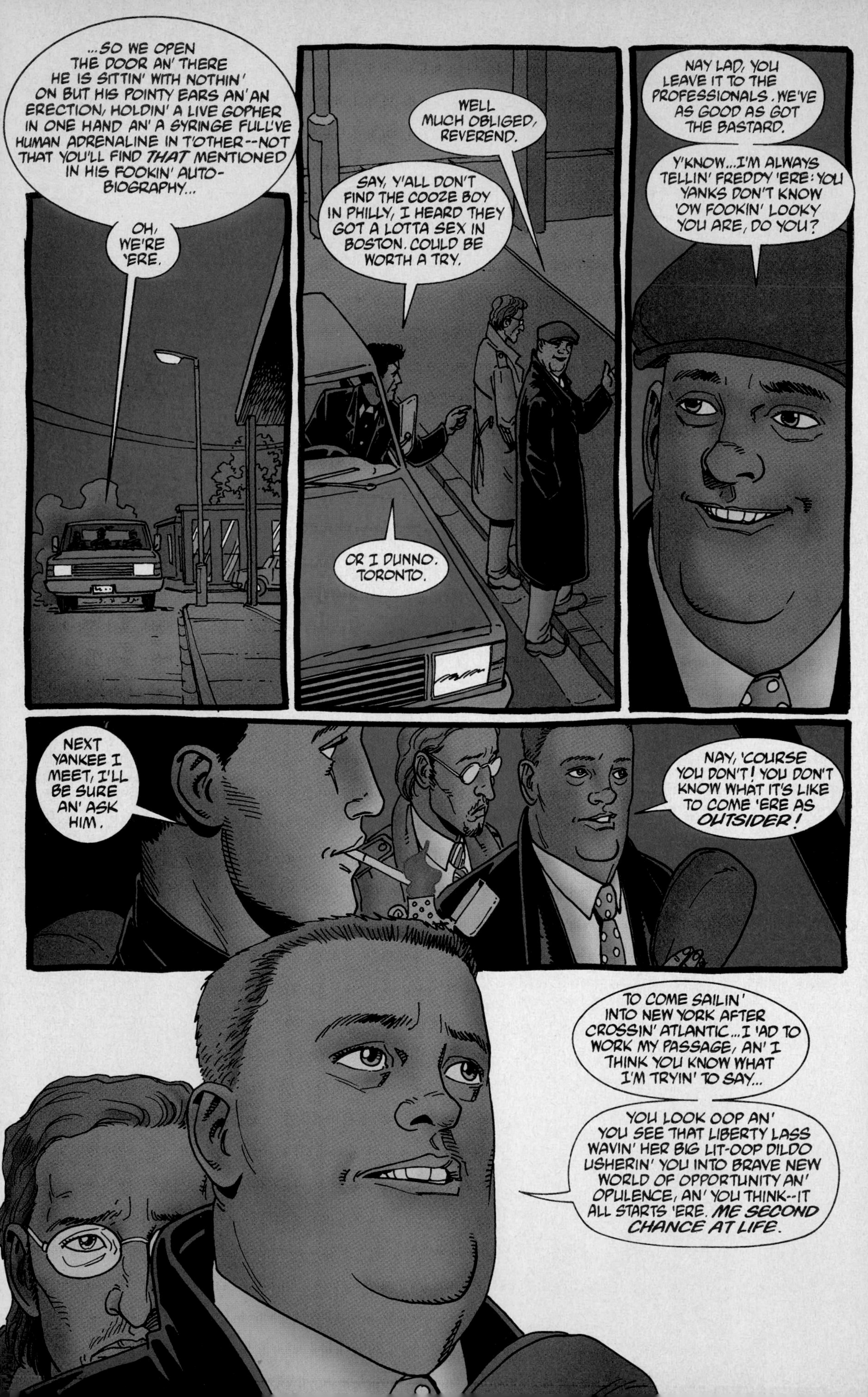
...SO WE OPEN THE DOOR AN' THERE HE IS SITTIN' WITH NOTHIN' ON BUT HIS POINTY EARS AN' AN ERECTION, HOLDIN' A LIVE GOPHER IN ONE HAND AN' A SYRINGE FULL'VE HUMAN ADRENALINE IN T'OTHER--NOT THAT YOU'LL FIND *THAT* MENTIONED IN HIS FOOKIN' AUTO-BIOGRAPHY...
OH, WE'RE 'ERE.
WELL MUCH OBLIGED, REVEREND.
SAY, Y'ALL DON'T FIND THE COOZE BOY IN PHILLY, I HEARD THEY GOT A LOTTA SEX IN BOSTON. COULD BE WORTH A TRY.
OR I DUNNO. TORONTO.
NAY LAD, YOU LEAVE IT TO THE PROFESSIONALS. WE'VE AS GOOD AS GOT THE BASTARD.
Y'KNOW...I'M ALWAYS TELLIN' FREDDY 'ERE: YOU YANKS DON'T KNOW 'OW FOOKIN' LOOKY YOU ARE, DO YOU?
NEXT YANKEE I MEET, I'LL BE SURE AN' ASK HIM.
NAY, 'COURSE YOU DON'T! YOU DON'T KNOW WHAT IT'S LIKE TO COME 'ERE AS *OUTSIDER!*
TO COME SAILIN' INTO NEW YORK AFTER CROSSIN' ATLANTIC...I 'AD TO WORK MY PASSAGE, AN' I THINK YOU KNOW WHAT I'M TRYIN' TO SAY...
YOU LOOK OOP AN' YOU SEE THAT LIBERTY LASS WAVIN' HER BIG LIT-OOP DILDO USHERIN' YOU INTO BRAVE NEW WORLD OF OPPORTUNITY AN' OPULENCE, AN' YOU THINK--IT ALL STARTS 'ERE. *ME SECOND CHANCE AT LIFE.*

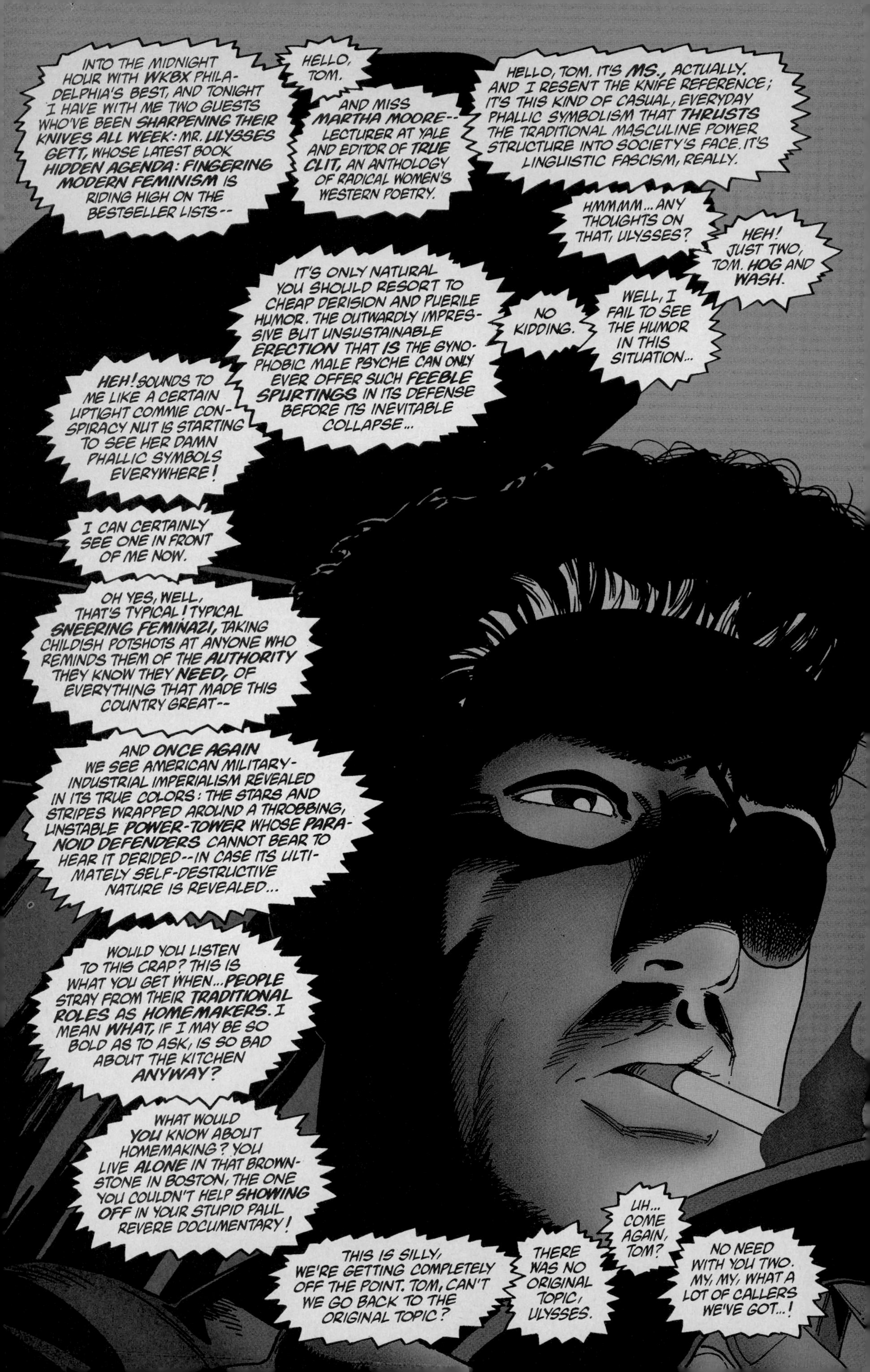
INTO THE MIDNIGHT HOUR WITH WKBX PHILADELPHIA'S BEST, AND TONIGHT I HAVE WITH ME TWO GUESTS WHO'VE BEEN SHARPENING THEIR KNIVES ALL WEEK: MR. ULYSSES GETT, WHOSE LATEST BOOK HIDDEN AGENDA: FINGERING MODERN FEMINISM IS RIDING HIGH ON THE BESTSELLER LISTS--
HELLO, TOM.
AND MISS MARTHA MOORE-- LECTURER AT YALE AND EDITOR OF TRUE CLIT, AN ANTHOLOGY OF RADICAL WOMEN'S WESTERN POETRY.
HELLO, TOM. IT'S MS., ACTUALLY. AND I RESENT THE KNIFE REFERENCE; IT'S THIS KIND OF CASUAL, EVERYDAY PHALLIC SYMBOLISM THAT THRUSTS THE TRADITIONAL MASCULINE POWER STRUCTURE INTO SOCIETY'S FACE. IT'S LINGUISTIC FASCISM, REALLY.
HMMMM... ANY THOUGHTS ON THAT, ULYSSES?
HEH! JUST TWO, TOM. HOG AND WASH.
WELL, I FAIL TO SEE THE HUMOR IN THIS SITUATION...
NO KIDDING.
IT'S ONLY NATURAL YOU SHOULD RESORT TO CHEAP DERISION AND PUERILE HUMOR. THE OUTWARDLY IMPRESSIVE BUT UNSUSTAINABLE ERECTION THAT IS THE GYNOPHOBIC MALE PSYCHE CAN ONLY EVER OFFER SUCH FEEBLE SPURTINGS IN ITS DEFENSE BEFORE ITS INEVITABLE COLLAPSE...
HEH! SOUNDS TO ME LIKE A CERTAIN UPTIGHT COMMIE CONSPIRACY NUT IS STARTING TO SEE HER DAMN PHALLIC SYMBOLS EVERYWHERE!
I CAN CERTAINLY SEE ONE IN FRONT OF ME NOW.
OH YES, WELL, THAT'S TYPICAL! TYPICAL SNEERING FEMINAZI, TAKING CHILDISH POTSHOTS AT ANYONE WHO REMINDS THEM OF THE AUTHORITY THEY KNOW THEY NEED, OF EVERYTHING THAT MADE THIS COUNTRY GREAT--
AND ONCE AGAIN WE SEE AMERICAN MILITARY-INDUSTRIAL IMPERIALISM REVEALED IN ITS TRUE COLORS: THE STARS AND STRIPES WRAPPED AROUND A THROBBING, UNSTABLE POWER-TOWER WHOSE PARANOID DEFENDERS CANNOT BEAR TO HEAR IT DERIDED--IN CASE ITS ULTIMATELY SELF-DESTRUCTIVE NATURE IS REVEALED...
WOULD YOU LISTEN TO THIS CRAP? THIS IS WHAT YOU GET WHEN... PEOPLE STRAY FROM THEIR TRADITIONAL ROLES AS HOMEMAKERS. I MEAN WHAT, IF I MAY BE SO BOLD AS TO ASK, IS SO BAD ABOUT THE KITCHEN ANYWAY?
WHAT WOULD YOU KNOW ABOUT HOMEMAKING? YOU LIVE ALONE IN THAT BROWNSTONE IN BOSTON, THE ONE YOU COULDN'T HELP SHOWING OFF IN YOUR STUPID PAUL REVERE DOCUMENTARY!
THIS IS SILLY, WE'RE GETTING COMPLETELY OFF THE POINT. TOM, CAN'T WE GO BACK TO THE ORIGINAL TOPIC?
THERE WAS NO ORIGINAL TOPIC, ULYSSES.
UH... COME AGAIN, TOM?
NO NEED WITH YOU TWO. MY, MY, WHAT A LOT OF CALLERS WE'VE GOT...!

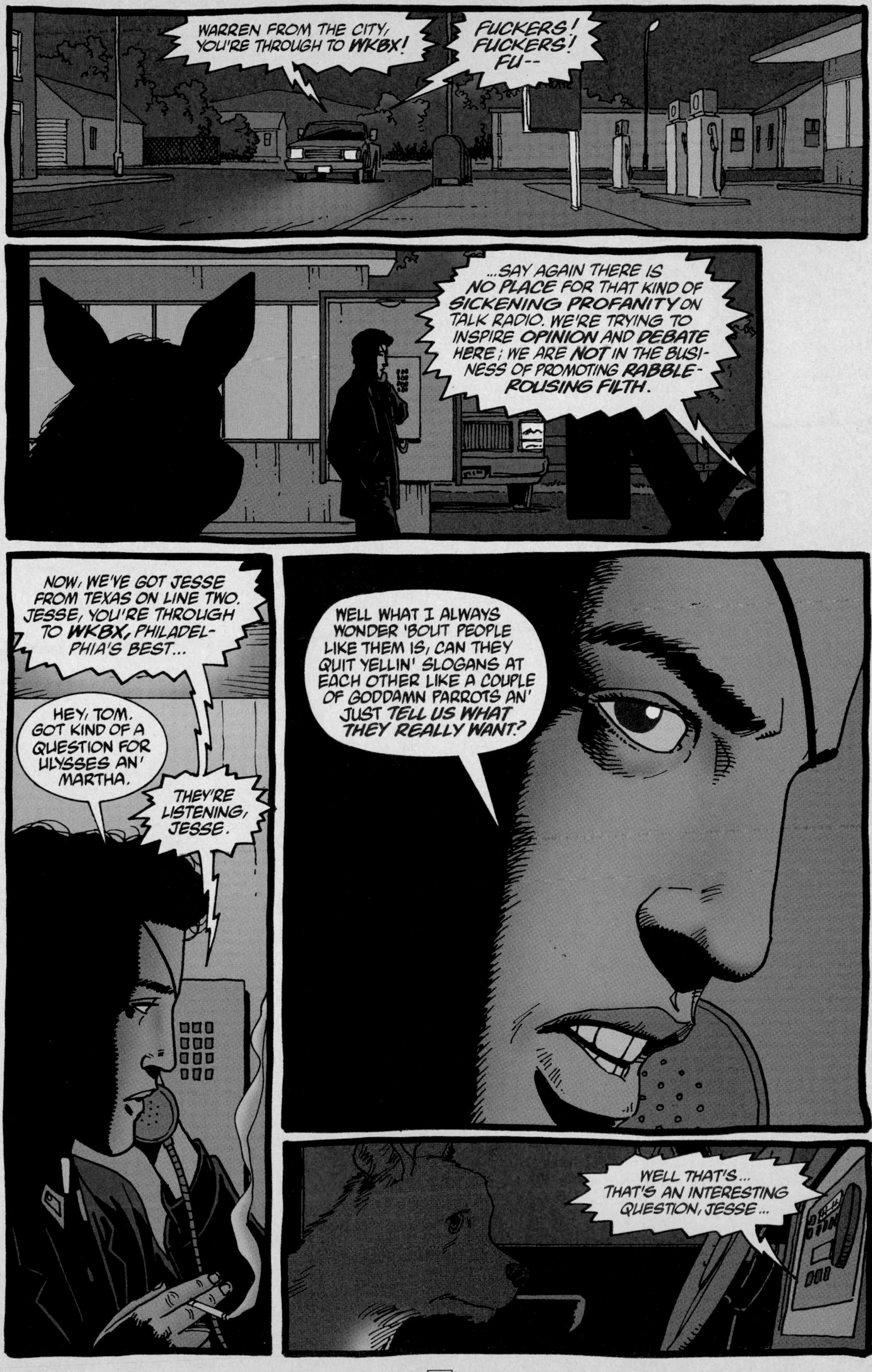
WARREN FROM THE CITY, YOU'RE THROUGH TO WKBX!
FUCKERS! FUCKERS! FU--
...SAY AGAIN THERE IS NO PLACE FOR THAT KIND OF SICKENING PROFANITY ON TALK RADIO. WE'RE TRYING TO INSPIRE OPINION AND DEBATE HERE; WE ARE NOT IN THE BUSINESS OF PROMOTING RABBLE-ROUSING FILTH.
NOW, WE'VE GOT JESSE FROM TEXAS ON LINE TWO. JESSE, YOU'RE THROUGH TO WKBX, PHILADELPHIA'S BEST...
HEY, TOM. GOT KIND OF A QUESTION FOR ULYSSES AN' MARTHA.
THEY'RE LISTENING, JESSE.
WELL WHAT I ALWAYS WONDER 'BOUT PEOPLE LIKE THEM IS, CAN THEY QUIT YELLIN' SLOGANS AT EACH OTHER LIKE A COUPLE OF GODDAMN PARROTS AN' JUST TELL US WHAT THEY REALLY WANT?
WELL THAT'S... THAT'S AN INTERESTING QUESTION, JESSE...

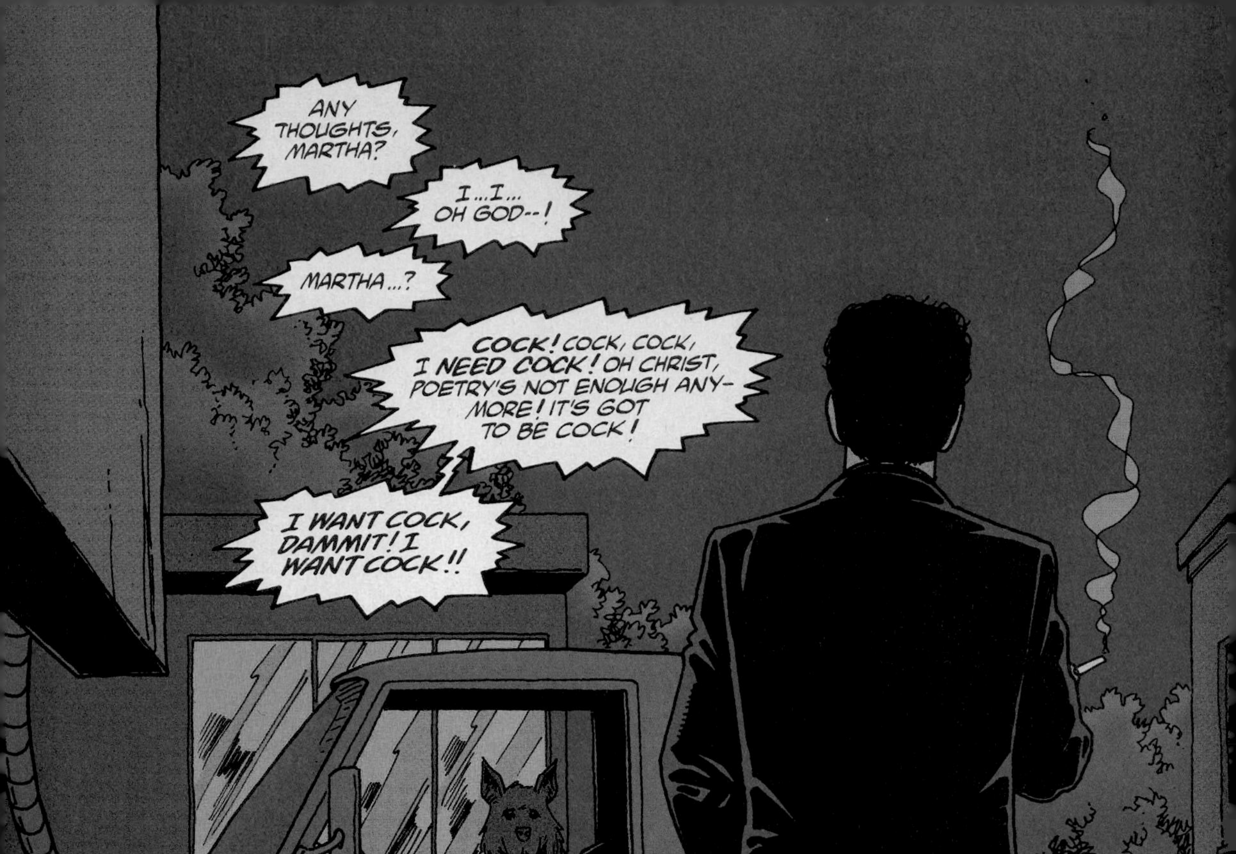
ANY THOUGHTS, MARTHA?
I...I... OH GOD--!
MARTHA...?
COCK! COCK, COCK, I NEED COCK! OH CHRIST, POETRY'S NOT ENOUGH ANY-MORE! IT'S GOT TO BE COCK!
I WANT COCK, DAMMIT! I WANT COCK!!
...WELL, ISN'T THAT A SURPRISE! HOW ABOUT YOU, ULYSSES?
MM?
ULYSSES?

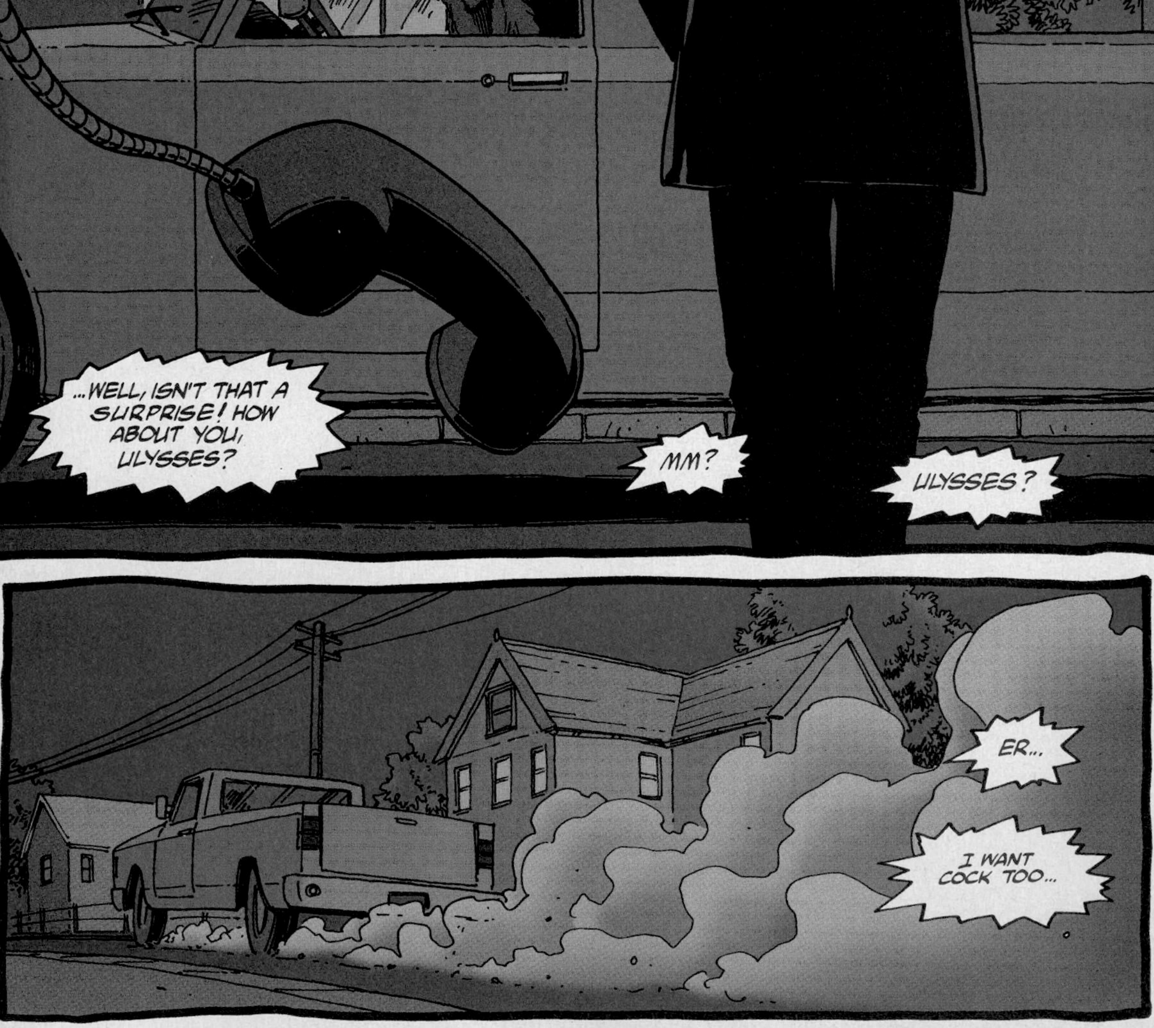
ER...
I WANT COCK TOO...

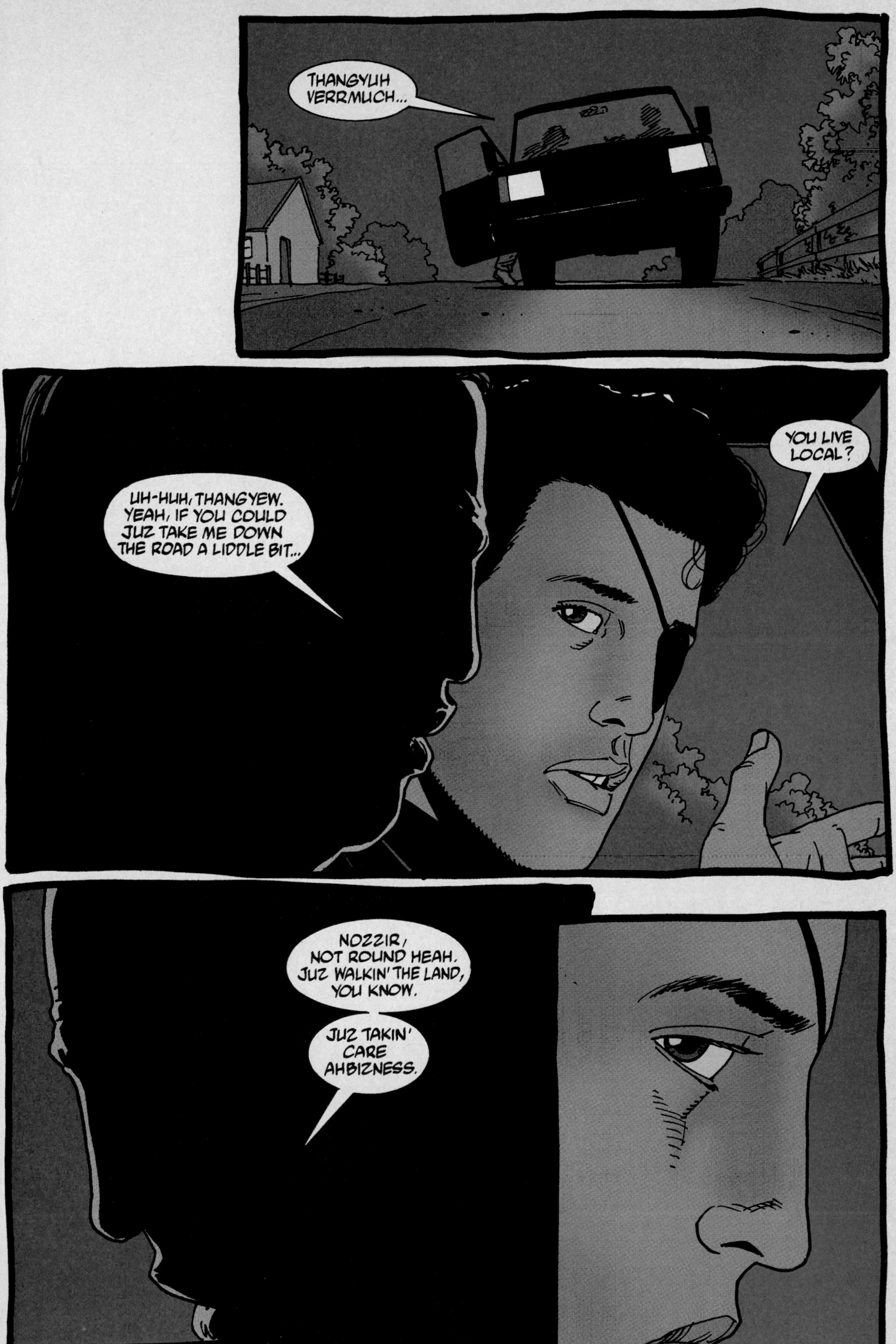
THANGYUH VERRMUCH...
UH-HUH, THANGYEW. YEAH, IF YOU COULD JUZ TAKE ME DOWN THE ROAD A LIDDLE BIT...
YOU LIVE LOCAL?
NOZZIR, NOT ROUND HEAH. JUZ WALKIN' THE LAND, YOU KNOW.
JUZ TAKIN' CARE AHBIZNESS.

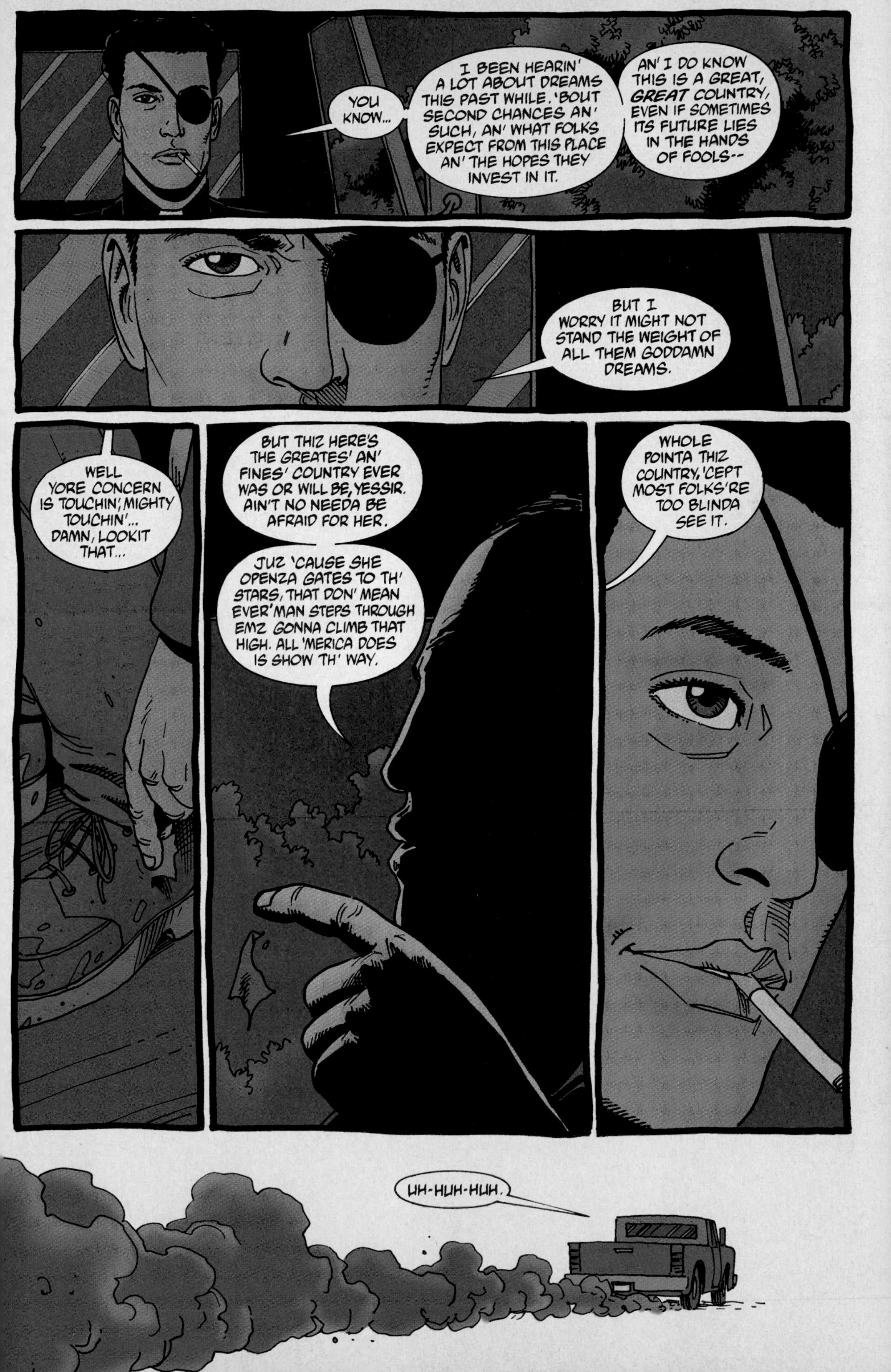
YOU KNOW...
I BEEN HEARIN' A LOT ABOUT DREAMS THIS PAST WHILE. 'BOUT SECOND CHANCES AN' SUCH, AN' WHAT FOLKS EXPECT FROM THIS PLACE AN' THE HOPES THEY INVEST IN IT.
AN' I DO KNOW THIS IS A GREAT, GREAT COUNTRY, EVEN IF SOMETIMES ITS FUTURE LIES IN THE HANDS OF FOOLS--
BUT I WORRY IT MIGHT NOT STAND THE WEIGHT OF ALL THEM GODDAMN DREAMS.
WELL YORE CONCERN IS TOUCHIN'; MIGHTY TOUCHIN'... DAMN, LOOKIT THAT...
BUT THIZ HERE'S THE GREATES' AN' FINES' COUNTRY EVER WAS OR WILL BE, YESSIR. AIN'T NO NEEDA BE AFRAID FOR HER.
JUZ 'CAUSE SHE OPENZA GATES TO TH' STARS, THAT DON' MEAN EVER'MAN STEPS THROUGH EMZ GONNA CLIMB THAT HIGH. ALL 'MERICA DOES IS SHOW TH' WAY.
WHOLE POINTA THIZ COUNTRY, 'CEPT MOST FOLKS'RE TOO BLINDA SEE IT.
UH-HUH-HUH.

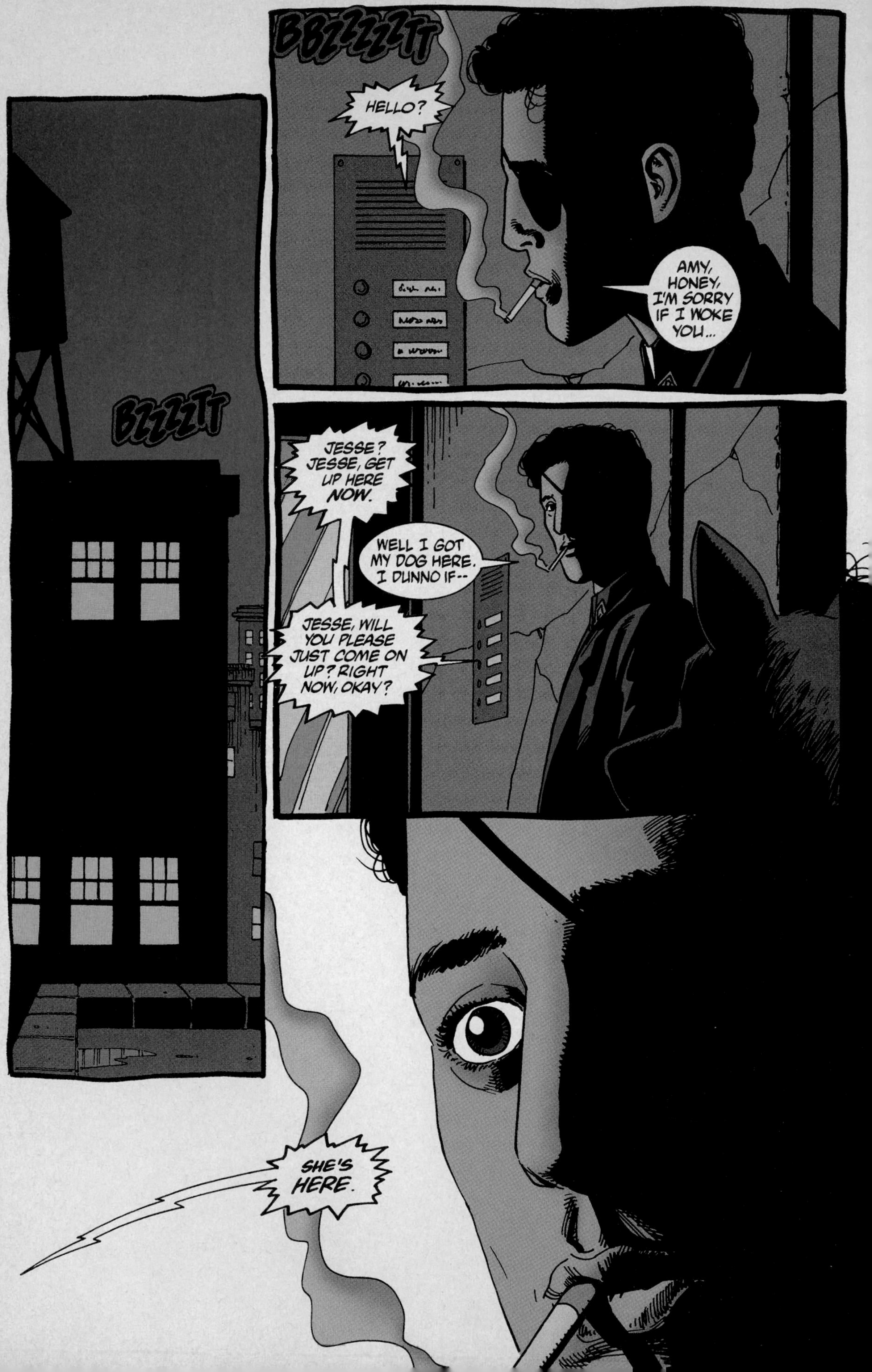
BZZZZTT
BBZZZZZZTT
HELLO?
AMY, HONEY, I'M SORRY IF I WOKE YOU...
JESSE? JESSE, GET UP HERE NOW.
WELL I GOT MY DOG HERE. I DUNNO IF--
JESSE, WILL YOU PLEASE JUST COME ON UP? RIGHT NOW, OKAY?
SHE'S HERE.

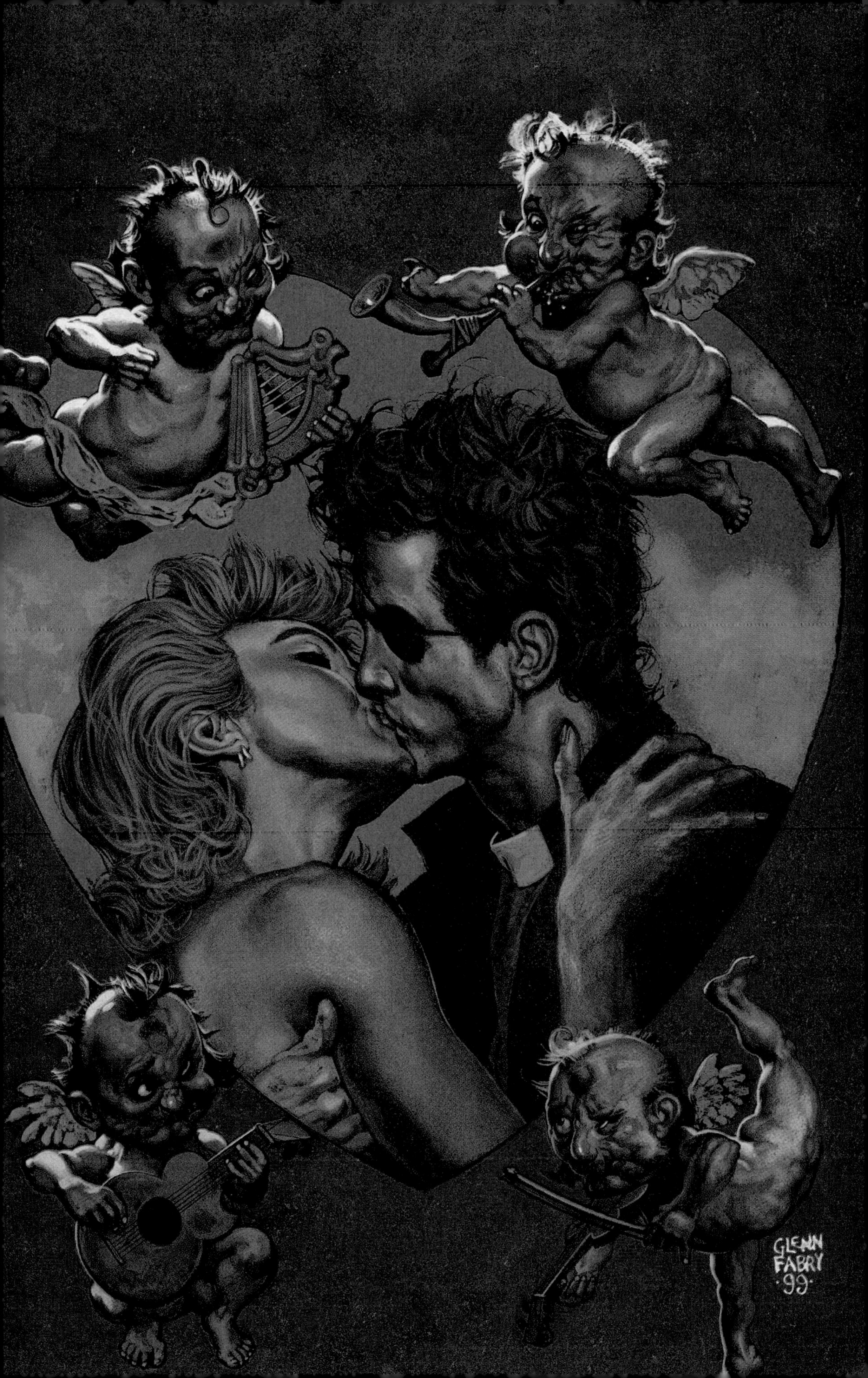
GLENN
FABRY
·99·

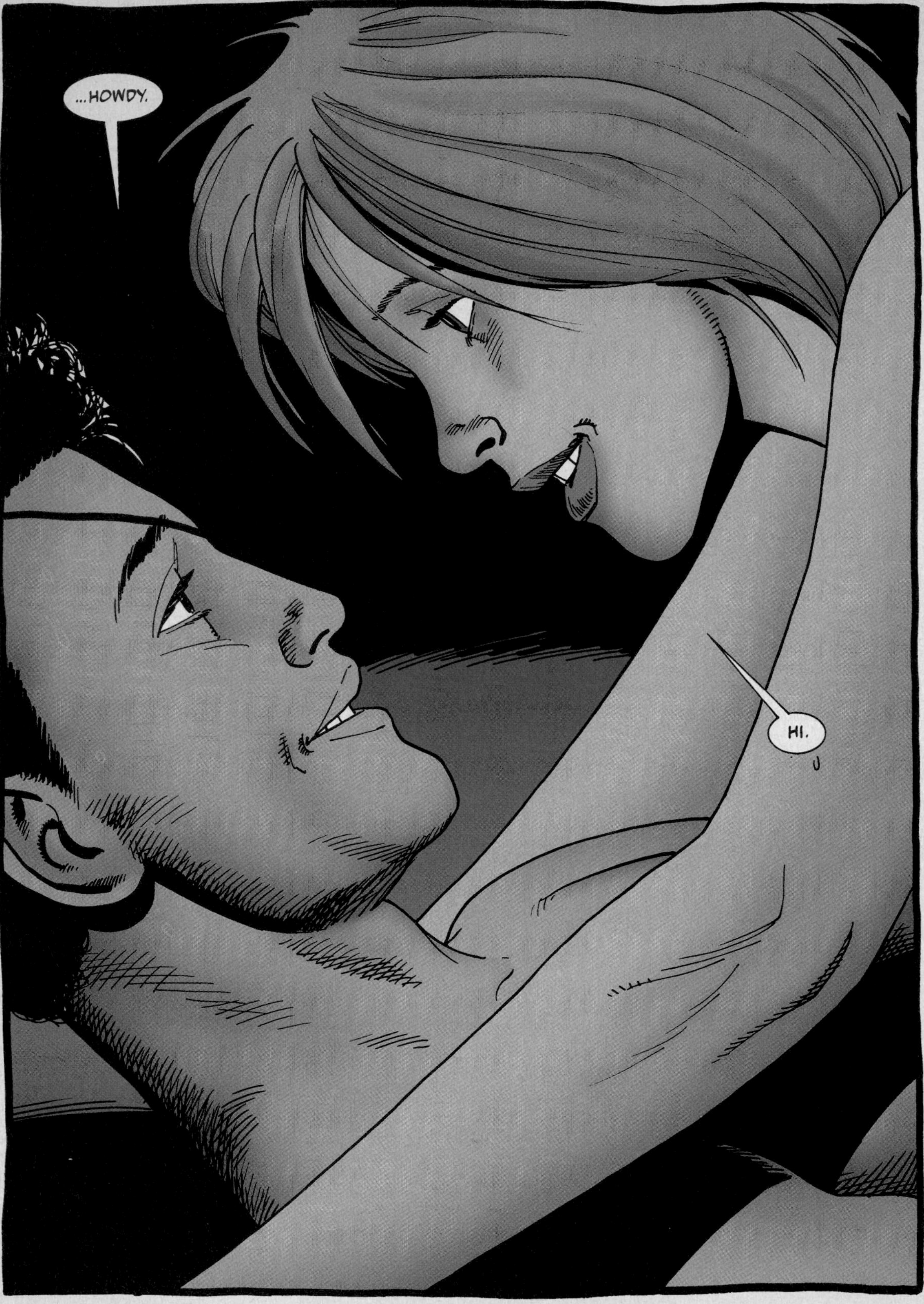
...HOWDY.
HI.

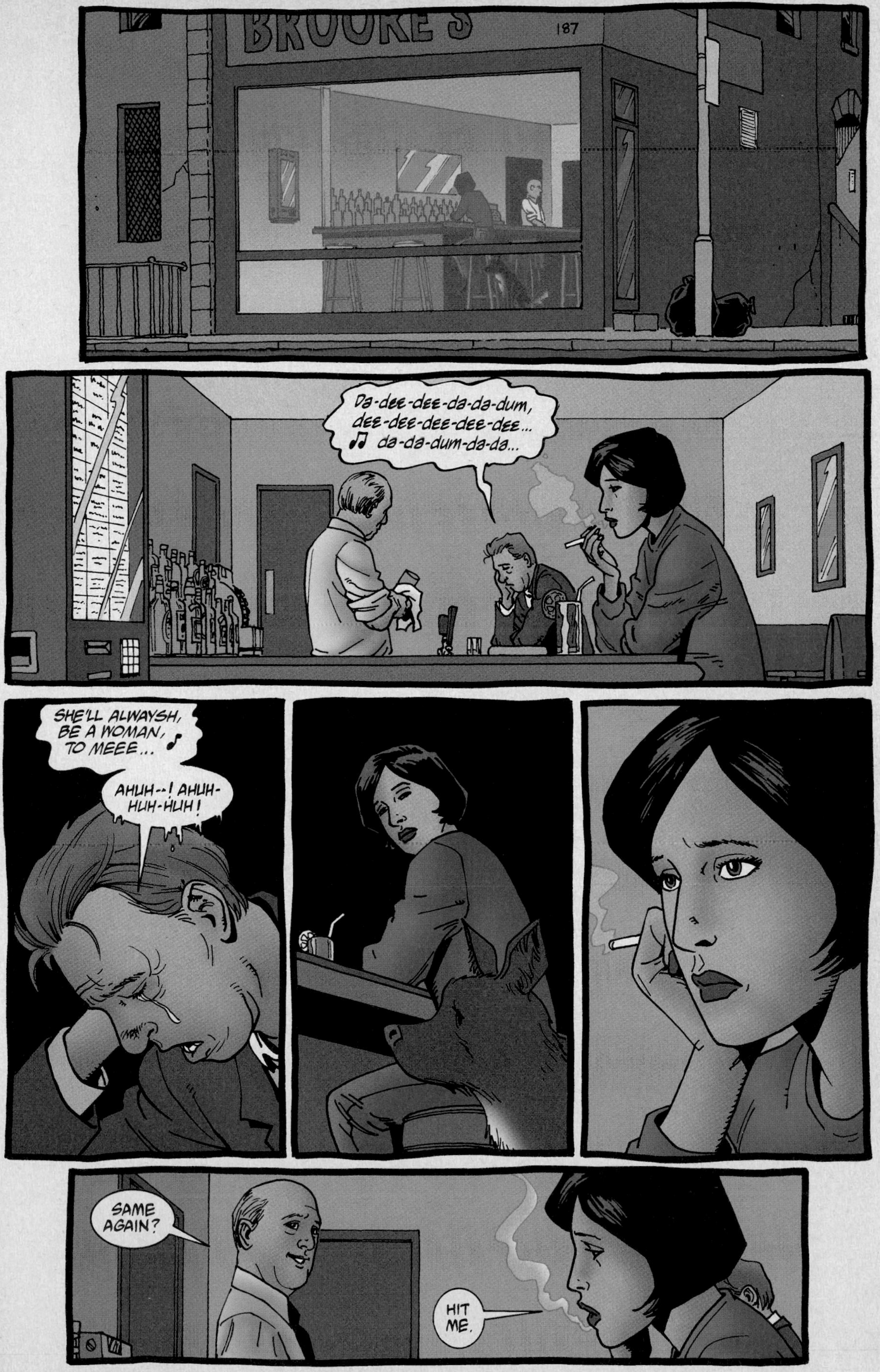
BROOKE'S
187
Da-dee-dee-da-da-dum, dee-dee-dee-dee-dee... ♫ da-da-dum-da-da...
SHE'LL ALWAYSH, BE A WOMAN, TO MEEE... ♪
AHUH--! AHUH-HUH-HUH!
SAME AGAIN?
HIT ME.

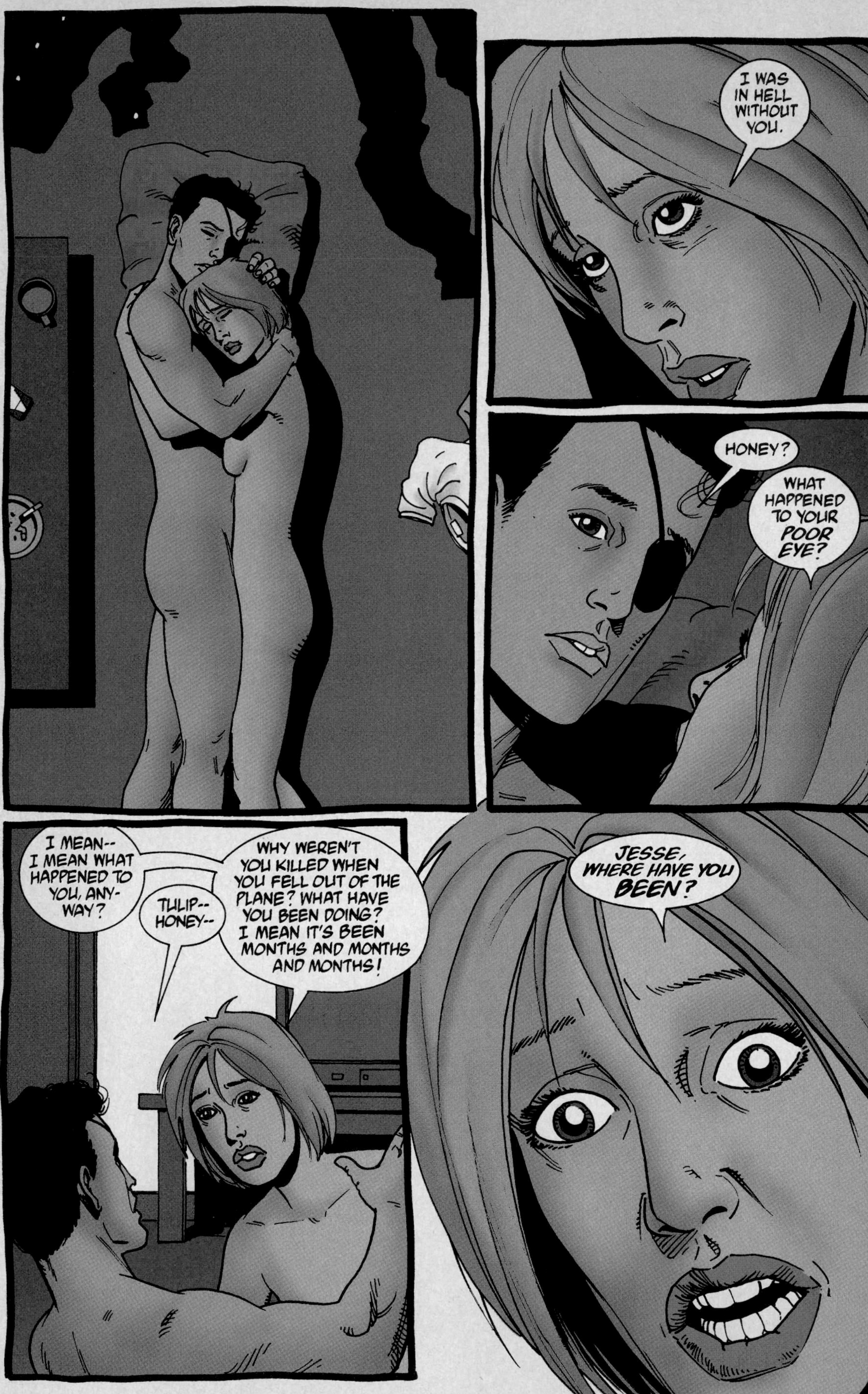
I WAS IN HELL WITHOUT YOU.
HONEY?
WHAT HAPPENED TO YOUR *POOR EYE?*
I MEAN-- I MEAN WHAT HAPPENED TO YOU, ANY-WAY?
WHY WEREN'T YOU KILLED WHEN YOU FELL OUT OF THE PLANE? WHAT HAVE YOU BEEN DOING? I MEAN IT'S BEEN MONTHS AND MONTHS AND MONTHS!
TULIP-- HONEY--
JESSE, WHERE HAVE YOU **BEEN?**

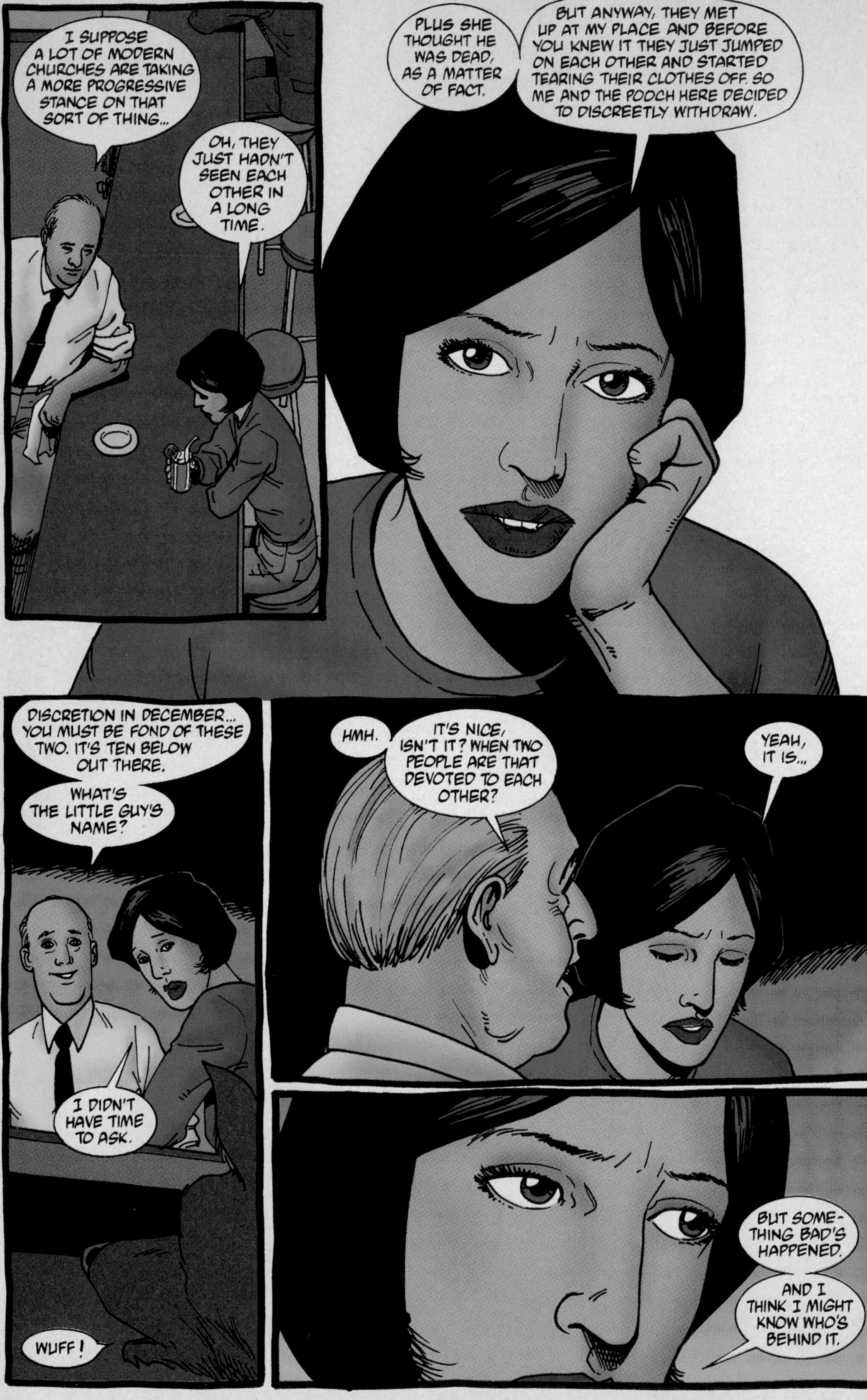
I SUPPOSE A LOT OF MODERN CHURCHES ARE TAKING A MORE PROGRESSIVE STANCE ON THAT SORT OF THING...
OH, THEY JUST HADN'T SEEN EACH OTHER IN A LONG TIME.
PLUS SHE THOUGHT HE WAS DEAD, AS A MATTER OF FACT.
BUT ANYWAY, THEY MET UP AT MY PLACE AND BEFORE YOU KNEW IT THEY JUST JUMPED ON EACH OTHER AND STARTED TEARING THEIR CLOTHES OFF. SO ME AND THE POOCH HERE DECIDED TO DISCREETLY WITHDRAW.
DISCRETION IN DECEMBER... YOU MUST BE FOND OF THESE TWO. IT'S TEN BELOW OUT THERE.
WHAT'S THE LITTLE GUY'S NAME?
I DIDN'T HAVE TIME TO ASK.
WUFF!
HMH.
IT'S NICE, ISN'T IT? WHEN TWO PEOPLE ARE THAT DEVOTED TO EACH OTHER?
YEAH, IT IS...
BUT SOMETHING BAD'S HAPPENED.
AND I THINK I MIGHT KNOW WHO'S BEHIND IT.

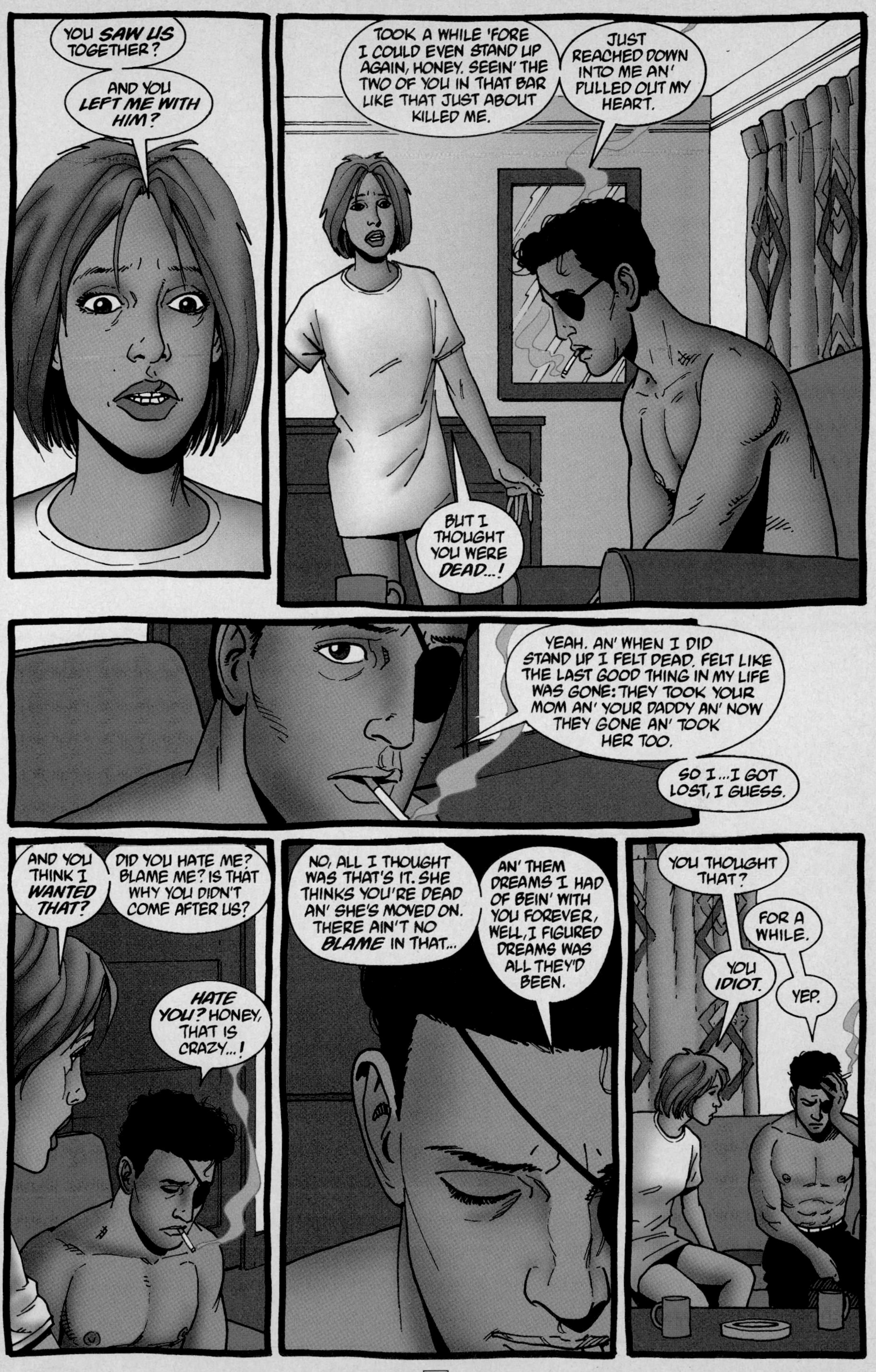

YOU SAW US TOGETHER?
AND YOU LEFT ME WITH HIM?
TOOK A WHILE 'FORE I COULD EVEN STAND UP AGAIN, HONEY. SEEIN' THE TWO OF YOU IN THAT BAR LIKE THAT JUST ABOUT KILLED ME.
JUST REACHED DOWN INTO ME AN' PULLED OUT MY HEART.
BUT I THOUGHT YOU WERE DEAD...!
YEAH. AN' WHEN I DID STAND UP I FELT DEAD. FELT LIKE THE LAST GOOD THING IN MY LIFE WAS GONE: THEY TOOK YOUR MOM AN' YOUR DADDY AN' NOW THEY GONE AN' TOOK HER TOO.
SO I...I GOT LOST, I GUESS.
AND YOU THINK I WANTED THAT?
DID YOU HATE ME? BLAME ME? IS THAT WHY YOU DIDN'T COME AFTER US?
HATE YOU? HONEY, THAT IS CRAZY...!
NO, ALL I THOUGHT WAS THAT'S IT. SHE THINKS YOU'RE DEAD AN' SHE'S MOVED ON. THERE AIN'T NO BLAME IN THAT...
AN' THEM DREAMS I HAD OF BEIN' WITH YOU FOREVER, WELL, I FIGURED DREAMS WAS ALL THEY'D BEEN.
YOU THOUGHT THAT?
FOR A WHILE.
YOU IDIOT.
YEP.

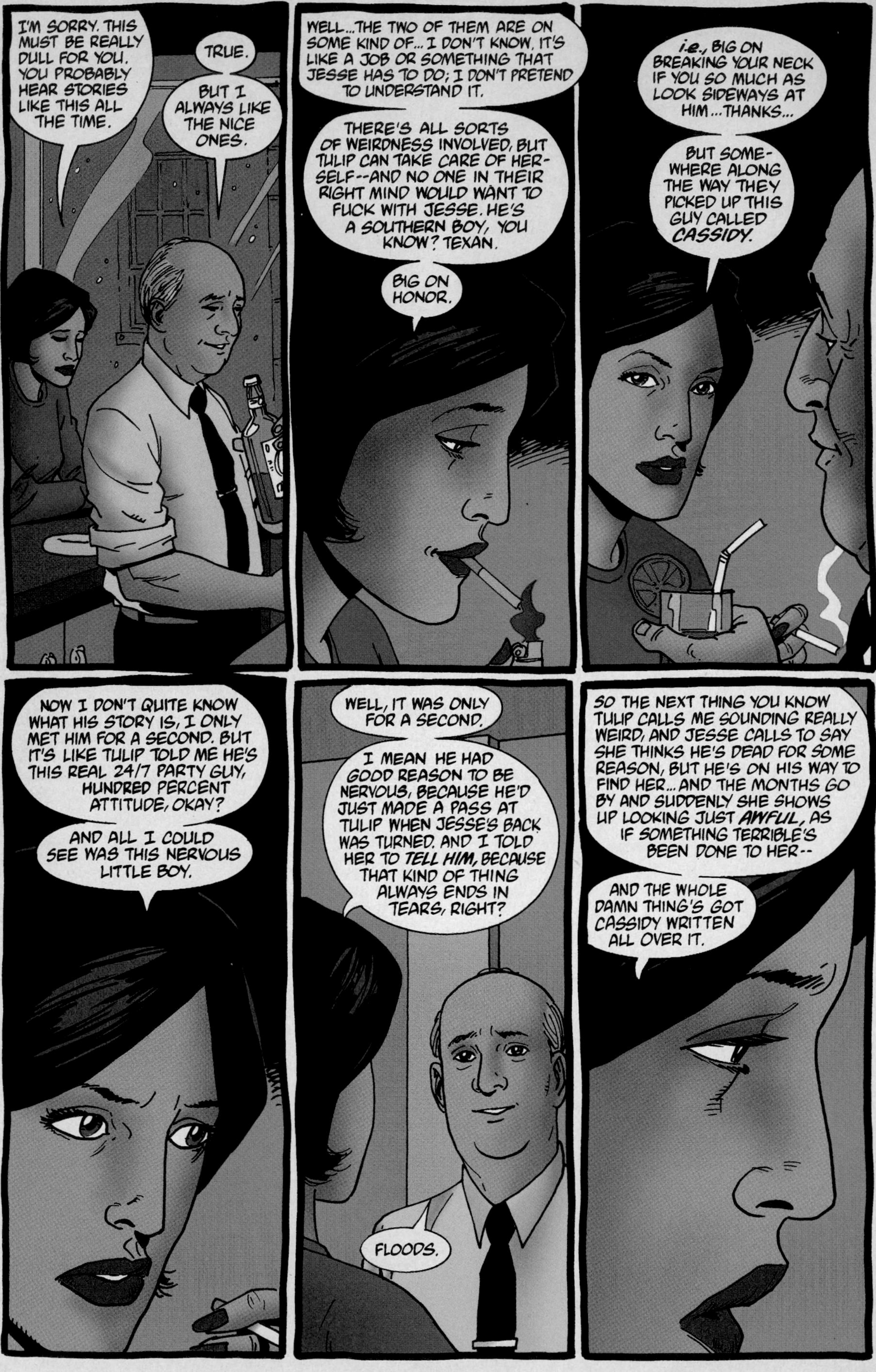
I'M SORRY. THIS MUST BE REALLY DULL FOR YOU. YOU PROBABLY HEAR STORIES LIKE THIS ALL THE TIME.
TRUE.
BUT I ALWAYS LIKE THE NICE ONES.
WELL... THE TWO OF THEM ARE ON SOME KIND OF... I DON'T KNOW, IT'S LIKE A JOB OR SOMETHING THAT JESSE HAS TO DO; I DON'T PRETEND TO UNDERSTAND IT.
THERE'S ALL SORTS OF WEIRDNESS INVOLVED, BUT TULIP CAN TAKE CARE OF HERSELF--AND NO ONE IN THEIR RIGHT MIND WOULD WANT TO FUCK WITH JESSE. HE'S A SOUTHERN BOY, YOU KNOW? TEXAN.
BIG ON HONOR.
i.e., BIG ON BREAKING YOUR NECK IF YOU SO MUCH AS LOOK SIDEWAYS AT HIM... THANKS...
BUT SOMEWHERE ALONG THE WAY THEY PICKED UP THIS GUY CALLED CASSIDY.
NOW I DON'T QUITE KNOW WHAT HIS STORY IS, I ONLY MET HIM FOR A SECOND. BUT IT'S LIKE TULIP TOLD ME HE'S THIS REAL 24/7 PARTY GUY, HUNDRED PERCENT ATTITUDE, OKAY?
AND ALL I COULD SEE WAS THIS NERVOUS LITTLE BOY.
WELL, IT WAS ONLY FOR A SECOND.
I MEAN HE HAD GOOD REASON TO BE NERVOUS, BECAUSE HE'D JUST MADE A PASS AT TULIP WHEN JESSE'S BACK WAS TURNED. AND I TOLD HER TO TELL HIM, BECAUSE THAT KIND OF THING ALWAYS ENDS IN TEARS, RIGHT?
FLOODS.
SO THE NEXT THING YOU KNOW TULIP CALLS ME SOUNDING REALLY WEIRD, AND JESSE CALLS TO SAY SHE THINKS HE'S DEAD FOR SOME REASON, BUT HE'S ON HIS WAY TO FIND HER... AND THE MONTHS GO BY AND SUDDENLY SHE SHOWS UP LOOKING JUST AWFUL, AS IF SOMETHING TERRIBLE'S BEEN DONE TO HER--
AND THE WHOLE DAMN THING'S GOT CASSIDY WRITTEN ALL OVER IT.

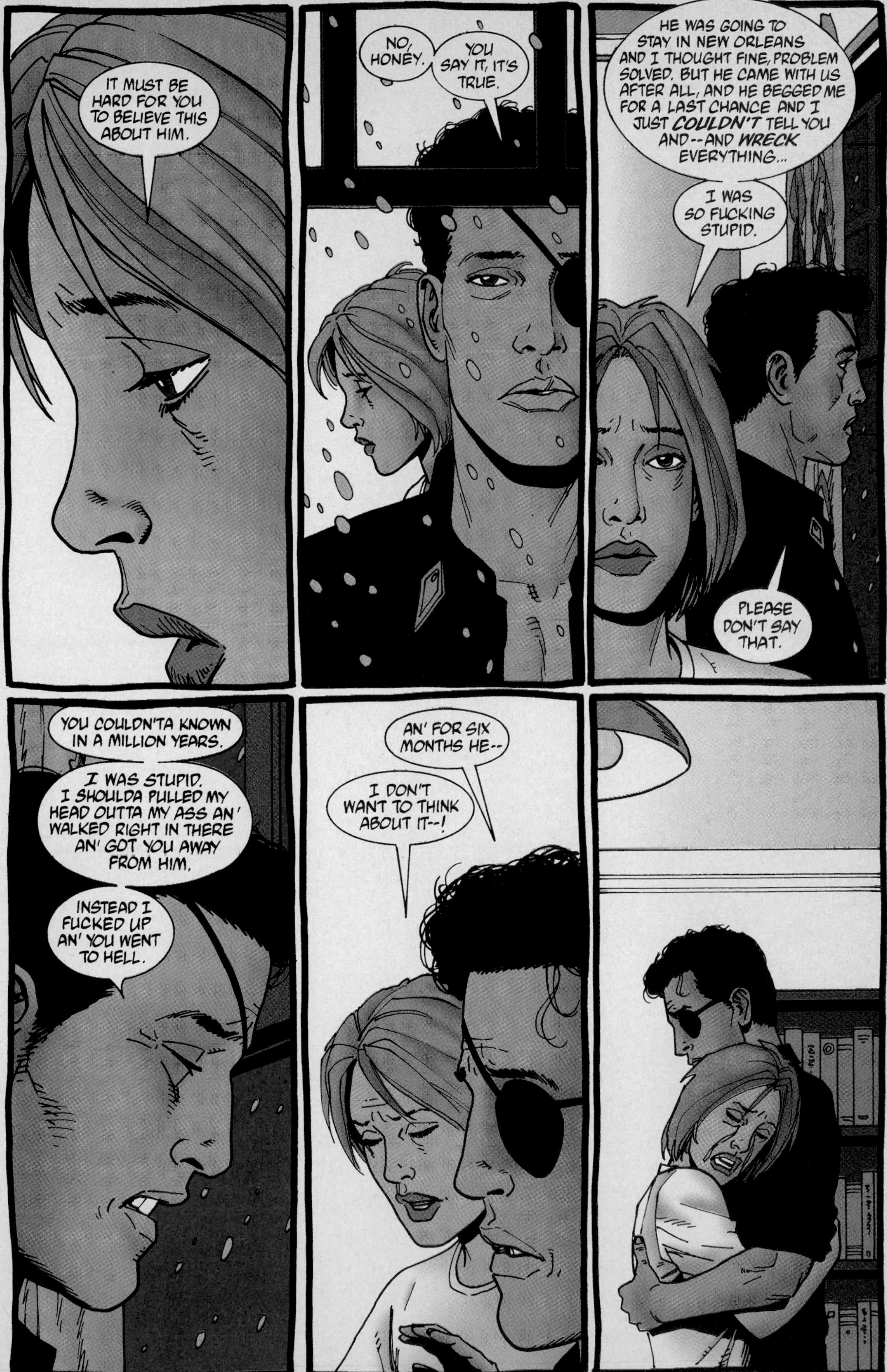
IT MUST BE HARD FOR YOU TO BELIEVE THIS ABOUT HIM.
NO, HONEY.
YOU SAY IT, IT'S TRUE.
HE WAS GOING TO STAY IN NEW ORLEANS AND I THOUGHT FINE, PROBLEM SOLVED. BUT HE CAME WITH US AFTER ALL, AND HE BEGGED ME FOR A LAST CHANCE AND I JUST **COULDN'T** TELL YOU AND--AND **WRECK** EVERYTHING...
I WAS SO FUCKING STUPID.
PLEASE DON'T SAY THAT.
YOU COULDN'TA KNOWN IN A MILLION YEARS.
I WAS STUPID. I SHOULDA PULLED MY HEAD OUTTA MY ASS AN' WALKED RIGHT IN THERE AN' GOT YOU AWAY FROM HIM.
INSTEAD I FUCKED UP AN' YOU WENT TO HELL.
AN' FOR SIX MONTHS HE--
I DON'T WANT TO THINK ABOUT IT--!

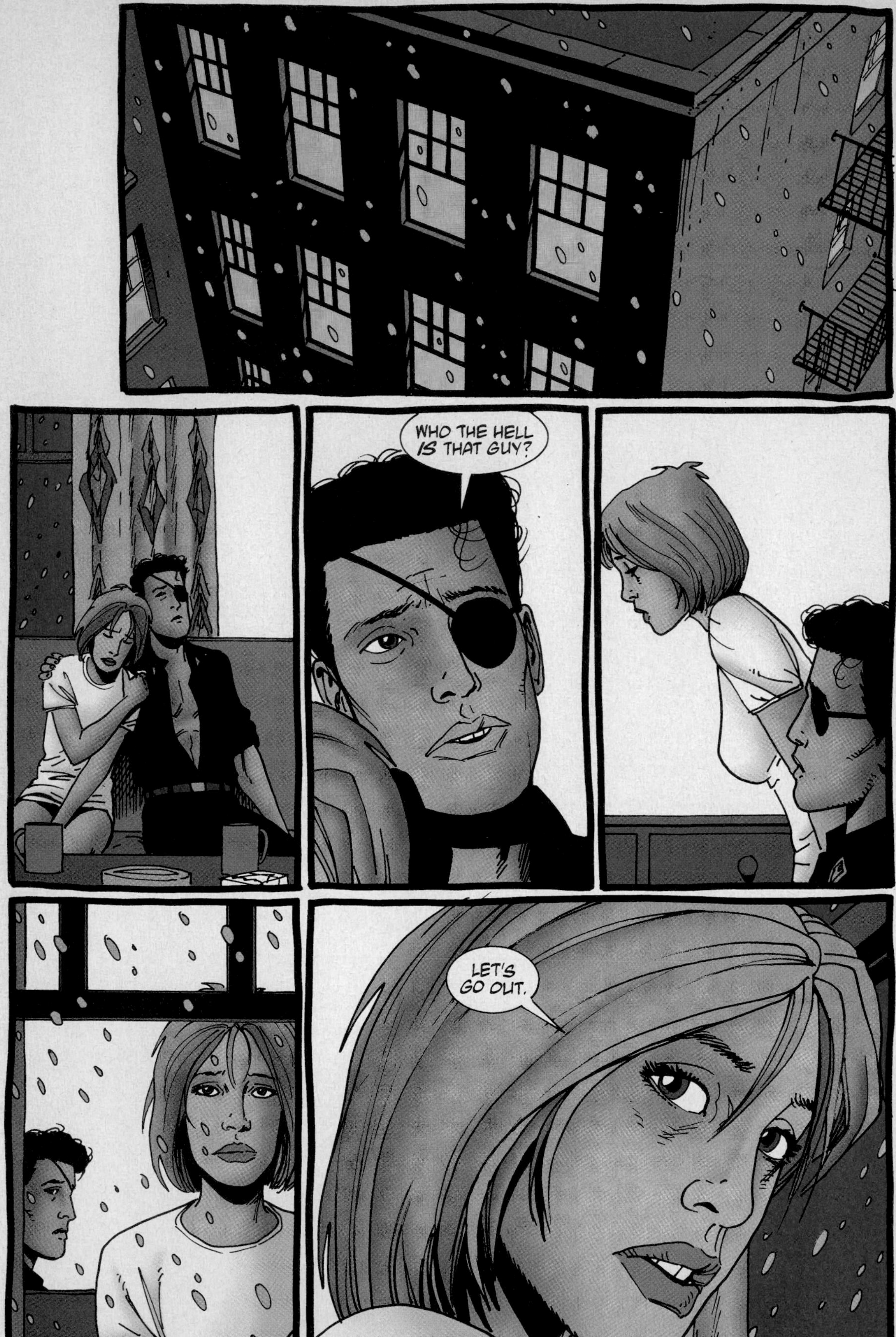
WHO THE HELL *IS* THAT GUY?
LET'S GO OUT.

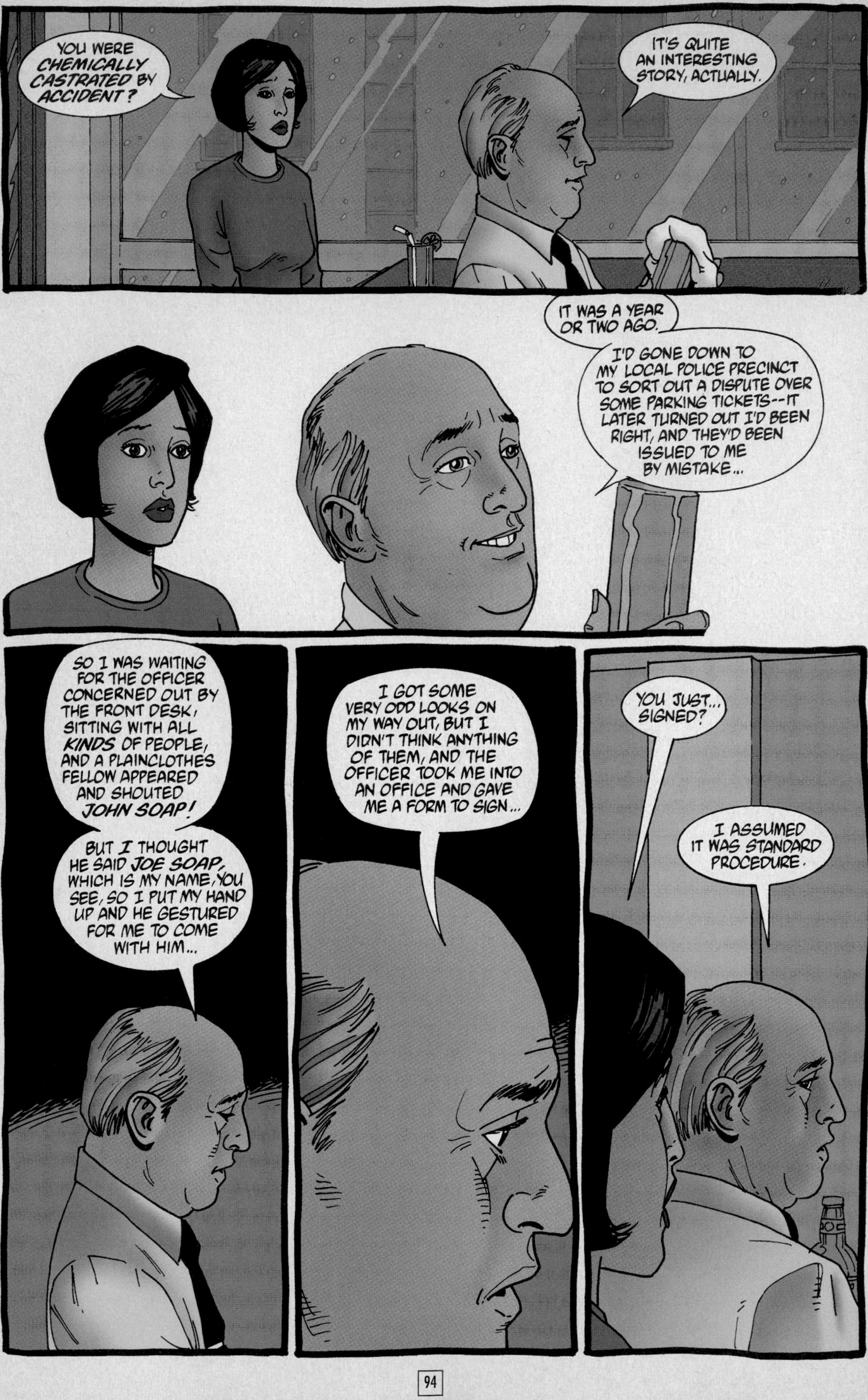
YOU WERE CHEMICALLY CASTRATED BY ACCIDENT?
IT'S QUITE AN INTERESTING STORY, ACTUALLY.
IT WAS A YEAR OR TWO AGO.
I'D GONE DOWN TO MY LOCAL POLICE PRECINCT TO SORT OUT A DISPUTE OVER SOME PARKING TICKETS--IT LATER TURNED OUT I'D BEEN RIGHT, AND THEY'D BEEN ISSUED TO ME BY MISTAKE...
SO I WAS WAITING FOR THE OFFICER CONCERNED OUT BY THE FRONT DESK, SITTING WITH ALL KINDS OF PEOPLE, AND A PLAINCLOTHES FELLOW APPEARED AND SHOUTED JOHN SOAP!
BUT I THOUGHT HE SAID JOE SOAP, WHICH IS MY NAME, YOU SEE, SO I PUT MY HAND UP AND HE GESTURED FOR ME TO COME WITH HIM...
I GOT SOME VERY ODD LOOKS ON MY WAY OUT, BUT I DIDN'T THINK ANYTHING OF THEM, AND THE OFFICER TOOK ME INTO AN OFFICE AND GAVE ME A FORM TO SIGN...
YOU JUST... SIGNED?
I ASSUMED IT WAS STANDARD PROCEDURE.

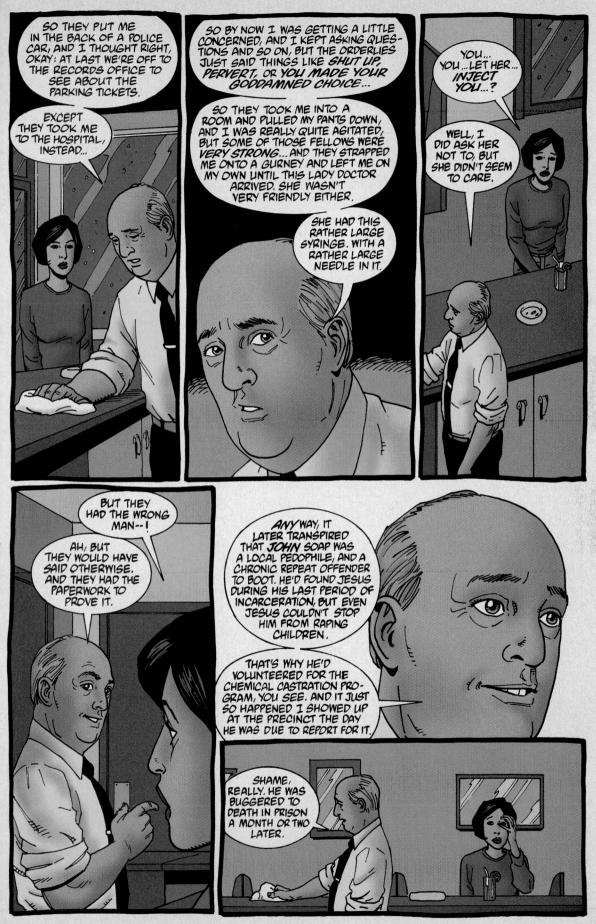

SO THEY PUT ME IN THE BACK OF A POLICE CAR, AND I THOUGHT RIGHT, OKAY: AT LAST WE'RE OFF TO THE RECORDS OFFICE TO SEE ABOUT THE PARKING TICKETS.

EXCEPT THEY TOOK ME TO THE HOSPITAL, INSTEAD...

SO BY NOW I WAS GETTING A LITTLE CONCERNED, AND I KEPT ASKING QUESTIONS AND SO ON, BUT THE ORDERLIES JUST SAID THINGS LIKE *SHUT UP, PERVERT,* OR *YOU MADE YOUR GODDAMNED CHOICE...*

SO THEY TOOK ME INTO A ROOM AND PULLED MY PANTS DOWN, AND I WAS REALLY QUITE AGITATED, BUT SOME OF THOSE FELLOWS WERE *VERY STRONG*... AND THEY STRAPPED ME ONTO A GURNEY AND LEFT ME ON MY OWN UNTIL THIS LADY DOCTOR ARRIVED. SHE WASN'T VERY FRIENDLY EITHER.

SHE HAD THIS RATHER LARGE SYRINGE, WITH A RATHER LARGE NEEDLE IN IT.

YOU... YOU...LET HER... *INJECT* YOU...?

WELL, I DID ASK HER NOT TO, BUT SHE DIDN'T SEEM TO CARE.

BUT THEY HAD THE WRONG MAN--!

AH, BUT THEY WOULD HAVE SAID OTHERWISE. AND THEY HAD THE PAPERWORK TO PROVE IT.

*ANY*WAY, IT LATER TRANSPIRED THAT *JOHN* SOAP WAS A LOCAL PEDOPHILE, AND A CHRONIC REPEAT OFFENDER TO BOOT. HE'D FOUND JESUS DURING HIS LAST PERIOD OF INCARCERATION, BUT EVEN JESUS COULDN'T STOP HIM FROM RAPING CHILDREN.

THAT'S WHY HE'D VOLUNTEERED FOR THE CHEMICAL CASTRATION PROGRAM, YOU SEE. AND IT JUST SO HAPPENED I SHOWED UP AT THE PRECINCT THE DAY HE WAS DUE TO REPORT FOR IT.

SHAME, REALLY. HE WAS BUGGERED TO DEATH IN PRISON A MONTH OR TWO LATER.

95

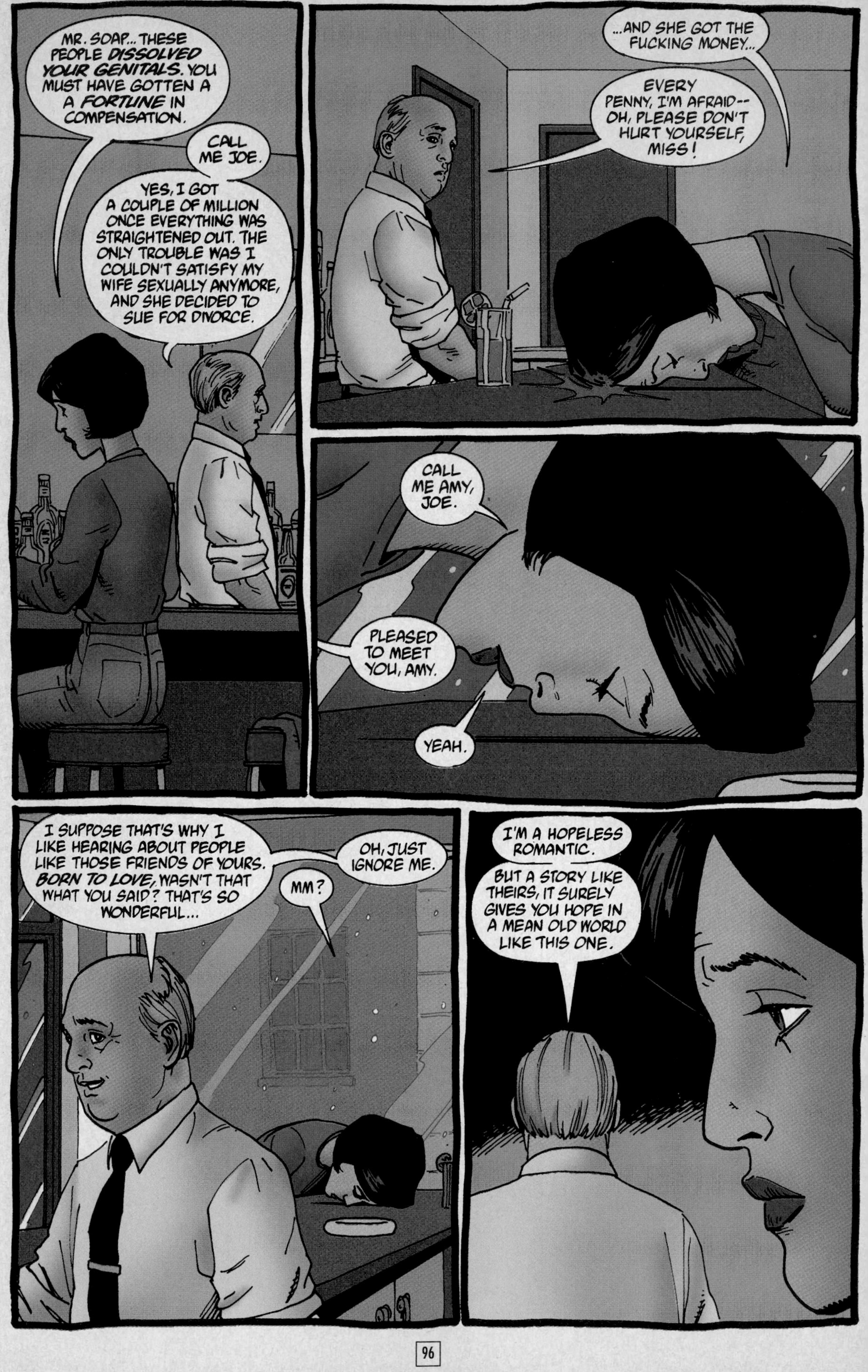

MR. SOAP... THESE PEOPLE DISSOLVED YOUR GENITALS. YOU MUST HAVE GOTTEN A A FORTUNE IN COMPENSATION.
CALL ME JOE.
YES, I GOT A COUPLE OF MILLION ONCE EVERYTHING WAS STRAIGHTENED OUT. THE ONLY TROUBLE WAS I COULDN'T SATISFY MY WIFE SEXUALLY ANYMORE, AND SHE DECIDED TO SUE FOR DIVORCE.
...AND SHE GOT THE FUCKING MONEY...
EVERY PENNY, I'M AFRAID-- OH, PLEASE DON'T HURT YOURSELF, MISS!
CALL ME AMY, JOE.
PLEASED TO MEET YOU, AMY.
YEAH.
I SUPPOSE THAT'S WHY I LIKE HEARING ABOUT PEOPLE LIKE THOSE FRIENDS OF YOURS. BORN TO LOVE, WASN'T THAT WHAT YOU SAID? THAT'S SO WONDERFUL...
MM?
OH, JUST IGNORE ME.
I'M A HOPELESS ROMANTIC.
BUT A STORY LIKE THEIRS, IT SURELY GIVES YOU HOPE IN A MEAN OLD WORLD LIKE THIS ONE.

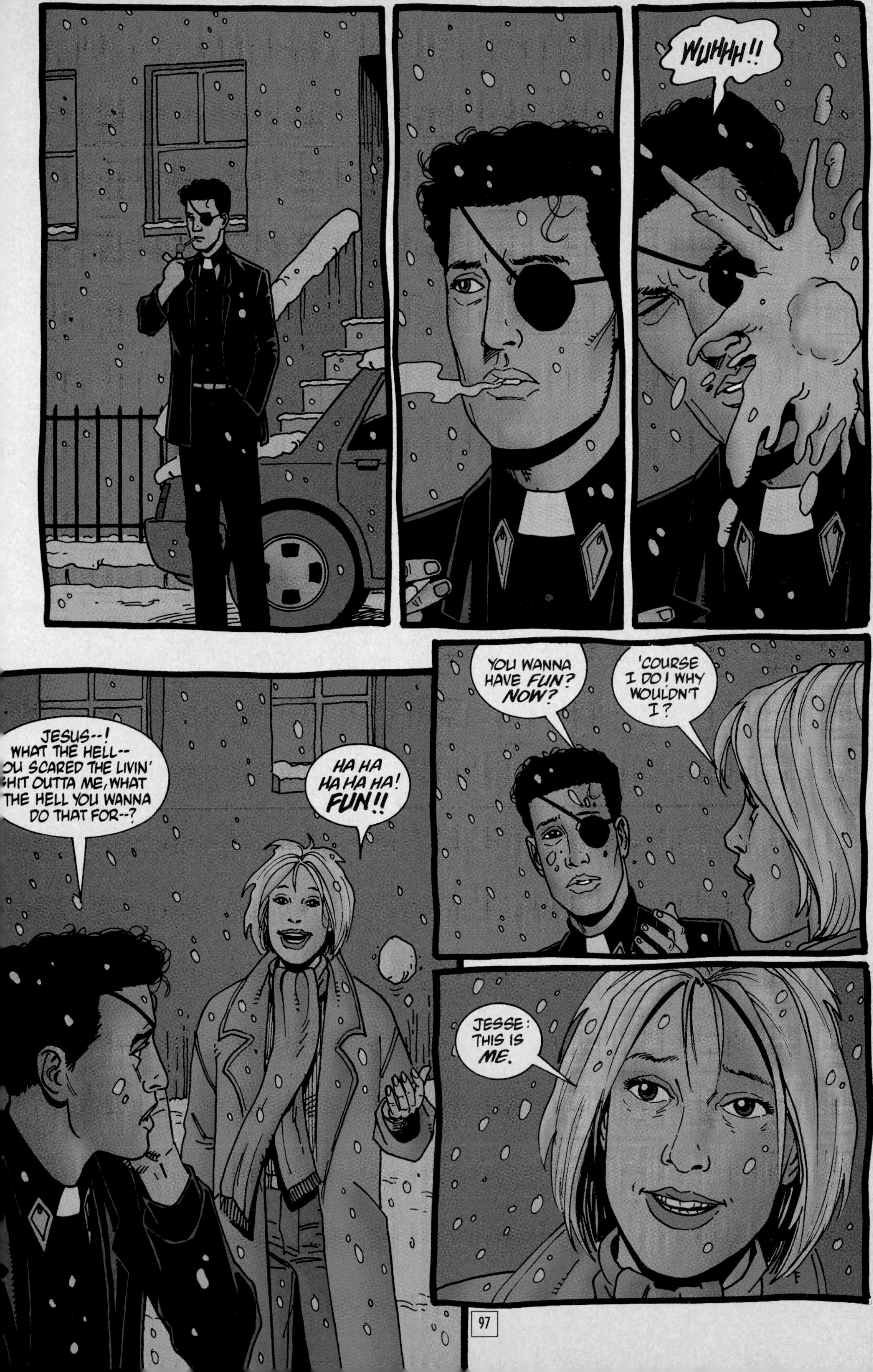
WUHHH!!
JESUS--! WHAT THE HELL-- OU SCARED THE LIVIN' HIT OUTTA ME, WHAT THE HELL YOU WANNA DO THAT FOR--?
HA HA HA HA HA! FUN!!
YOU WANNA HAVE FUN? NOW?
'COURSE I DO! WHY WOULDN'T I?
JESSE: THIS IS ME.

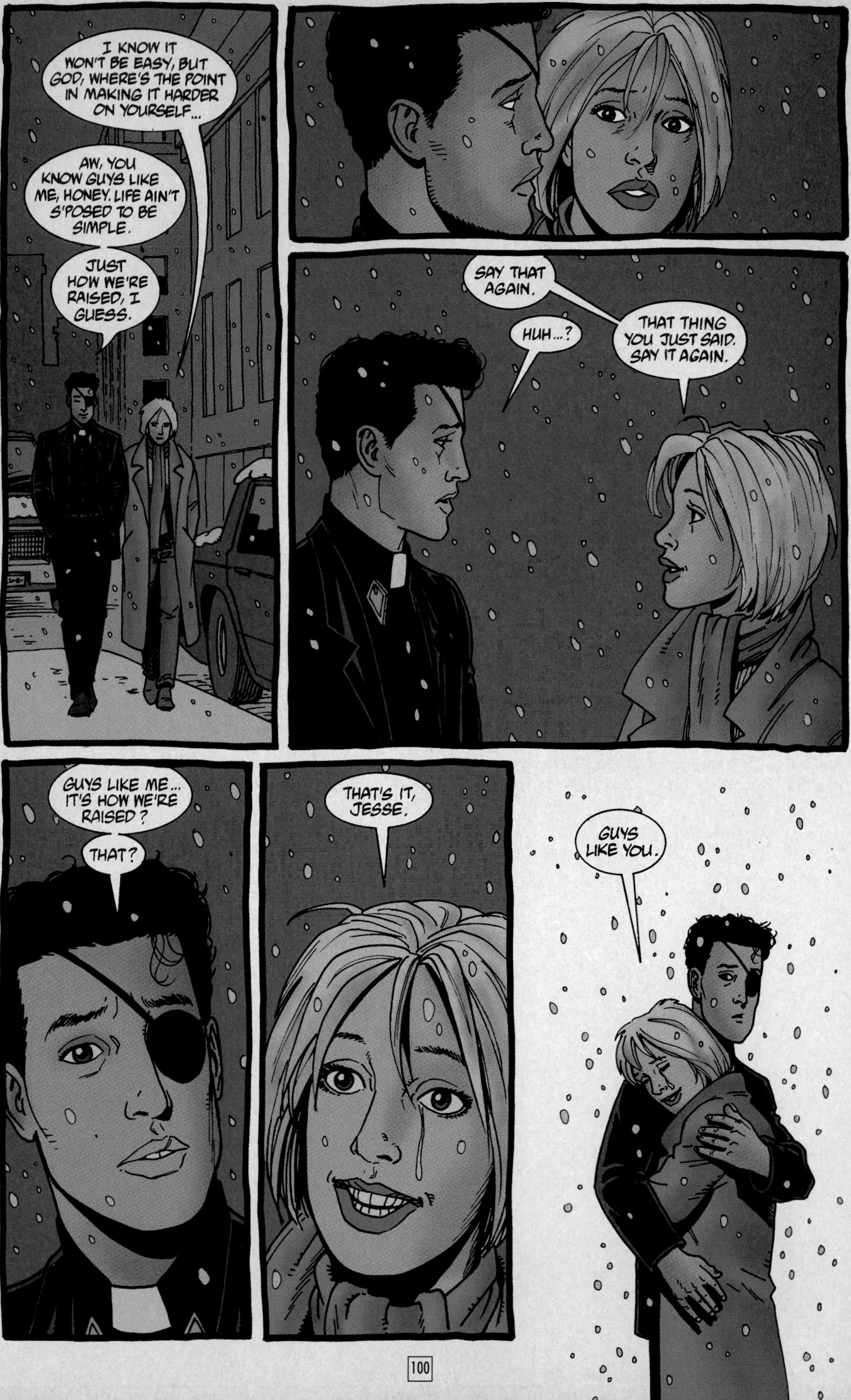
I KNOW IT WON'T BE EASY, BUT GOD, WHERE'S THE POINT IN MAKING IT HARDER ON YOURSELF...
AW, YOU KNOW GUYS LIKE ME, HONEY. LIFE AIN'T S'POSED TO BE SIMPLE.
JUST HOW WE'RE RAISED, I GUESS.
SAY THAT AGAIN.
HUH...?
THAT THING YOU JUST SAID. SAY IT AGAIN.
GUYS LIKE ME... IT'S HOW WE'RE RAISED?
THAT?
THAT'S IT, JESSE.
GUYS LIKE YOU.

I MEAN THEY TOOK YOUR *BALLS,* JOE, I CAN'T BELIEVE YOU CAN STILL FEEL *ROMANTIC* AFTER SOMETHING LIKE THAT...

AND HOPE? HOW DO YOU FIND *HOPE* IN ANYTHING, AFTER WHAT'S HAPPENED TO YOU?

I HAVE TO.

LOOK AT THESE FRIENDS OF YOURS, THE PREACHER AND HIS YOUNG LADY. DON'T YOU SEE HOW THEY KEEP ON *FINDING* EACH OTHER?

THEY GET SPLIT UP BUT THEY'RE REUNITED, AND THEN THEY GET SPLIT UP AGAIN-- AND EVEN THOUGH ONE THINKS THE OTHER'S DEAD, EVEN WITH ALL THIS CASSIDY FELLOW CAN DO TO THEM, *THEY FIND EACH OTHER AGAIN...*

BECAUSE AS YOU YOUR-SELF SAID, THE WORLD IS NOT AN IRREDEEMABLY BAD PLACE, AND IT'S THINGS LIKE THIS THAT PROVE IT.

AND IF YOU DON'T BELIEVE ME, ASK YOUR-SELF THIS: WHAT KEEPS THEM TOGETHER? WHY DID JESSE COME LOOKING FOR TULIP AFTER ALL THIS TIME?

OKAY, JOE. 'CAUSE THERE'S HOPE.

'CAUSE *IN THE HALLS OF HIS MEMORY STILL ECHOED HER EYES.*

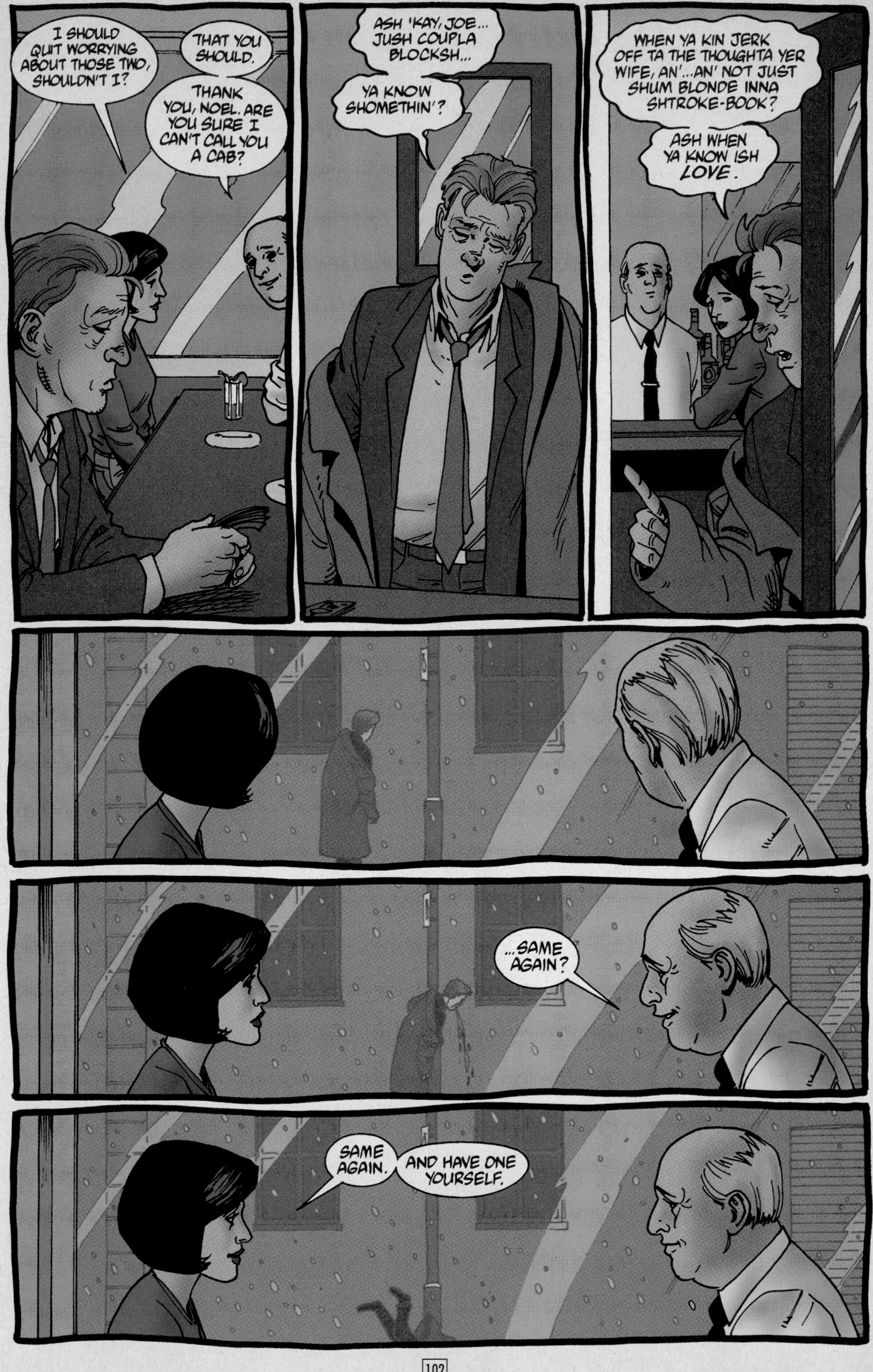
I SHOULD QUIT WORRYING ABOUT THOSE TWO, SHOULDN'T I?
THAT YOU SHOULD.
THANK YOU, NOEL. ARE YOU SURE I CAN'T CALL YOU A CAB?
ASH 'KAY, JOE... JUSH COUPLA BLOCKSH...
YA KNOW SHOMETHIN'?
WHEN YA KIN JERK OFF TA THE THOUGHTA YER WIFE, AN'...AN' NOT JUST SHUM BLONDE INNA SHTROKE-BOOK?
ASH WHEN YA KNOW ISH *LOVE*.
...SAME AGAIN?
SAME AGAIN.
AND HAVE ONE YOURSELF.

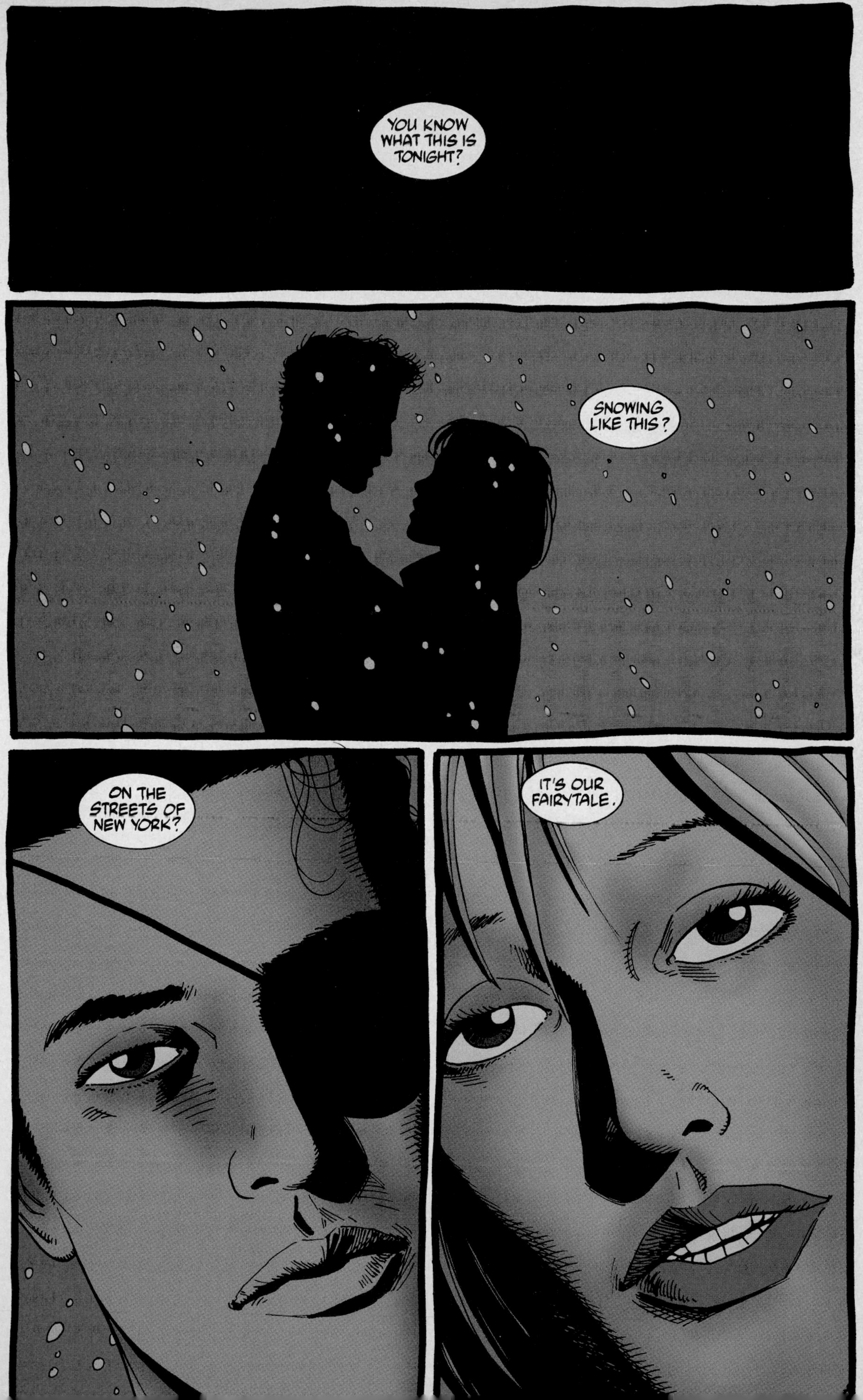
YOU KNOW WHAT THIS IS TONIGHT?
SNOWING LIKE THIS?
ON THE STREETS OF NEW YORK?
IT'S OUR FAIRYTALE.

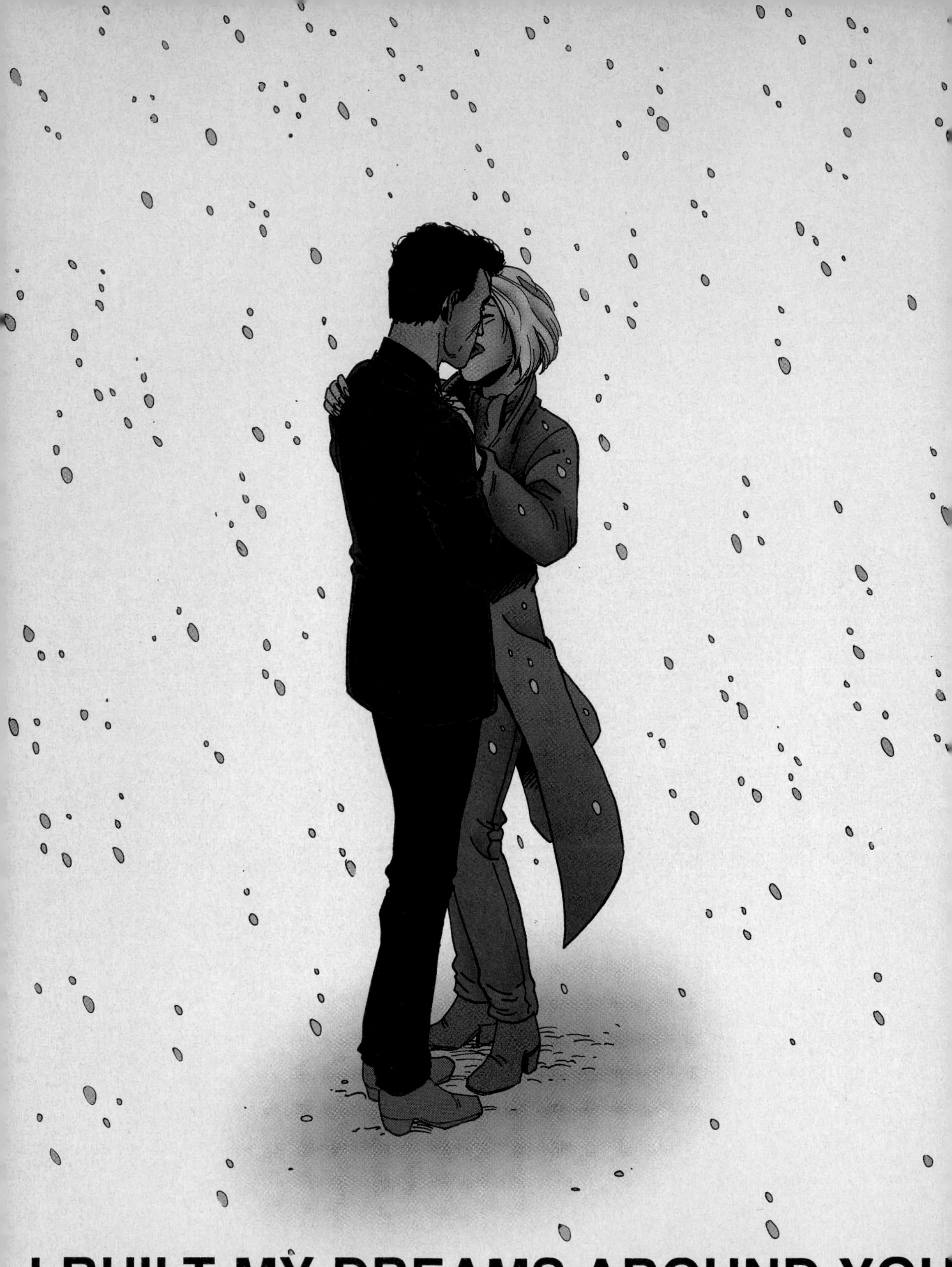

I BUILT MY DREAMS AROUND YOU

GARTH ENNIS - Writer STEVE DILLON - Artist

PAMELA RAMBO - Colorist CLEM ROBINS - Letterer AXEL ALONSO - Editor

PREACHER created by GARTH ENNIS and STEVE DILLON

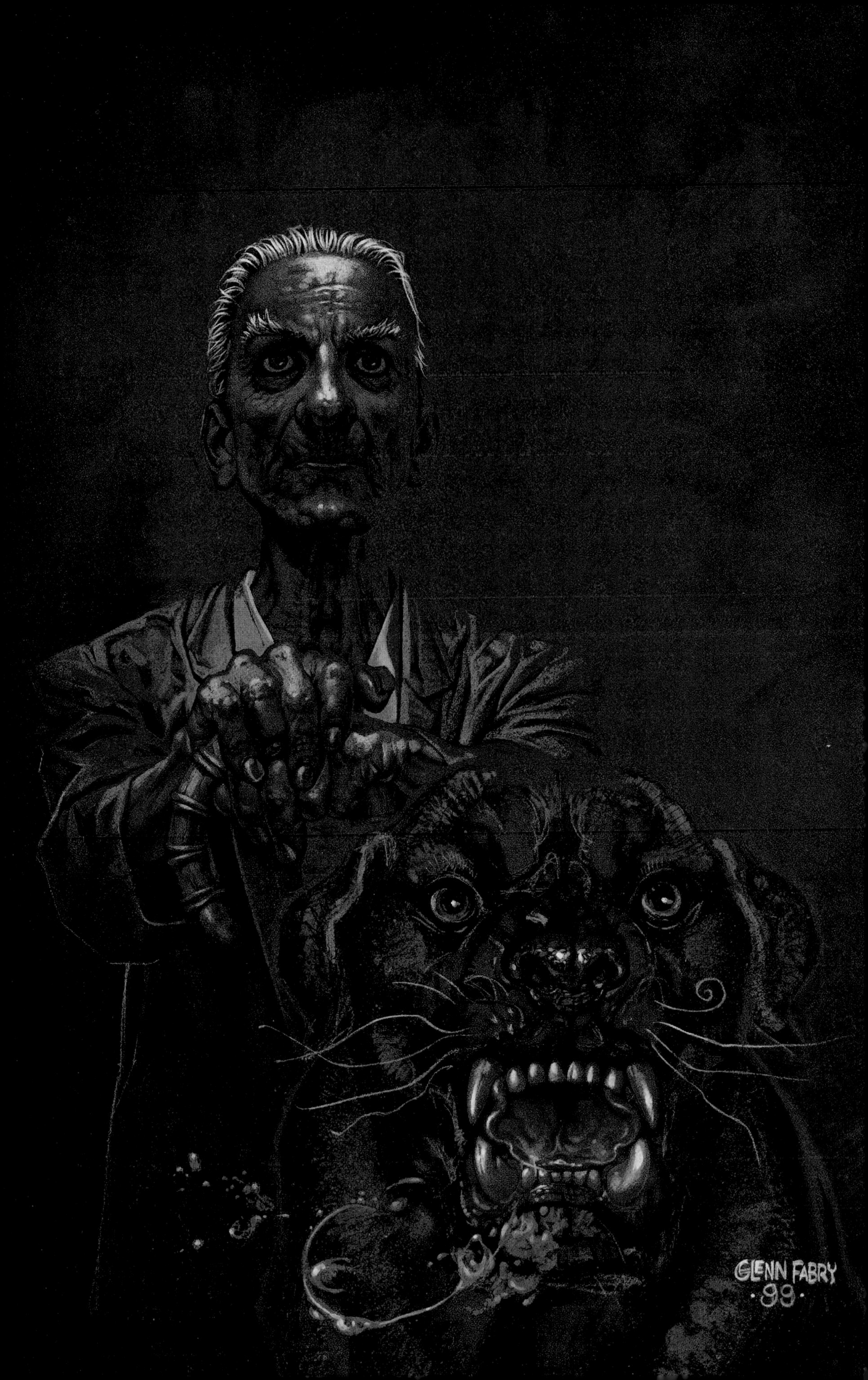
GLENN FABRY
·99·

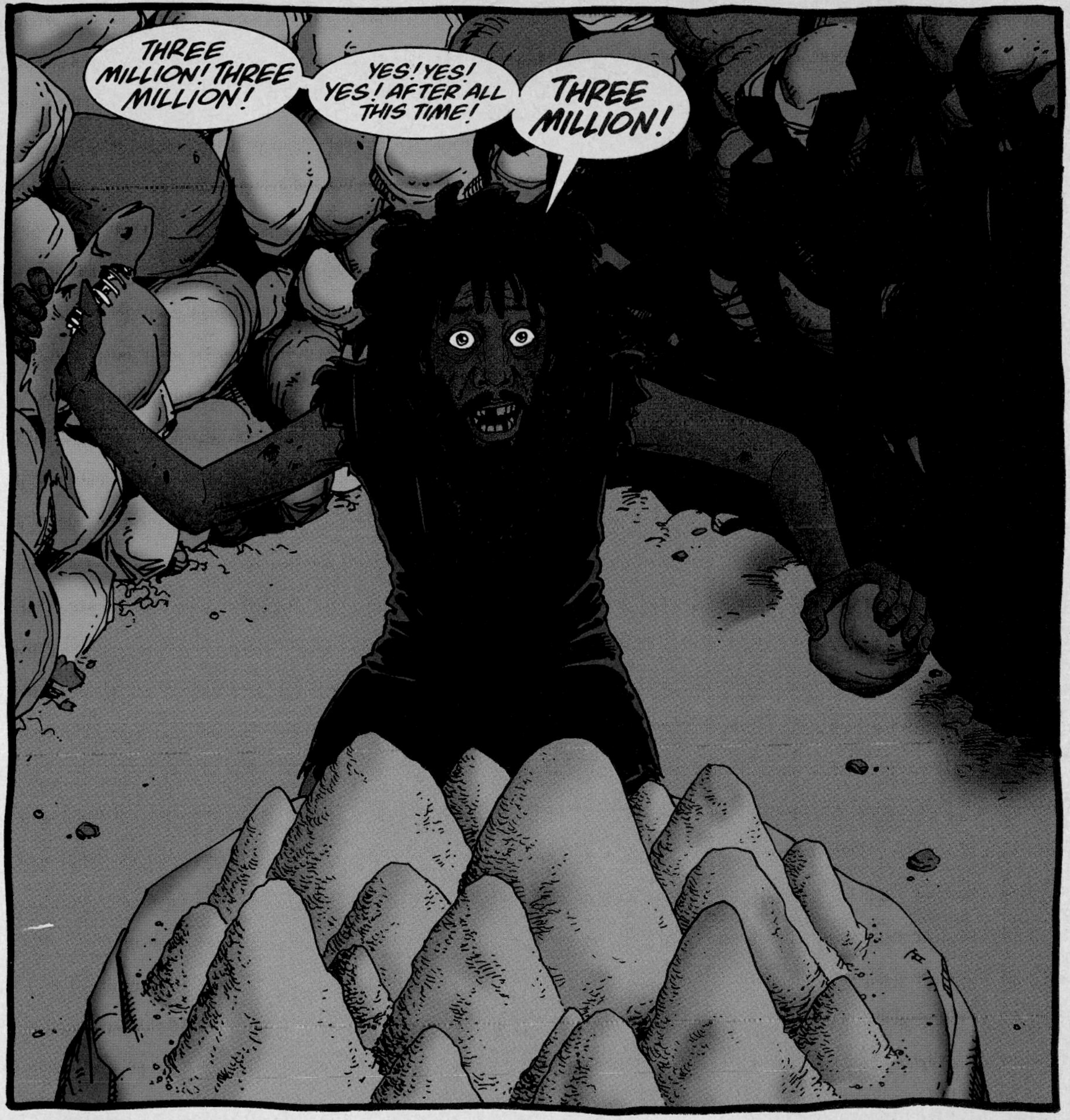
THREE MILLION! THREE MILLION!
YES! YES! YES! AFTER ALL THIS TIME!
THREE MILLION!

HARBINGER

GARTH ENNIS - Writer STEVE DILLON - Artist
PAMELA RAMBO - Colorist CLEM ROBINS - Letterer AXEL ALONSO - Editor
PREACHER created by GARTH ENNIS and STEVE DILLON

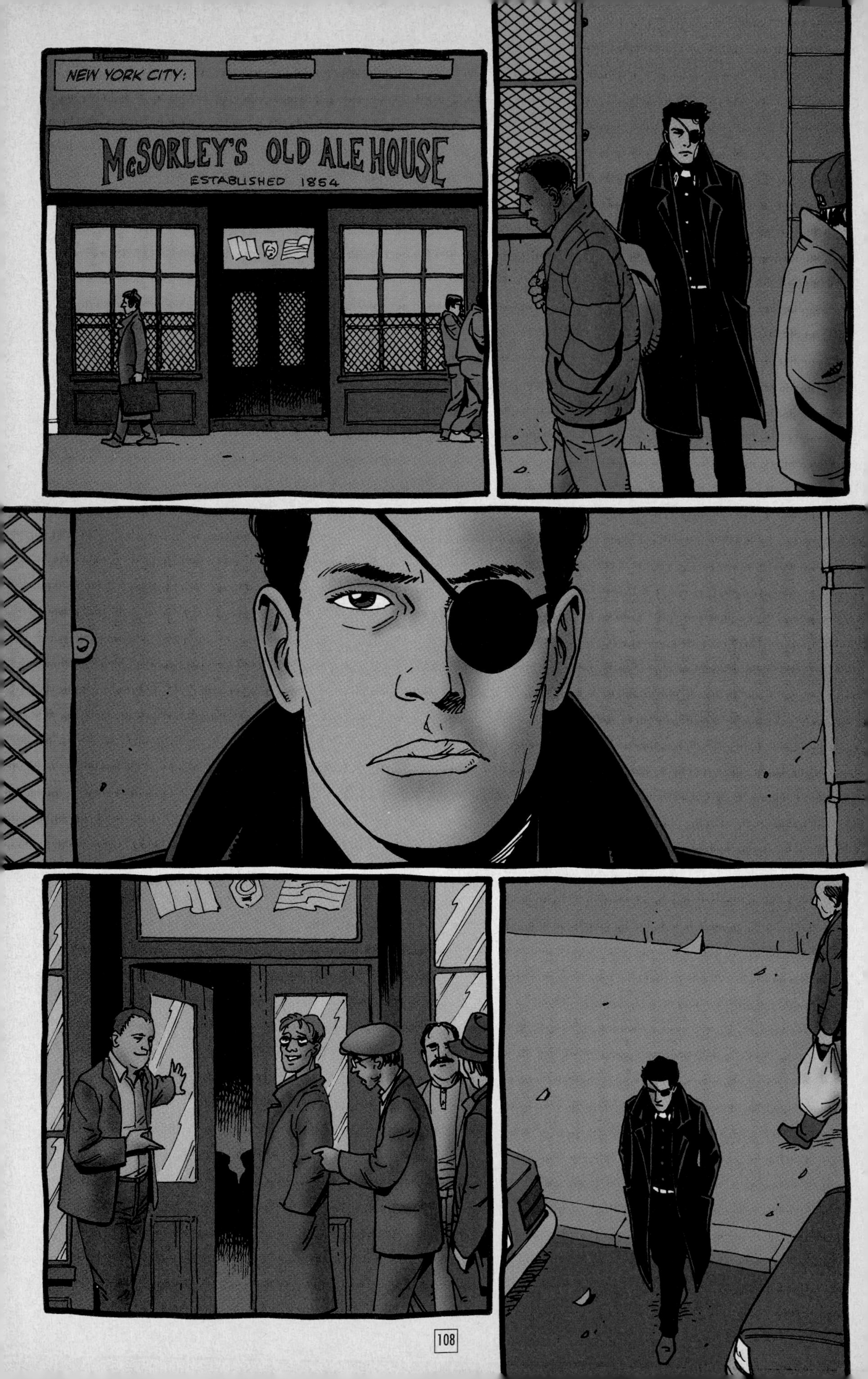
NEW YORK CITY:
McSORLEY'S OLD ALE HOUSE
ESTABLISHED 1854

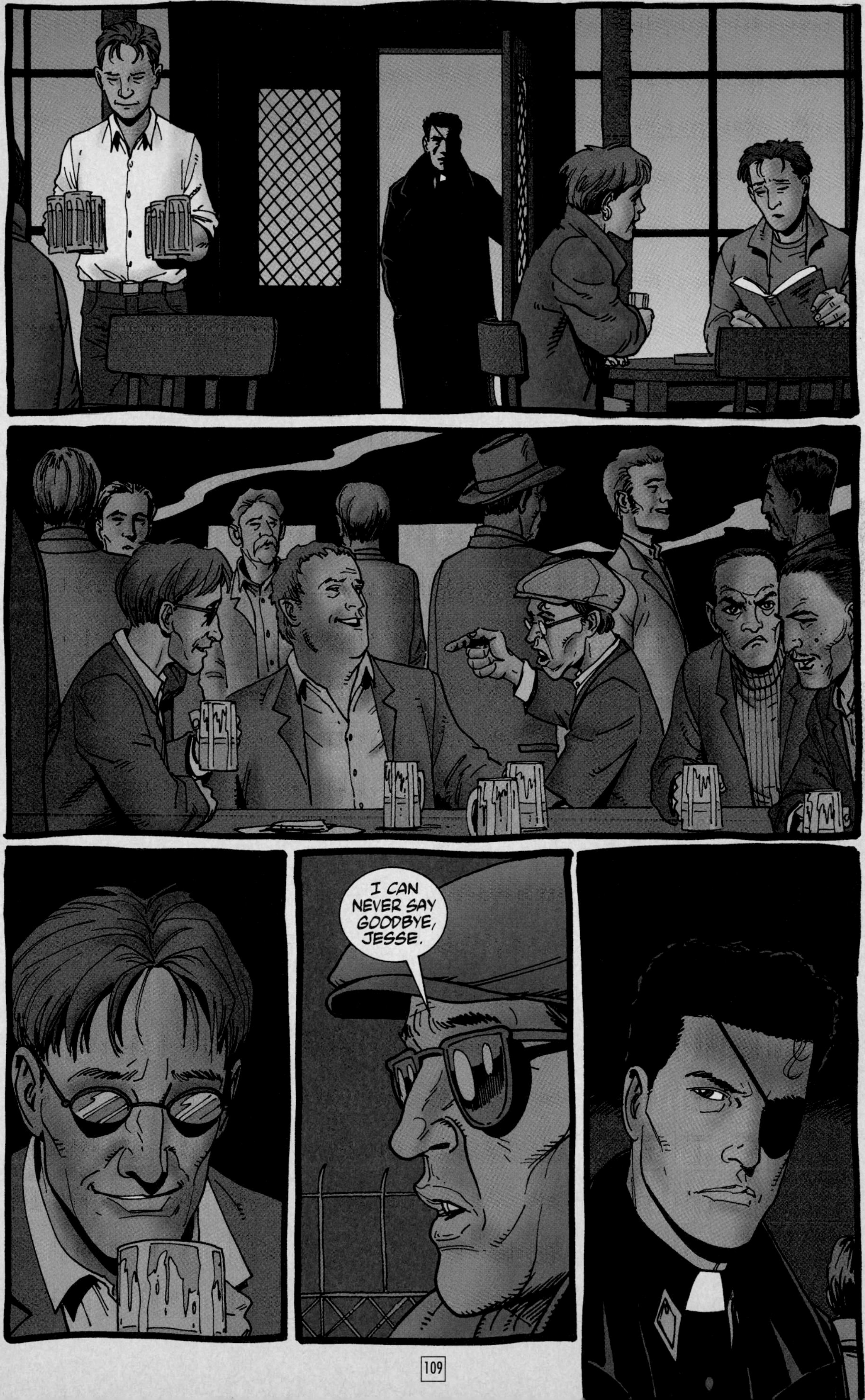
I CAN NEVER SAY GOODBYE, JESSE.

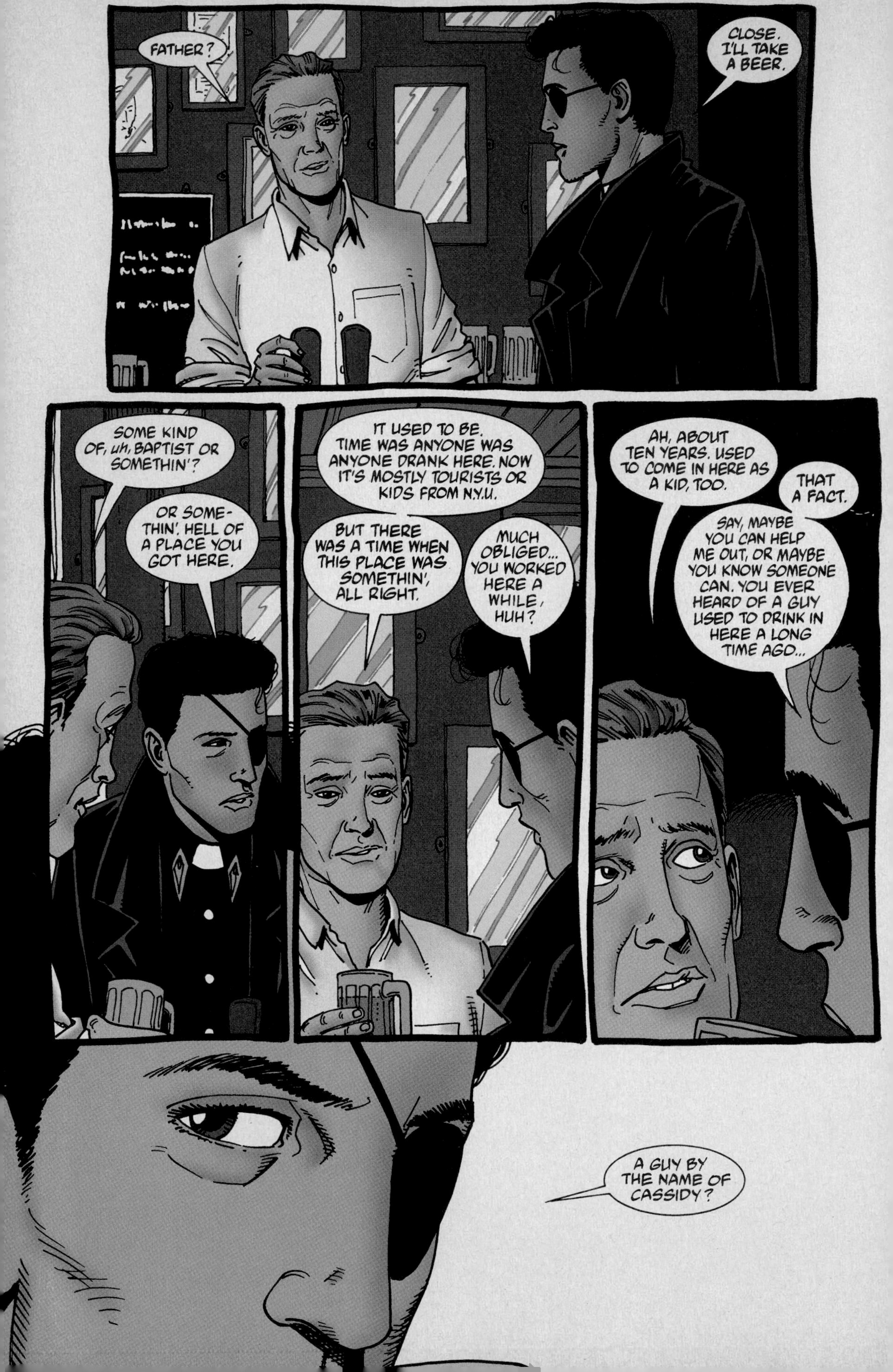
FATHER?
CLOSE. I'LL TAKE A BEER.
SOME KIND OF, uh, BAPTIST OR SOMETHIN'?
OR SOMETHIN'. HELL OF A PLACE YOU GOT HERE.
IT USED TO BE. TIME WAS ANYONE WAS ANYONE DRANK HERE. NOW IT'S MOSTLY TOURISTS OR KIDS FROM N.Y.U.
BUT THERE WAS A TIME WHEN THIS PLACE WAS SOMETHIN', ALL RIGHT.
MUCH OBLIGED... YOU WORKED HERE A WHILE, HUH?
AH, ABOUT TEN YEARS. USED TO COME IN HERE AS A KID, TOO.
THAT A FACT.
SAY, MAYBE YOU CAN HELP ME OUT, OR MAYBE YOU KNOW SOMEONE CAN. YOU EVER HEARD OF A GUY USED TO DRINK IN HERE A LONG TIME AGO...
A GUY BY THE NAME OF CASSIDY?

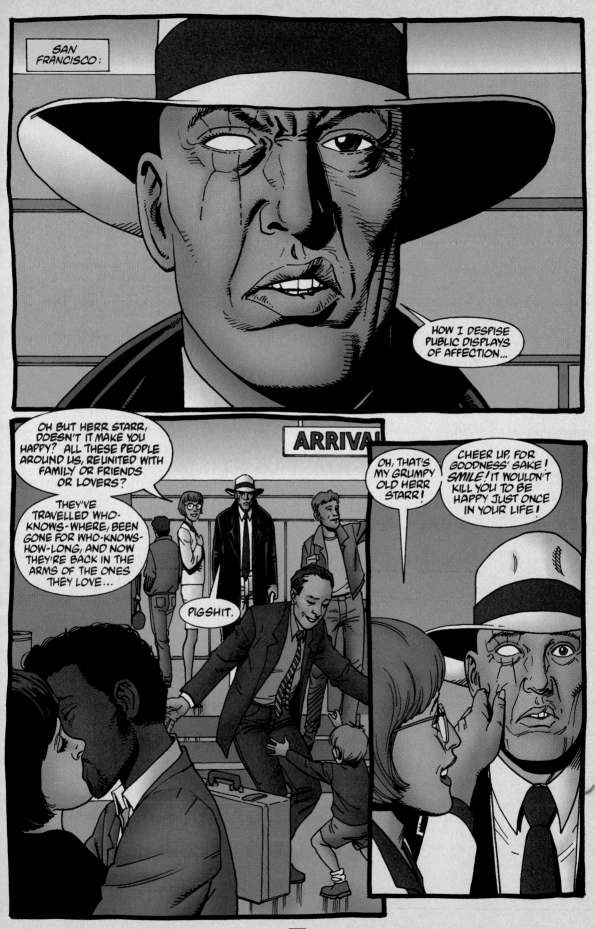

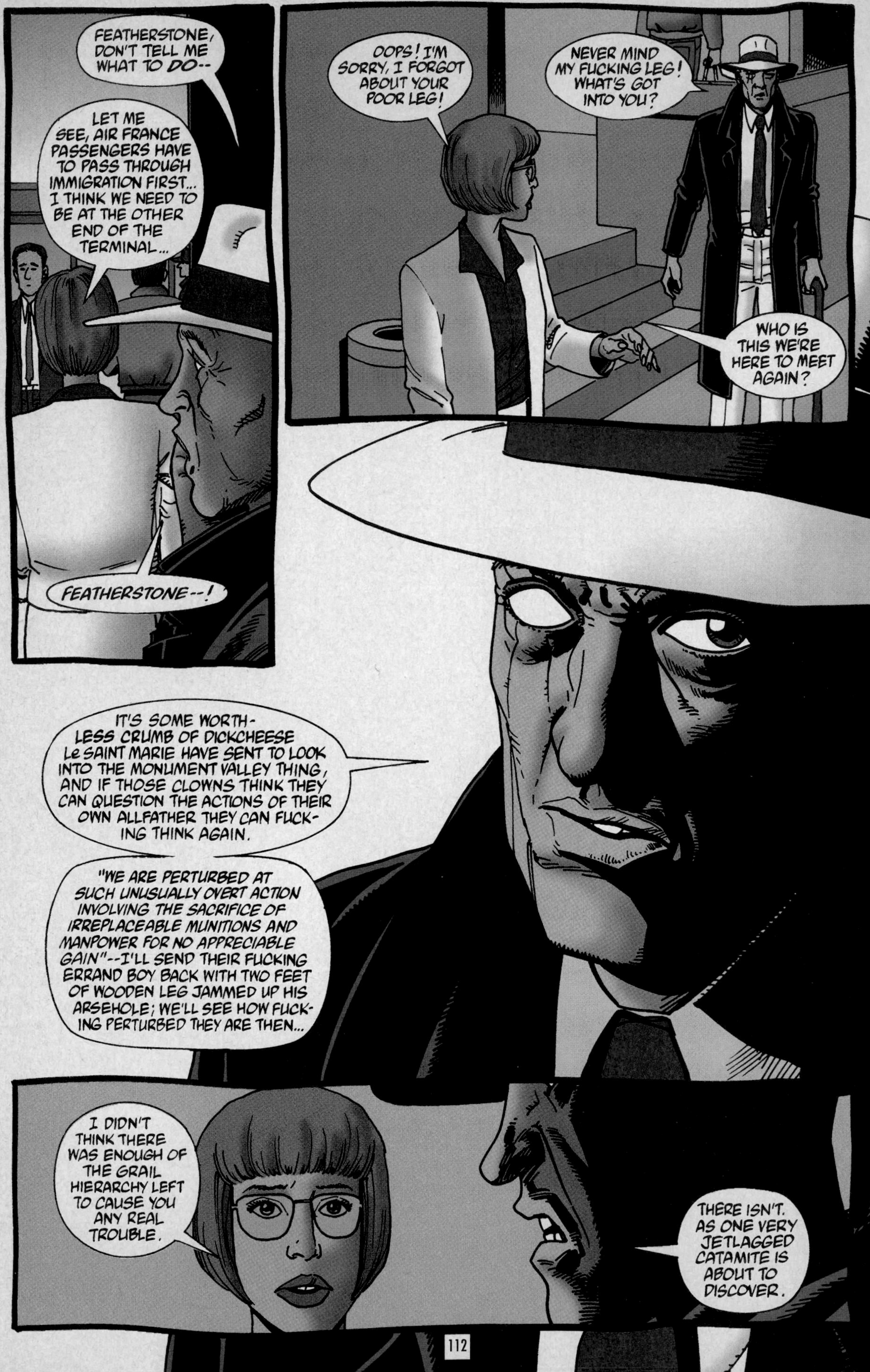

FEATHERSTONE, DON'T TELL ME WHAT TO DO--
LET ME SEE, AIR FRANCE PASSENGERS HAVE TO PASS THROUGH IMMIGRATION FIRST... I THINK WE NEED TO BE AT THE OTHER END OF THE TERMINAL...
FEATHERSTONE--!
OOPS! I'M SORRY, I FORGOT ABOUT YOUR POOR LEG!
NEVER MIND MY FUCKING LEG! WHAT'S GOT INTO YOU?
WHO IS THIS WE'RE HERE TO MEET AGAIN?
IT'S SOME WORTH-LESS CRUMB OF DICKCHEESE Le SAINT MARIE HAVE SENT TO LOOK INTO THE MONUMENT VALLEY THING, AND IF THOSE CLOWNS THINK THEY CAN QUESTION THE ACTIONS OF THEIR OWN ALLFATHER THEY CAN FUCK-ING THINK AGAIN.
"WE ARE PERTURBED AT SUCH UNUSUALLY OVERT ACTION INVOLVING THE SACRIFICE OF IRREPLACEABLE MUNITIONS AND MANPOWER FOR NO APPRECIABLE GAIN"--I'LL SEND THEIR FUCKING ERRAND BOY BACK WITH TWO FEET OF WOODEN LEG JAMMED UP HIS ARSEHOLE; WE'LL SEE HOW FUCK-ING PERTURBED THEY ARE THEN...
I DIDN'T THINK THERE WAS ENOUGH OF THE GRAIL HIERARCHY LEFT TO CAUSE YOU ANY REAL TROUBLE.
THERE ISN'T. AS ONE VERY JETLAGGED CATAMITE IS ABOUT TO DISCOVER.

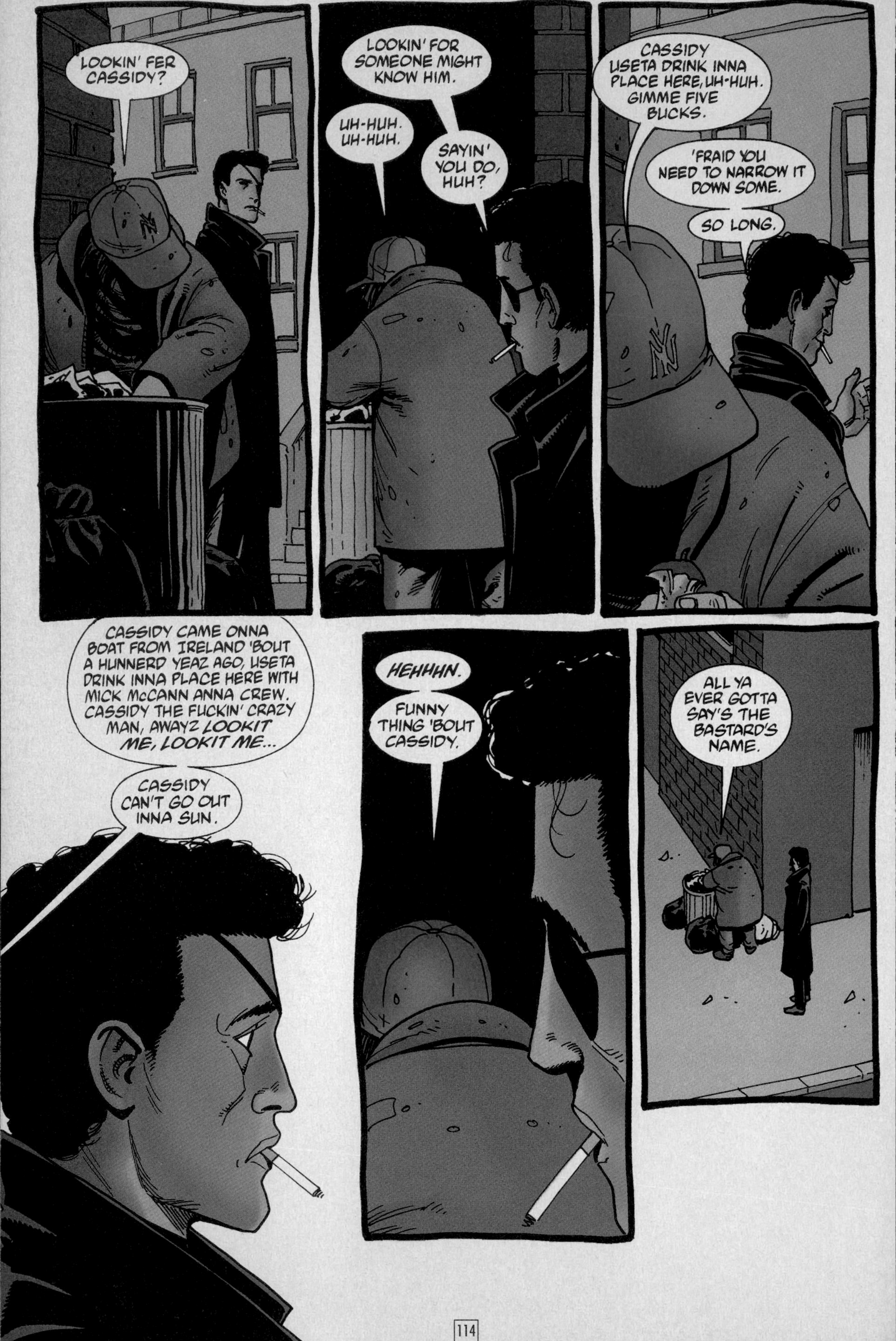
LOOKIN' FER CASSIDY?
LOOKIN' FOR SOMEONE MIGHT KNOW HIM.
UH-HUH. UH-HUH.
SAYIN' YOU DO, HUH?
CASSIDY USETA DRINK INNA PLACE HERE, UH-HUH. GIMME FIVE BUCKS.
'FRAID YOU NEED TO NARROW IT DOWN SOME.
SO LONG.
CASSIDY CAME ONNA BOAT FROM IRELAND 'BOUT A HUNNERD YEAZ AGO, USETA DRINK INNA PLACE HERE WITH MICK McCANN ANNA CREW. CASSIDY THE FUCKIN' CRAZY MAN, AWAYZ *LOOKIT ME, LOOKIT ME*...
CASSIDY CAN'T GO OUT INNA SUN.
HEHHHN.
FUNNY THING 'BOUT CASSIDY.
ALL YA EVER GOTTA SAY'S THE BASTARD'S NAME.

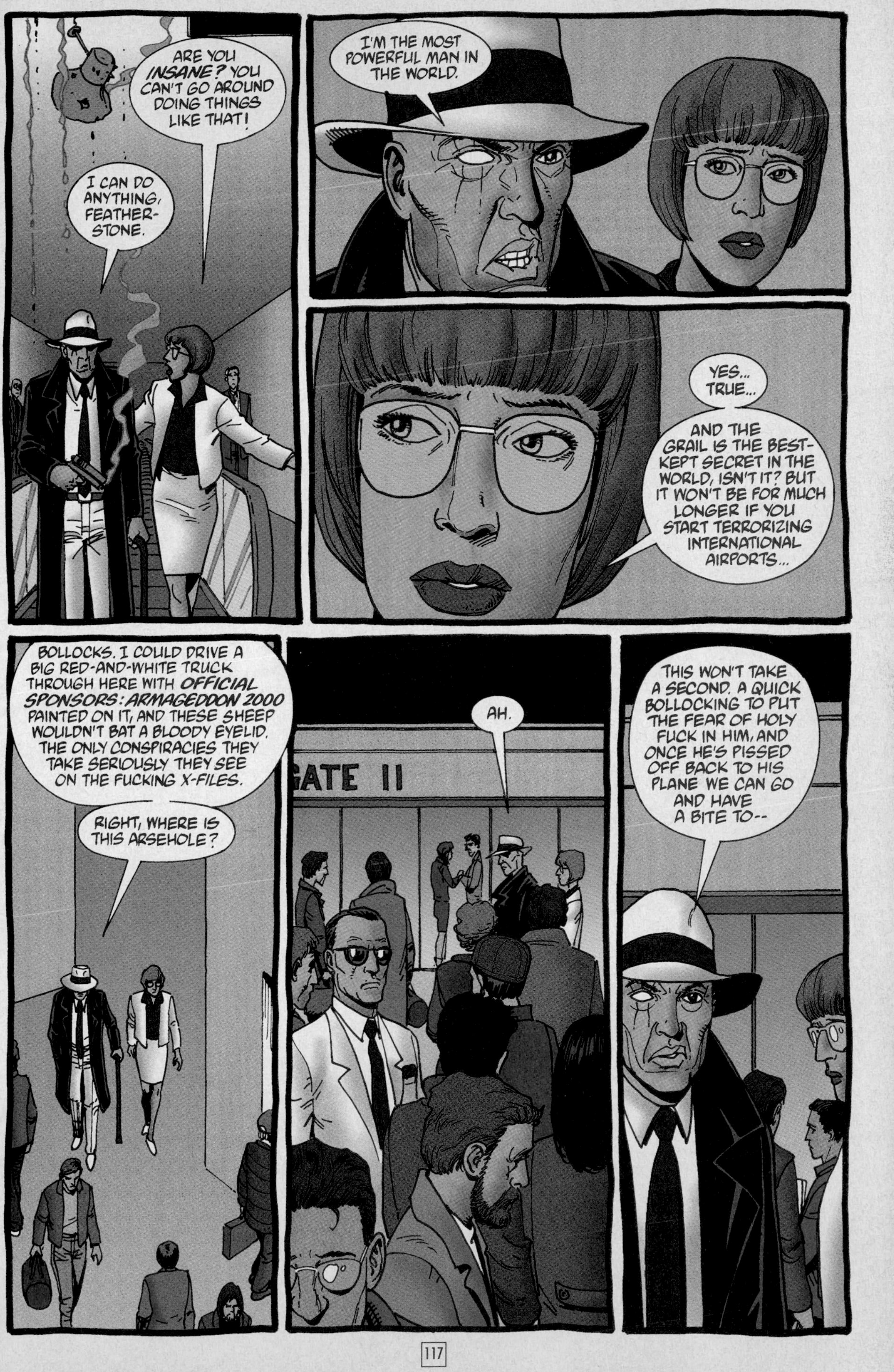
ARE YOU INSANE? YOU CAN'T GO AROUND DOING THINGS LIKE THAT!
I CAN DO ANYTHING, FEATHER-STONE.
I'M THE MOST POWERFUL MAN IN THE WORLD.
YES... TRUE...
AND THE GRAIL IS THE BEST-KEPT SECRET IN THE WORLD, ISN'T IT? BUT IT WON'T BE FOR MUCH LONGER IF YOU START TERRORIZING INTERNATIONAL AIRPORTS...
BOLLOCKS. I COULD DRIVE A BIG RED-AND-WHITE TRUCK THROUGH HERE WITH OFFICIAL SPONSORS: ARMAGEDDON 2000 PAINTED ON IT, AND THESE SHEEP WOULDN'T BAT A BLOODY EYELID. THE ONLY CONSPIRACIES THEY TAKE SERIOUSLY THEY SEE ON THE FUCKING X-FILES.
RIGHT, WHERE IS THIS ARSEHOLE?
AH.
GATE 11
THIS WON'T TAKE A SECOND. A QUICK BOLLOCKING TO PUT THE FEAR OF HOLY FUCK IN HIM, AND ONCE HE'S PISSED OFF BACK TO HIS PLANE WE CAN GO AND HAVE A BITE TO--

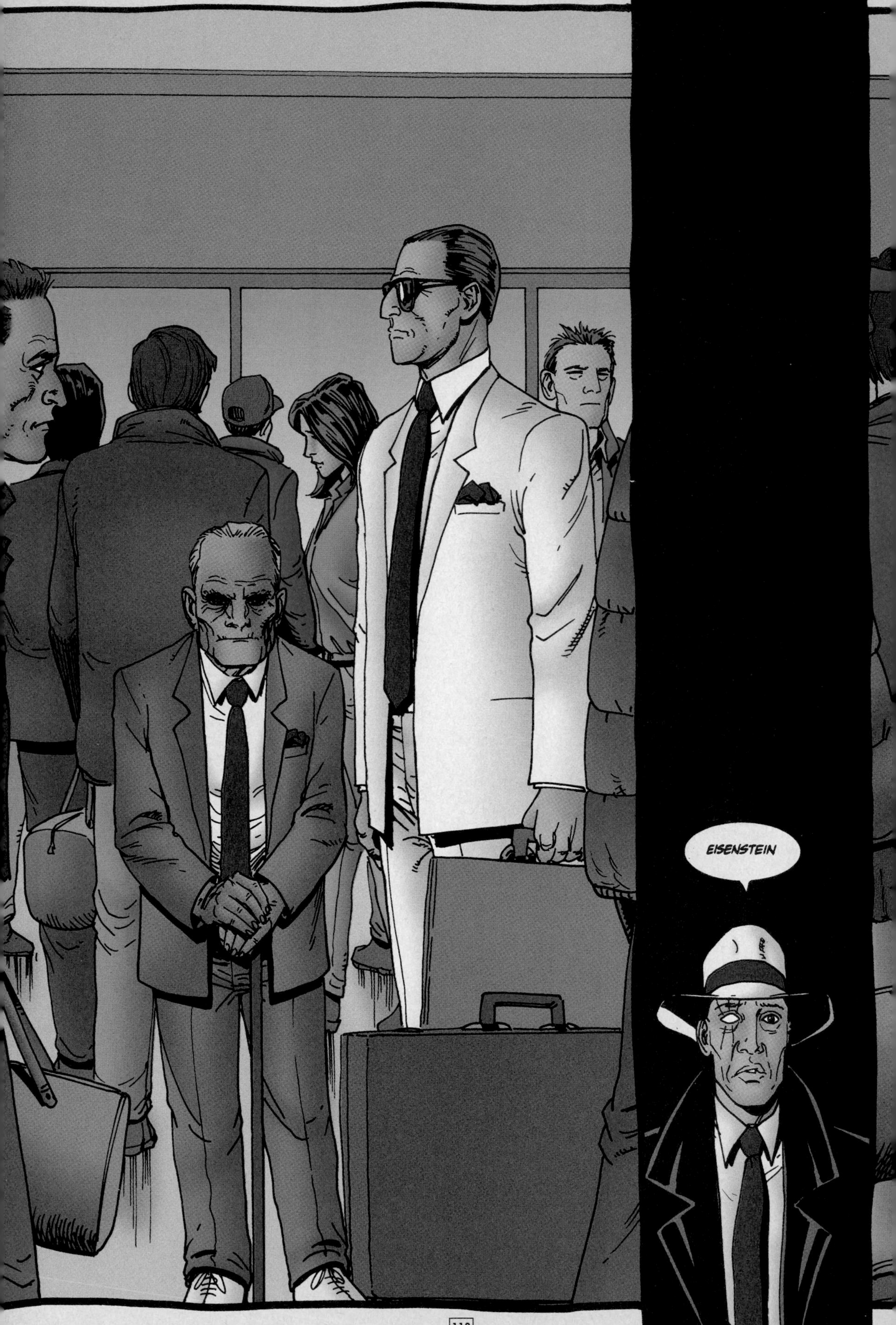
EISENSTEIN

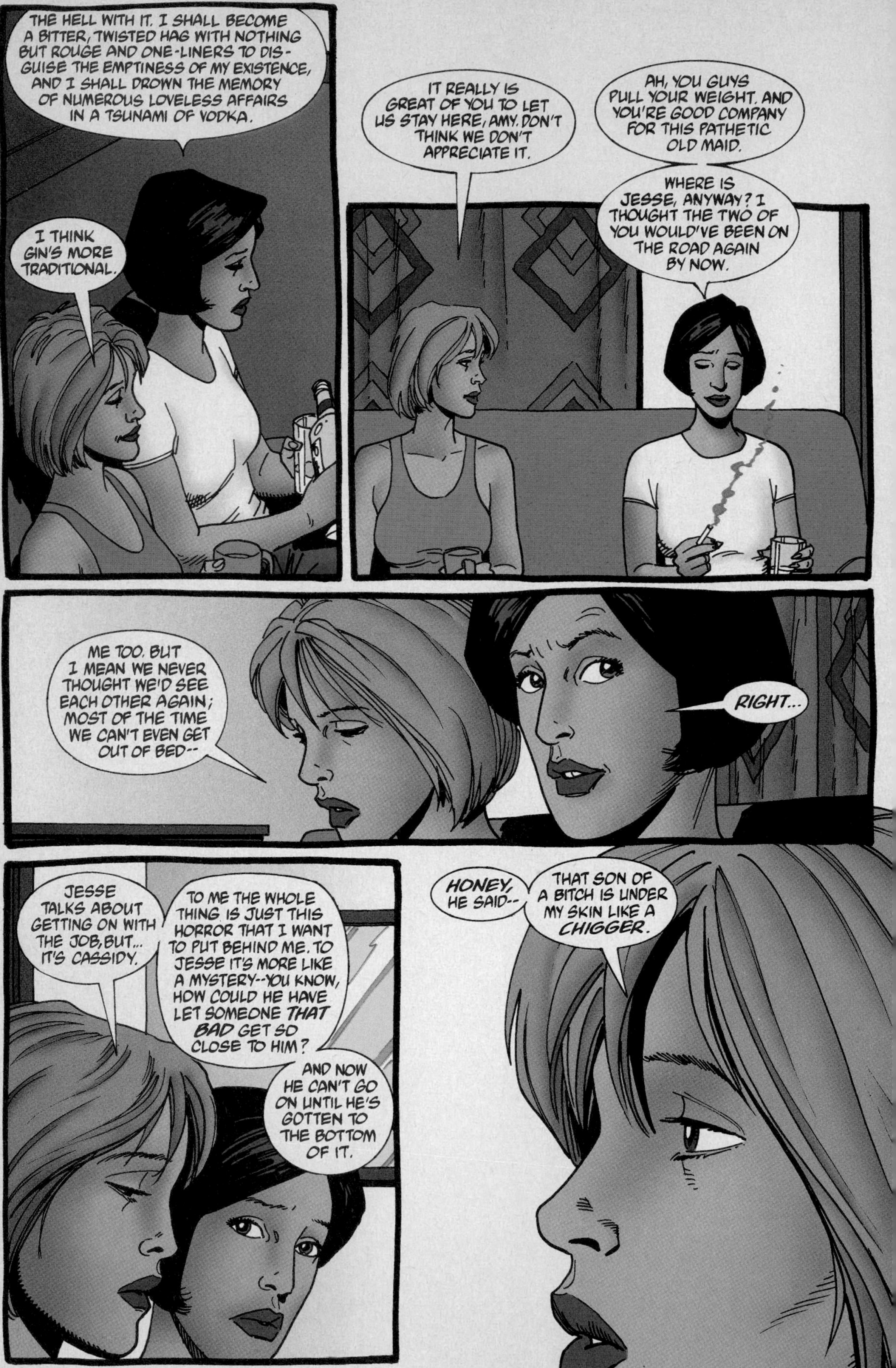
THE HELL WITH IT. I SHALL BECOME A BITTER, TWISTED HAG WITH NOTHING BUT ROUGE AND ONE-LINERS TO DIS-GUISE THE EMPTINESS OF MY EXISTENCE, AND I SHALL DROWN THE MEMORY OF NUMEROUS LOVELESS AFFAIRS IN A TSUNAMI OF VODKA.
I THINK GIN'S MORE TRADITIONAL.
IT REALLY IS GREAT OF YOU TO LET US STAY HERE, AMY. DON'T THINK WE DON'T APPRECIATE IT.
AH, YOU GUYS PULL YOUR WEIGHT. AND YOU'RE GOOD COMPANY FOR THIS PATHETIC OLD MAID.
WHERE IS JESSE, ANYWAY? I THOUGHT THE TWO OF YOU WOULD'VE BEEN ON THE ROAD AGAIN BY NOW.
ME TOO. BUT I MEAN WE NEVER THOUGHT WE'D SEE EACH OTHER AGAIN; MOST OF THE TIME WE CAN'T EVEN GET OUT OF BED--
RIGHT...
JESSE TALKS ABOUT GETTING ON WITH THE JOB, BUT... IT'S CASSIDY.
TO ME THE WHOLE THING IS JUST THIS HORROR THAT I WANT TO PUT BEHIND ME. TO JESSE IT'S MORE LIKE A MYSTERY--YOU KNOW, HOW COULD HE HAVE LET SOMEONE THAT BAD GET SO CLOSE TO HIM?
AND NOW HE CAN'T GO ON UNTIL HE'S GOTTEN TO THE BOTTOM OF IT.
HONEY, HE SAID--
THAT SON OF A BITCH IS UNDER MY SKIN LIKE A CHIGGER.

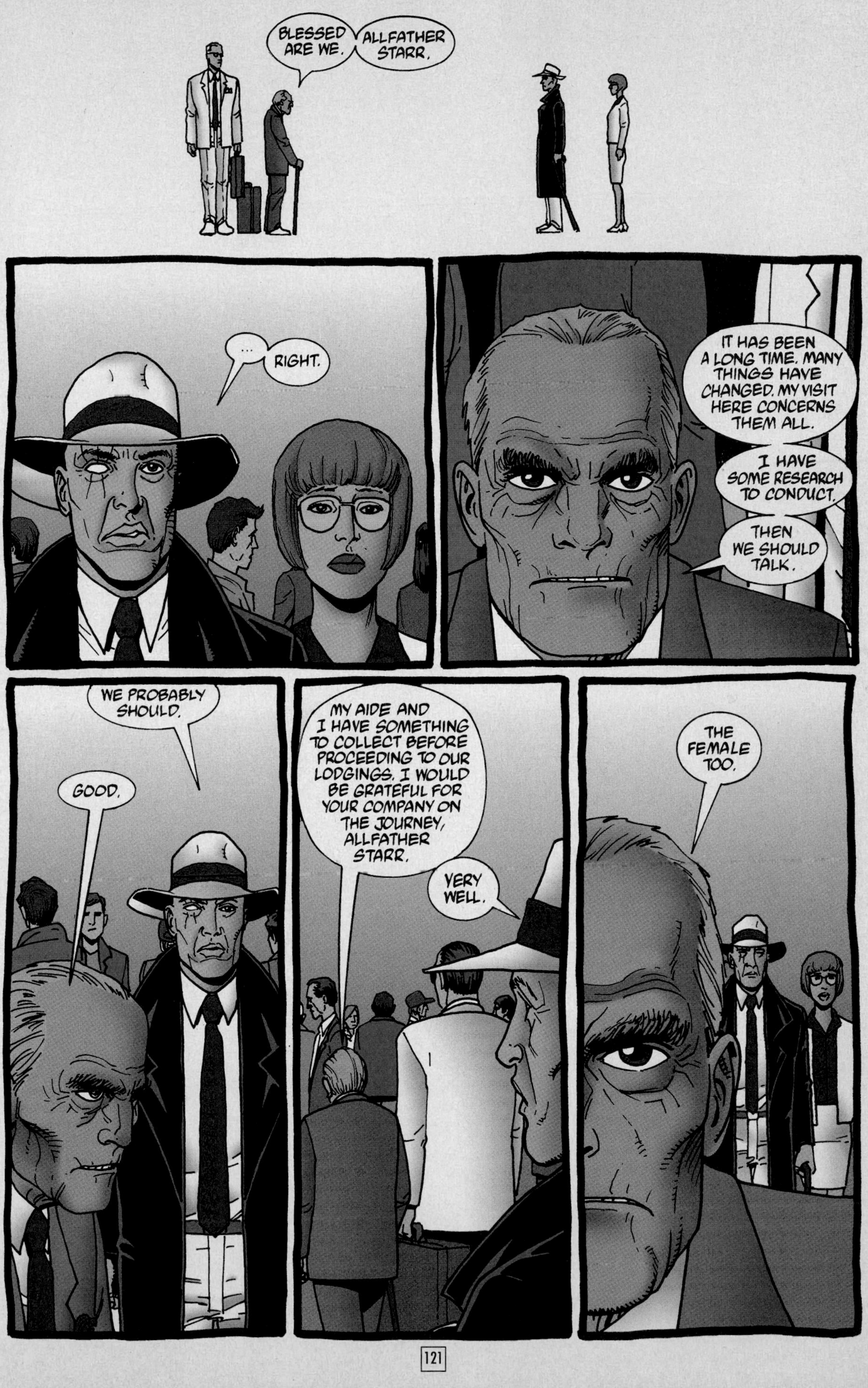
BLESSED ARE WE.
ALLFATHER STARR.
...
RIGHT.
IT HAS BEEN A LONG TIME. MANY THINGS HAVE CHANGED. MY VISIT HERE CONCERNS THEM ALL.
I HAVE SOME RESEARCH TO CONDUCT.
THEN WE SHOULD TALK.
WE PROBABLY SHOULD.
GOOD.
MY AIDE AND I HAVE SOMETHING TO COLLECT BEFORE PROCEEDING TO OUR LODGINGS. I WOULD BE GRATEFUL FOR YOUR COMPANY ON THE JOURNEY, ALLFATHER STARR.
VERY WELL.
THE FEMALE TOO.

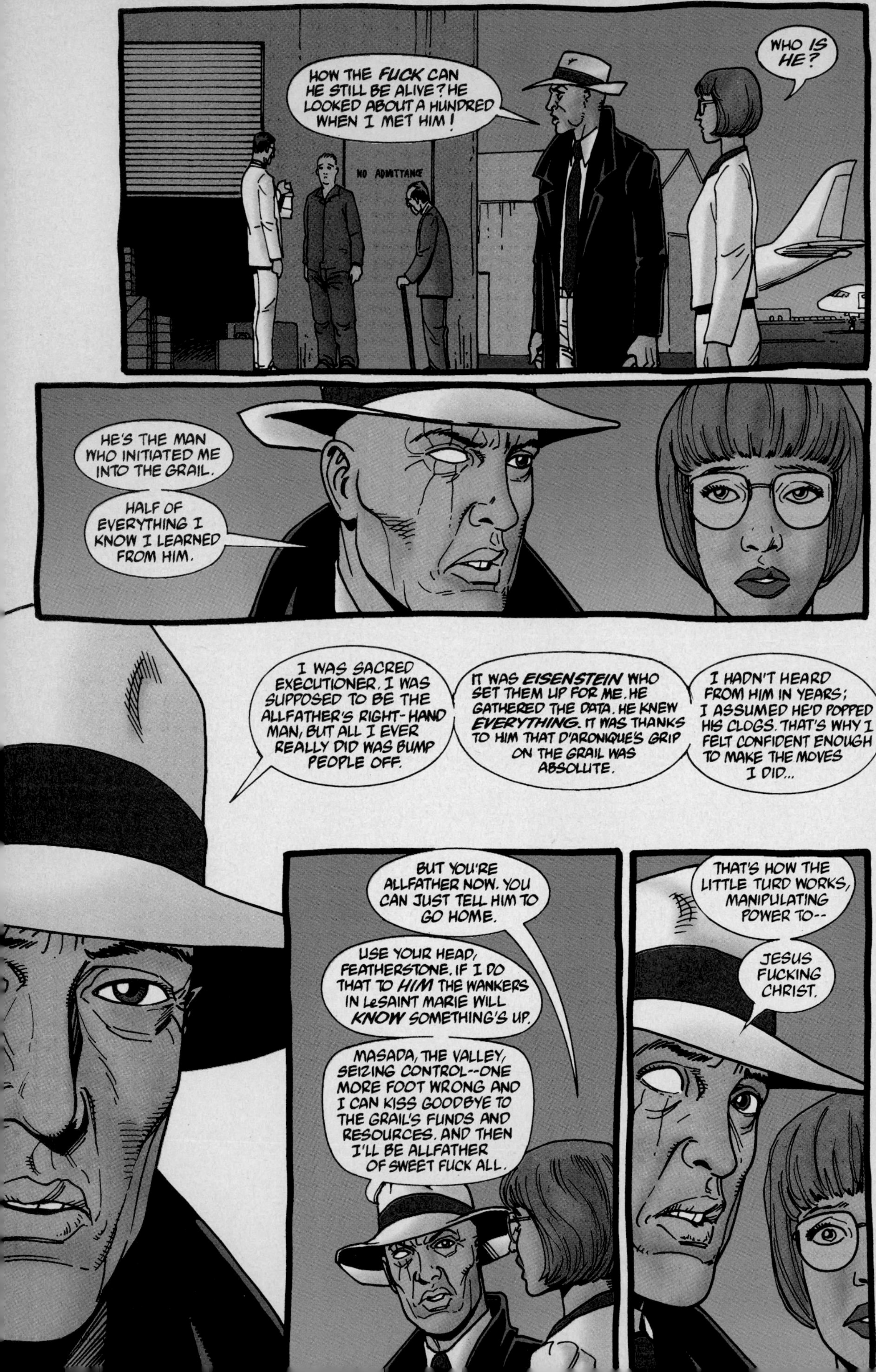
HOW THE FUCK CAN HE STILL BE ALIVE? HE LOOKED ABOUT A HUNDRED WHEN I MET HIM!
WHO IS HE?
NO ADMITTANCE
HE'S THE MAN WHO INITIATED ME INTO THE GRAIL.
HALF OF EVERYTHING I KNOW I LEARNED FROM HIM.
I WAS SACRED EXECUTIONER. I WAS SUPPOSED TO BE THE ALLFATHER'S RIGHT-HAND MAN, BUT ALL I EVER REALLY DID WAS BUMP PEOPLE OFF.
IT WAS EISENSTEIN WHO SET THEM UP FOR ME. HE GATHERED THE DATA. HE KNEW EVERYTHING. IT WAS THANKS TO HIM THAT D'ARONIQUE'S GRIP ON THE GRAIL WAS ABSOLUTE.
I HADN'T HEARD FROM HIM IN YEARS; I ASSUMED HE'D POPPED HIS CLOGS. THAT'S WHY I FELT CONFIDENT ENOUGH TO MAKE THE MOVES I DID...
BUT YOU'RE ALLFATHER NOW. YOU CAN JUST TELL HIM TO GO HOME.
USE YOUR HEAD, FEATHERSTONE. IF I DO THAT TO HIM THE WANKERS IN LeSAINT MARIE WILL KNOW SOMETHING'S UP.
MASADA, THE VALLEY, SEIZING CONTROL--ONE MORE FOOT WRONG AND I CAN KISS GOODBYE TO THE GRAIL'S FUNDS AND RESOURCES. AND THEN I'LL BE ALLFATHER OF SWEET FUCK ALL.
THAT'S HOW THE LITTLE TURD WORKS, MANIPULATING POWER TO--
JESUS FUCKING CHRIST.

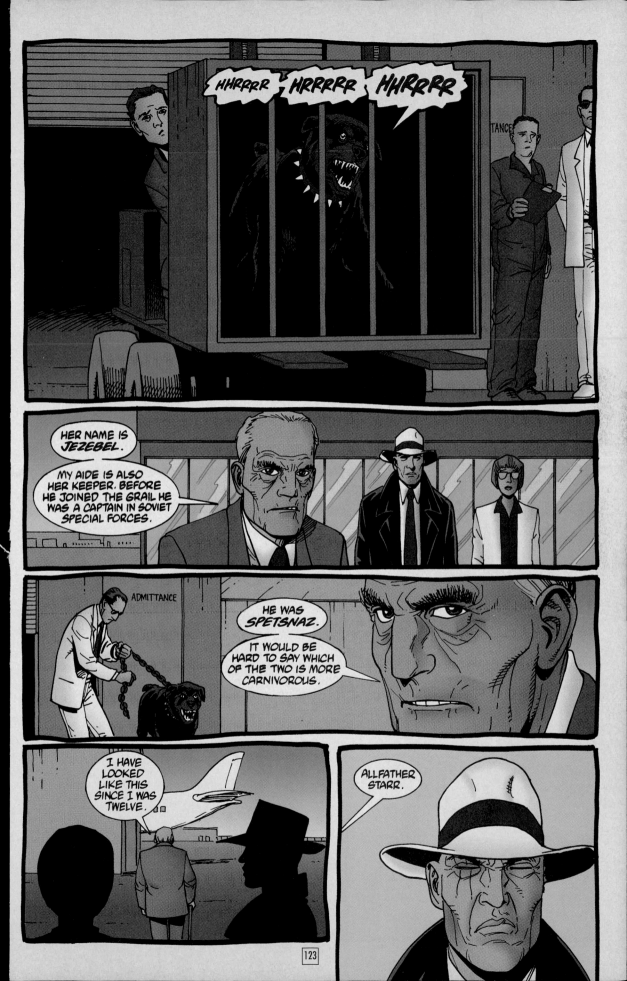

HHRRRR HRRRRR HHRRRR

HER NAME IS *JEZEBEL.*

MY AIDE IS ALSO HER KEEPER. BEFORE HE JOINED THE GRAIL HE WAS A CAPTAIN IN SOVIET SPECIAL FORCES.

ADMITTANCE

HE WAS *SPETSNAZ.*

IT WOULD BE HARD TO SAY WHICH OF THE TWO IS MORE CARNIVOROUS.

I HAVE LOOKED LIKE THIS SINCE I WAS TWELVE.

ALLFATHER STARR.

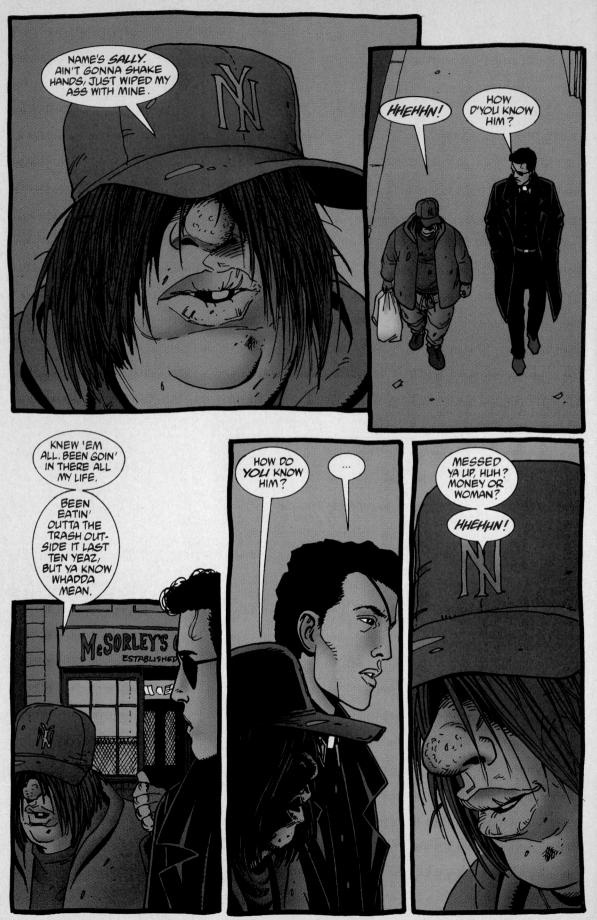

NAME'S *SALLY*. AIN'T GONNA SHAKE HANDS, JUST WIPED MY ASS WITH MINE.

HHEHHN!

HOW D'YOU KNOW HIM?

KNEW 'EM ALL. BEEN GOIN' IN THERE ALL MY LIFE.

BEEN EATIN' OUTTA THE TRASH OUTSIDE IT LAST TEN YEAZ, BUT YA KNOW WHADDA MEAN.

HOW DO *YOU* KNOW HIM?

...

MESSED YA UP, HUH? MONEY OR WOMAN?

HHEHHN!

McSORLEY'S
ESTABLISHED

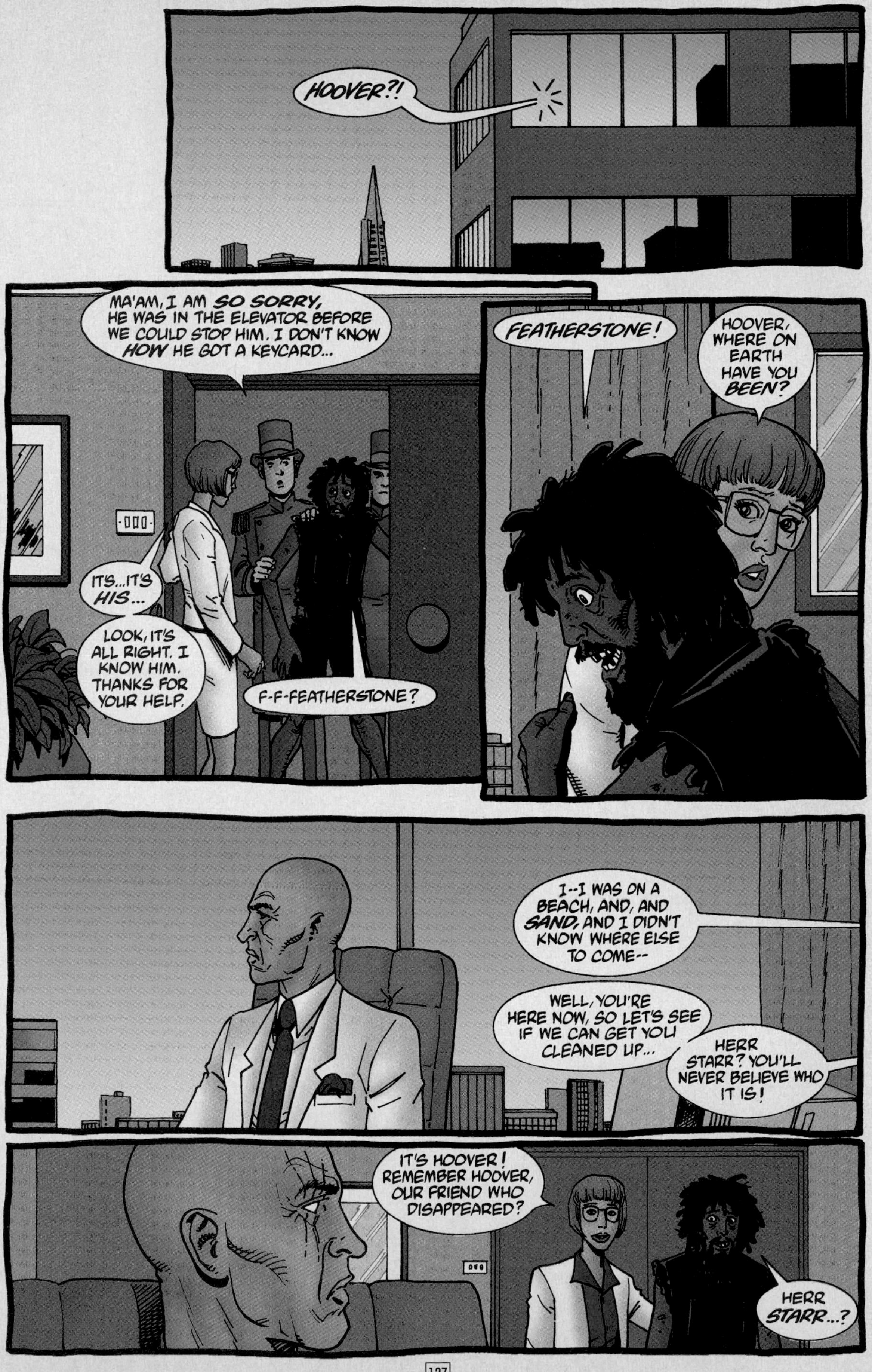
HOOVER?!
MA'AM, I AM SO SORRY, HE WAS IN THE ELEVATOR BEFORE WE COULD STOP HIM. I DON'T KNOW HOW HE GOT A KEYCARD...
IT'S...IT'S HIS...
LOOK, IT'S ALL RIGHT. I KNOW HIM. THANKS FOR YOUR HELP.
F-F-FEATHERSTONE?
FEATHERSTONE!
HOOVER, WHERE ON EARTH HAVE YOU BEEN?
I--I WAS ON A BEACH, AND, AND SAND, AND I DIDN'T KNOW WHERE ELSE TO COME--
WELL, YOU'RE HERE NOW, SO LET'S SEE IF WE CAN GET YOU CLEANED UP...
HERR STARR? YOU'LL NEVER BELIEVE WHO IT IS!
IT'S HOOVER! REMEMBER HOOVER, OUR FRIEND WHO DISAPPEARED?
HERR STARR...?

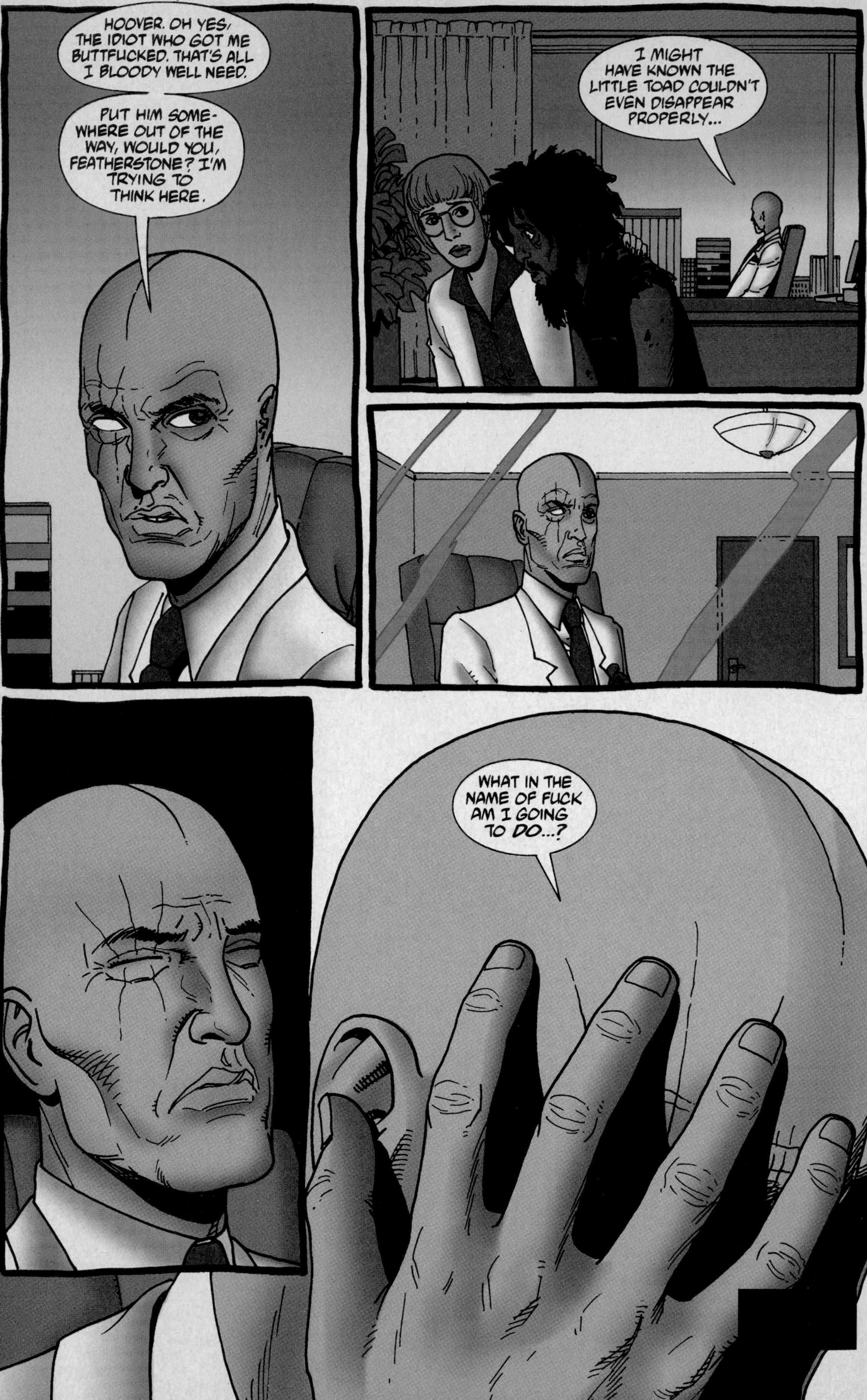
HOOVER. OH YES, THE IDIOT WHO GOT ME BUTTFUCKED. THAT'S ALL I BLOODY WELL NEED.
PUT HIM SOME-WHERE OUT OF THE WAY, WOULD YOU, FEATHERSTONE? I'M TRYING TO THINK HERE.
I MIGHT HAVE KNOWN THE LITTLE TOAD COULDN'T EVEN DISAPPEAR PROPERLY...
WHAT IN THE NAME OF FUCK AM I GOING TO *DO*...?

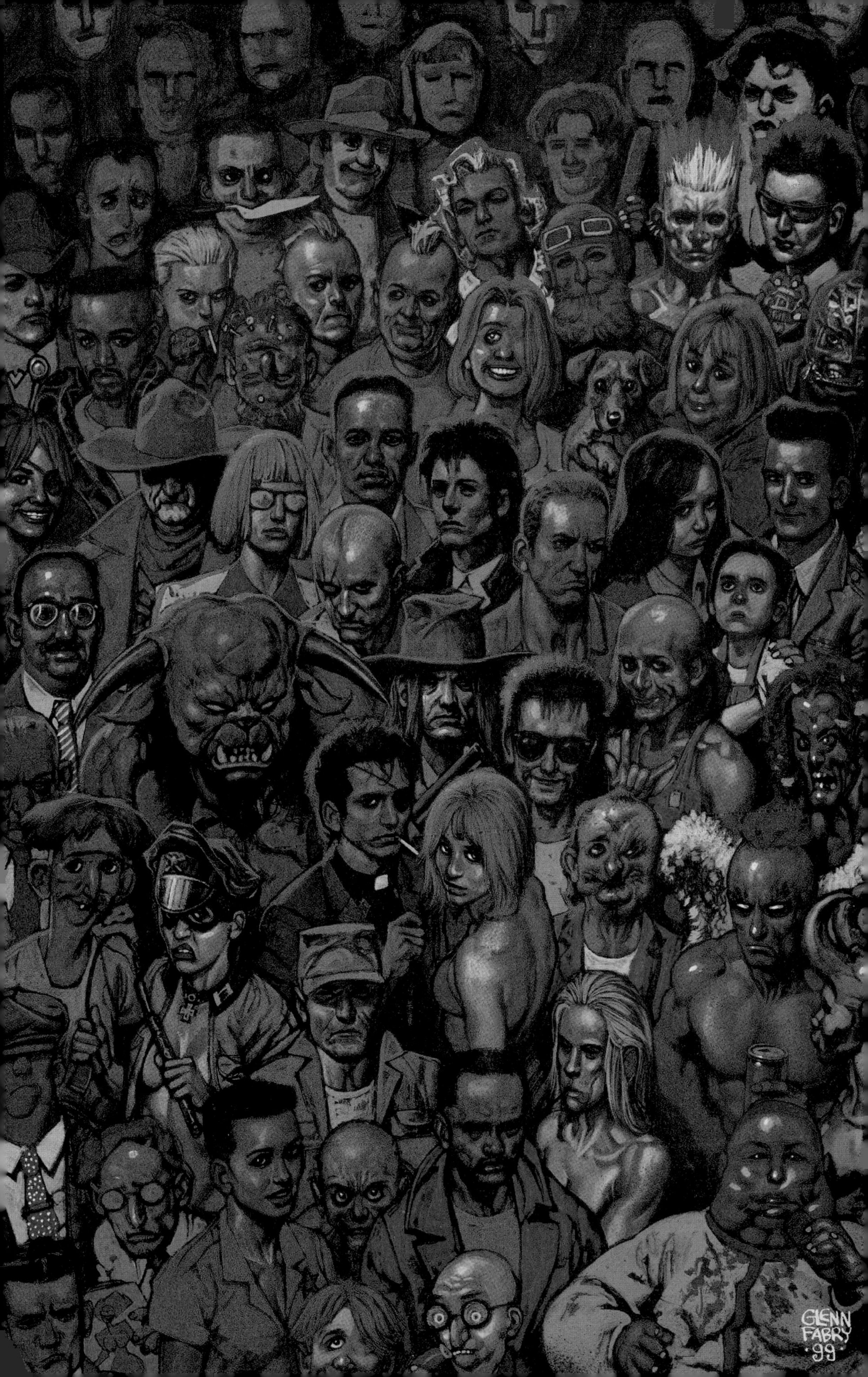
GLENN FABRY ·99·

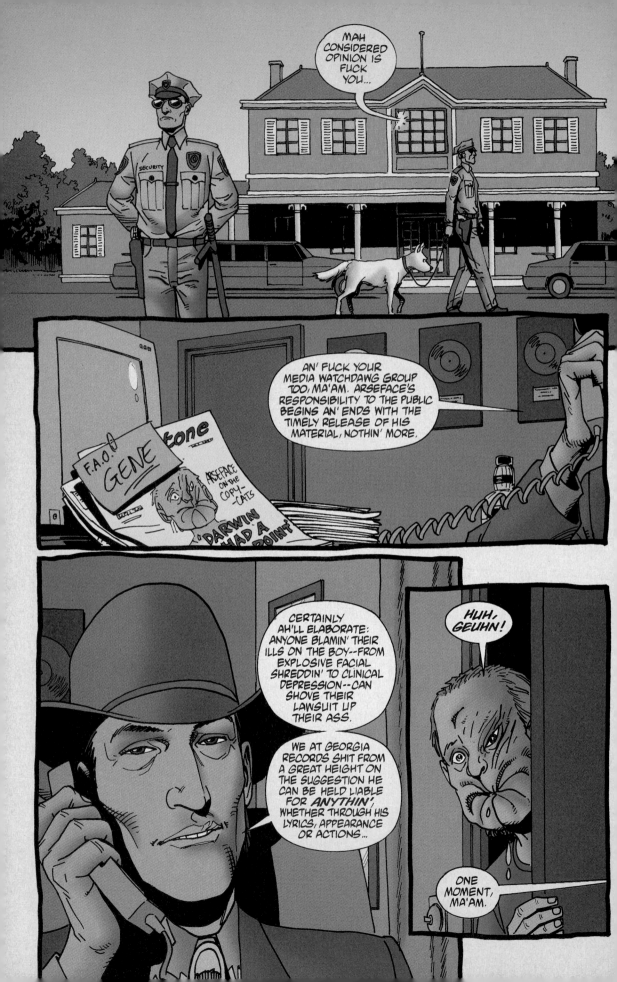

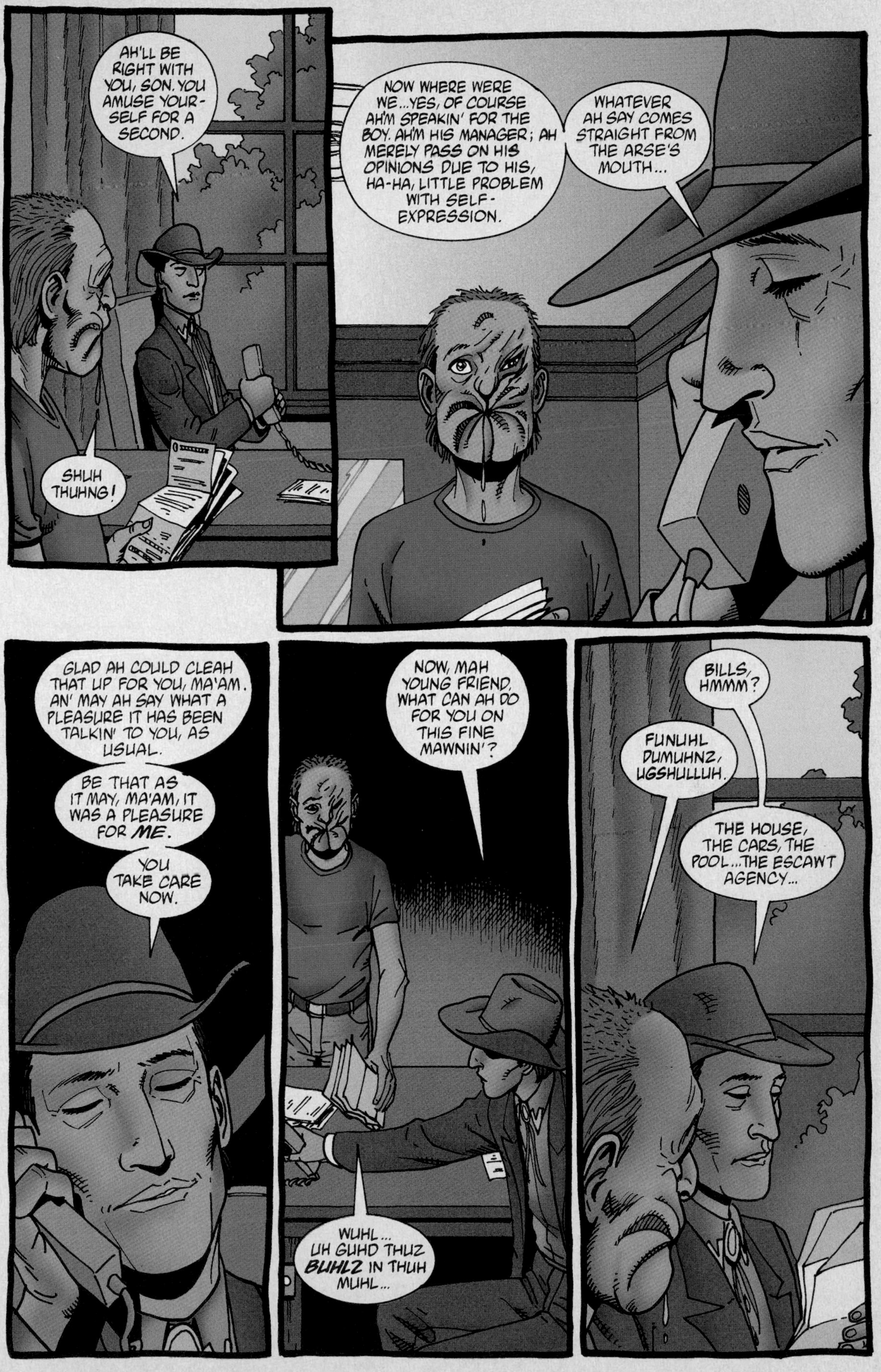
AH'LL BE RIGHT WITH YOU, SON. YOU AMUSE YOURSELF FOR A SECOND.
SHUH THUHNG!
NOW WHERE WERE WE...YES, OF COURSE AH'M SPEAKIN' FOR THE BOY. AH'M HIS MANAGER; AH MERELY PASS ON HIS OPINIONS DUE TO HIS, HA-HA, LITTLE PROBLEM WITH SELF-EXPRESSION.
WHATEVER AH SAY COMES STRAIGHT FROM THE ARSE'S MOUTH...
GLAD AH COULD CLEAH THAT UP FOR YOU, MA'AM. AN' MAY AH SAY WHAT A PLEASURE IT HAS BEEN TALKIN' TO YOU, AS USUAL.
BE THAT AS IT MAY, MA'AM, IT WAS A PLEASURE FOR ME.
YOU TAKE CARE NOW.
NOW, MAH YOUNG FRIEND, WHAT CAN AH DO FOR YOU ON THIS FINE MAWNIN'?
WUHL... UH GUHD THUZ BUHLZ IN THUH MUHL...
BILLS, HMMM?
FUNUHL DUMUHNZ, UGSHULLUH.
THE HOUSE, THE CARS, THE POOL...THE ESCAWT AGENCY...

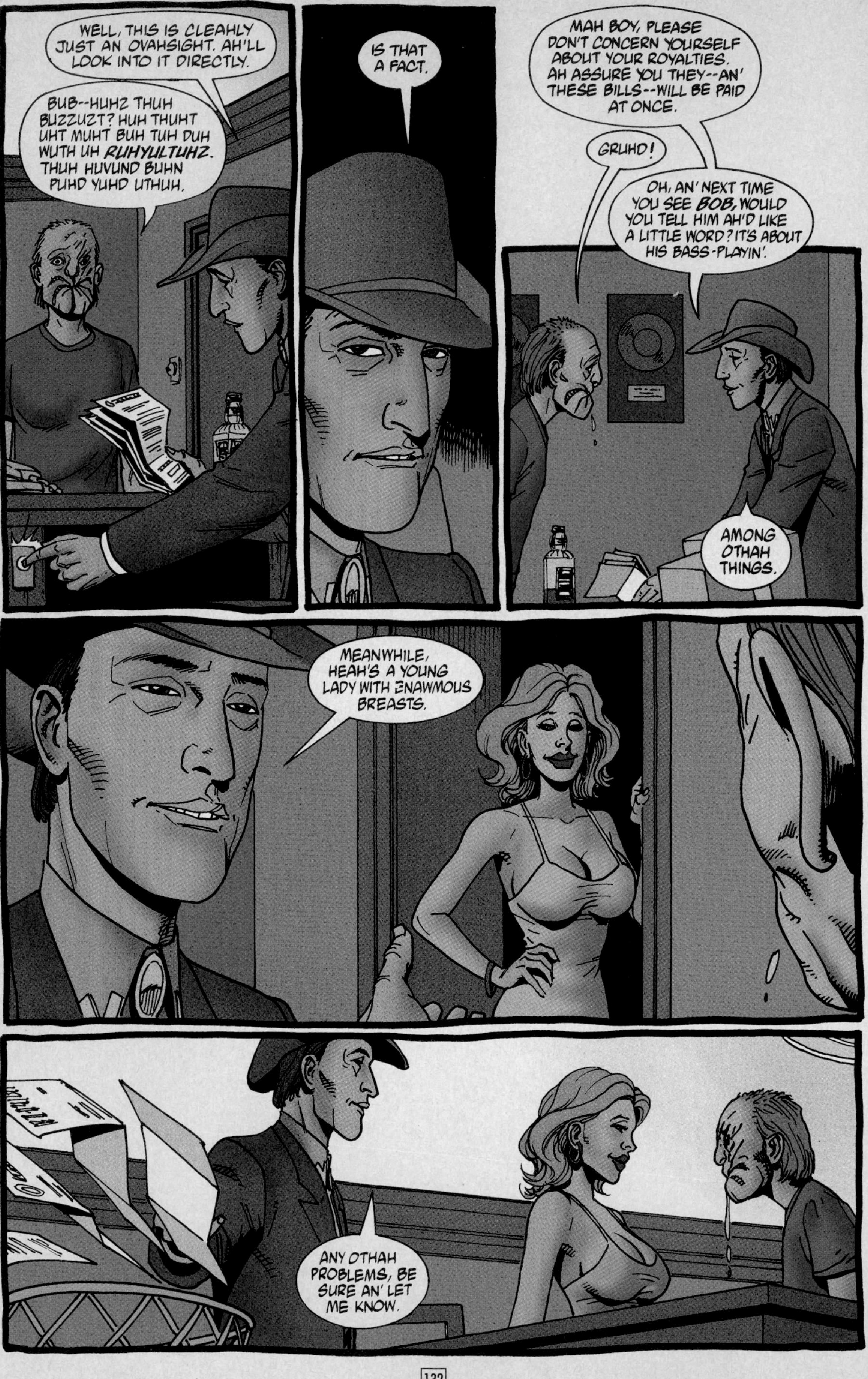
WELL, THIS IS CLEAHLY JUST AN OVAHSIGHT. AH'LL LOOK INTO IT DIRECTLY.
BUB--HUHZ THUH BUZZUZT? HUH THUHT UHT MUHT BUH TUH DUH WUTH UH RUHYULTUHZ. THUH HUVUND BUHN PUHD YUHD UTHUH.
IS THAT A FACT.
MAH BOY, PLEASE DON'T CONCERN YOURSELF ABOUT YOUR ROYALTIES. AH ASSURE YOU THEY--AN' THESE BILLS--WILL BE PAID AT ONCE.
GRUHD!
OH, AN' NEXT TIME YOU SEE BOB, WOULD YOU TELL HIM AH'D LIKE A LITTLE WORD? IT'S ABOUT HIS BASS-PLAYIN'.
AMONG OTHAH THINGS.
MEANWHILE, HEAH'S A YOUNG LADY WITH ENAWMOUS BREASTS.
!
ANY OTHAH PROBLEMS, BE SURE AN' LET ME KNOW.

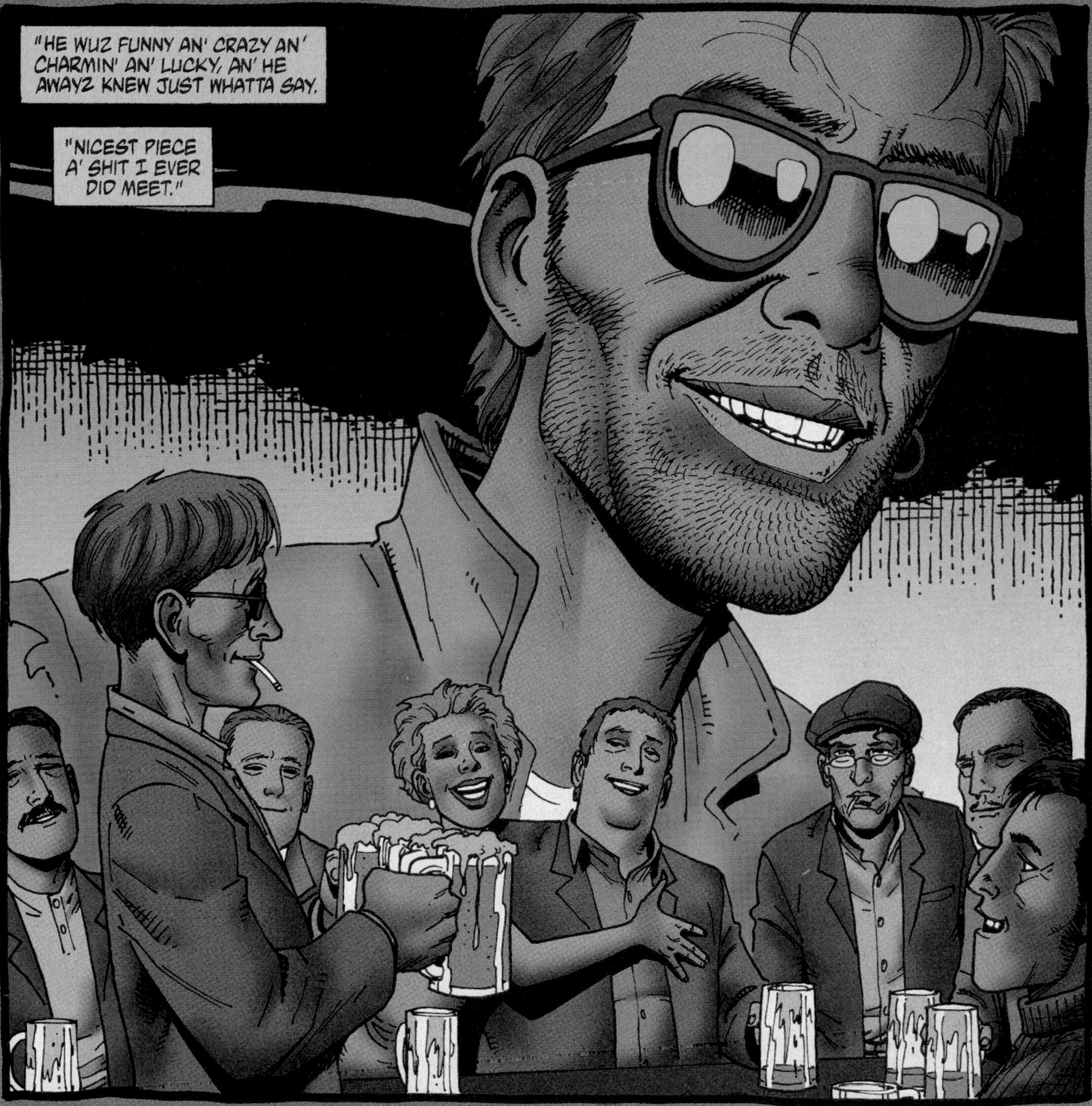
"HE WUZ FUNNY AN' CRAZY AN' CHARMIN' AN' LUCKY, AN' HE AWAYZ KNEW JUST WHATTA SAY.
"NICEST PIECE A' SHIT I EVER DID MEET."

SMILE LIKE THE GATES OF HELL

GARTH ENNIS - Writer STEVE DILLON - Artist

PAMELA RAMBO - Colorist CLEM ROBINS - Letterer AXEL ALONSO - Editor

PREACHER created by GARTH ENNIS and STEVE DILLON

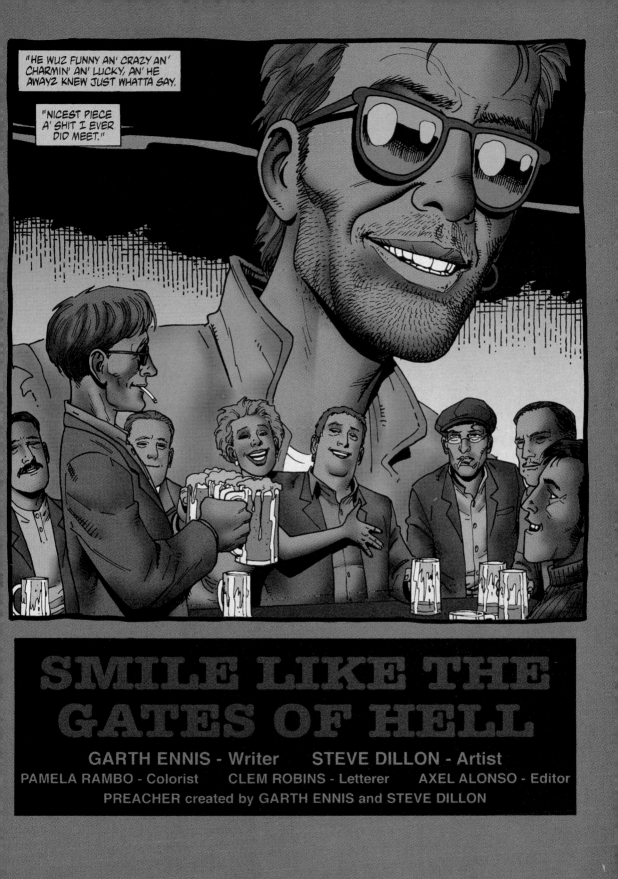

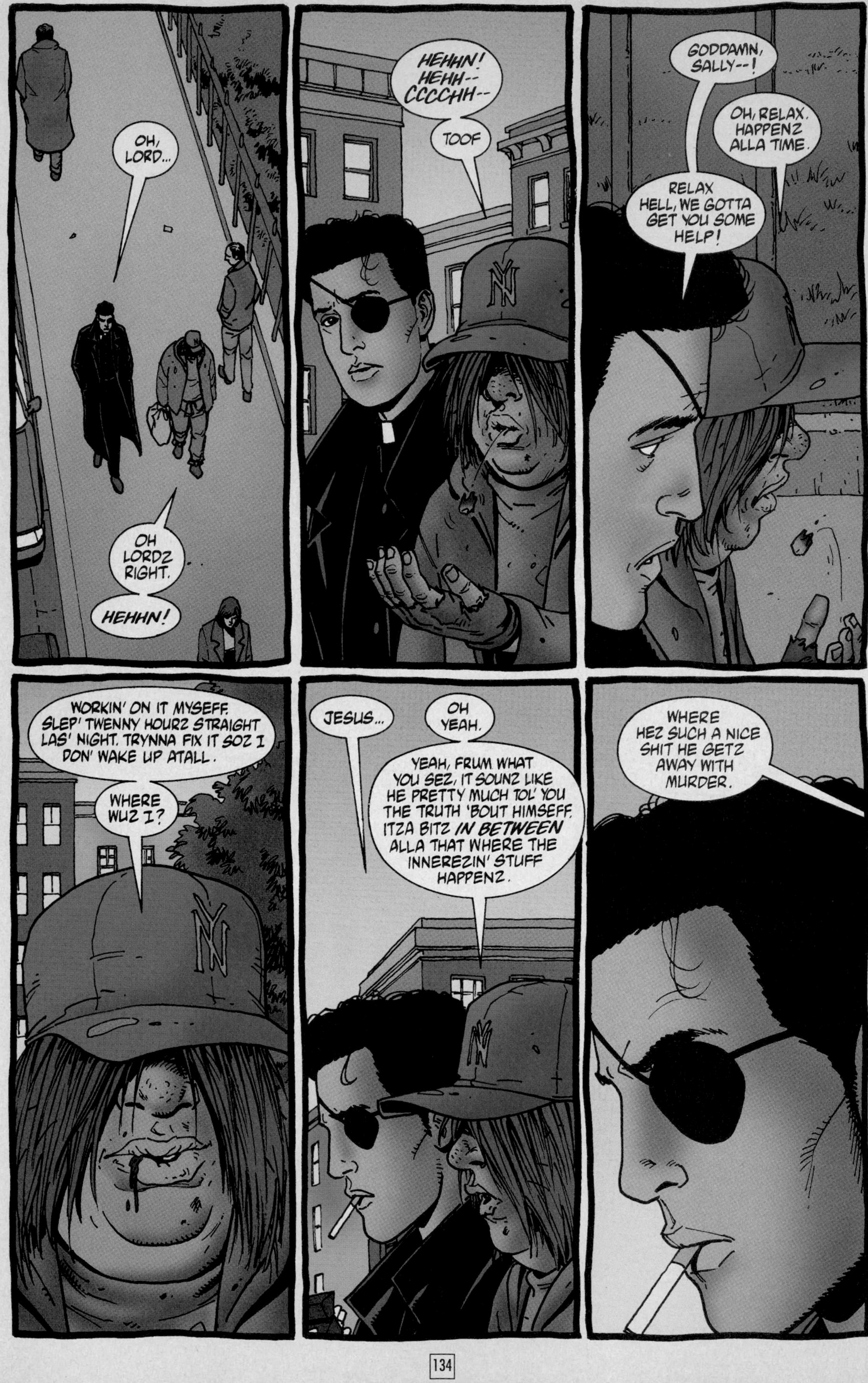
OH, LORD...
OH LORDZ RIGHT.
HEHHN!
HEHHN! HEHH-- CCCCHH--
TOOF
GODDAMN, SALLY--!
OH, RELAX. HAPPENZ ALLA TIME.
RELAX HELL, WE GOTTA GET YOU SOME HELP!
WORKIN' ON IT MYSEFF. SLEP' TWENNY HOURZ STRAIGHT LAS' NIGHT. TRYNNA FIX IT SOZ I DON' WAKE UP ATALL.
WHERE WUZ I?
JESUS...
OH YEAH.
YEAH, FRUM WHAT YOU SEZ, IT SOUNZ LIKE HE PRETTY MUCH TOL' YOU THE TRUTH 'BOUT HIMSEFF. ITZA BITZ IN BETWEEN ALLA THAT WHERE THE INNEREZIN' STUFF HAPPENZ.
WHERE HEZ SUCH A NICE SHIT HE GETZ AWAY WITH MURDER.

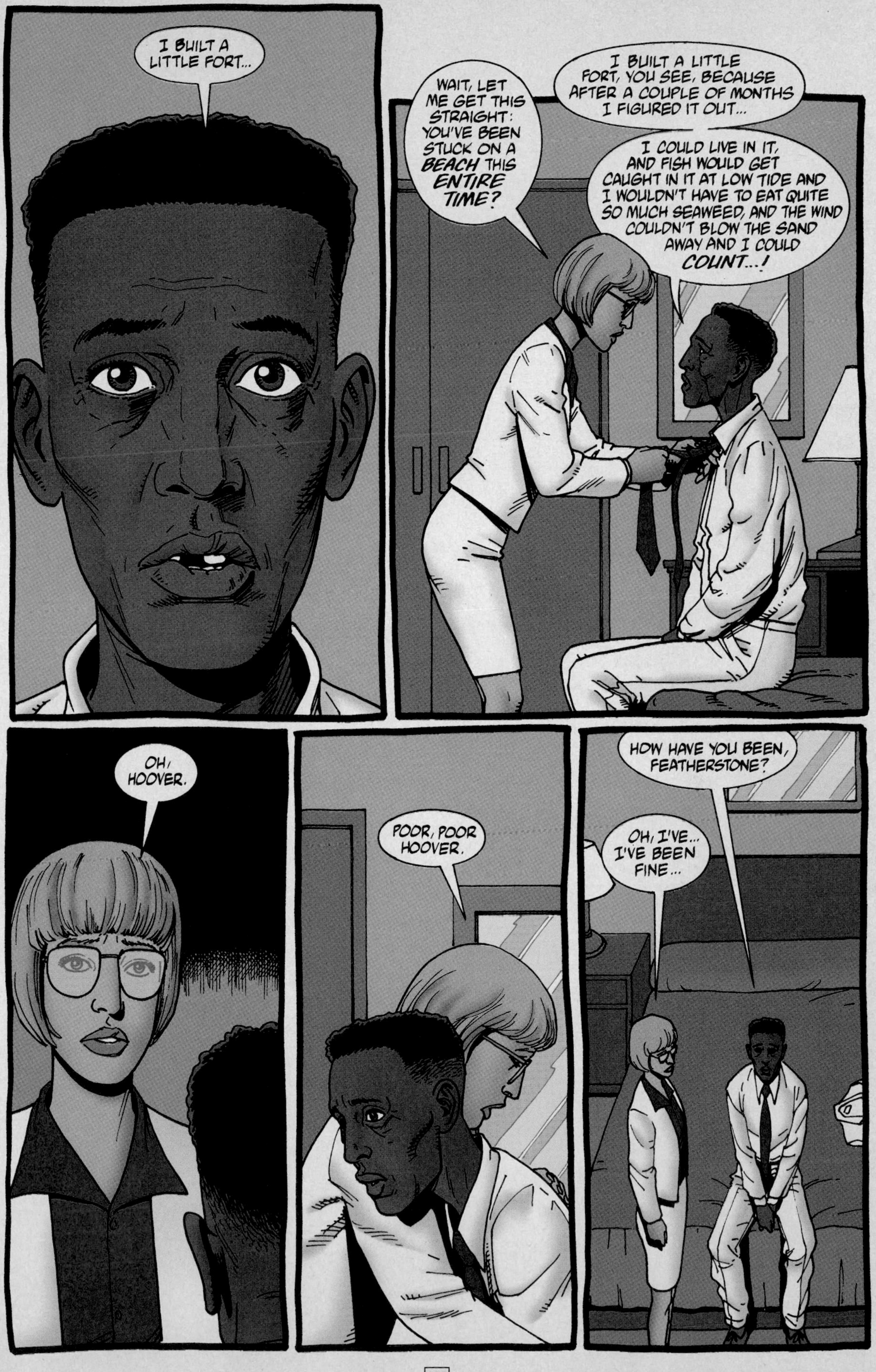
I BUILT A LITTLE FORT...
WAIT, LET ME GET THIS STRAIGHT: YOU'VE BEEN STUCK ON A BEACH THIS ENTIRE TIME?
I BUILT A LITTLE FORT, YOU SEE, BECAUSE AFTER A COUPLE OF MONTHS I FIGURED IT OUT...
I COULD LIVE IN IT, AND FISH WOULD GET CAUGHT IN IT AT LOW TIDE AND I WOULDN'T HAVE TO EAT QUITE SO MUCH SEAWEED, AND THE WIND COULDN'T BLOW THE SAND AWAY AND I COULD COUNT...!
OH, HOOVER.
POOR, POOR HOOVER.
HOW HAVE YOU BEEN, FEATHERSTONE?
OH, I'VE... I'VE BEEN FINE...

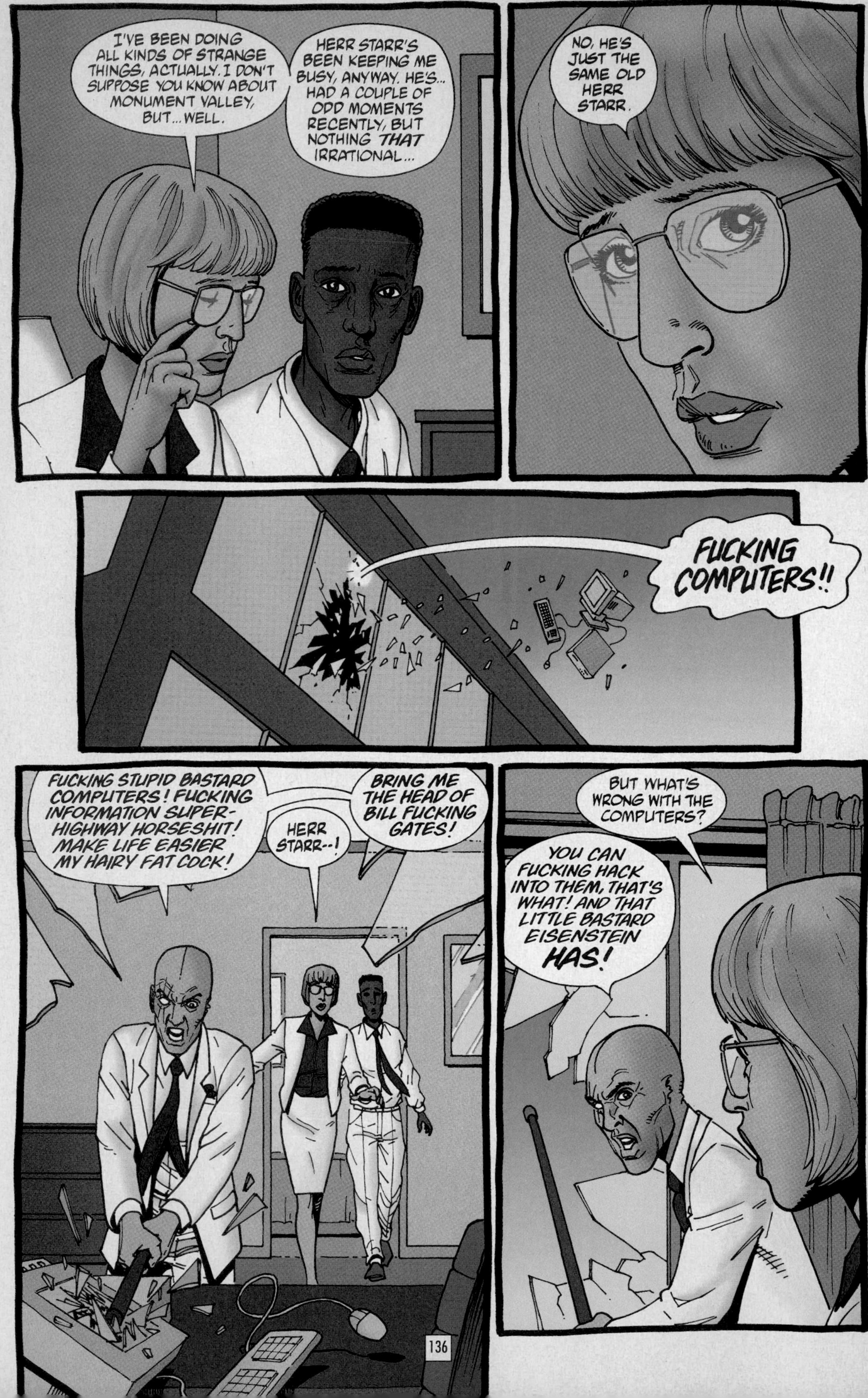
I'VE BEEN DOING ALL KINDS OF STRANGE THINGS, ACTUALLY. I DON'T SUPPOSE YOU KNOW ABOUT MONUMENT VALLEY, BUT... WELL.
HERR STARR'S BEEN KEEPING ME BUSY, ANYWAY. HE'S... HAD A COUPLE OF ODD MOMENTS RECENTLY, BUT NOTHING THAT IRRATIONAL...
NO, HE'S JUST THE SAME OLD HERR STARR.
FUCKING COMPUTERS!!
FUCKING STUPID BASTARD COMPUTERS! FUCKING INFORMATION SUPER-HIGHWAY HORSESHIT! MAKE LIFE EASIER MY HAIRY FAT COCK!
HERR STARR--!
BRING ME THE HEAD OF BILL FUCKING GATES!
BUT WHAT'S WRONG WITH THE COMPUTERS?
YOU CAN FUCKING HACK INTO THEM, THAT'S WHAT! AND THAT LITTLE BASTARD EISENSTEIN HAS!

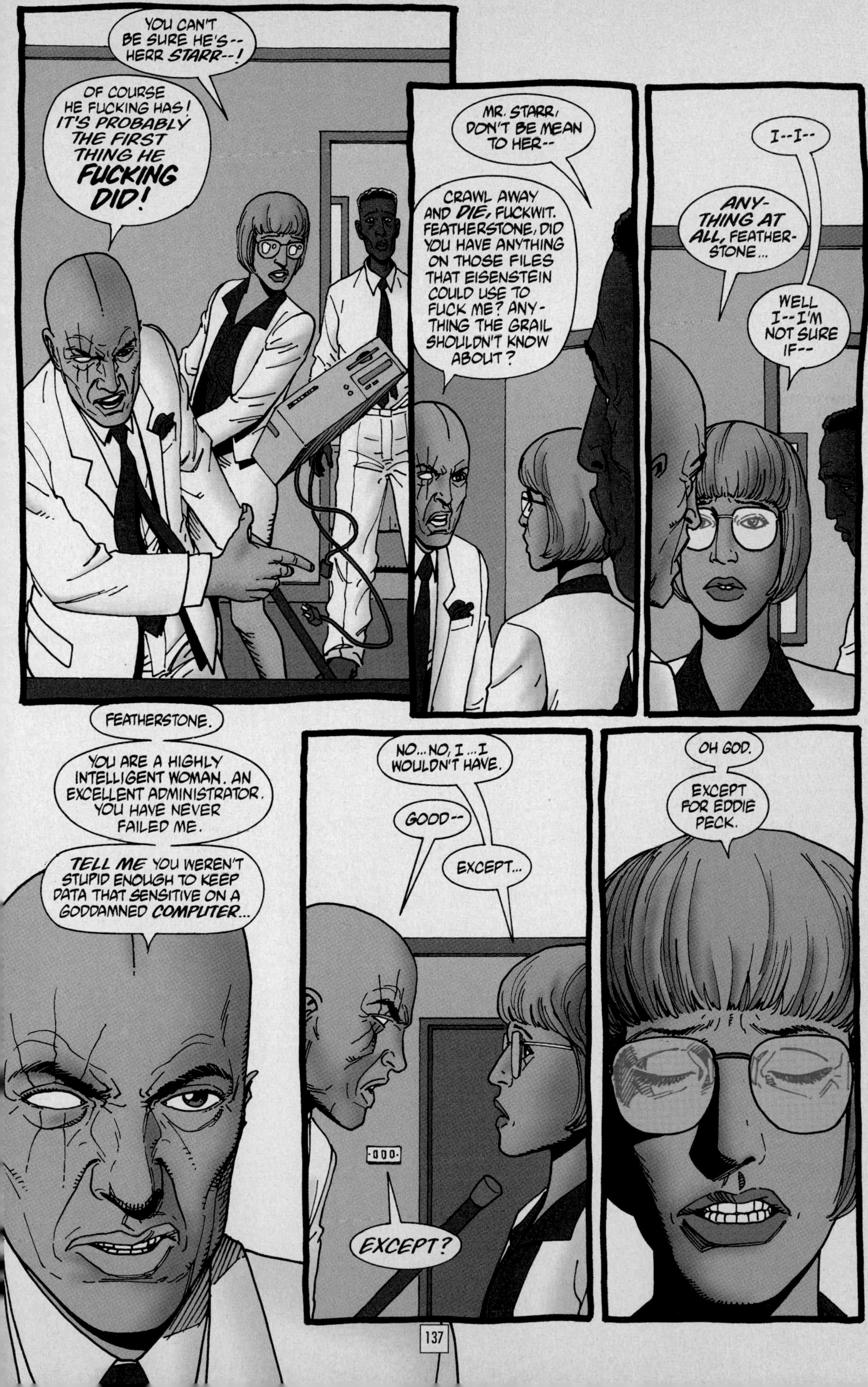
YOU CAN'T BE SURE HE'S-- HERR STARR--!
OF COURSE HE FUCKING HAS! IT'S PROBABLY THE FIRST THING HE FUCKING DID!
MR. STARR, DON'T BE MEAN TO HER--
CRAWL AWAY AND DIE, FUCKWIT. FEATHERSTONE, DID YOU HAVE ANYTHING ON THOSE FILES THAT EISENSTEIN COULD USE TO FUCK ME? ANY-THING THE GRAIL SHOULDN'T KNOW ABOUT?
I--I--
ANY-THING AT ALL, FEATHER-STONE...
WELL I--I'M NOT SURE IF--
FEATHERSTONE.
YOU ARE A HIGHLY INTELLIGENT WOMAN. AN EXCELLENT ADMINISTRATOR. YOU HAVE NEVER FAILED ME.
TELL ME YOU WEREN'T STUPID ENOUGH TO KEEP DATA THAT SENSITIVE ON A GODDAMNED COMPUTER...
NO...NO, I...I WOULDN'T HAVE.
GOOD--
EXCEPT...
EXCEPT?
OH GOD.
EXCEPT FOR EDDIE PECK.

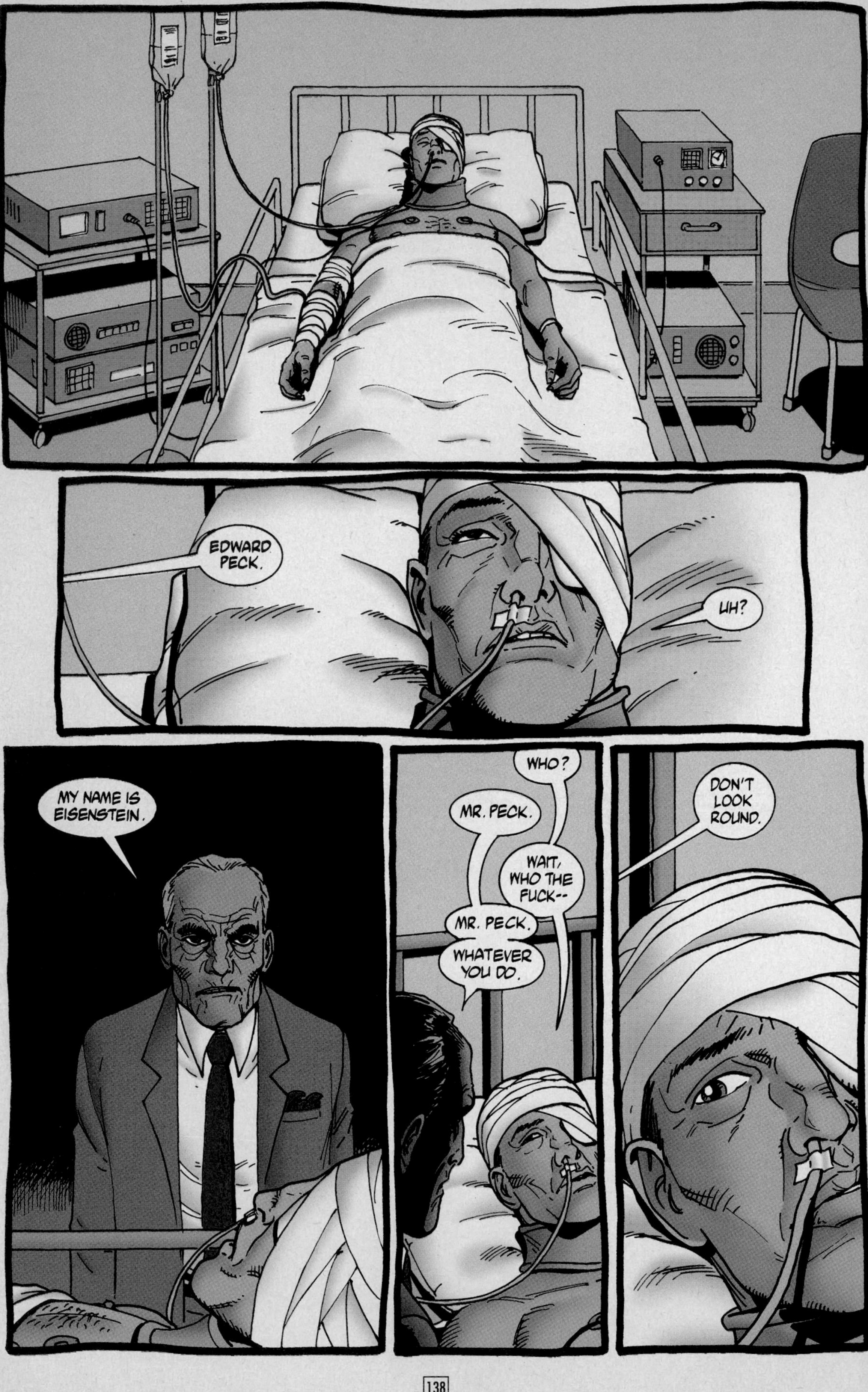
EDWARD PECK.
UH?
MY NAME IS EISENSTEIN.
MR. PECK.
WHO?
WAIT, WHO THE FUCK--
MR. PECK.
WHATEVER YOU DO.
DON'T LOOK ROUND.

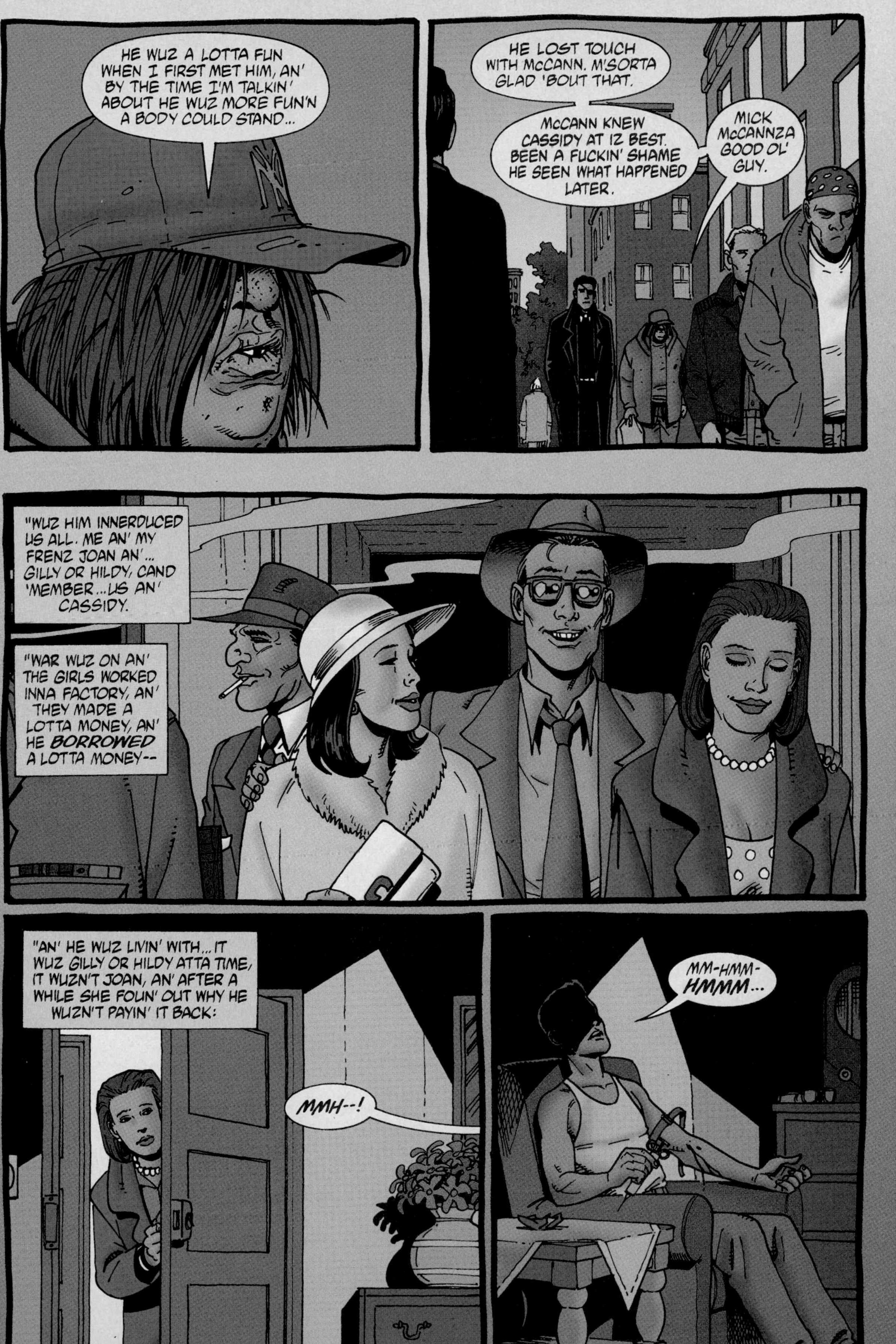
HE WUZ A LOTTA FUN WHEN I FIRST MET HIM, AN' BY THE TIME I'M TALKIN' ABOUT HE WUZ MORE FUN'N A BODY COULD STAND...
HE LOST TOUCH WITH McCANN. M'SORTA GLAD 'BOUT THAT.
McCANN KNEW CASSIDY AT IZ BEST. BEEN A FUCKIN' SHAME HE SEEN WHAT HAPPENED LATER.
MICK McCANNZA GOOD OL' GUY.
"WUZ HIM INNERDUCED US ALL. ME AN' MY FRENZ JOAN AN'... GILLY OR HILDY, CAND 'MEMBER... US AN' CASSIDY.
"WAR WUZ ON AN' THE GIRLS WORKED INNA FACTORY, AN' THEY MADE A LOTTA MONEY, AN' HE BORROWED A LOTTA MONEY--
"AN' HE WUZ LIVIN' WITH... IT WUZ GILLY OR HILDY ATTA TIME, IT WUZN'T JOAN, AN' AFTER A WHILE SHE FOUN' OUT WHY HE WUZN'T PAYIN' IT BACK:
MMH--!
MM-HMM-HMMM...

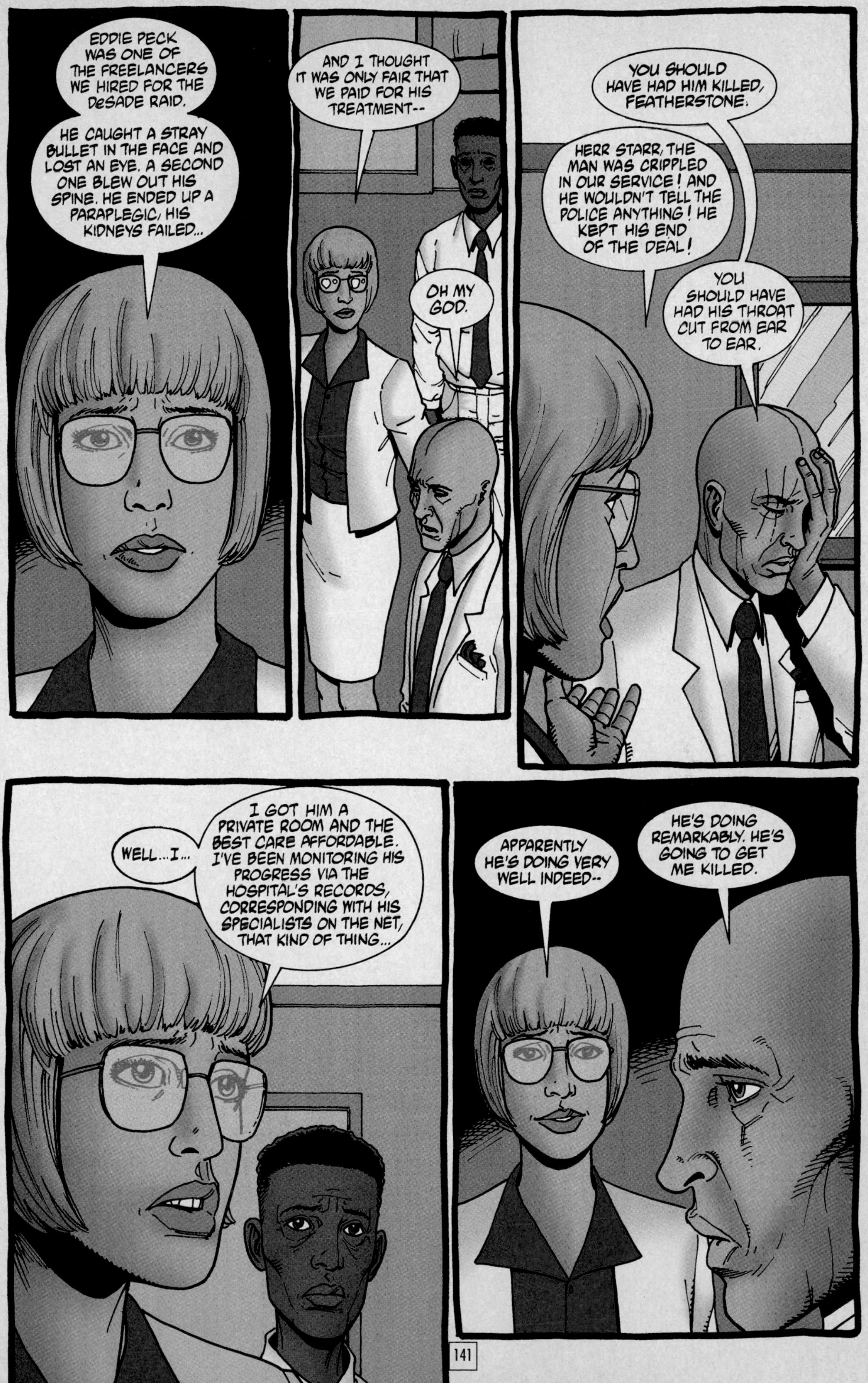
EDDIE PECK WAS ONE OF THE FREELANCERS WE HIRED FOR THE DeSADE RAID.
HE CAUGHT A STRAY BULLET IN THE FACE AND LOST AN EYE. A SECOND ONE BLEW OUT HIS SPINE. HE ENDED UP A PARAPLEGIC, HIS KIDNEYS FAILED...
AND I THOUGHT IT WAS ONLY FAIR THAT WE PAID FOR HIS TREATMENT--
OH MY GOD.
YOU SHOULD HAVE HAD HIM KILLED, FEATHERSTONE.
HERR STARR, THE MAN WAS CRIPPLED IN OUR SERVICE! AND HE WOULDN'T TELL THE POLICE ANYTHING! HE KEPT HIS END OF THE DEAL!
YOU SHOULD HAVE HAD HIS THROAT CUT FROM EAR TO EAR.
WELL... I...
I GOT HIM A PRIVATE ROOM AND THE BEST CARE AFFORDABLE. I'VE BEEN MONITORING HIS PROGRESS VIA THE HOSPITAL'S RECORDS, CORRESPONDING WITH HIS SPECIALISTS ON THE NET, THAT KIND OF THING...
APPARENTLY HE'S DOING VERY WELL INDEED--
HE'S DOING REMARKABLY. HE'S GOING TO GET ME KILLED.

ONCE EISENSTEIN GETS TO PECK HE'S GOING TO DISCOVER THAT I LED A TEAM OF ARMED THUGS, ALL UNAFFILIATED WITH THE GRAIL. INTO A PRIVATE RESIDENCE PACKED WITH SEVERAL HUNDRED WITNESSES.

LOOKING FOR SOMEONE CALLED JESSE CUSTER.

HE'S GOING TO FIND OUT THAT AMONG OTHER DISTINGUISHING FEATURES I RELATED TO SAID THUGS, CUSTER ENJOYS THE MIRACULOUS ABILITY TO SPEAK WITH THE WORD OF GOD: TO HAVE ALL HIS COMMANDS OBEYED WITHOUT QUESTION.

ARMED WITH THIS NUGGET, EISENSTEIN WILL RECALL THE DEATH OF OUR OWN *MIRACLE WORKER*-- THAT FUCKING CHIMP'S AFTERBIRTH THE GRAIL SOMEHOW RAISED AS A CHILD-- IN THE DESTRUCTION OF MASADA, THE CONFLA-GRATION THAT I ALONE SURVIVED.

HE WILL CONSIDER HOW THE CHILD WAS INTENDED TO BE REVEALED AS THE MESSIAH DURING *ARMAGEDDON*, THE WORLD-SHATTERING EVENT THAT I AM SUPPOSED TO BE ORCHESTRATING--

AND HE WILL THEN PUT TWO AND TWO TOGETHER AND COME UP WITH MY BALLS ON A STICK.

CUSTER... *MIGHT* HAVE DIED IN THE VALLEY...

CUSTER SURVIVED. WHO D'YOU THINK *SHERIFF JESSE CUSTER* WAS ON THAT NAMESEARCH YOU DID ON YOUR STUPID FUCKING COMPUTER?

CUSTER *SURVIVED*, PECK WILL *TALK*, EISENSTEIN WILL *KNOW*...

ANY OTHER ACTS OF KINDNESS YOU WANT TO TELL ME ABOUT, FEATHERSTONE? SET UP A RELIEF FUND FOR THE POOR IRRADIATED NAVAJO WITH MY FUCKING NAME ON IT, ANYTHING LIKE THAT?

NO?

GOOD.

WELL, I'M GOING TO SPEND SOME TIME WITH MY SCROTUM. WE MAY AS WELL ENJOY OUR LAST COUPLE OF HOURS TOGETHER.

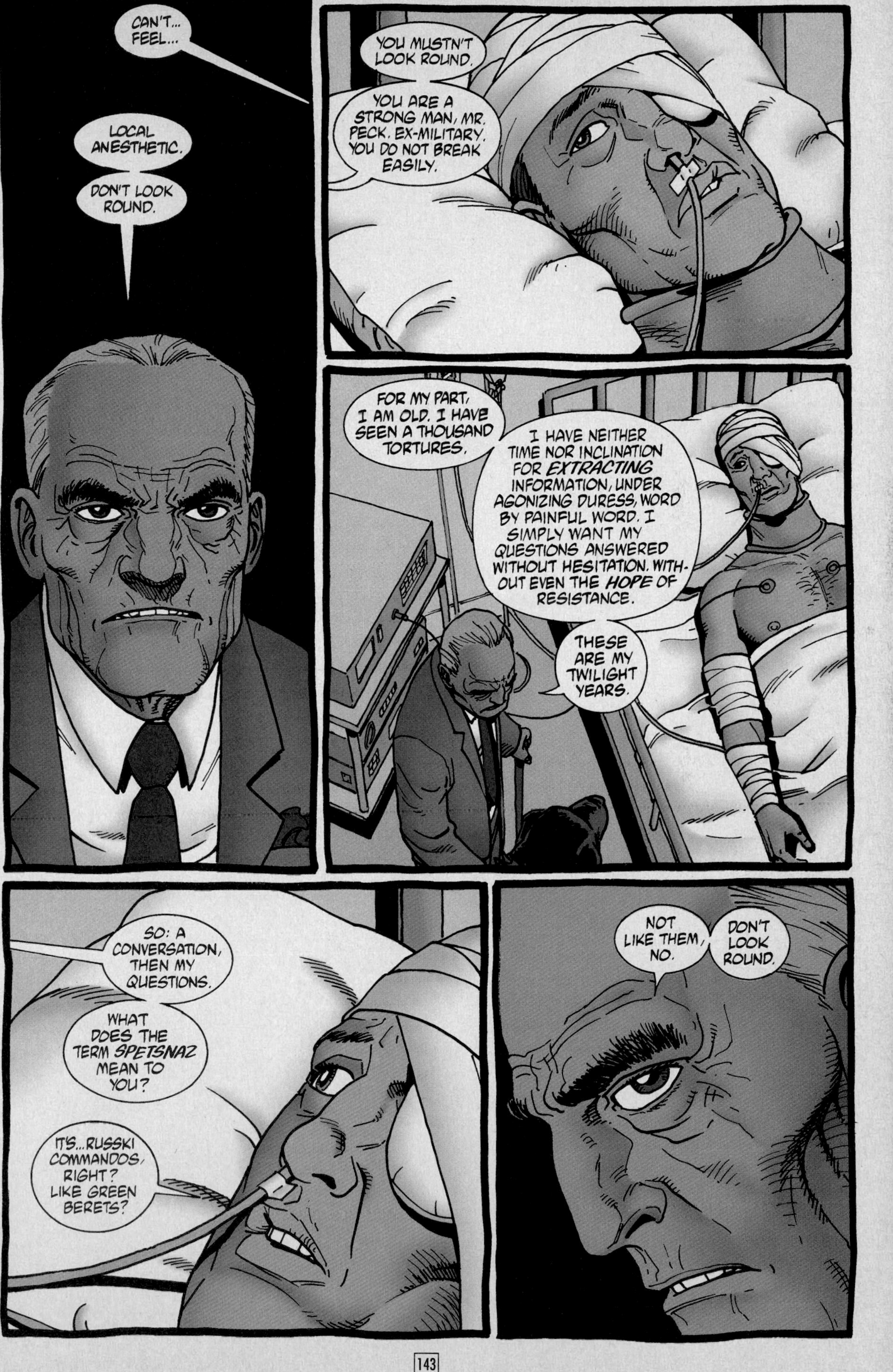
CAN'T... FEEL...
YOU MUSTN'T LOOK ROUND.
YOU ARE A STRONG MAN, MR. PECK. EX-MILITARY. YOU DO NOT BREAK EASILY.
LOCAL ANESTHETIC.
DON'T LOOK ROUND.
FOR MY PART, I AM OLD. I HAVE SEEN A THOUSAND TORTURES.
I HAVE NEITHER TIME NOR INCLINATION FOR EXTRACTING INFORMATION, UNDER AGONIZING DURESS, WORD BY PAINFUL WORD. I SIMPLY WANT MY QUESTIONS ANSWERED WITHOUT HESITATION. WITH-OUT EVEN THE HOPE OF RESISTANCE.
THESE ARE MY TWILIGHT YEARS.
SO: A CONVERSATION, THEN MY QUESTIONS.
WHAT DOES THE TERM SPETSNAZ MEAN TO YOU?
IT'S...RUSSKI COMMANDOS, RIGHT? LIKE GREEN BERETS?
NOT LIKE THEM, NO.
DON'T LOOK ROUND.

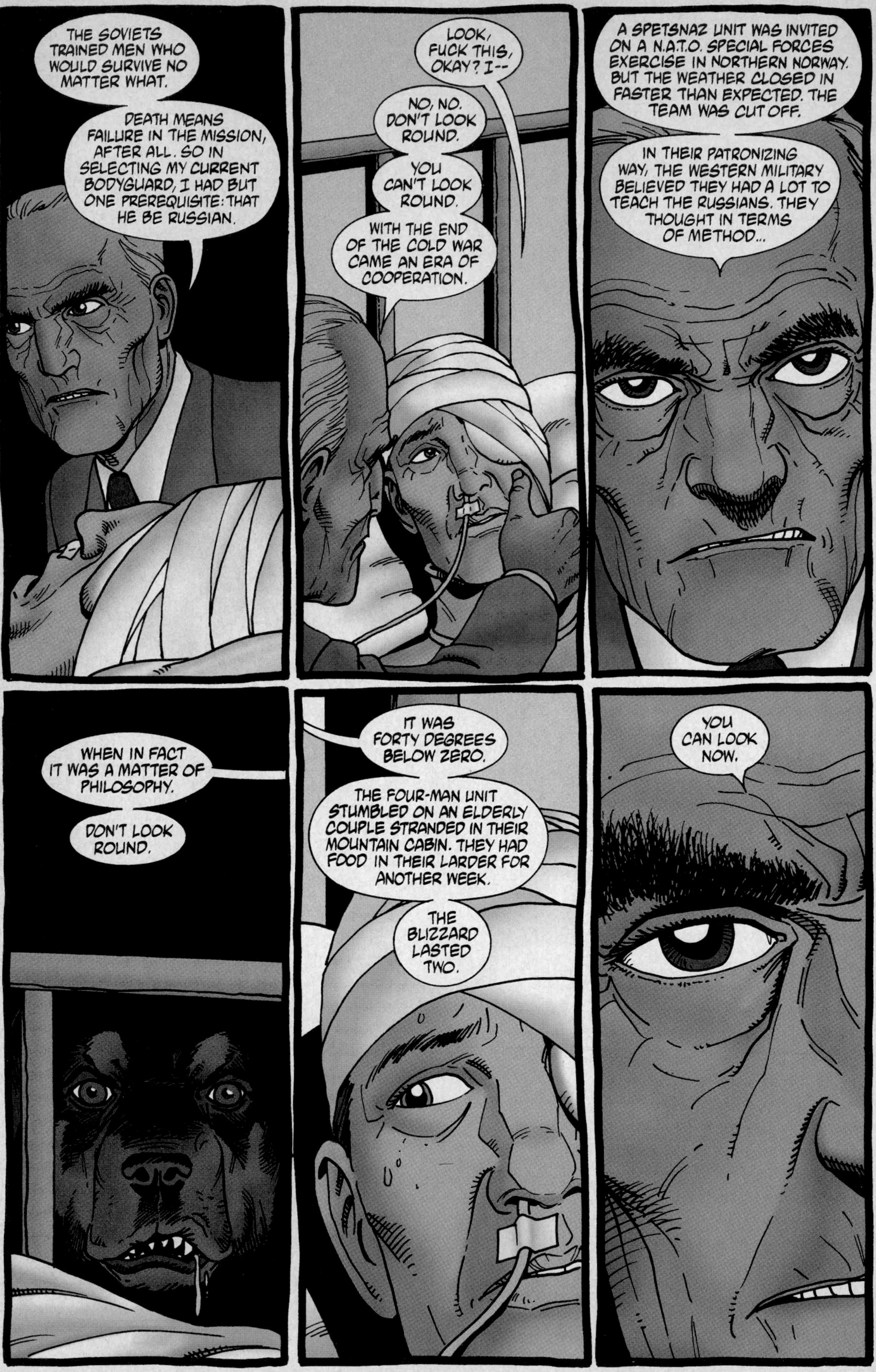
THE SOVIETS TRAINED MEN WHO WOULD SURVIVE NO MATTER WHAT.
DEATH MEANS FAILURE IN THE MISSION, AFTER ALL. SO IN SELECTING MY CURRENT BODYGUARD, I HAD BUT ONE PREREQUISITE: THAT HE BE RUSSIAN.
LOOK, FUCK THIS, OKAY? I--
NO, NO. DON'T LOOK ROUND.
YOU CAN'T LOOK ROUND.
WITH THE END OF THE COLD WAR CAME AN ERA OF COOPERATION.
A SPETSNAZ UNIT WAS INVITED ON A N.A.T.O. SPECIAL FORCES EXERCISE IN NORTHERN NORWAY. BUT THE WEATHER CLOSED IN FASTER THAN EXPECTED. THE TEAM WAS CUT OFF.
IN THEIR PATRONIZING WAY, THE WESTERN MILITARY BELIEVED THEY HAD A LOT TO TEACH THE RUSSIANS. THEY THOUGHT IN TERMS OF METHOD...
WHEN IN FACT IT WAS A MATTER OF PHILOSOPHY.
DON'T LOOK ROUND.
IT WAS FORTY DEGREES BELOW ZERO.
THE FOUR-MAN UNIT STUMBLED ON AN ELDERLY COUPLE STRANDED IN THEIR MOUNTAIN CABIN. THEY HAD FOOD IN THEIR LARDER FOR ANOTHER WEEK.
THE BLIZZARD LASTED TWO.
YOU CAN LOOK NOW.

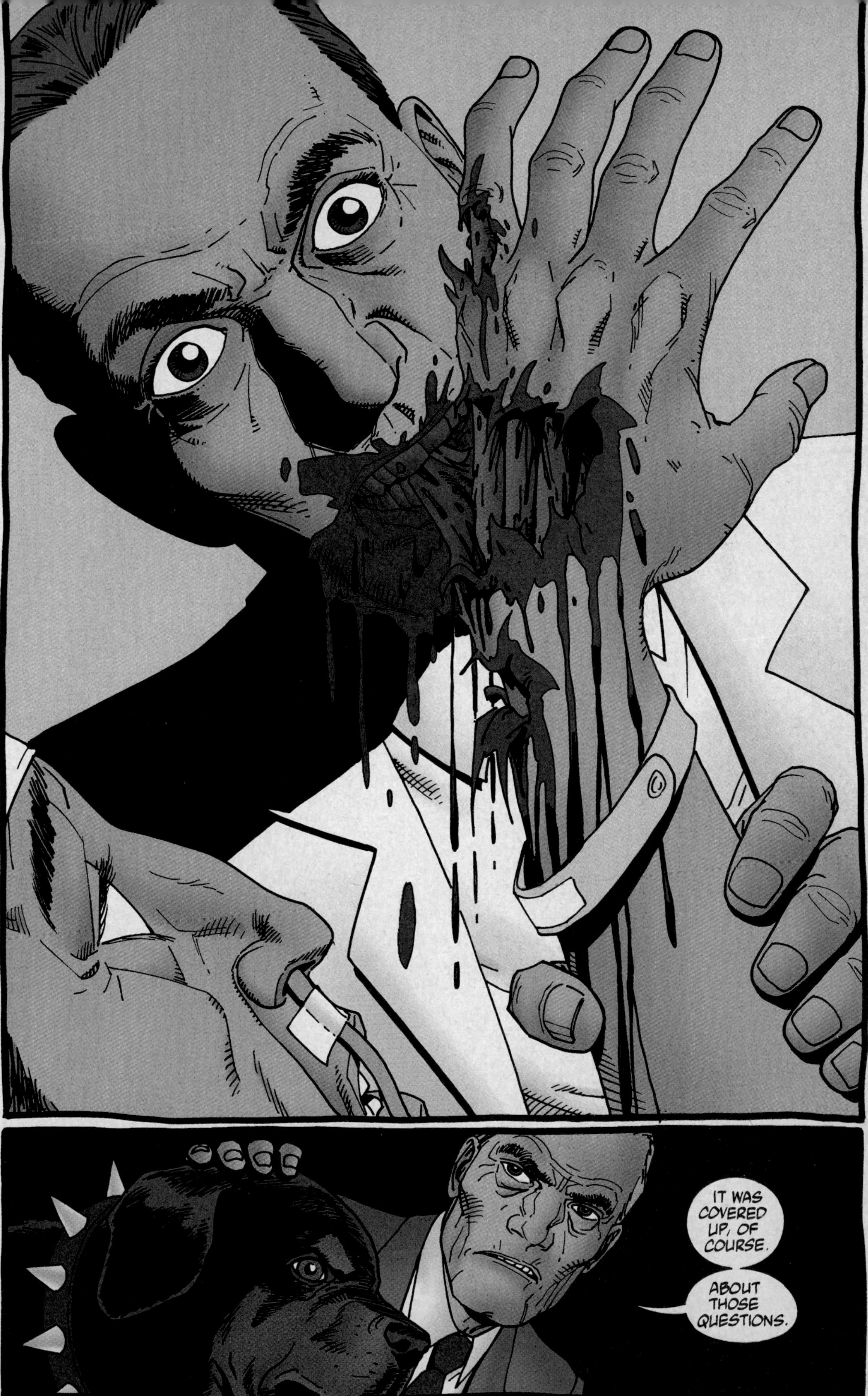
IT WAS COVERED UP, OF COURSE.
ABOUT THOSE QUESTIONS.

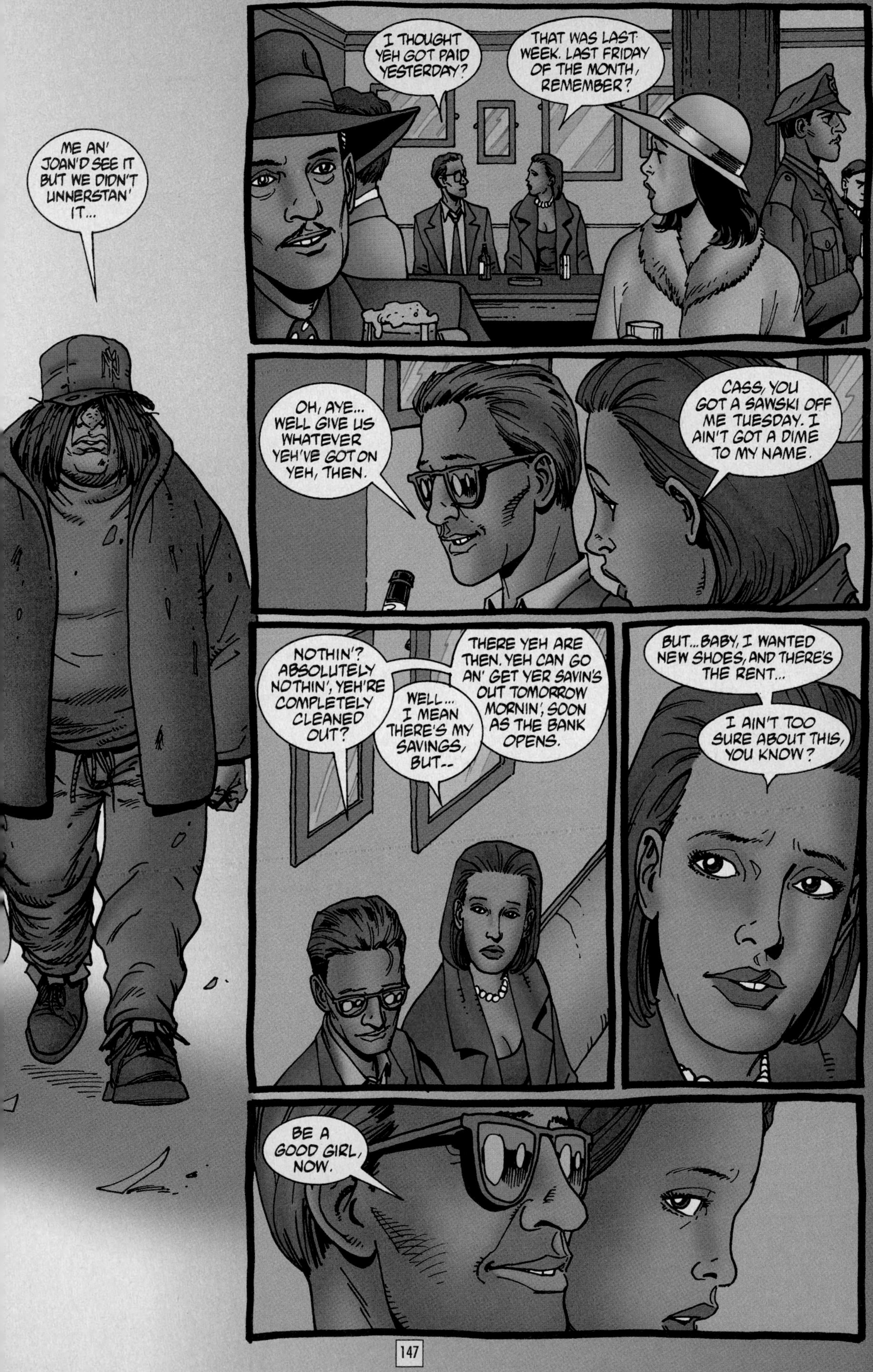

ME AN' JOAN'D SEE IT BUT WE DIDN'T UNNERSTAN' IT...
I THOUGHT YEH GOT PAID YESTERDAY?
THAT WAS LAST WEEK. LAST FRIDAY OF THE MONTH, REMEMBER?
OH, AYE... WELL GIVE US WHATEVER YEH'VE GOT ON YEH, THEN.
CASS, YOU GOT A SAWSKI OFF ME TUESDAY. I AIN'T GOT A DIME TO MY NAME.
NOTHIN'? ABSOLUTELY NOTHIN', YEH'RE COMPLETELY CLEANED OUT?
WELL... I MEAN THERE'S MY SAVINGS, BUT--
THERE YEH ARE THEN. YEH CAN GO AN' GET YER SAVIN'S OUT TOMORROW MORNIN', SOON AS THE BANK OPENS.
BUT...BABY, I WANTED NEW SHOES, AND THERE'S THE RENT...
I AIN'T TOO SURE ABOUT THIS, YOU KNOW?
BE A GOOD GIRL, NOW.

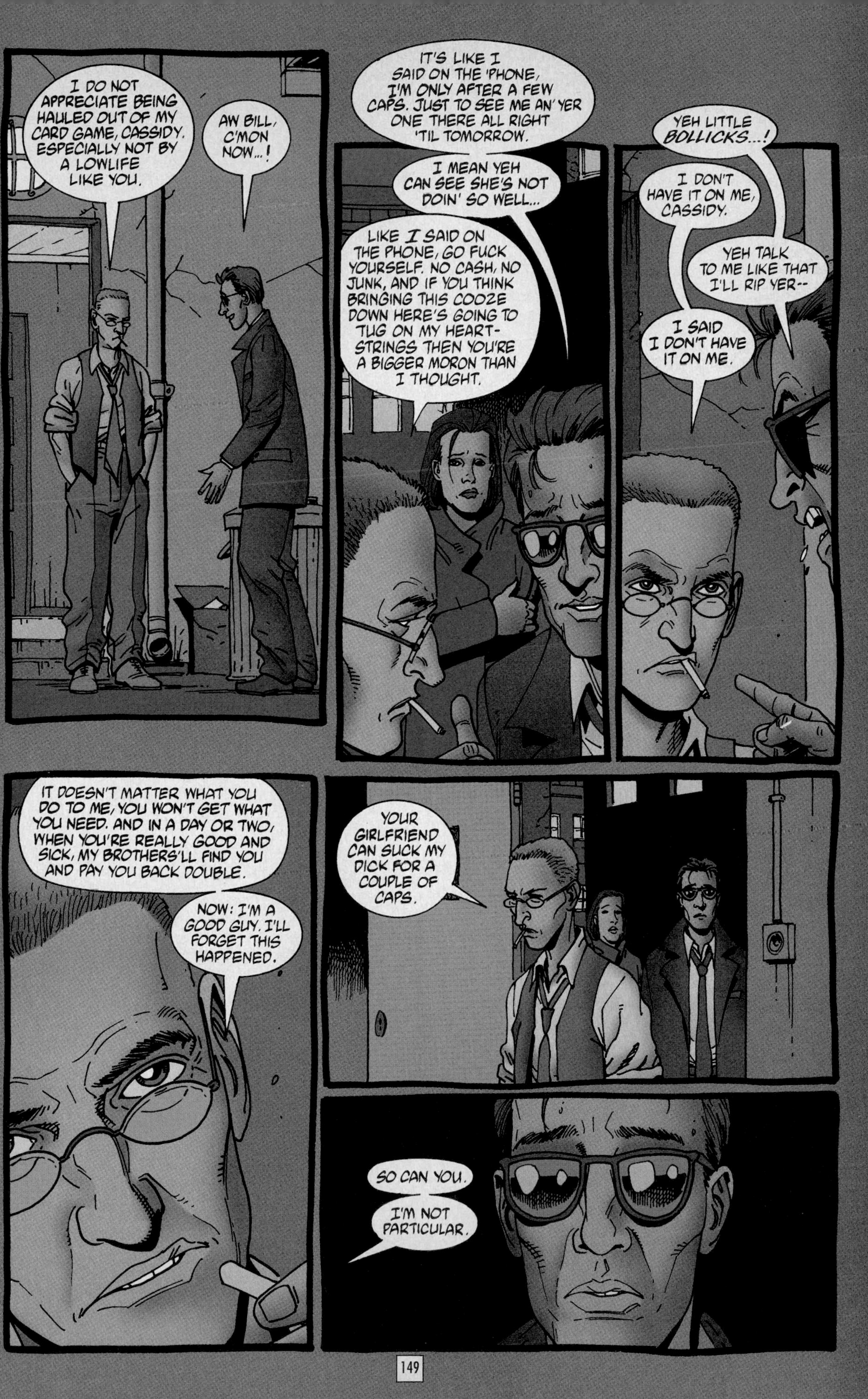
I DO NOT APPRECIATE BEING HAULED OUT OF MY CARD GAME, CASSIDY. ESPECIALLY NOT BY A LOWLIFE LIKE YOU.
AW BILL, C'MON NOW...!
IT'S LIKE I SAID ON THE 'PHONE, I'M ONLY AFTER A FEW CAPS. JUST TO SEE ME AN' YER ONE THERE ALL RIGHT 'TIL TOMORROW.
I MEAN YEH CAN SEE SHE'S NOT DOIN' SO WELL...
LIKE I SAID ON THE PHONE, GO FUCK YOURSELF. NO CASH, NO JUNK, AND IF YOU THINK BRINGING THIS COOZE DOWN HERE'S GOING TO TUG ON MY HEART-STRINGS THEN YOU'RE A BIGGER MORON THAN I THOUGHT.
YEH LITTLE BOLLICKS...!
I DON'T HAVE IT ON ME, CASSIDY.
YEH TALK TO ME LIKE THAT I'LL RIP YER--
I SAID I DON'T HAVE IT ON ME.
IT DOESN'T MATTER WHAT YOU DO TO ME, YOU WON'T GET WHAT YOU NEED. AND IN A DAY OR TWO, WHEN YOU'RE REALLY GOOD AND SICK, MY BROTHERS'LL FIND YOU AND PAY YOU BACK DOUBLE.
NOW: I'M A GOOD GUY. I'LL FORGET THIS HAPPENED.
YOUR GIRLFRIEND CAN SUCK MY DICK FOR A COUPLE OF CAPS.
SO CAN YOU.
I'M NOT PARTICULAR.

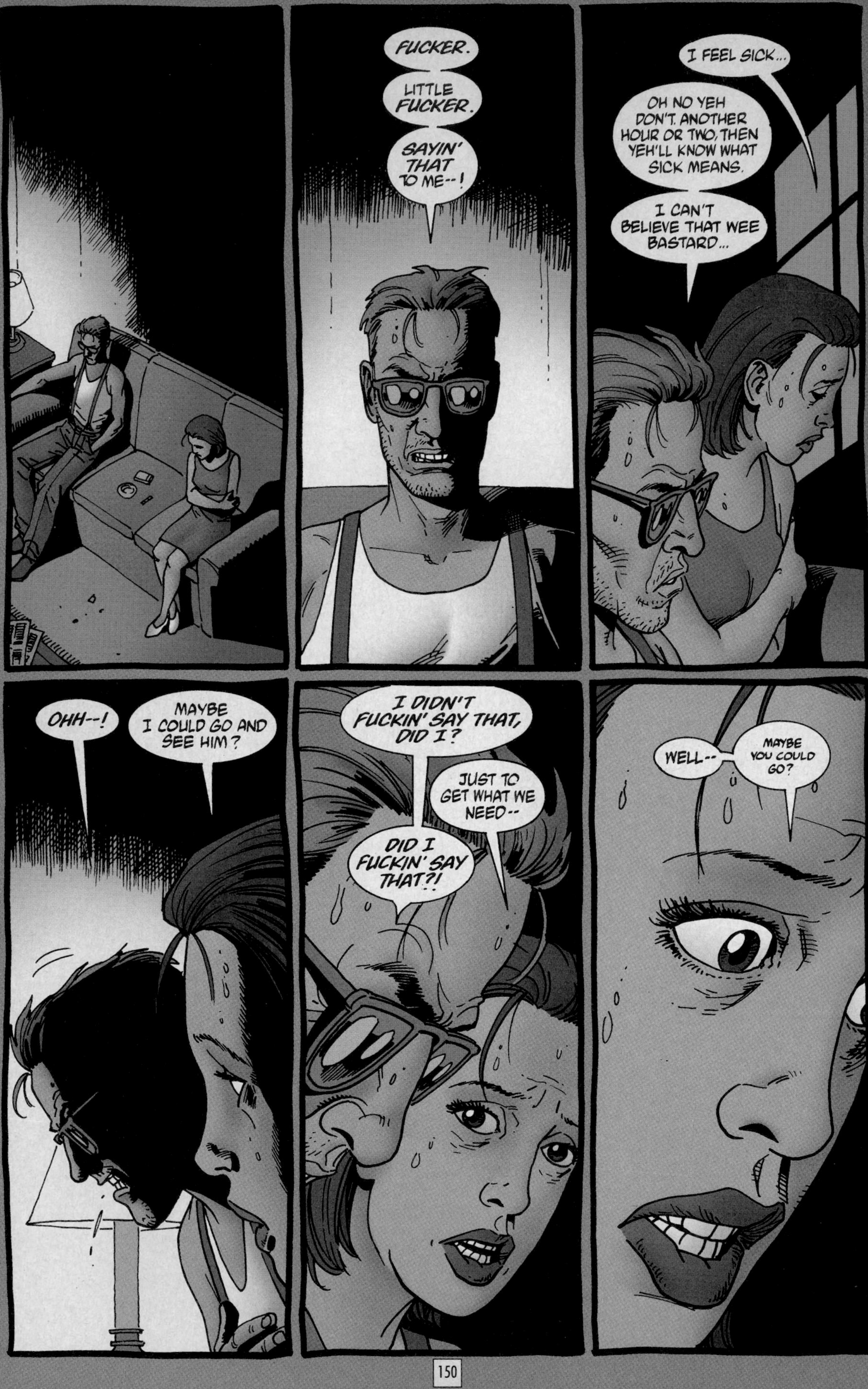
FUCKER.
LITTLE FUCKER.
SAYIN' THAT TO ME--!
I FEEL SICK...
OH NO YEH DON'T. ANOTHER HOUR OR TWO, THEN YEH'LL KNOW WHAT SICK MEANS.
I CAN'T BELIEVE THAT WEE BASTARD...
OHH--!
MAYBE I COULD GO AND SEE HIM?
I DIDN'T FUCKIN' SAY THAT, DID I?
JUST TO GET WHAT WE NEED--
DID I FUCKIN' SAY THAT?!
WELL--
MAYBE YOU COULD GO?

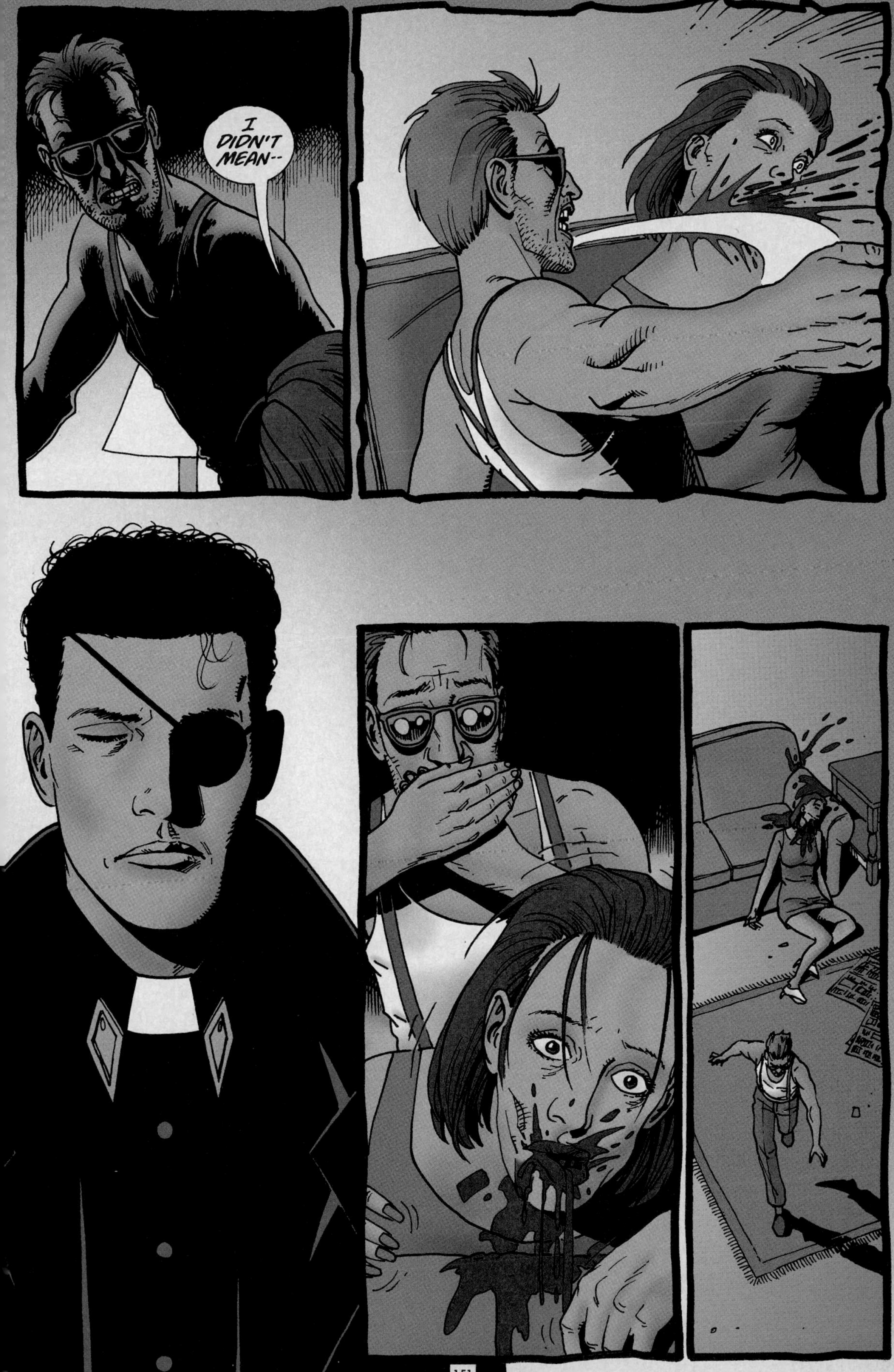
I DIDN'T MEAN--

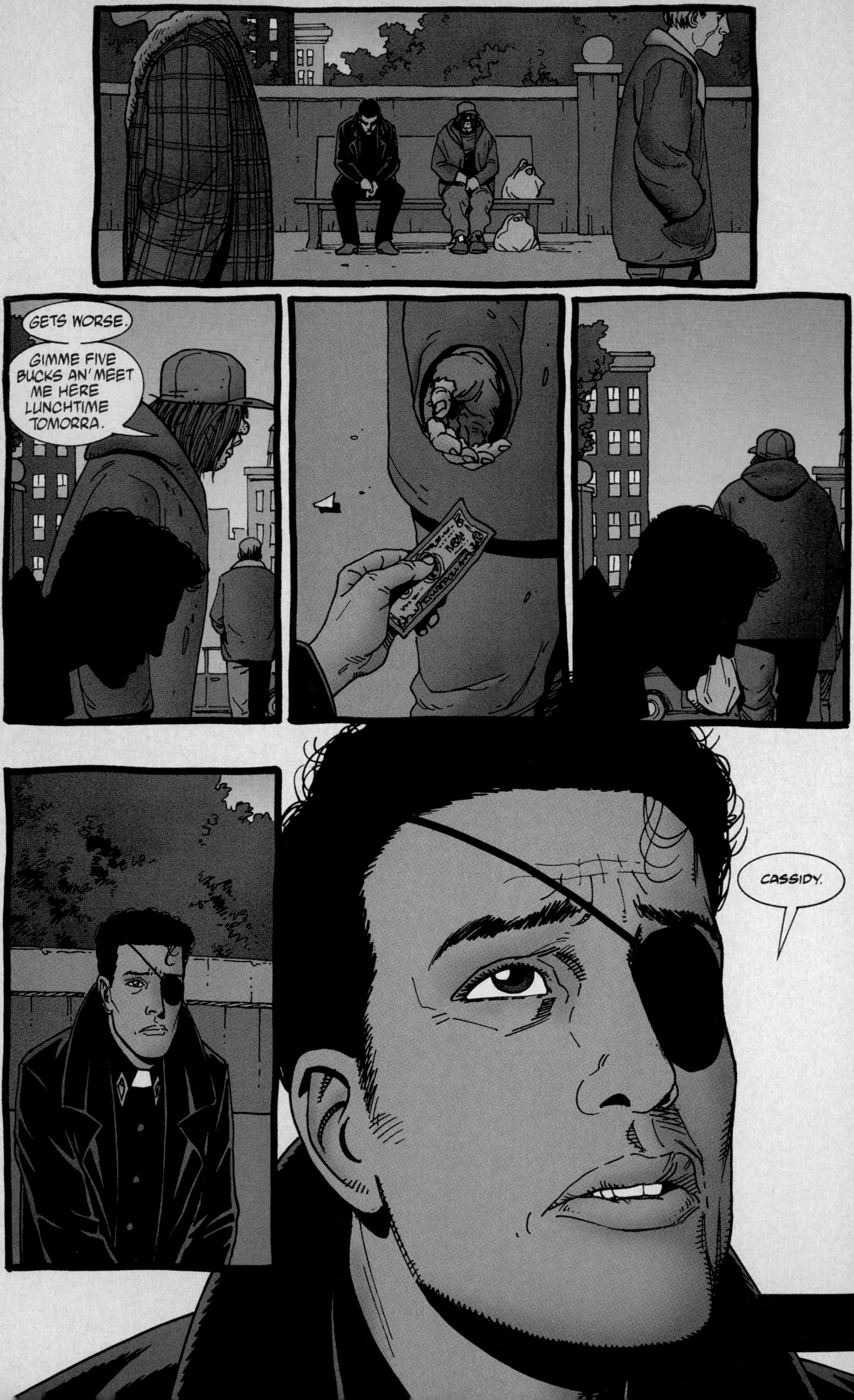

GETS WORSE.
GIMME FIVE BUCKS AN' MEET ME HERE LUNCHTIME TOMORRA.
CASSIDY.

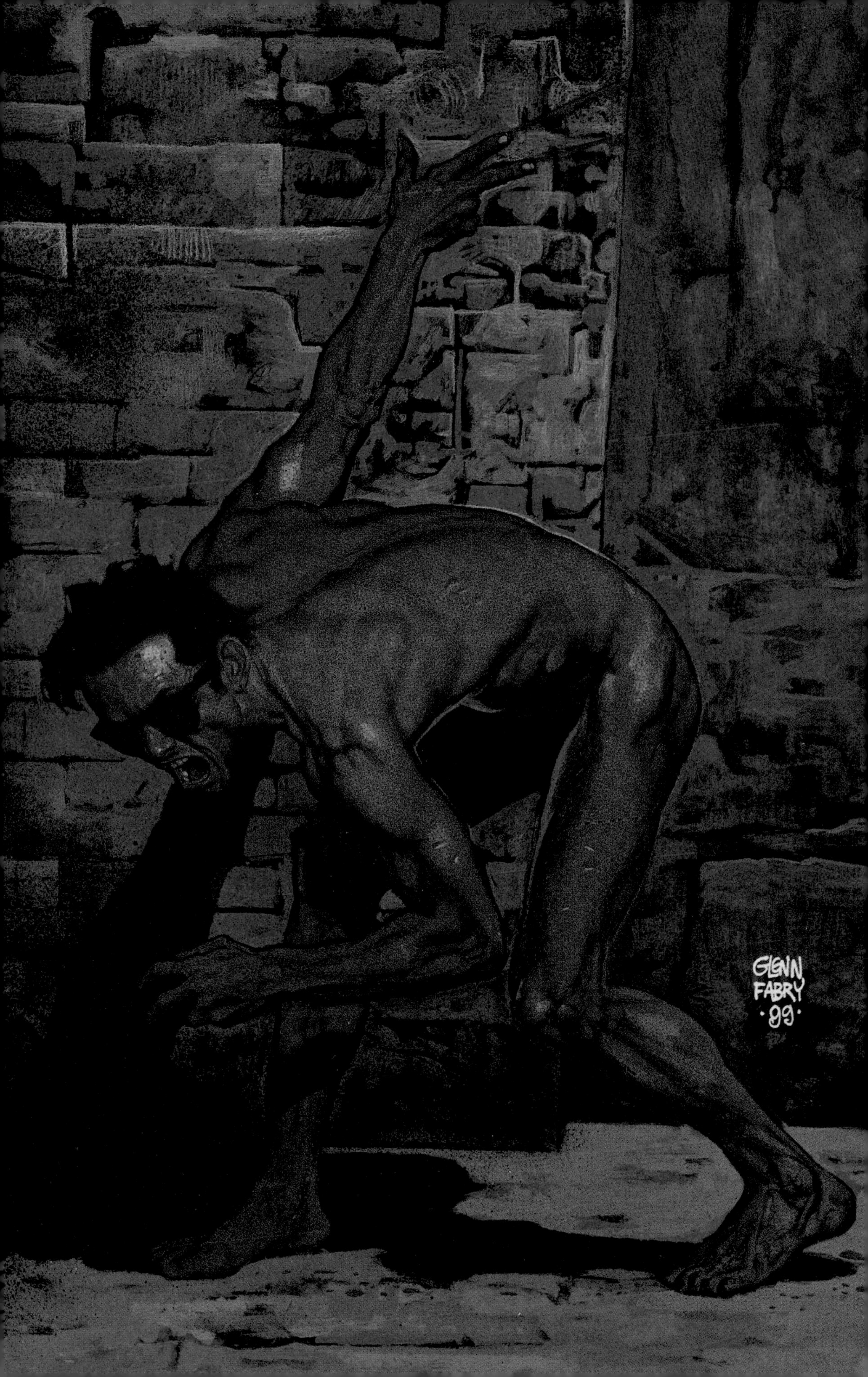
GLENN
FABRY
·99·

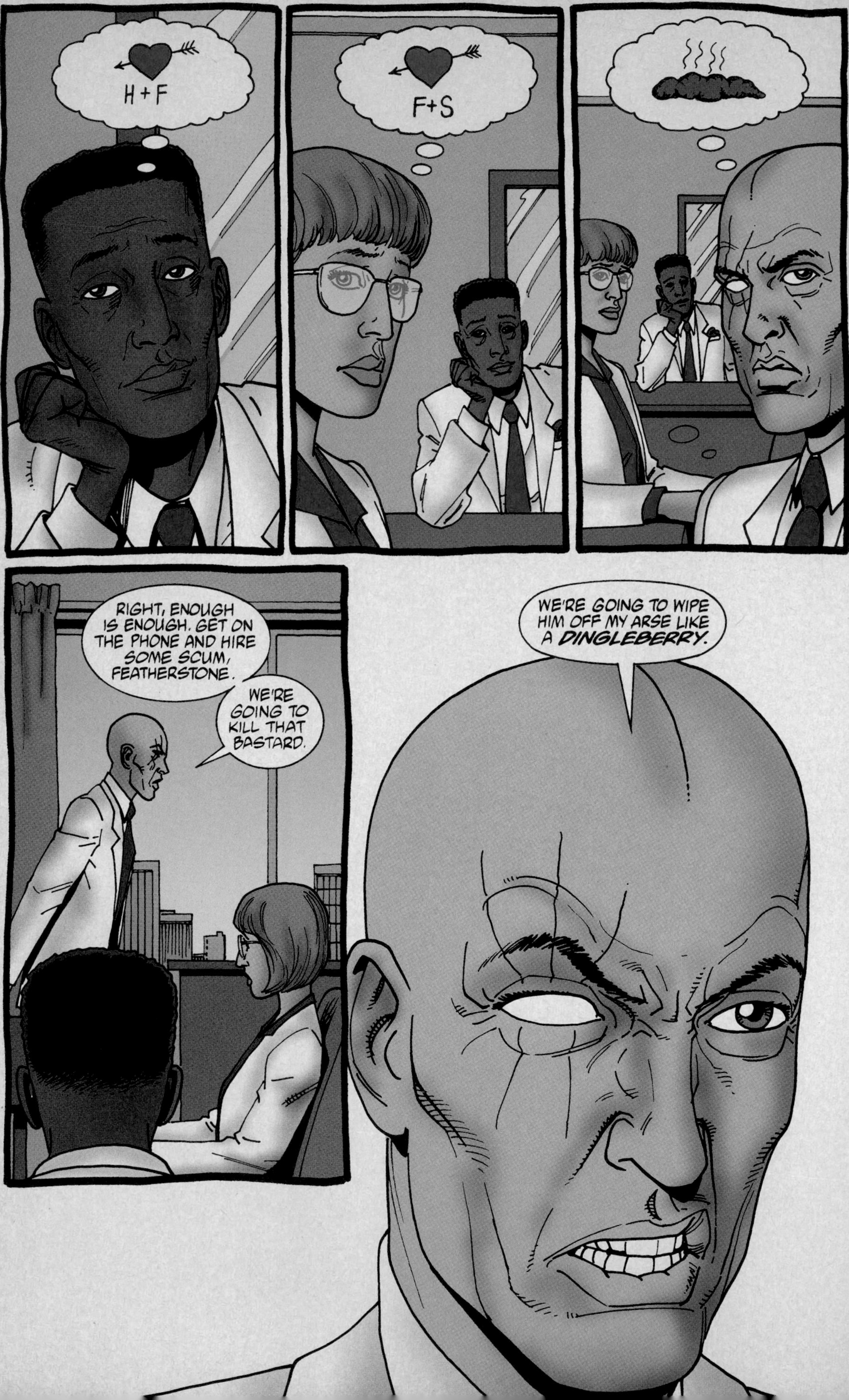
H + F
F+S
RIGHT, ENOUGH IS ENOUGH. GET ON THE PHONE AND HIRE SOME SCUM, FEATHERSTONE.
WE'RE GOING TO KILL THAT BASTARD.
WE'RE GOING TO WIPE HIM OFF MY ARSE LIKE A DINGLEBERRY.

OF THE IRISH
IN AMERICA

GARTH ENNIS - Writer   STEVE DILLON - Artist

PAMELA RAMBO - Colorist   CLEM ROBINS - Letterer   AXEL ALONSO - Editor

PREACHER created by GARTH ENNIS and STEVE DILLON

157

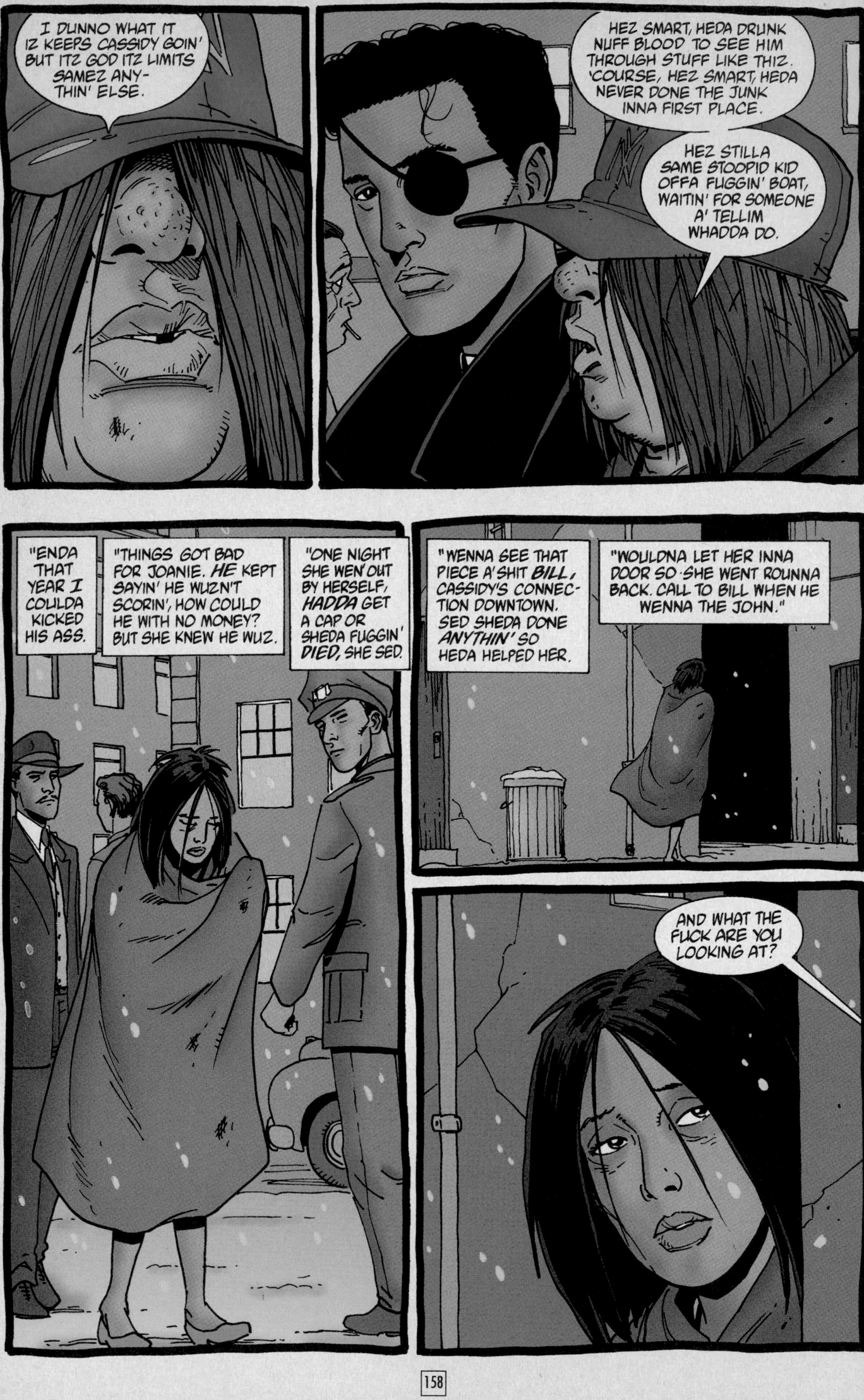

I DUNNO WHAT IT IZ KEEPS CASSIDY GOIN' BUT ITZ GOD ITZ LIMITS SAMEZ ANY-THIN' ELSE.
HEZ SMART, HEDA DRUNK NUFF BLOOD TO SEE HIM THROUGH STUFF LIKE THIZ. 'COURSE, HEZ SMART, HEDA NEVER DONE THE JUNK INNA FIRST PLACE.
HEZ STILLA SAME STOOPID KID OFFA FUGGIN' BOAT, WAITIN' FOR SOMEONE A' TELLIM WHADDA DO.
"ENDA THAT YEAR I COULDA KICKED HIS ASS.
"THINGS GOT BAD FOR JOANIE. HE KEPT SAYIN' HE WUZN'T SCORIN', HOW COULD HE WITH NO MONEY? BUT SHE KNEW HE WUZ.
"ONE NIGHT SHE WEN' OUT BY HERSELF, HADDA GET A CAP OR SHEDA FUGGIN' DIED, SHE SED.
"WENNA SEE THAT PIECE A' SHIT BILL, CASSIDY'S CONNECTION DOWNTOWN. SED SHEDA DONE ANYTHIN' SO HEDA HELPED HER.
"WOULDNA LET HER INNA DOOR SO SHE WENT ROUNNA BACK. CALL TO BILL WHEN HE WENNA THE JOHN."
AND WHAT THE FUCK ARE YOU LOOKING AT?

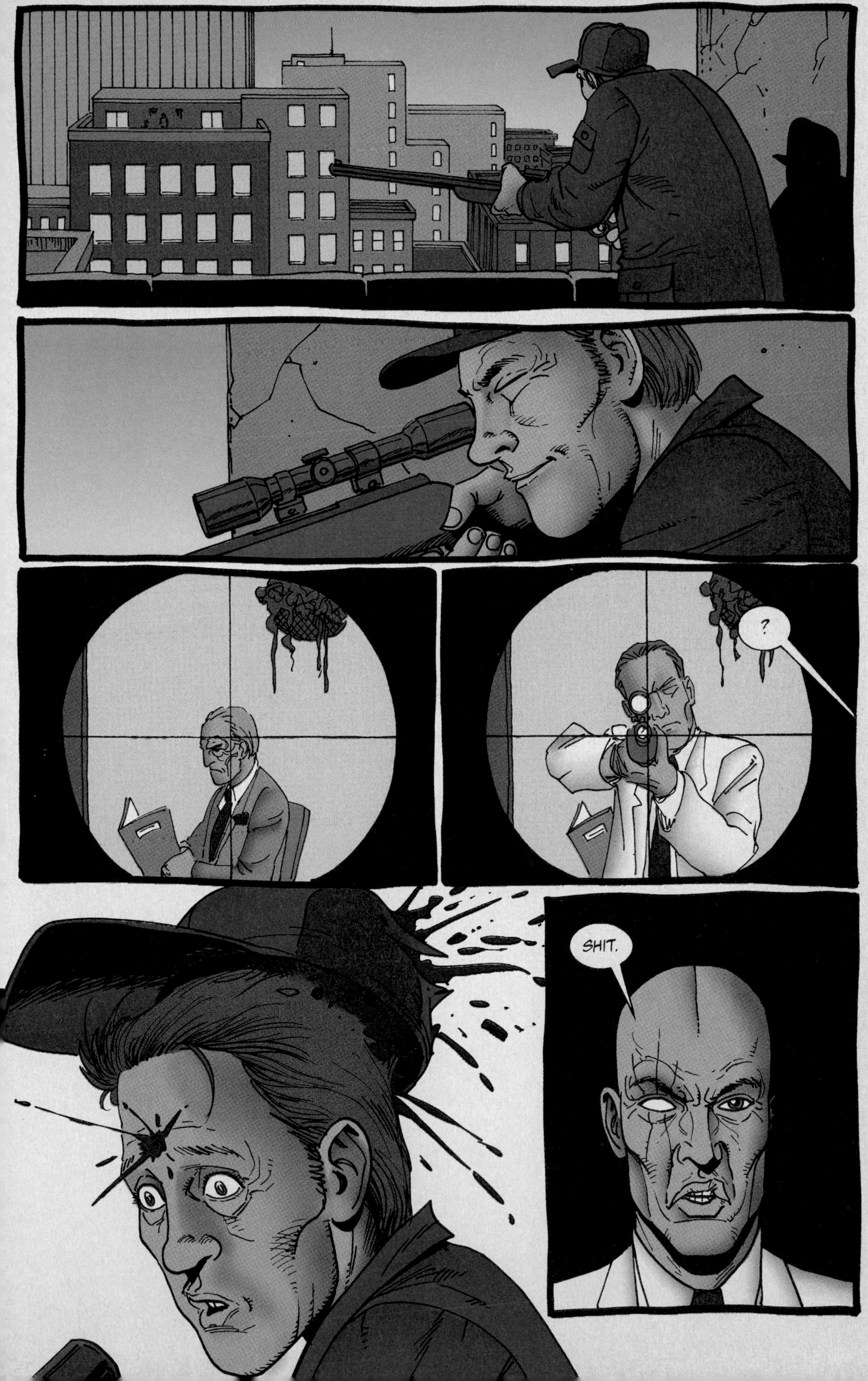
?
SHIT.

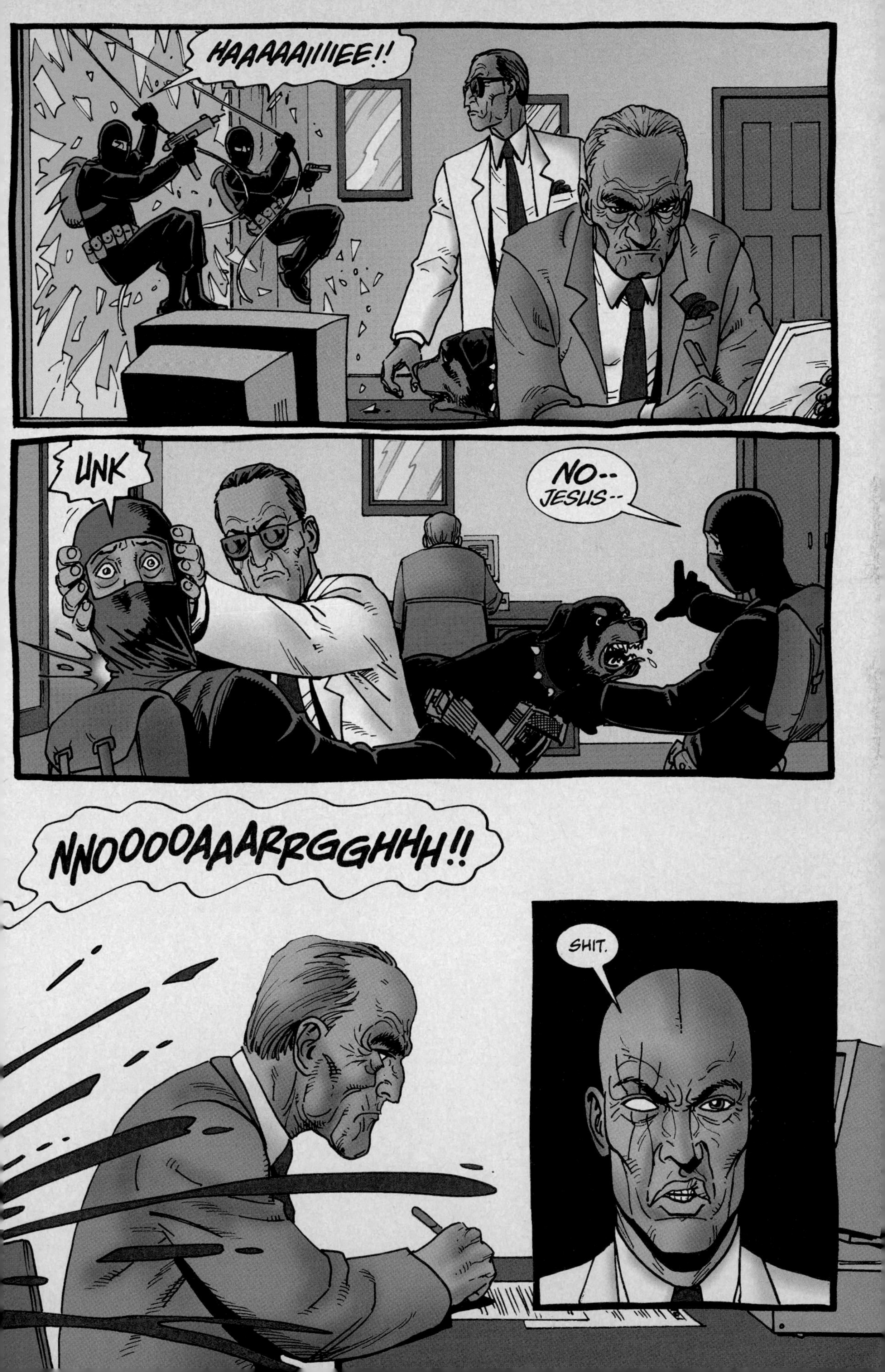
HAAAAAIIIIEE!!
UNK
NO--
JESUS--
NNOOOOAAARRGGHHH!!
SHIT.

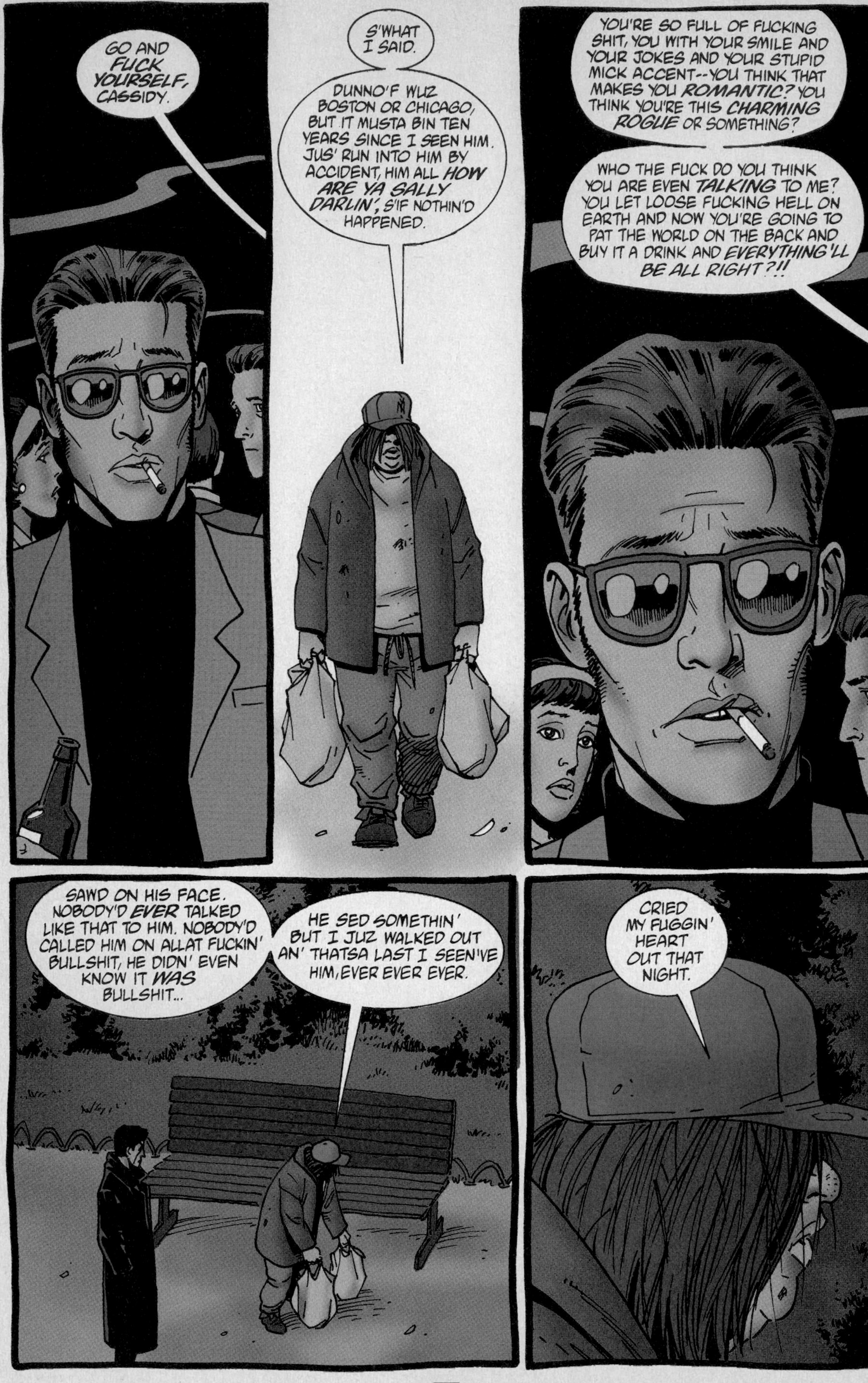
GO AND FUCK YOURSELF, CASSIDY.
S'WHAT I SAID.
DUNNO'F WUZ BOSTON OR CHICAGO, BUT IT MUSTA BIN TEN YEARS SINCE I SEEN HIM. JUS' RUN INTO HIM BY ACCIDENT, HIM ALL HOW ARE YA SALLY DARLIN', S'IF NOTHIN'D HAPPENED.
YOU'RE SO FULL OF FUCKING SHIT, YOU WITH YOUR SMILE AND YOUR JOKES AND YOUR STUPID MICK ACCENT--YOU THINK THAT MAKES YOU ROMANTIC? YOU THINK YOU'RE THIS CHARMING ROGUE OR SOMETHING?
WHO THE FUCK DO YOU THINK YOU ARE EVEN TALKING TO ME? YOU LET LOOSE FUCKING HELL ON EARTH AND NOW YOU'RE GOING TO PAT THE WORLD ON THE BACK AND BUY IT A DRINK AND EVERYTHING'LL BE ALL RIGHT?!!
SAWD ON HIS FACE. NOBODY'D EVER TALKED LIKE THAT TO HIM. NOBODY'D CALLED HIM ON ALLAT FUCKIN' BULLSHIT, HE DIDN' EVEN KNOW IT WAS BULLSHIT...
HE SED SOMETHIN' BUT I JUZ WALKED OUT AN' THATSA LAST I SEEN'VE HIM, EVER EVER EVER.
CRIED MY FUGGIN' HEART OUT THAT NIGHT.

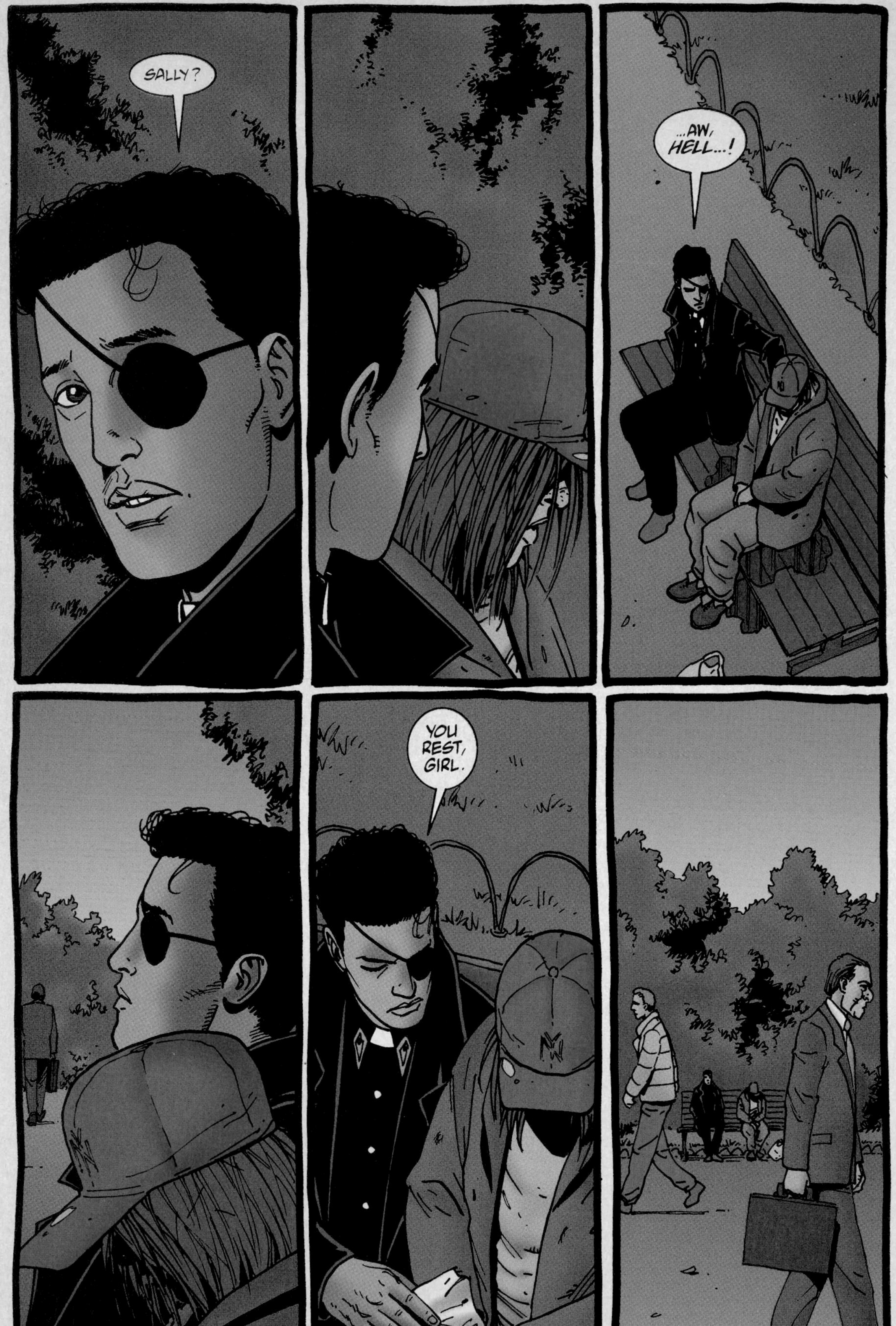
SALLY?
...AW, HELL...!
YOU REST, GIRL.

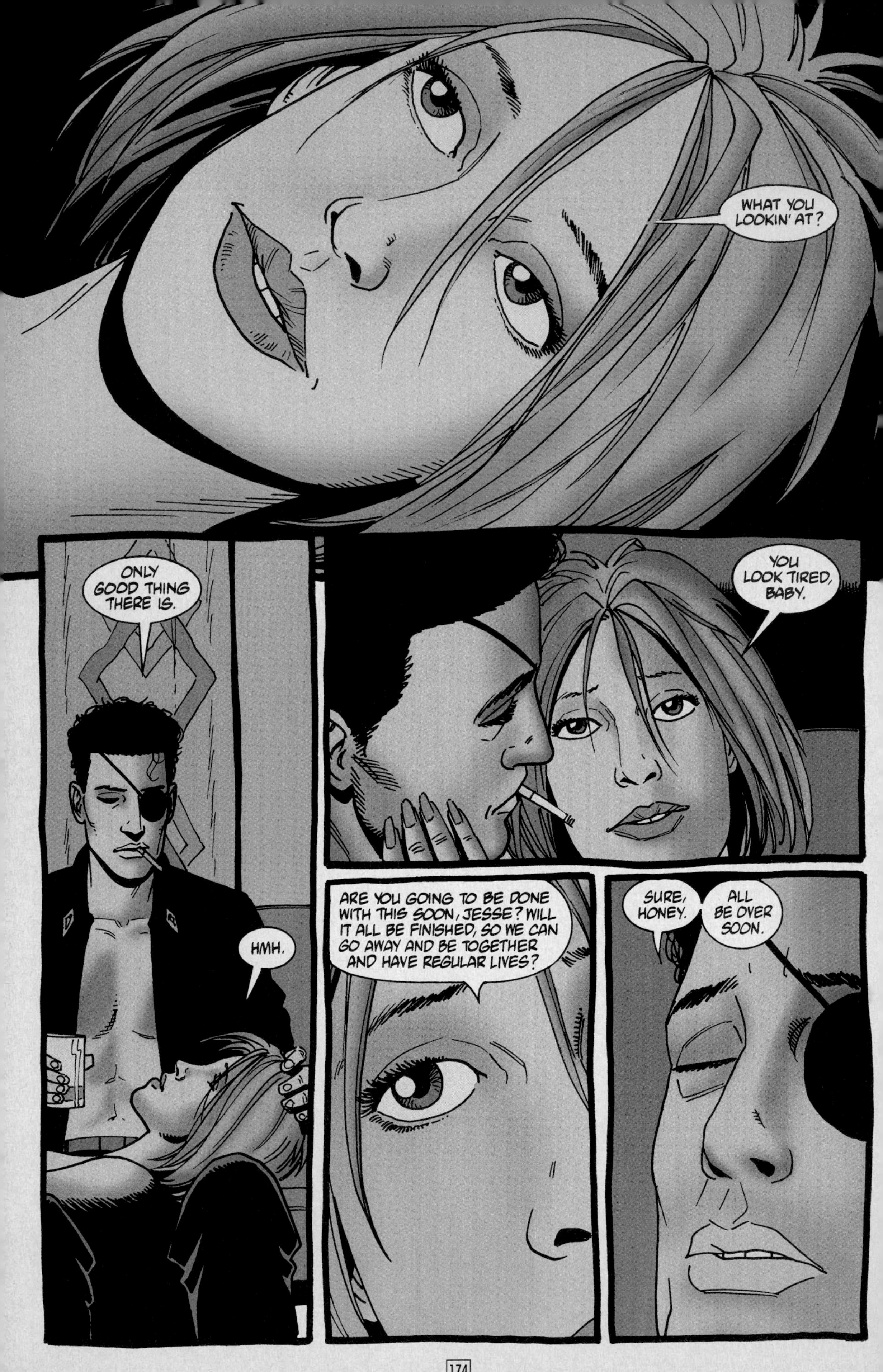
WHAT YOU LOOKIN' AT?
ONLY GOOD THING THERE IS.
YOU LOOK TIRED, BABY.
HMH.
ARE YOU GOING TO BE DONE WITH THIS SOON, JESSE? WILL IT ALL BE FINISHED, SO WE CAN GO AWAY AND BE TOGETHER AND HAVE REGULAR LIVES?
SURE, HONEY.
ALL BE OVER SOON.

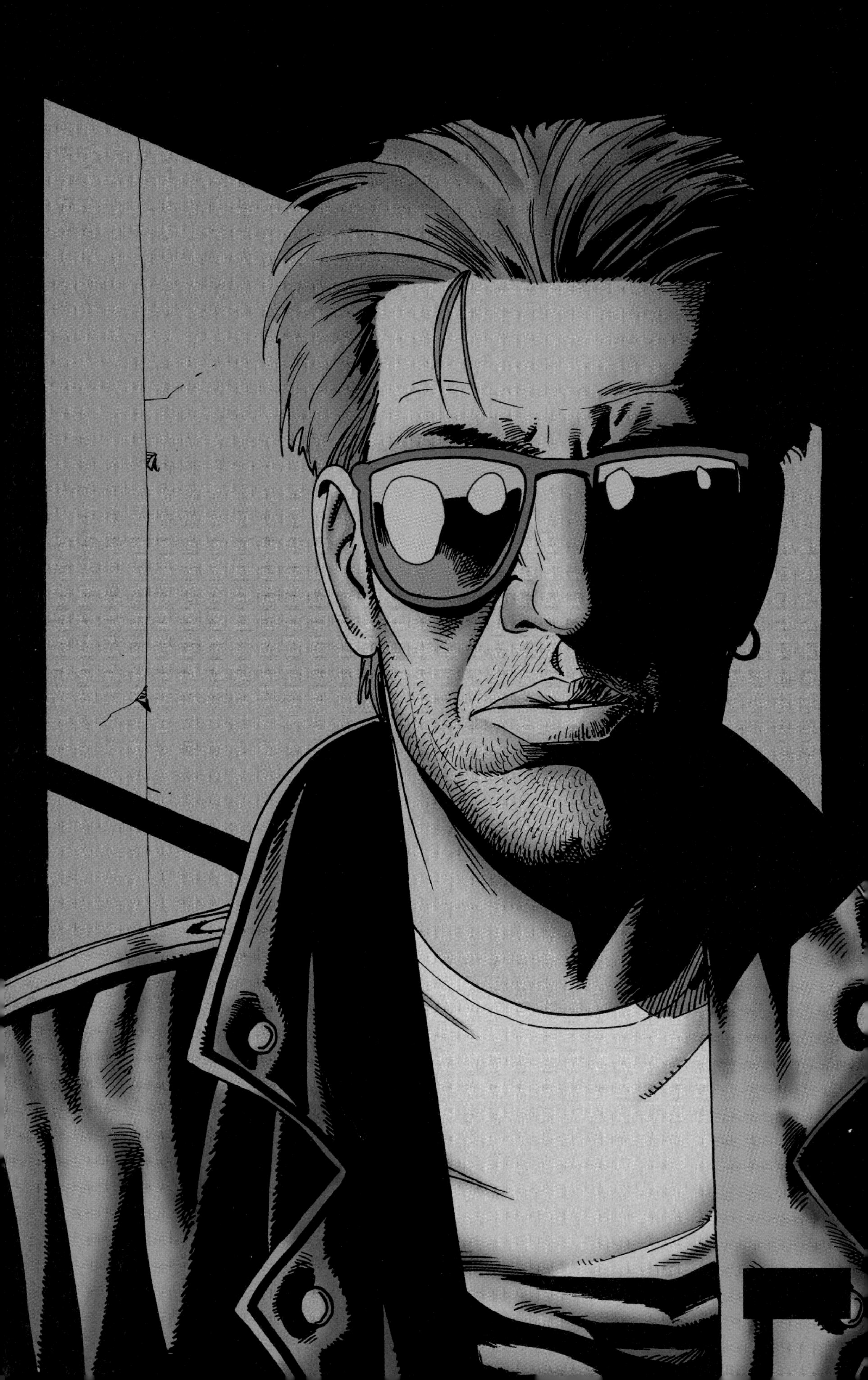

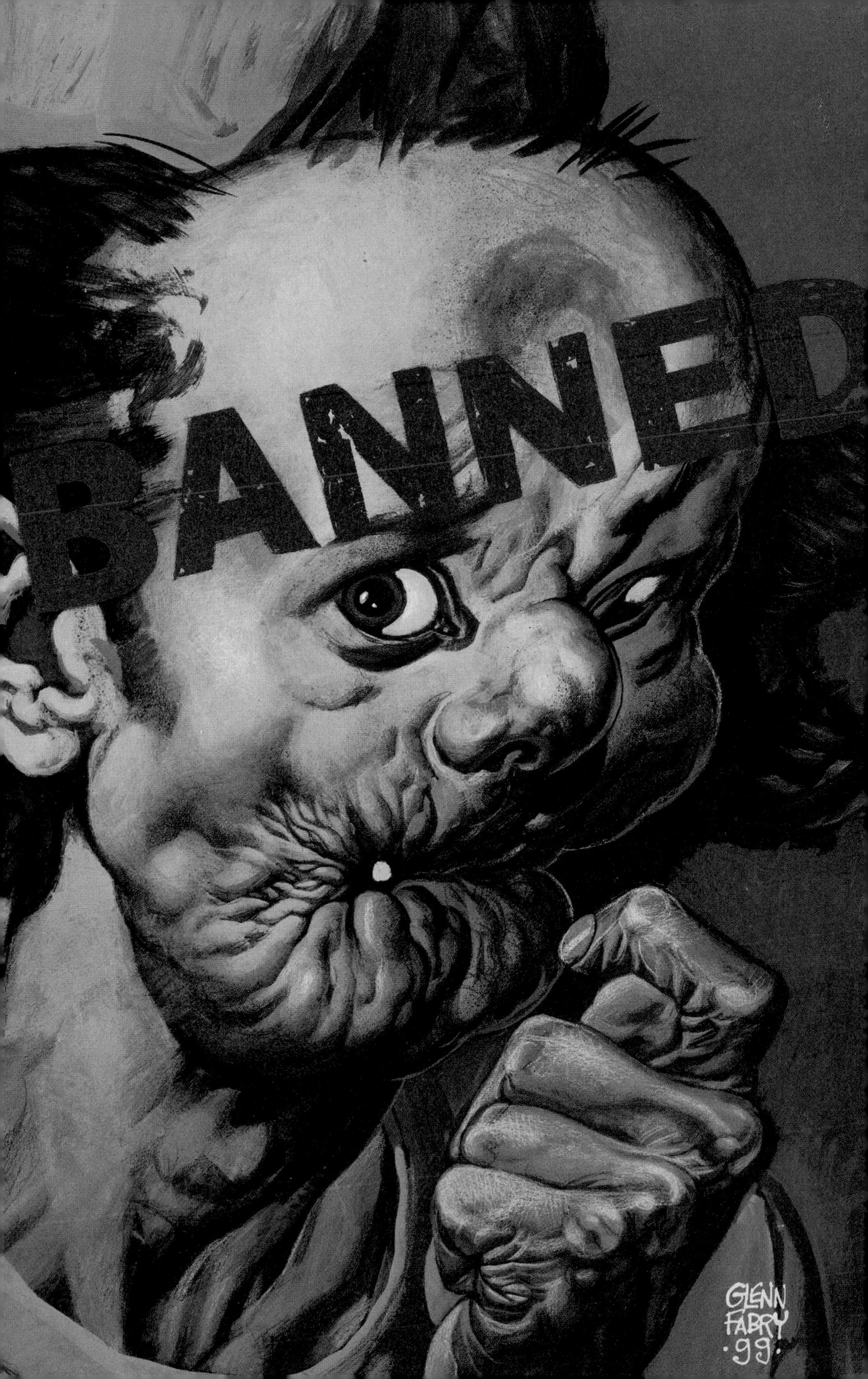
BANNED
GLENN FABRY ·99·

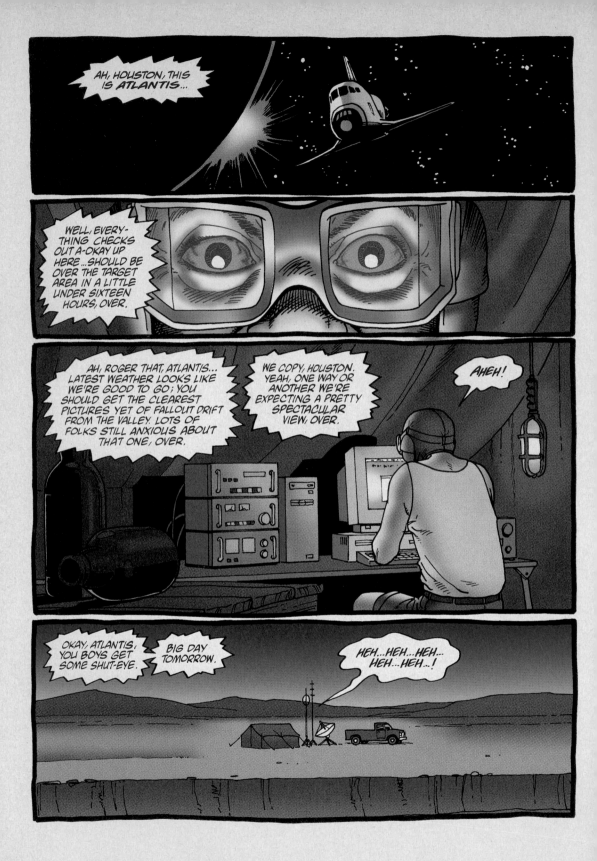

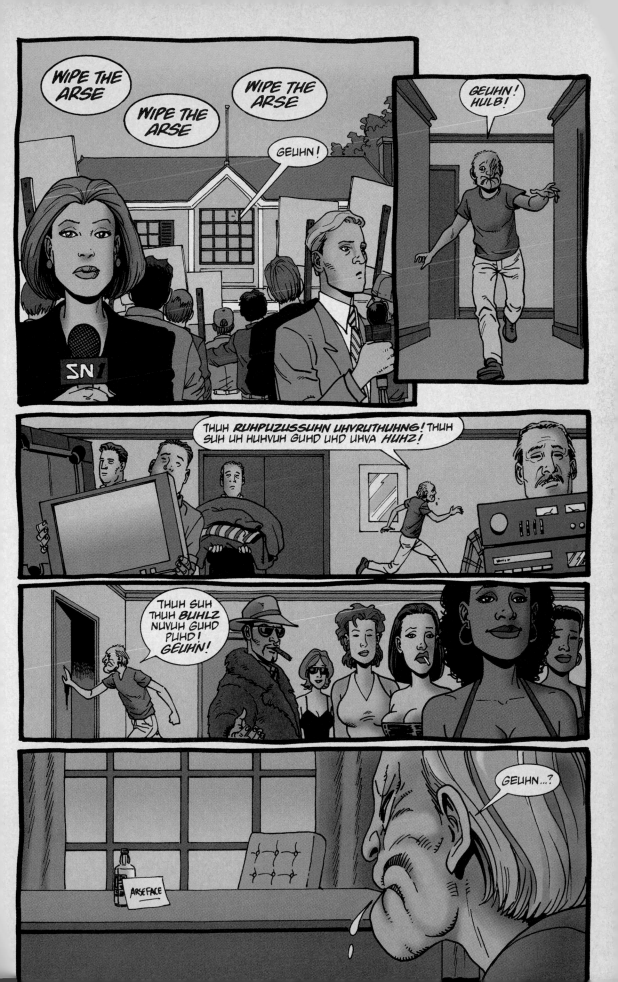

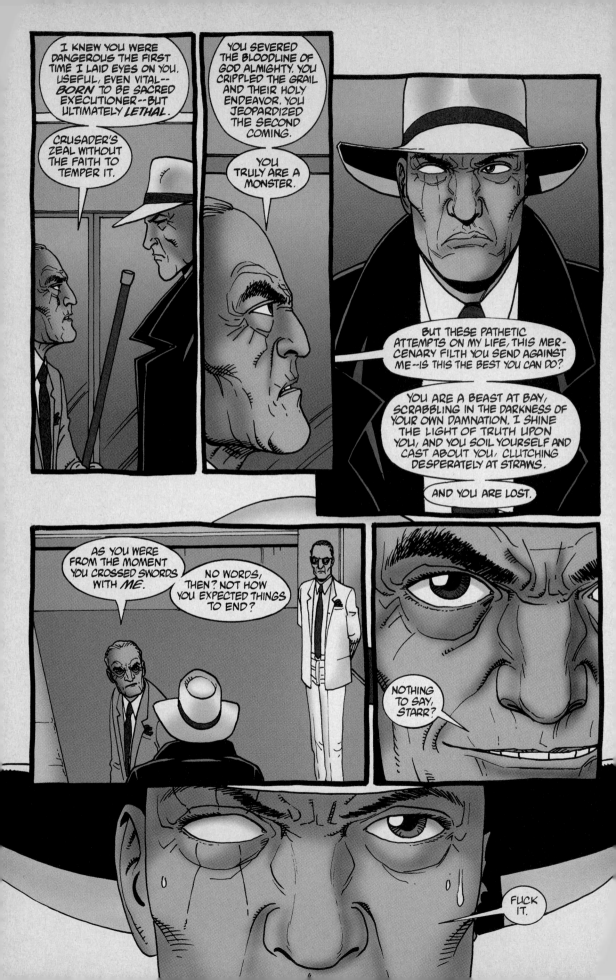

I KNEW YOU WERE DANGEROUS THE FIRST TIME I LAID EYES ON YOU. USEFUL, EVEN VITAL-- *BORN* TO BE SACRED EXECUTIONER--BUT ULTIMATELY *LETHAL*.

CRUSADER'S ZEAL WITHOUT THE FAITH TO TEMPER IT.

YOU SEVERED THE BLOODLINE OF GOD ALMIGHTY. YOU CRIPPLED THE GRAIL AND THEIR HOLY ENDEAVOR. YOU JEOPARDIZED THE SECOND COMING.

YOU TRULY ARE A MONSTER.

BUT THESE PATHETIC ATTEMPTS ON MY LIFE, THIS MERCENARY FILTH YOU SEND AGAINST ME--IS THIS THE BEST YOU CAN DO?

YOU ARE A BEAST AT BAY, SCRABBLING IN THE DARKNESS OF YOUR OWN DAMNATION. I SHINE THE LIGHT OF TRUTH UPON YOU, AND YOU SOIL YOURSELF AND CAST ABOUT YOU, CLUTCHING DESPERATELY AT STRAWS.

AND YOU ARE LOST.

AS YOU WERE FROM THE MOMENT YOU CROSSED SWORDS WITH *ME*.

NO WORDS, THEN? NOT HOW YOU EXPECTED THINGS TO END?

NOTHING TO SAY, STARR?

FUCK IT.

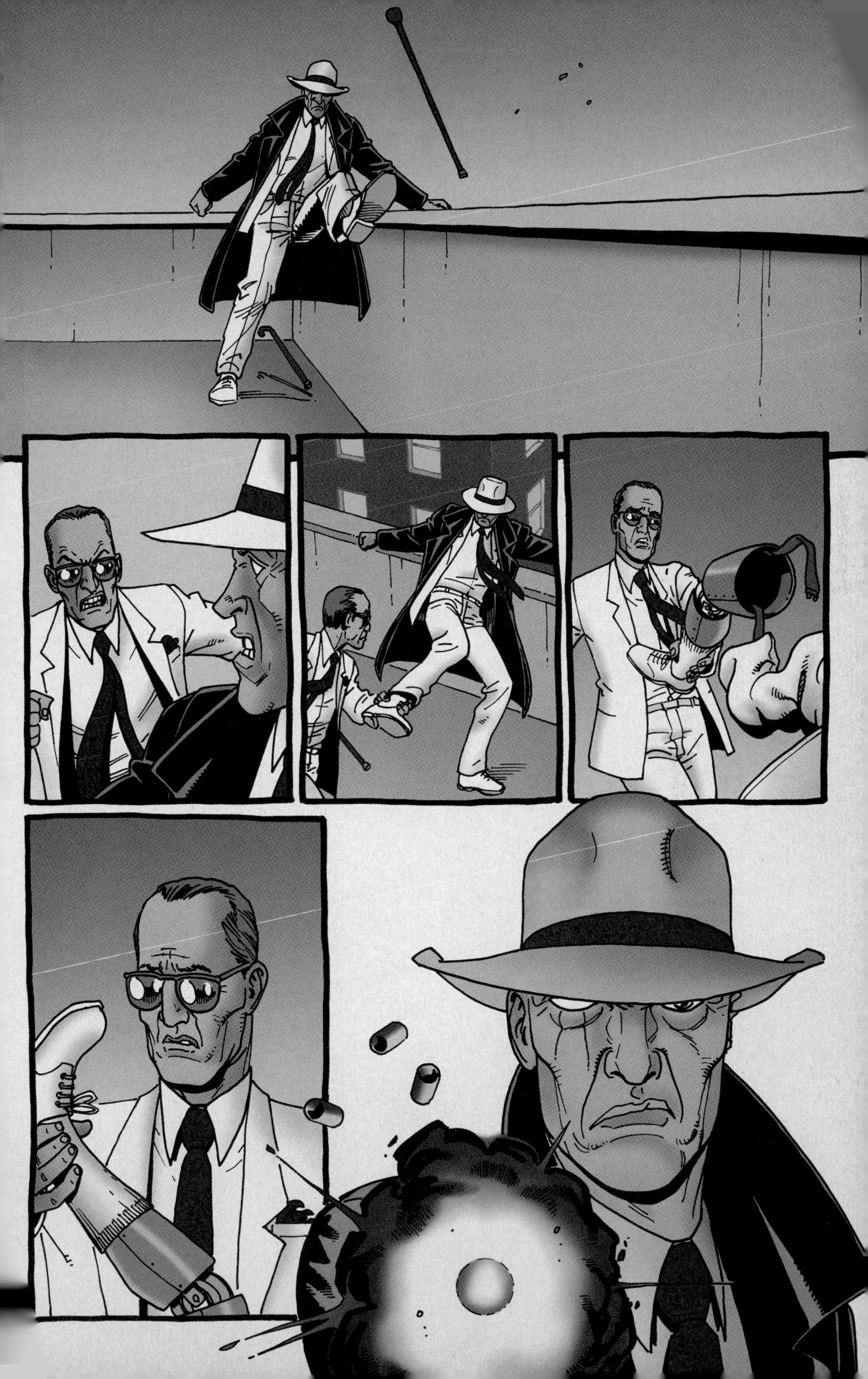

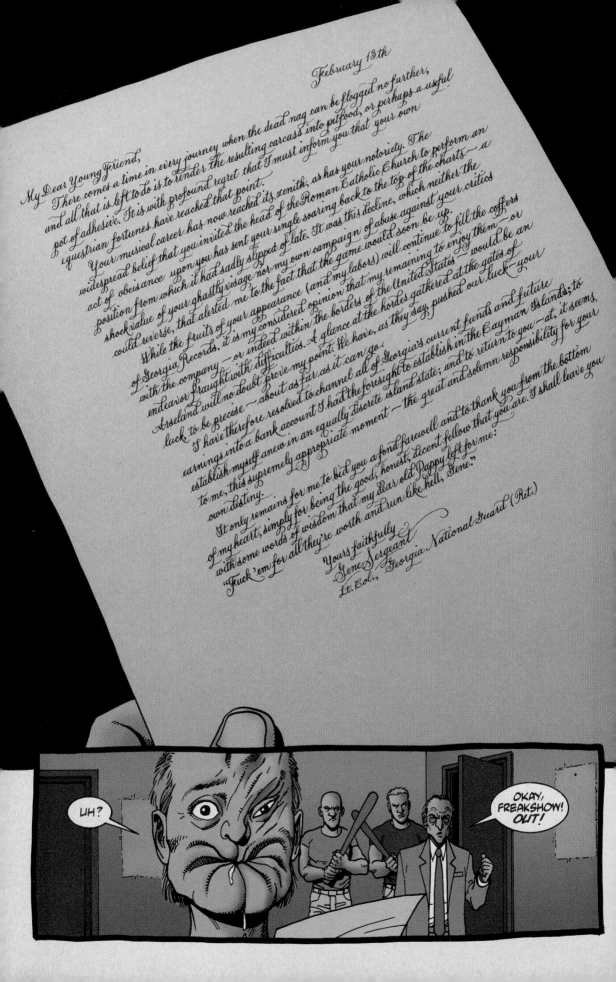

February 13th

My Dear Young Friend,

There comes a time in every journey when the dead nag can be flogged no further, and all that is left to do is to render the resulting carcass into petfood, or perhaps a useful pot of adhesive. It is with profound regret that I must inform you that your own equestrian fortunes have reached that point.

Your musical career has now reached its zenith, as has your notoriety. The widespread belief that you invited the head of the Roman Catholic Church to perform an act of obeisance upon you has sent your single soaring back to the top of the charts — a position from which it had sadly slipped of late. It was this decline, which neither the shock value of your ghastly visage nor my own campaign of abuse against your critics could reverse, that alerted me to the fact that the game would soon be up.

While the fruits of your appearance — or indeed within the borders of the United States — would be an with the company — or indeed within the borders of the United States — would be an endeavor fraught with difficulties. A glance at the hordes gathered at the gates of Arseland will no doubt prove my point. We have, as they say, pushed our luck — your luck, to be precise — about as far as it can go.

I have therefore resolved to channel all of Georgia's current funds and future earnings into a bank account I had the foresight to establish in the Cayman Islands; to establish myself anew in an equally discrete island state; and to return to you — at, it seems to me, this supremely appropriate moment — the great and solemn responsibility for your own destiny.

It only remains for me to bid you a fond farewell and to thank you from the bottom of my heart, simply for being the good, honest, decent fellow that you are. I shall leave you with some words of wisdom that my dear old Pappy left for me:

"Fuck 'em for all they're worth and run like hell, Gene."

Yours faithfully
Gene Sergeant
Lt. Col., Georgia National Guard (Ret.)

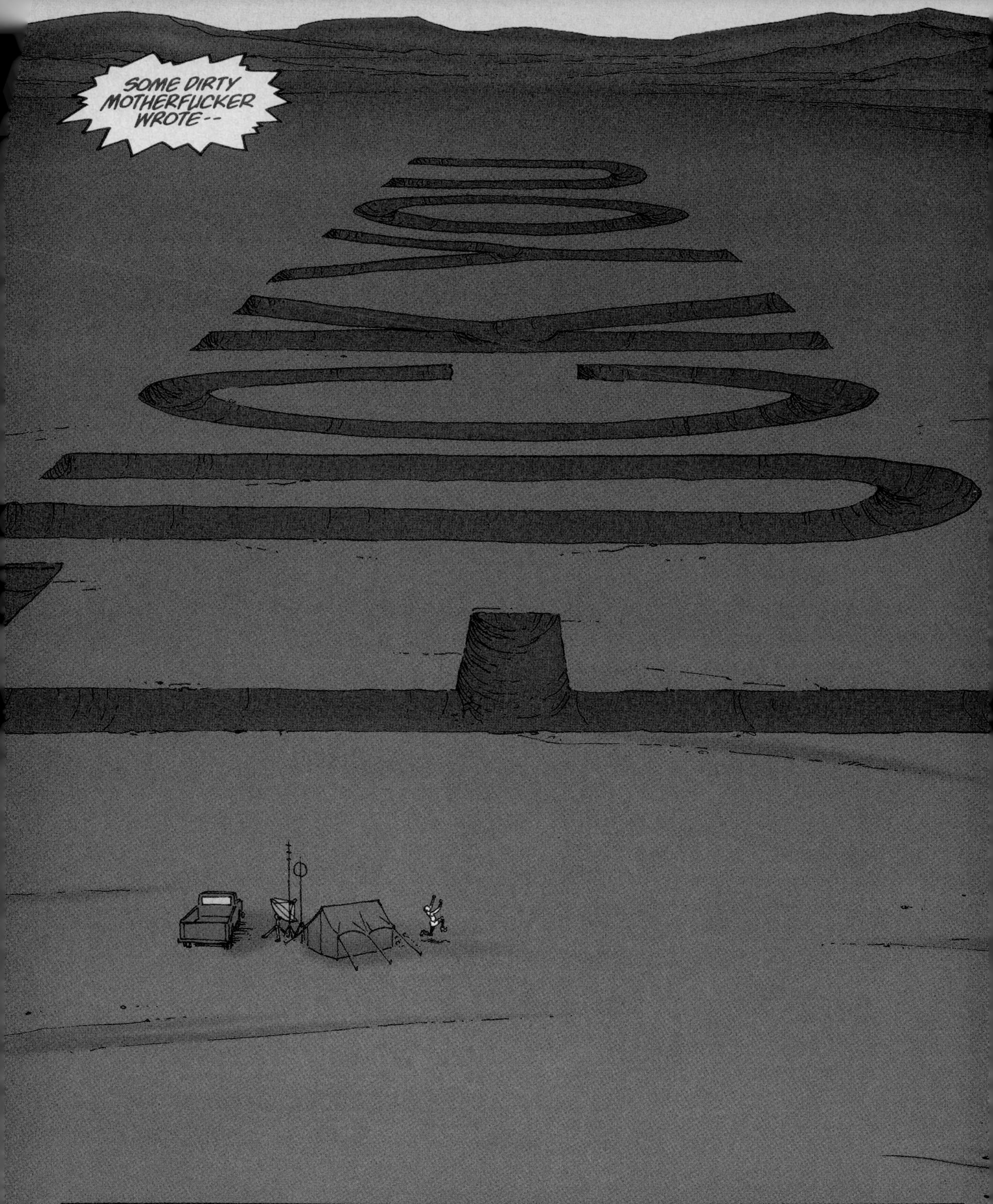
SOME DIRTY MOTHERFUCKER WROTE--

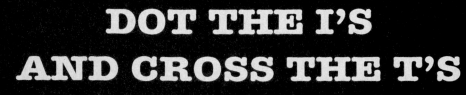

DOT THE I'S AND CROSS THE T'S

GARTH ENNIS - Writer STEVE DILLON - Artist
PAMELA RAMBO - Colorist (pages 2-8) • PATRICIA MULVILHILL - Colorist (pages 1,9-23)
CLEM ROBINS - Letter • AXEL ALONSO - Editor
PREACHER created by GARTH ENNIS and STEVE DILLON

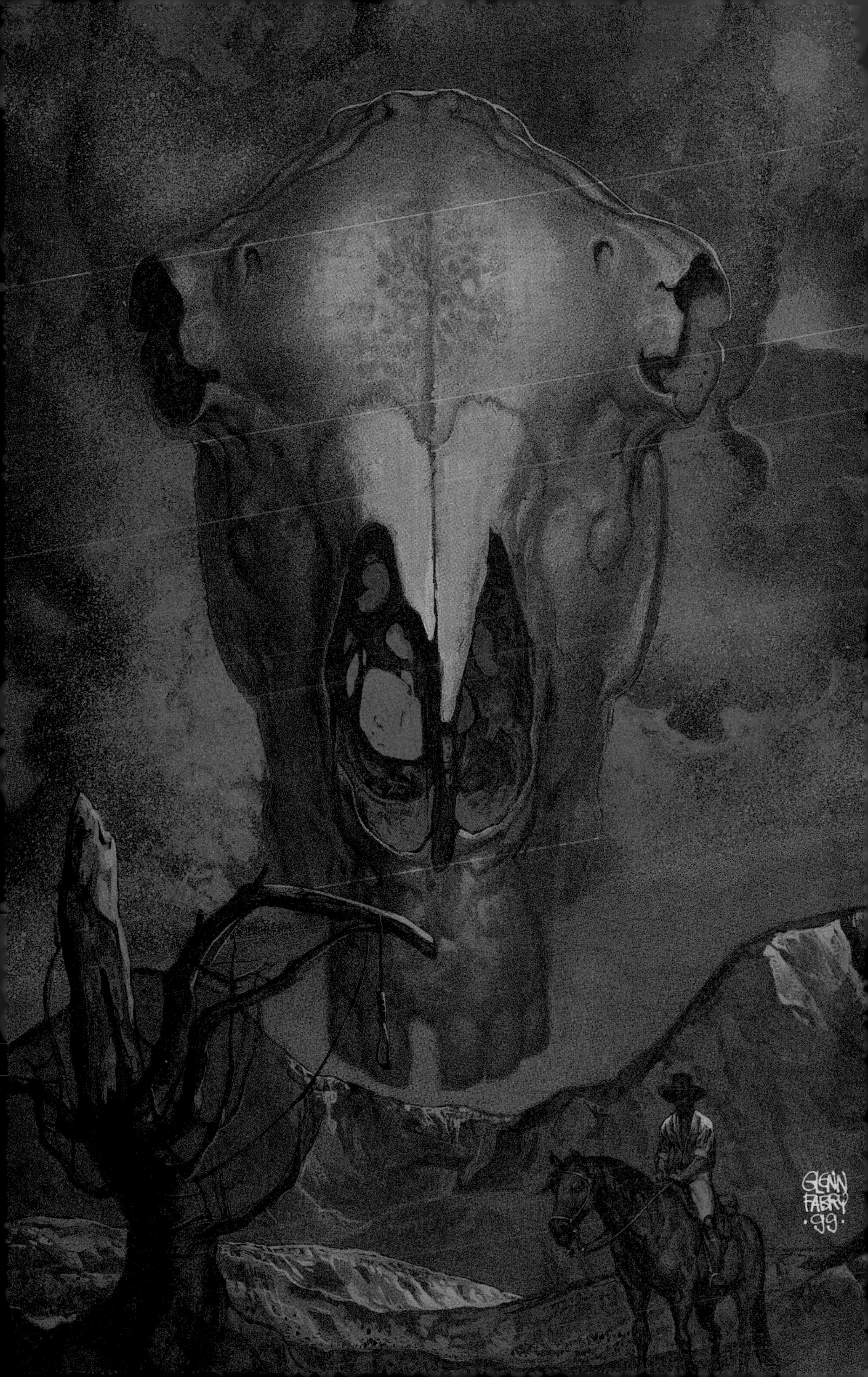
GLENN FABRY ·99·

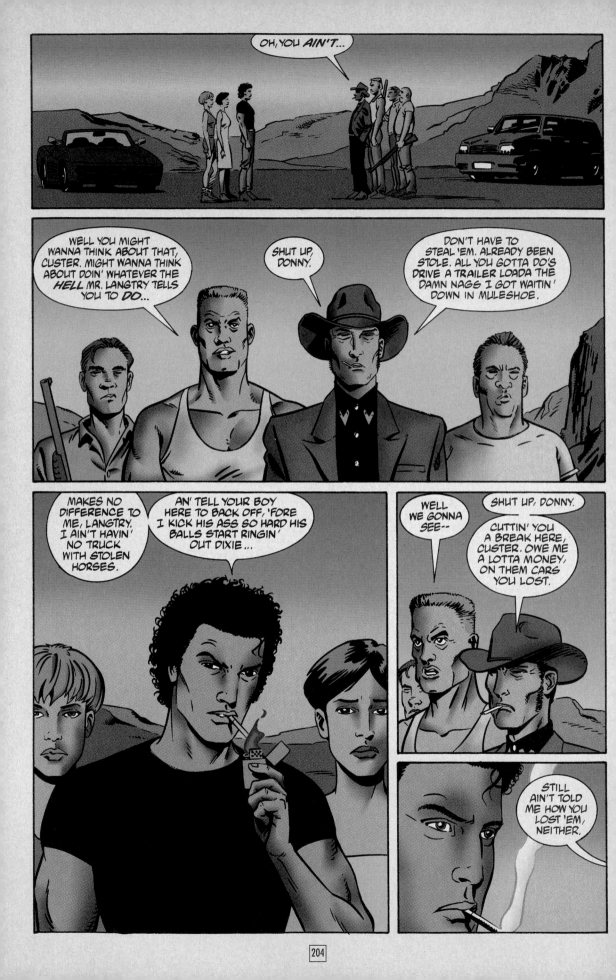

OH, YOU *AIN'T*...

WELL YOU MIGHT WANNA THINK ABOUT THAT, CUSTER. MIGHT WANNA THINK ABOUT DOIN' WHATEVER THE *HELL* MR. LANGTRY TELLS YOU TO *DO*...

SHUT UP, DONNY.

DON'T HAVE TO STEAL 'EM. ALREADY BEEN STOLE. ALL YOU GOTTA DO'S DRIVE A TRAILER LOADA THE DAMN NAGS I GOT WAITIN' DOWN IN MULESHOE.

MAKES NO DIFFERENCE TO ME, LANGTRY. I AIN'T HAVIN' NO TRUCK WITH STOLEN HORSES.

AN' TELL YOUR BOY HERE TO BACK OFF, 'FORE I KICK HIS ASS SO HARD HIS BALLS START RINGIN' OUT DIXIE...

WELL WE GONNA SEE--

SHUT UP, DONNY.

CUTTIN' YOU A BREAK HERE, CUSTER. OWE ME A LOTTA MONEY, ON THEM CARS YOU LOST.

STILL AIN'T TOLD ME HOW YOU LOST 'EM, NEITHER.

204

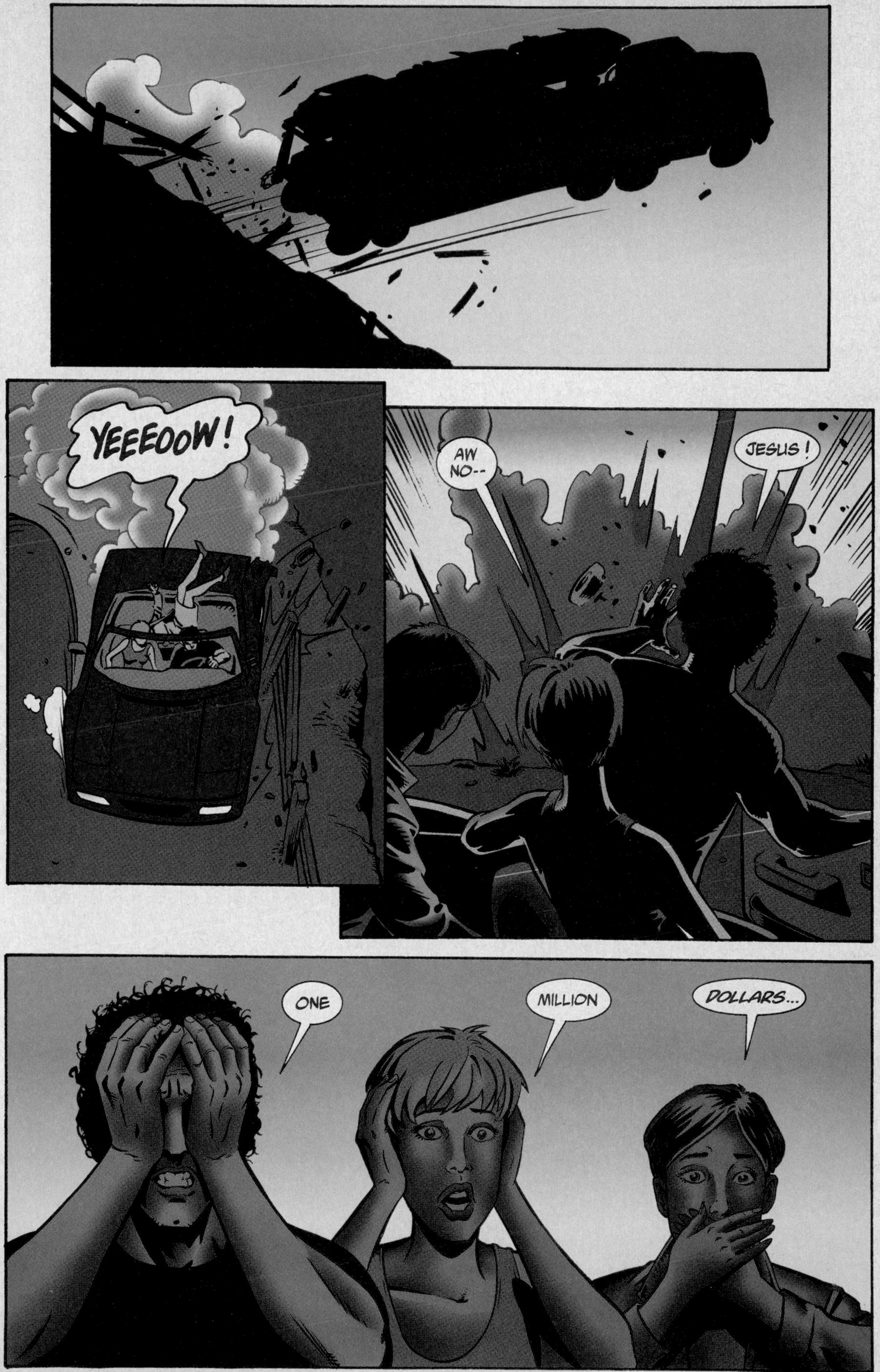
YEEEOOW!
AW NO--
JESUS!
ONE
MILLION
DOLLARS...

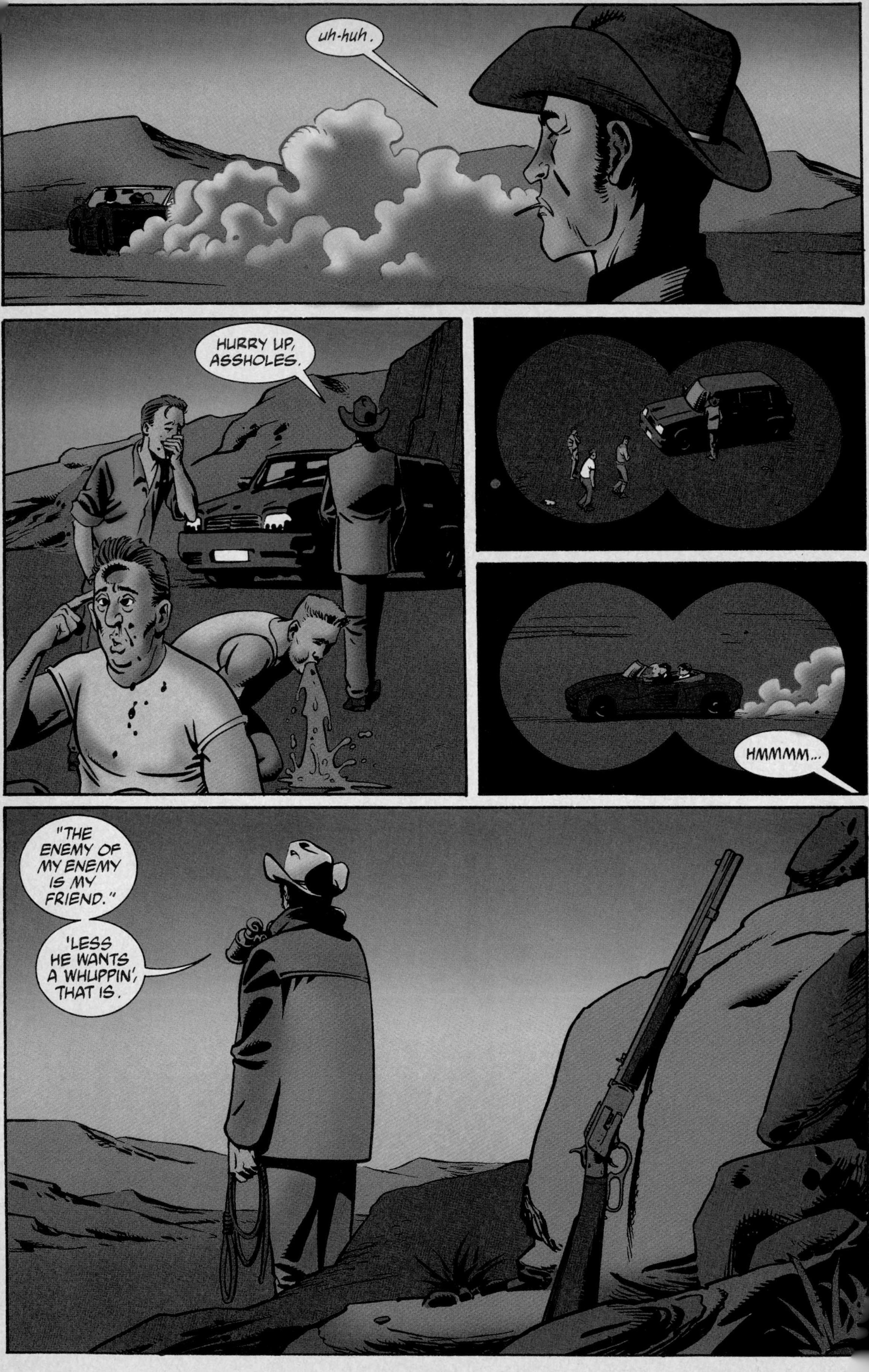
uh-huh.
HURRY UP, ASSHOLES.
HMMMM...
"THE ENEMY OF MY ENEMY IS MY FRIEND."
'LESS HE WANTS A WHUPPIN', THAT IS.

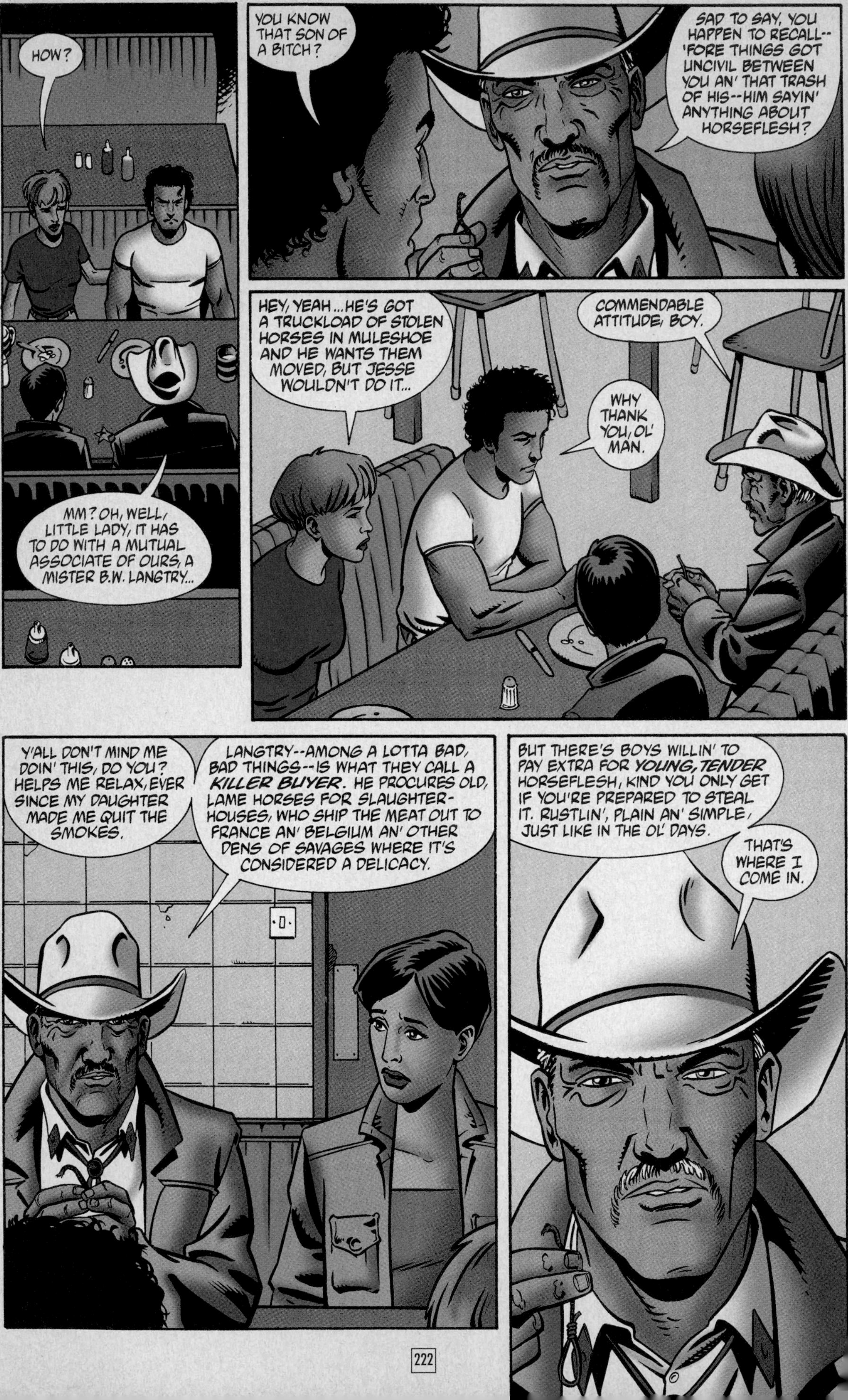

HOW?

YOU KNOW THAT SON OF A BITCH?

SAD TO SAY, YOU HAPPEN TO RECALL-- 'FORE THINGS GOT UNCIVIL BETWEEN YOU AN' THAT TRASH OF HIS--HIM SAYIN' ANYTHING ABOUT HORSEFLESH?

MM? OH, WELL, LITTLE LADY, IT HAS TO DO WITH A MUTUAL ASSOCIATE OF OURS, A MISTER B.W. LANGTRY...

HEY, YEAH...HE'S GOT A TRUCKLOAD OF STOLEN HORSES IN MULESHOE AND HE WANTS THEM MOVED, BUT JESSE WOULDN'T DO IT...

COMMENDABLE ATTITUDE, BOY.

WHY THANK YOU, OL' MAN.

Y'ALL DON'T MIND ME DOIN' THIS, DO YOU? HELPS ME RELAX, EVER SINCE MY DAUGHTER MADE ME QUIT THE SMOKES.

LANGTRY--AMONG A LOTTA BAD, BAD THINGS--IS WHAT THEY CALL A *KILLER BUYER.* HE PROCURES OLD, LAME HORSES FOR SLAUGHTERHOUSES, WHO SHIP THE MEAT OUT TO FRANCE AN' BELGIUM AN' OTHER DENS OF SAVAGES WHERE IT'S CONSIDERED A DELICACY.

BUT THERE'S BOYS WILLIN' TO PAY EXTRA FOR *YOUNG, TENDER* HORSEFLESH, KIND YOU ONLY GET IF YOU'RE PREPARED TO STEAL IT. RUSTLIN', PLAIN AN' SIMPLE, JUST LIKE IN THE OL' DAYS.

THAT'S WHERE I COME IN.

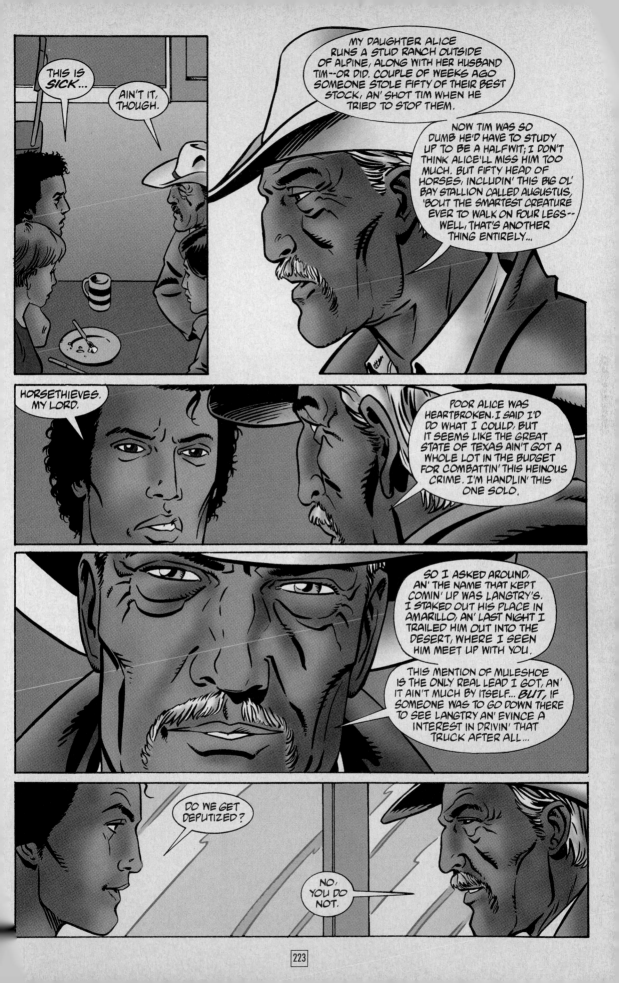

MY DAUGHTER ALICE RUNS A STUD RANCH OUTSIDE OF ALPINE, ALONG WITH HER HUSBAND TIM--OR DID. COUPLE OF WEEKS AGO SOMEONE STOLE FIFTY OF THEIR BEST STOCK, AN' SHOT TIM WHEN HE TRIED TO STOP THEM.

NOW TIM WAS SO DUMB HE'D HAVE TO STUDY UP TO BE A HALFWIT; I DON'T THINK ALICE'LL MISS HIM TOO MUCH. BUT FIFTY HEAD OF HORSES, INCLUDIN' THIS BIG OL' BAY STALLION CALLED AUGUSTUS, 'BOUT THE SMARTEST CREATURE EVER TO WALK ON FOUR LEGS-- WELL, THAT'S ANOTHER THING ENTIRELY...

THIS IS *SICK*...

AIN'T IT, THOUGH.

HORSETHIEVES. MY LORD.

POOR ALICE WAS HEARTBROKEN. I SAID I'D DO WHAT I COULD, BUT IT SEEMS LIKE THE GREAT STATE OF TEXAS AIN'T GOT A WHOLE LOT IN THE BUDGET FOR COMBATTIN' THIS HEINOUS CRIME. I'M HANDLIN' THIS ONE SOLO.

SO I ASKED AROUND, AN' THE NAME THAT KEPT COMIN' UP WAS LANGTRY'S. I STAKED OUT HIS PLACE IN AMARILLO, AN' LAST NIGHT I TRAILED HIM OUT INTO THE DESERT, WHERE I SEEN HIM MEET UP WITH YOU.

THIS MENTION OF MULESHOE IS THE ONLY REAL LEAD I GOT, AN' IT AIN'T MUCH BY ITSELF... *BUT*, IF SOMEONE WAS TO GO DOWN THERE TO SEE LANGTRY AN' EVINCE A INTEREST IN DRIVIN' THAT TRUCK AFTER ALL...

DO WE GET DEPUTIZED?

NO, YOU DO NOT.

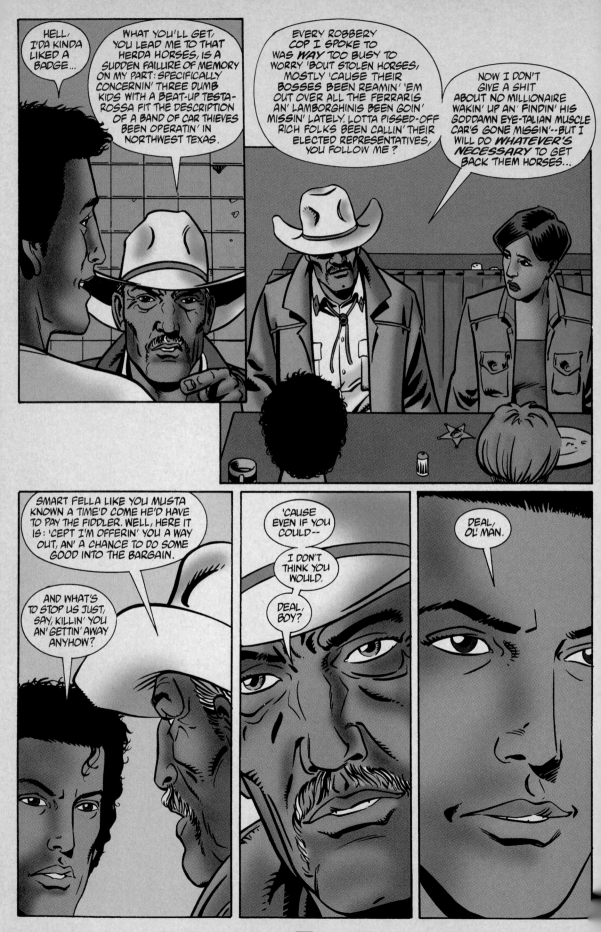

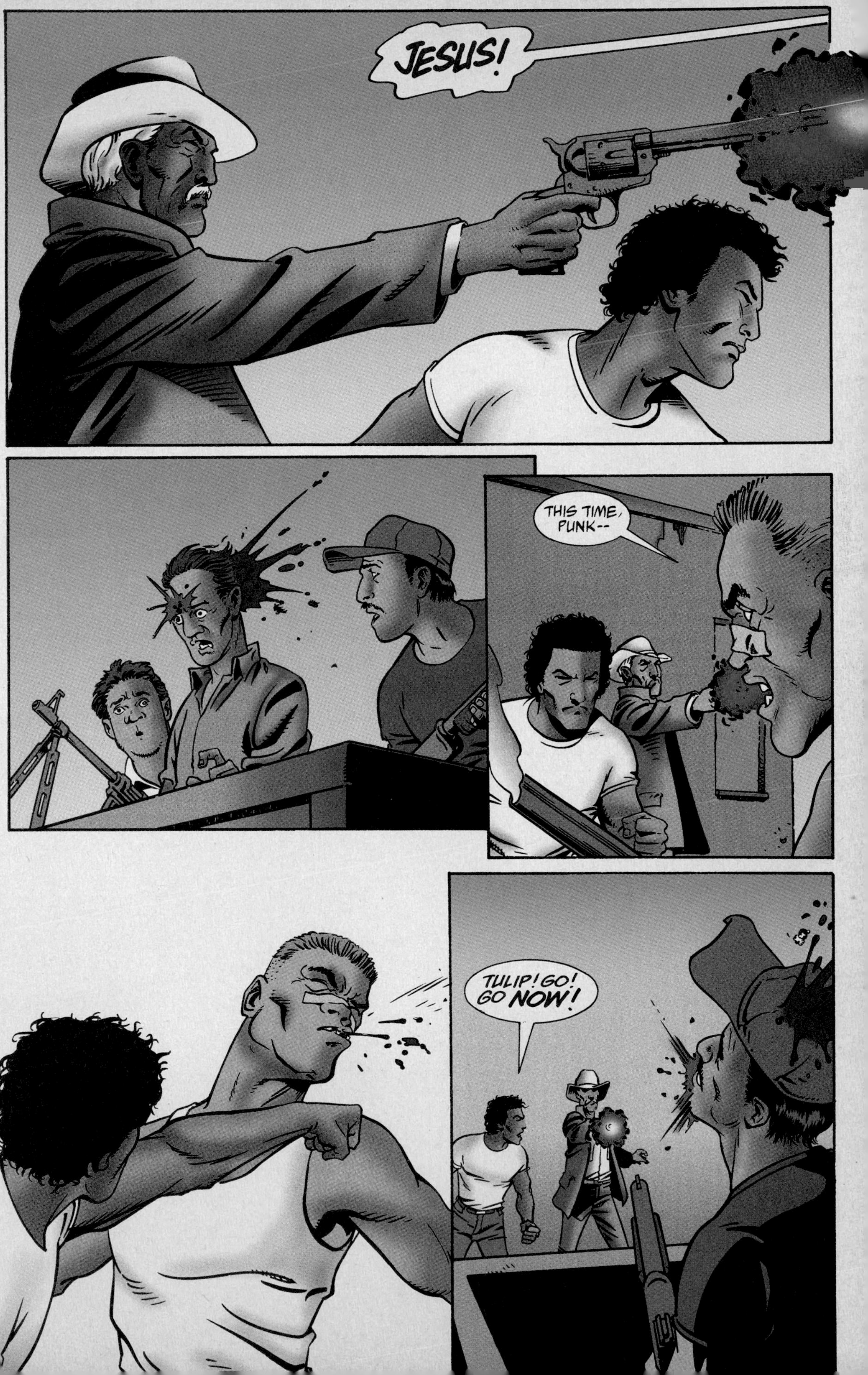
JESUS!
THIS TIME, PUNK--
TULIP! GO! GO NOW!

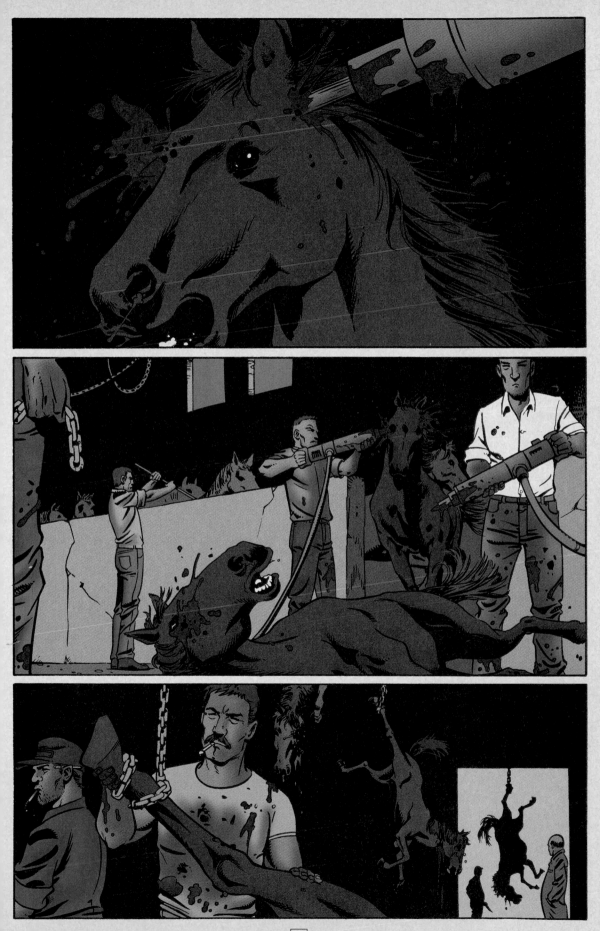

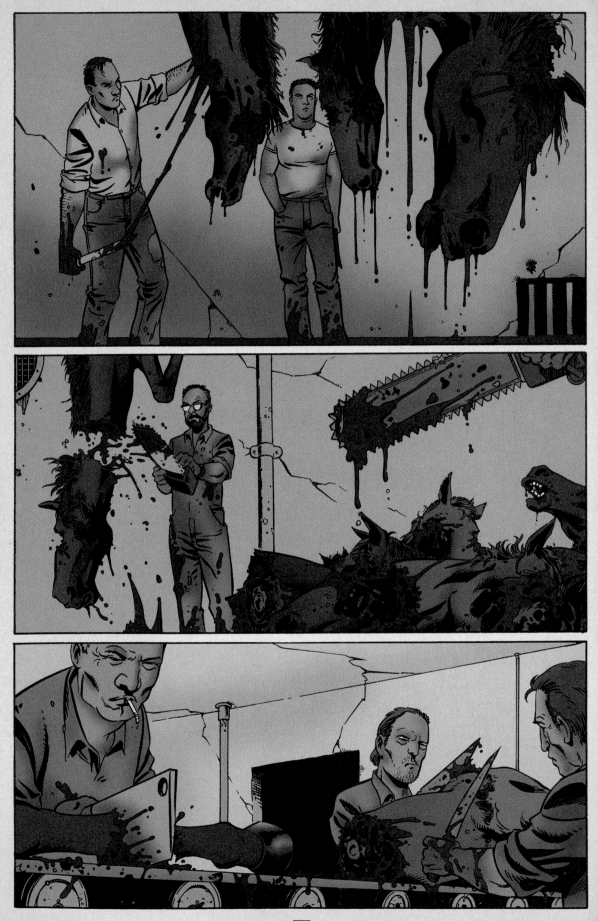

UHHNNHH...

SHOT...SHOT A DOZEN SONS A BITCHES WITH THAT DAMN PEACEMAKER. NEVER FIGURED ON IT ENDIN' UP KILLIN' ME.

YOU AIN'T KILLED.

HEH.

I'M GUTSHOT. MY OWN SHIT'S GONNA POISON ME TO DEATH.

GODDAMN, I WAS SO SURE I WAS GONNA BRING ALICE BACK HER HORSES...

AN' THAT BIG OL' FELLA WITH THE ONE WHITE EAR THERE? THAT'S AUGUSTUS.

RECKON I CAN TAKE CARE OF IT.

DON'T YOU MEAN, "I CAN TAKE CARE OF IT-- OL' MAN"?

NO SIR, I DO NOT.

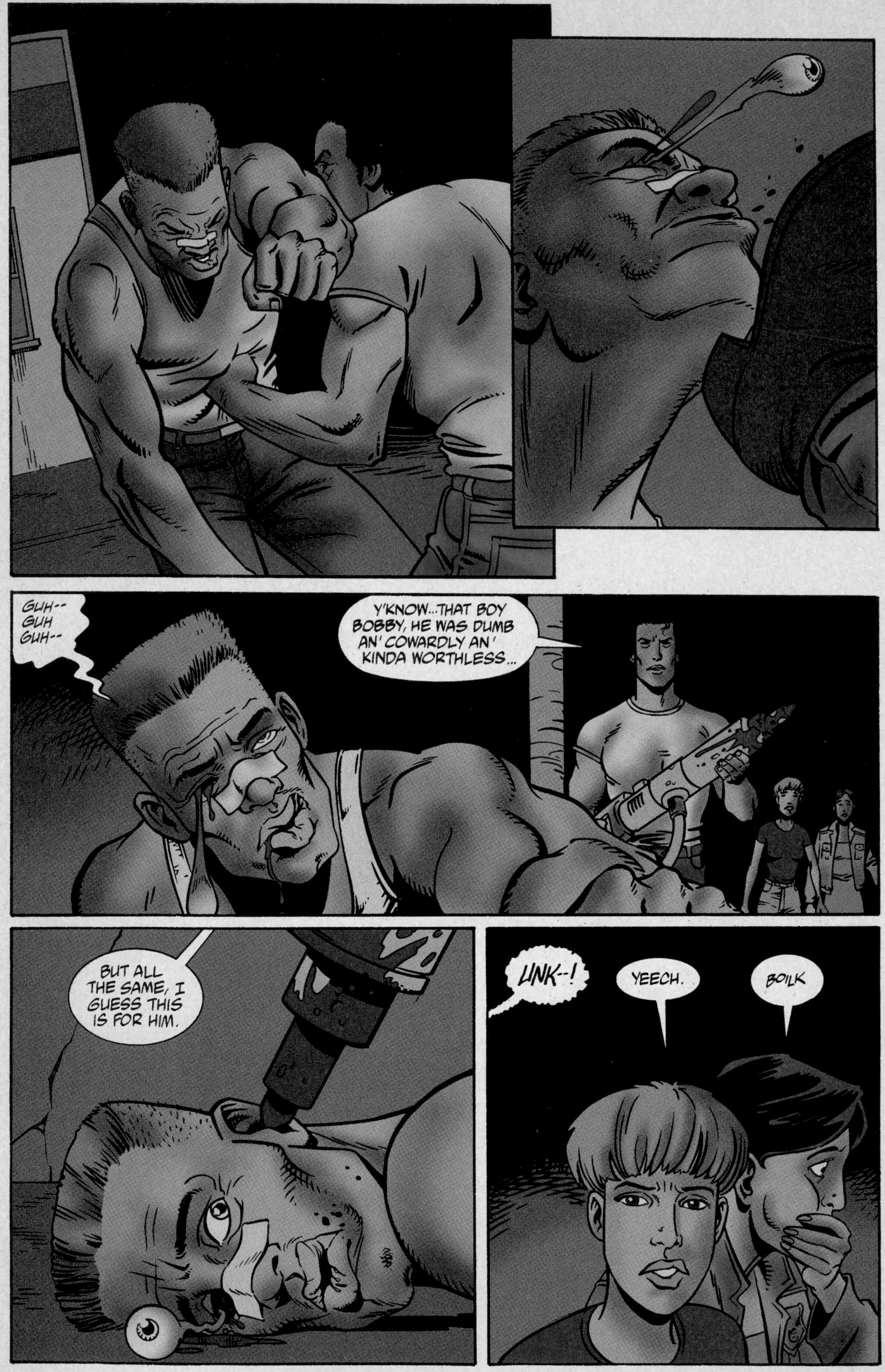
GUH--
GUH
GUH--
Y'KNOW...THAT BOY BOBBY, HE WAS DUMB AN' COWARDLY AN' KINDA WORTHLESS...
BUT ALL THE SAME, I GUESS THIS IS FOR HIM.
UNK--!
YEECH.
BOILK

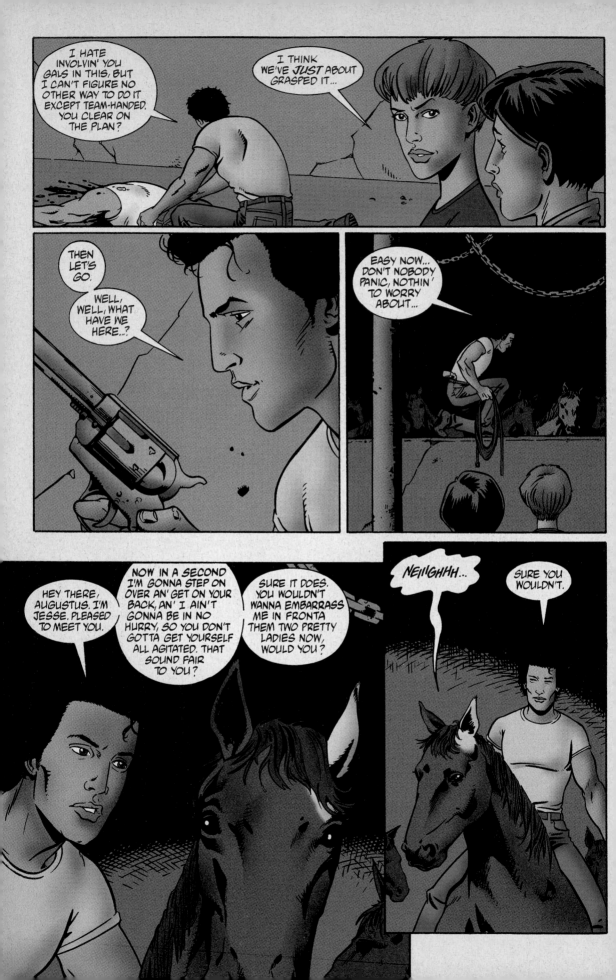

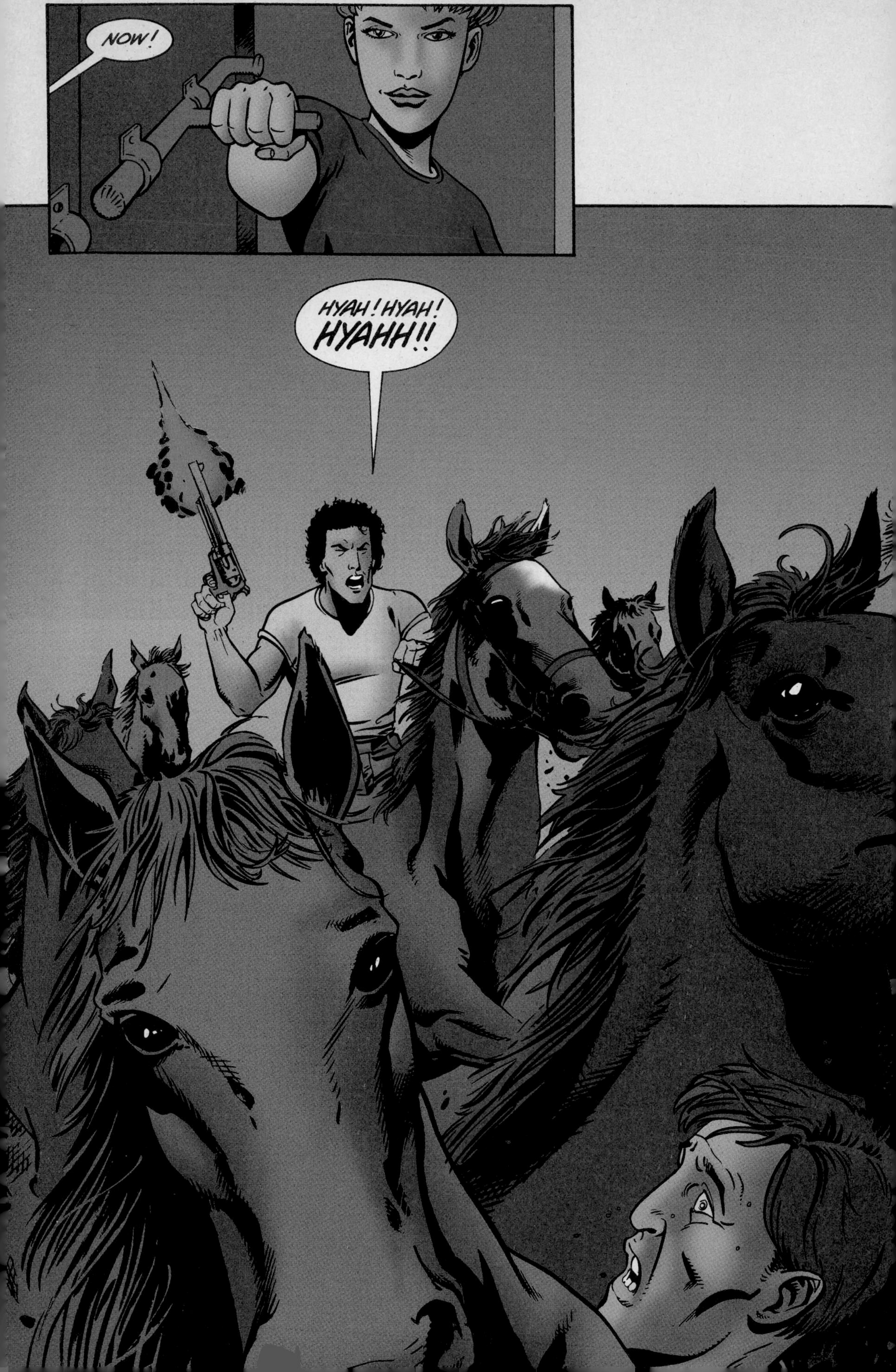
NOW!
HYAH! HYAH! HYAHH!!

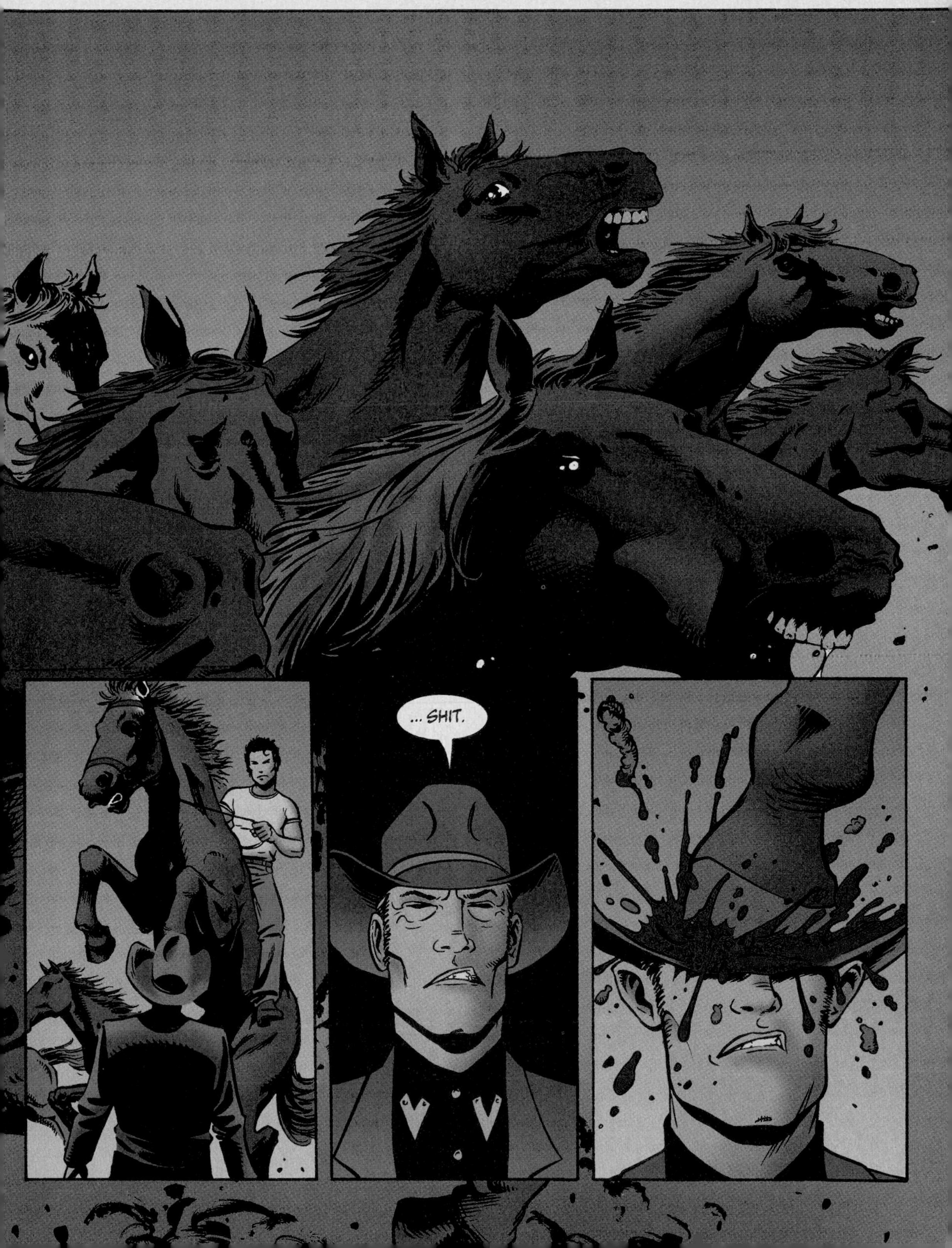
... SHIT.

SO HERE'S HOW IT IS, MONSEWER...

HUNDRED YEARS OR MORE AGO HERE IN TEXAS, YOU STOLE A FELLA'S HORSE AN' YOU DID MORE'N JUST TAKE AWAY HIS TRANSPORT OR HIS LIVELIHOOD, YOU ALL BUT CONDEMNED HIM TO DEATH.

YOU LIKE AS NOT STRANDED HIM IN THE DESERT, SEE, ALL ALONE IN A HOSTILE WILDERNESS FULLA SNAKES AN' SPIKES AN' VICIOUS CRITTERS AN' INJUNS READY TO SCALP HIM...

WH-WH-WHAT ARE YOU GOING TO DO TO ME?

HEY, NOW DON'T INTERRUPT.

WITHOUT HIS HORSE HE WAS GOOD AS DEAD. WASN'T NO BREAKDOWN SERVICE HE COULD CALL--HELL, WASN'T EVEN NO HIGHWAY. AN' THERE SURE AS SHIT WASN'T NO GODDAMN INSURANCE, NEITHER...

SO STEALIN' HORSES WAS TAKEN PRETTY DAMN SERIOUSLY BACK IN THEM DAYS.

AN' HORSE-THIEVES...

WELL, THE OUTLOOK FOR THEM WAS GENERALLY KINDA BLEAK.

OH MY GOD.

YOU WOULDN'T.

247

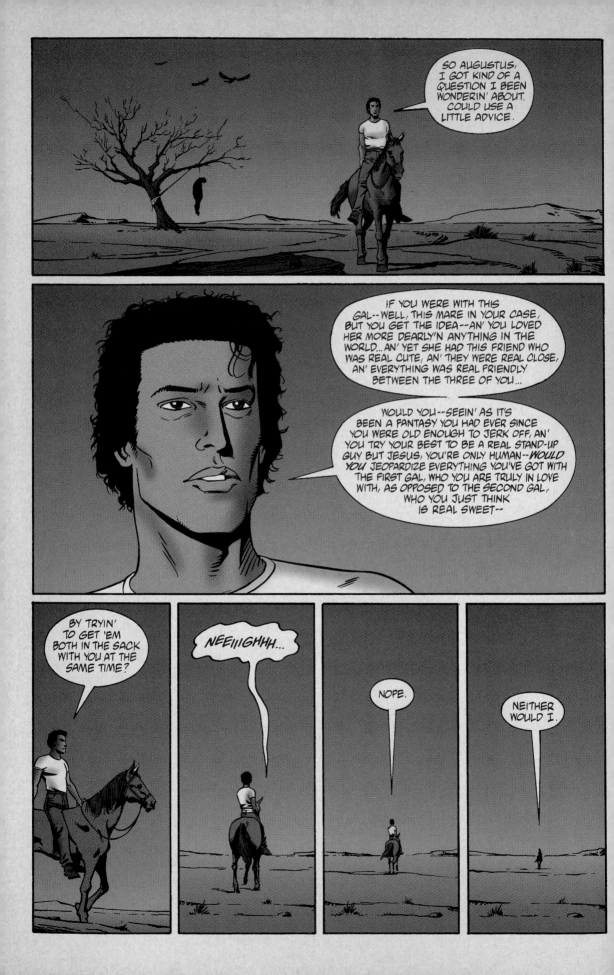

THE INVISIBLES:
KISSING MR. QUIMPER
G. Morrison/C. Weston/
I. Reis/various

MICHAEL MOORCOCK'S
MULTIVERSE
M. Moorcock/W. Simonson/
J. Ridgway/M. Reeve

MERCY
J.M. DeMatteis/Paul Johnson

NEIL GAIMAN & CHARLES VESS'
STARDUST
Neil Gaiman/Charles Vess

NEIL GAIMAN'S
MIDNIGHT DAYS
N. Gaiman/T. Kristiansen/
S. Bissette/J. Totleben/
M. Mignola/various

NEVADA
S. Gerber/P. Winslade/
S. Leialoha/D. Giordano

PREACHER: GONE TO TEXAS
Garth Ennis/Steve Dillon

PREACHER: UNTIL THE END OF
THE WORLD
Garth Ennis/Steve Dillon

PREACHER: PROUD AMERICANS
Garth Ennis/Steve Dillon

PREACHER: ANCIENT HISTORY
G. Ennis/S. Pugh/C. Ezquerra/
R. Case

PREACHER: DIXIE FRIED
Garth Ennis/Steve Dillon

PREACHER: SALVATION
Garth Ennis/Steve Dillon

PREACHER: WAR IN
THE SUN
Garth Ennis/Steve Dillon/
Peter Snejbjerg

THE SYSTEM
Peter Kuper

SWAMP THING: SAGA OF
THE SWAMP THING
Alan Moore/Steve Bissette/
John Totleben

SWAMP THING: LOVE AND
DEATH
A. Moore/S. Bissette/
J. Totleben/S. McManus

SWAMP THING: ROOTS
Jon J Muth

TERMINAL CITY
Dean Motter/Michael Lark

TRANSMETROPOLITAN:
BACK ON THE STREET
Warren Ellis/Darick Robertson/
various

TRANSMETROPOLITAN:
LUST FOR LIFE
Warren Ellis/Darick Robertson/
various

TRANSMETROPOLITAN:
YEAR OF THE BASTARD
Warren Ellis/Darick Robertson/
Rodney Ramos

TRUE FAITH
Garth Ennis/Warren Pleece

UNCLE SAM
Steve Darnall/Alex Ross

UNKNOWN SOLDIER
Garth Ennis/Kilian Plunkett

V FOR VENDETTA
Alan Moore/David Lloyd

VAMPS
Elaine Lee/William Simpson

WITCHCRAFT
J. Robinson/P. Snejbjerg/
M. Zulli/S. Yeowell/
T. Kristiansen

the Sandman library

THE SANDMAN:
PRELUDES & NOCTURNES
N. Gaiman/S. Kieth/
M. Dringenberg/M. Jones

THE SANDMAN: THE DOLL'S
HOUSE
N. Gaiman/M. Dringenberg/
M. Jones/C. Bachalo/
M. Zulli/S. Parkhouse

THE SANDMAN: DREAM
COUNTRY
N. Gaiman/K. Jones/C. Vess/
C. Doran/M. Jones

THE SANDMAN:
THE DREAM HUNTERS
Neil Gaiman/Yoshitaka Amano

THE SANDMAN: SEASON OF
MISTS
N. Gaiman/K. Jones/
M. Dringenberg/M. Jones/
various

THE SANDMAN: A GAME
OF YOU
Neil Gaiman/Shawn McManus/
various

THE SANDMAN:
FABLES AND REFLECTIONS
Neil Gaiman/various

THE SANDMAN: BRIEF LIVES
Neil Gaiman/Jill Thompson/
Vince Locke

THE SANDMAN: WORLDS' END
Neil Gaiman/various

THE SANDMAN:
THE KINDLY ONES
N. Gaiman/M. Hempel/R. Case/
various

THE SANDMAN: THE WAKE
N. Gaiman/M. Zulli/J. Muth/
C. Vess

DUSTCOVERS-THE COLLECTED
SANDMAN COVERS 1989 - 1997
Dave McKean/Neil Gaiman

THE SANDMAN COMPANION
Hy Bender

To find more collected editions and monthly comic books from DC Comics,
call 1-888-COMIC BOOK for the nearest comics shop or go to your local book store.

Visit us at www.dccomics.com